D1593483

Genealogical Fictions

Genealogical Fictions

Cultural Periphery and Historical Change in the Modern Novel

JOBST WELGE

Johns Hopkins University Press

Baltimore

© 2015 Johns Hopkins University Press
All rights reserved. Published 2015
Printed in the United States of America on acid-free paper
2 4 6 8 9 7 5 3 1

Johns Hopkins University Press
2715 North Charles Street
Baltimore, Maryland 21218-4363
www.press.jhu.edu

Library of Congress Cataloging-in-Publication Data

Welge, Jobst, 1969–
Genealogical fictions : cultural periphery and historical change in the modern
novel / Jobst Welge.
pages cm
Includes bibliographical references and index.
ISBN 978-1-4214-1435-5 (hardcover) — ISBN 978-1-4214-1436-2 (electronic) —
ISBN 1-4214-1435-X (hardcover) — ISBN 1-4214-1436-8 (electronic)
1. European fiction—19th century—History and criticism.   2. European
fiction—20th century—History and criticism.   3. Brazilian fiction—19th
century—History and criticism.   4. Brazilian fiction—20th century—History
and criticism.   5. Families in literature.   6. Social change in
literature.   7. Social change—Europe.   8. Social change—Brazil.
9. Genealogy—Social aspects.   10. Literature and history.   I. Title.
II. Title: Cultural periphery and historical change in the modern
novel.   III. Title: Historical change in the modern novel.
PN3499.W45 2014
809.3'9355—dc23   2014011205

A catalog record for this book is available from the British Library.

Special discounts are available for bulk purchases of this book. For more information,
please contact Special Sales at 410-516-6936 or specialsales@press.jhu.edu.

Johns Hopkins University Press uses environmentally friendly book materials,
including recycled text paper that is composed of at least 30 percent post-
consumer waste, whenever possible.

CONTENTS

Unless otherwise noted, translations are my own.

CR   Maria Edgeworth. *Castle Rackrent; an Hibernian Tale, Taken from Facts, and from the Manners of the Irish Squires, before the Year 1782.* Edited by George Watson. Oxford: Oxford University Press, 1999.

EJ   Joaquim Maria Machado de Assis. *Esaú e Jacó.* Rio de Janeiro: Garnier, 2005.

FJ   Benito Pérez Galdós. *Fortunata y Jacinta: Dos historias de casadas.* Edited by Francisco Caudet, 2 vols. Madrid: Cátedra, 2002.

G   Giuseppe Tomasi di Lampedusa. *Il gattopardo.* Milan: Feltrinelli Editore, 2003.

HC   Joaquim Maria Machado de Assis. *Esau and Jacob.* Translated by Helen Caldwell. Berkeley: University of California Press, 1965.

L   Giuseppe Tomasi di Lampedusa. *The Leopard.* Translated by Archibald Colquhoun. New York: Pantheon, 1988.

LMN   Emilia Pardo Bazán. *La madre naturaleza.* Edited by Ignacio Javier López. Madrid: Cátedra, 2007.

LPU   Emilia Pardo Bazán. *Los Pazos de Ulloa.* Edited by Marina Mayoral. Madrid: Clásicos Castalia, 1986.

ME   José Lins do Rego. *Menino de engenho.* Rio de Janeiro: José Olympio, 2008.

MV   Giovanni Verga. *I Malavoglia.* Edited by Ferruccio Cecco. Turin: Einaudi, 1997.

OM   Eça de Queirós. *Os Maias: Episódios da vida romântica.* Lisbon: Porto Editora, 2002.

TM   Eça de Queirós. *The Maias: Episodes from Romantic Life.* Translated by Margaret Jull Costa. New Directions: New York, 2007.

VR   Federico de Roberto. *I Viceré.* Turin: Einaudi, 1990.

W   Walter Scott. *Waverley; or, 'Tis Sixty Years Since.* Edited by Andrew Hook. London: Penguin, 1985.

This book certainly has a genealogy of its own. The remote beginnings may be traced back to the time when I lectured on Italian cultural history at the University of Santa Barbara, in the year 2004. When in this context I was teaching Tomasi di Lampedusa's *Il Gattopardo*, I first began to explore the novel's wider connections with the history of the European novel—little suspecting in which directions it would take me in the following years. At the Freie Universität Berlin the book was conceived and realized in the form of a German *Habilitation*. The final stages of rearrangement and revision for its present form were carried out at my present position at the University of Konstanz. In its various incarnations, then, the book has accompanied me to many different places—the first draft of the chapter on Machado de Assis was written in the Library Machado de Assis at the Academia Brasileira das Letras in Rio de Janeiro, and several other chapters were written in the study room of the Kungliga Biblioteket, Stockholm or in the library of the Ibero-Amerikanisches Institut, Berlin.

The present form of the book owes much to the critical comments and helpful suggestions of Joachim Küpper, Helmut Pfeiffer, and Jeffrey Schnapp, all of whom have accompanied, supported, and inspired me on my academic trajectory, for which I am deeply grateful. Individual chapters have also benefited from the expertise and advice of Oliver Lubrich, João Cezar de Castro Rocha, and Berthold Zilly. Their companionship and encouragement over the years has been invaluable. For their interest and insightful input at various junctures I would like to thank Pedro Almeida Magalhães, Esther Kilchmann, Elisabeth Lack, and Marie Naumann. I would also like to acknowledge the helpful comments of the anonymous reader for Johns Hopkins University Press, as well as Carrie Watterson for her superb copyediting work. Special thanks to Thomas Jorion for his generous permission to use his evocative photography for the cover art. Last but not least, I thank Robert Buch for unfailing friendship and the careful reading of the entire manuscript. Since the final stages and beyond, a more incalculable debt is due to my wife Katrin and my daughter Carla Mia.

A different version of chapter 4 was published (in German), as "Nation, Genealogie und Geschichte in Benito Pérez Galdós' *Fortunata y Jacinta*," *Romanistisches Jahrbuch* 57 (Berlin: De Gruyter, 2006), 378–402. An earlier version of a portion of chapter 5 was published (in Spanish) as "Degeneración y crisis de la provincia en *Los Pazos de Ulloa*," in *Narrar la pluralidad cultural: Crisis de modernidad y funciones de lo popular en la novela en lengua española*, edited by Wolfgang Matzat and Max Grosse (Madrid: Iberoamericana; Frankfurt: Vervuert, 2012), 213–25. A slightly different version of chapter 7 is forthcoming as "Machado de Assis' *Esaú e Jacó* and the Problem of Historical Representation" in the *Luso-Brazilian Review*. © 2014 by the Board of Regents of the University of Wisconsin System. Reproduced courtesy of the University of Wisconsin Press. I thank the publishers for the permission to reprint.

Genealogical Fictions

CHAPTER ONE

Introduction

This book emerged through a series of questions that I asked myself when studying and teaching Tomasi di Lampedusa's novel *Il Gattopardo* (1958). While that text, one of the great novels of the twentieth century, has for various reasons often been seen as a rather isolated and "eccentric" phenomenon in the panorama of Italian literature during the 1950s, I began to notice certain similarities between it and Gabriel García Márquez's *Cien años de soledad* (1967), as well as other novels of the twentieth century, notably Thomas Mann's *Buddenbrooks* (1901). What these novels had in common was a concern with family history that is echoed by the formal and structural makeup of this type of "genealogical" novel. Given these similarities among different novels of the twentieth century, I set out to formulate questions such as these: How can we define the genealogical novel, and what is generally the function of genealogy and family history in the form and history of the novel? Are there possible connections between the theme of genealogical decline and the location in a geographical periphery (Sicily, Macondo, Lübeck)?[1] How are family history, genealogical succession, and generational experience related to a bigger history, the history of the nation, as well as to social change and modernization?

However, it soon occurred to me that what I had initially observed as a phenomenon of the twentieth-century novel could be explained only by retreating in time, by looking at the history and geography of the novel in the nineteenth century. Although *Il Gattopardo* was my first stepping stone to address these problems, my analysis of this novel stands at the end of this book. I would now claim that Lampedusa's novel represents a culmination and summa of a constellation of themes originating in a certain tradition of the nineteenth-century novel, involving the nation, the (regional) periphery, familial genealogy, and the question of historical change. The readings of these novels inform each other and reveal similarities and differences across a broad temporal and geographical range. *Il Gattopardo* is a book about a transitional period in which a geographical periphery is annexed to a central nation-state. In fact, all the novels discussed here are concerned with a moment of historical transition during which a remote, or "backward," area is confronted with the homogenizing but also liberating forces of modernity. This is not to say that my study presents necessarily a "genealogical" account of the type of novel represented by *Il Gattopardo*, but it shows that the central coordinates of this novel replay earlier constellations of the nineteenth-century novel. The point of the following case studies is not primarily the question of literary influence but rather a more indirect sense of "family resemblance" among the different texts analyzed here.

Genealogy, Time, and Narrative

Throughout the nineteenth century, the notions of family and pedigree have served as powerful images for the discourse of nationhood, the emergence or transformation of collective identities and communities, especially during those moments when the continuity of succession came under threat.[2] I assume that the figure of the family lends itself so much to the sense of nationhood because it is a convenient device to represent the synchronic group of an "imagined community" as well as the cross-generational succession that links private and public history.[3] The refraction of a national theme through the structural device of familial succession introduces a *distinctive* temporality into the novel—for, in fact, the representation of temporal development has always been a characteristic feature of the novelistic genre and of the practice of narration as such. That is to say, in a century of historicism and the circulation of the Darwinian model of science, the nineteenth-century novel participates in the general epistemological attempt, at the intersection of biology and history, to explain evolutionally how things came to be the way they are and thus to confront the present with chronological retrospections and the search for origins, antecedents, predecessors, or archetypes. Insofar as genealogical narratives are necessarily developmental in nature, they are oriented toward both the past and the future, and thus they often take on a certain recursive direction, where, for instance, decline is the flip side of inheritance: "developmental histories always enact a double movement, they organize their narrative material simultaneously forward and backward, toward the imagined endpoint and away from it."[4]

In the nineteenth century, the conception of time itself becomes fully historicized. As Janet L. Beizer has put it, "We must understand the nineteenth-century imagination as properly chronological; newly condemned to exist in time, it seeks its logic in temporal designs and its authority in genealogical tracings."[5] In a similar vein, Michel Foucault has characterized the intellectual situation of the nineteenth century: "from the nineteenth-century onward [. . .], a profound historicity penetrates into the heart of things, isolates and defines them in their own coherence, imposes upon them the forms of order implied by the continuity of time."[6] As a matter of fact, the profound connection between genealogy and narrative has long been recognized and studied by literary historians with regard to a number of genres and periods, particularly the nineteenth century novel.[7] In her important study of the genealogical imperative in the modern novel, Patricia Drechsel Tobin has defined this term as the correspondence between the temporal form of the novel and the linear structure of the dynastic, patriarchal family. According to this logic, deeply rooted in Western culture, the individual is situated in a lineage that establishes a causal relation to its particular place in time. As Tobin insists, this "genealogical imperative" is not simply natural but a cause of meaning production:

> By an analogy of function, events in time come to be perceived as begetting other events within a line of causality similar to the line of generations, with the prior event earning a special prestige as it is seen to originate, control, and predict future events. When in some such manner ontological priority is conferred upon mere temporal anteriority, the historical consciousness is born, and time is understood as a linear manifestation of the genealogical destiny of events.[8]

Tobin focuses her study primarily on examples of the twentieth-century family saga (Mann, Faulkner, Márquez, etc.), although she also includes a few examples of nineteenth-century novels (Brontë, Butler), those that she sees as anticipatory of the modern novel's tendency to disrupt linearity and traditional patrilineal succession. Despite the great merits of her study, this book differs from Tobin's in two respects. First, her discussion of what she designates as "eccentric" examples of the nineteenth-century novel rests on the assumption that the novel of this period *normally* confirms to the linear structure of genealogical continuity. In fact, many, if not most, examples of the nineteenth-century family novel involve a crisis of patrilineal succession, even if this crisis rarely affects the principle of *narrative* continuity, as will indeed be characteristic for the novel of the twentieth century. Such a critical narrative about the transformation of a supposedly stable order into the dissolution of order is of course typical of the discourse of modernity, which always has to posit the past as its own opposite.[9] The genealogical novels of the nineteenth century establish and reinforce precisely such a narrative of modernity, understood in either positive or negative terms. Second, Tobin's study devotes much effort to the novel's particular modelling and sequencing of time, but the question of history and space appears only in a generic, abstract way, with little consideration of the local context.

The interrelation of space and time is characteristic of the nineteenth century as a whole, but the decadent inflection of family narratives (and the deferred potential for a possible regeneration) will be the specific mark of the naturalist novel, in the wake of Émile Zola's monumental Rougon-Macquart cycle of novels (1871–93). The enormous influence of his work on the literature of the latter part of the nineteenth century has been frequently remarked, yet it is intriguing that Zola's predominantly urban, Parisian model of naturalism had particularly significant repercussions in peripheral spaces, such as Italy and Spain (this influence will be discussed in chapters 3 and 4).[10] In the European (and American) periphery, Zola's model worked as a powerful—and highly controversial—model of literary innovation. If Zola used a tainted family history to dramatize what he saw as the decadence of the society of the Second Empire in France, many of his followers related the dying out of a family line to the dying out of the lifeworld of a particular region under the forces of modernity. In British literature, Thomas Hardy's regional novels are another prominent example for this conjunction of genealogy and geographical periphery, in this case within the fictional entity of Wessex (in Southwest England), whose specific local difference represents an "otherness" with respect to central English modernity but also, in a sense, a last reservoir of authentic national values.[11] As Sophie Gilmartin has written, "A failure of the 'dynastic principle' is connected to a dying out of regionalism in these novels. Hardy so often wrote of a threshold in time when the distinct customs and character of a region were yet intact, but about to be forgotten within the next generation or two."[12] In novels such as *Tess of the d'Urbervilles* (1891) and *Jude the Obscure* (1895), genealogy signifies a traditional means of legitimization that, just like the self-identity of the region, is under threat because of the levelling forces of modernity.

Hardy, however, was less interested in the question of biological heredity, the self-declared "scientific" component of Zola's naturalism, which toward the end of the century also informed the European phenomenon of social Darwinism.[13] In his novel *By the Open Sea* (*I Havsbandet*, 1890), Hardy's Swedish contemporary August Strindberg, influenced here by both Nietzsche and Darwin, presents the reader with an aristocratically aloof scientist and fishing inspector, Axel Borg, who was sent to the outskirts of the Swedish archipelago, which serves as a metonymy for what Strindberg saw as the peripheral condition of Sweden as a whole.[14] After a failed romantic relationship, Borg develops a eugenic fantasy of male celibate reproduction as the supposed remedy to the crisis of patriarchal continuity and racial degeneration. Even though this absurd plan obviously fails, Borg's ultimate suicide is associated with images of cosmic regeneration. This, then, is a typical fin de siècle novel to the extent that the "primitive" forces of regional, "maternal" nature resist the scientific ideas of progress and at the same time are envisioned as a possible antidote to the regressive fears of a self-doubting modernity and masculinity.

These examples illustrate how the ingredients of literary naturalism and Zola's dialectic of decadence and regeneration reflect a profound crisis of patriarchy at the end of the century, as well as modernity's experience of temporal and spatial asymmetries.[15] Moreover, they show that the reception and variation of naturalism, with its preference for narratives of decadence, provides a matrix for the international proliferation of the plot of familial decline, which as such might be said to be relatively stable, although the style, ideological implications, and local color change.[16] Throughout the nineteenth century, the common frame of reference for spatial and temporal gradations remains the idea of the nation.

Nation, Periphery, and Modernization

As is well known, Benedict Anderson has claimed that the nineteenth-century realist novel is bound up with the imaginary production of the modern nation-state.[17] The generality of this well-known argument regarding the novel's form and materiality, however, does not concern the specificity of a novel's content or plot. Anderson asserts that the homology among family, social groups, the state, and certain narrative forms, notably the novel and the newspaper, rests on a changed conception of time, the idea of secular, "neutral" time (as opposed to an earlier "messianic" time—a conception taken up from Walter Benjamin): "the idea of a sociological organism moving through homogeneous, empty time is a precise analogue of the idea of the nation, which also is conceived as a solid community moving steadily down (or up) in history."[18] The idea of an "empty" time, writes Anderson, can be contrasted with "those prefatory genealogies, often ascending to the origin of man, which are so characteristic a feature of ancient chronicles, legends, and holy books."[19] Modern novels indeed do not refer to the origin of man, but their conception of time is deeply historical, insofar as empty time is shaped by different cultural coordinates, period habits, breaks, repetitions, and so forth.[20]

In this sense Homi Bhaba has elaborated on Anderson's ideas. According to Bhaba, the national imagination works by integrating the idea of the people into a continuity of past and present, and he sees the specific modernity of this situation in the potential conflict between narratives of original foundation and the focus on the contemporary, day-to-day iterations that affirm the existence of a nation as a living place. The boundaries and the visual concreteness of the community are affirmed by its insertion into a given *space* of the nation: "national time becomes concrete and visible in the chronotype [*sic*] of the local, particular, graphic, from beginning to end."[21] In other words, one of the fundamental tasks in the representation of the nation is to make time visible by locating it in a given space.

Anderson's and Bhaba's comments, then, posit a fundamental, but very general, relation among the form of the novel, its modelling of time, and the imagined community of the nation. Yet, even in the specific case of the nineteenth-century novel, it is readily apparent that not all novels are both formally and *thematically* concerned with the question of nationhood to the same degree. To be sure, many of the great and representative novels of the nineteenth century, from *Middlemarch* to *Madame Bovary*, from *Oliver Twist* to *Effi Briest*, are centrally concerned with the individual's relation to society and hence also with the respective nation. Yet, in a deeper sense, the state of the nation is obviously not their central concern. The significance of nationhood for peripheral literature leads undoubtedly to a stronger "allegorical" encoding, which is to say that family constellations or narratives of private histories refer more or less directly to questions of national identity formation.[22]

Thus the thematization of the problem of nationhood occurs especially in those countries or regions that come to be associated with a peripheral, "belated" status in the context of (European) modernity. This has certainly to do with the fact that the more established nation-states (notably France and England) are also distinguished by a higher degree of autonomy of the literary field, as Pascale Casanova would have it.[23] Yet, even if we stay within the confines of the nineteenth century and the cultural practice of the novel, it would be misleading to simply assign the terms "center" and "periphery" to specific places or nations. Rather, these terms must be understood in a relational and mobile sense, as applied to specific historical and cultural circumstances. Yet at the same time the dynamic of center and periphery is a crucial ingredient for the self-understanding of the nineteenth-century world, and it is also central for the spatial imagination of the novel. Take the example of *Madame Bovary*, a novel produced in France, the cultural center at this time, and yet a novel *about* life in the provinces.

I share the view articulated by Mads R. Thomsen, who defends the new paradigm of world literature against certain conceptual shortcomings of a long-dominant version of postcolonial criticism: "the lack of interest in seeing postcolonial literature as part of the same system as the literature of the West, as well as literature from the West that could qualify as post-colonial literature, remains a problem, by creating an irrational divide between the objects of comparative literature and post-colonial studies."[24] As a matter of fact, the idea of Europe is based on the existence of its *internal* peripheries. Since the eighteenth century this internal difference between modern nationhood and provincial marginality has been mapped unto the axis of North versus South (which in turn might be understood as the reconfiguration of a former opposition between West and East), and the rhetoric of cultural difference has been shaped, most influentially, by the likes of Montesquieu and Madame de Staël.[25] In this regard, Roberto Dainotto has recently argued that the spatial mapping of a Eurocentric imaginary is coextensive with the European theorization of history, which accounts in turn for the alleged backwardness of the various European peripheries, notably the South.[26] This means, for instance, that the eighteenth-century understanding of history amounts to a contrasting of the different temporalities of different geographical areas. Yet if the production and representation of internal peripheries is part of the European identity formation, we will have to study not only the external discourses about these spaces as evident, for instance, in travelogues and political-geographical discourses, but also the literary self-representations of these spaces. In fact, the emphasis on economic inequalities in world-systems theory has increasingly been complemented with an awareness of the importance of cultural representations as symbolic responses to the process of globalization.[27]

During the nineteenth century, England and France were the undisputed centers of literary production, especially in the realm of the novel. Accordingly, the emergence or consolidation of literary realism in peripheral spaces of cultural production (Italy, Spain, Portugal) must be understood in terms of the specifically cultural dynamics of central and peripheral spaces. The novels of the nineteenth century constitute a rich archive about the internal geographies and temporalities of the Western world during a time of the consolidation and crisis of national identities.

The spatial aspect of my argument has been strongly influenced by the work of Pascale Casanova and Franco Moretti, the two critics most associated today with inserting literary studies into a paradigm of cultural geography. It might be useful to present here some of their central arguments, as pertaining to the dynamic between center and periphery. Starting with the notion of cultural capital and the premise of the internal differentiation of the literary space, Casanova's innovative study develops a wide-ranging metatheory about the relation of literature to the politics of nationhood, according to which different geographical manifestations enter into a complex field of competition and rivalry, without necessarily being ancillary to (or being entirely independent of) the entity of the nation-state. On the contrary, Casanova argues, the space of literary economy is actually "constituting itself as a distinct world in opposition to the nation and nationalism."[28] This potentially autonomous literary field knows its own dynamics of power, according to which literary authority is measured by its distance from what is perceived as the center (or the centers) of literary production and consecration. While literature is "not a pure emanation of national identity," it necessarily enters into a space that is characterized by international relations: "given, then, that literary capital is national, and that there exists a relation of dependence with regard first to the state, then to the nation, it becomes possible to connect the idea of an economy peculiar to the literary world with the notion of a literary geopolitics."[29]

Although I think that Casanova somewhat overstates the central role that Paris played for centuries as the literary capital of the world (this might itself be a Franco-centric bias), her basic point is suggestive: "in France, the volume of accumulated capital was so great, and the literary domination exerted over the whole of Europe from the eighteenth century onward so uncontested (and indeed incontestable), that it became the most autonomous literary space of all, which is to say the freest in relation to political and national institutions."[30] The notion of literature's potential autonomy, then, is itself a historical result that has to be gradually achieved in divesting the practice of literature of external, political interests. Therefore, if the literatures of the geographical periphery are "lagging behind" in achieving such autonomy, the question of nationhood and a self-perceived backwardness in relation to a cultural center become an explicit concern of the form of the novel.

While Casanova's book is interested in the force fields of globalized literature generally, Franco Moretti has advanced several theses about the relation between the dynamic of center and periphery and the specific form of the modern novel, as well as innovative proposals of how to study its international diffusion. In a much-discussed article, "Conjectures on World Literature," Moretti, basing himself on an eclectic mix of evolutionary and world-systems theory, has argued for a more globalized approach to the question of the emergence of the novel, asserting the "universal" law according to which "the modern novel first arises not as an autonomous development, but as a compromise between a Western formal influence (usually French or English) and local materials."[31] In an earlier work, about the nineteenth-century novel, Moretti had similarly underscored the role of France (Paris) and England (London) as literary export centers with which almost all other European countries had to cope in one form or another. The novel, asserts Moretti, is a "centralized" genre insofar as the majority of European countries are on the receiving side: "provincialism is not so much a question of *difference* from the centre, but rather of *enforced similarity* (and always a little belated)."[32] Since Moretti tends to be more interested in the geographical dynamics of the emergence and diffusion of specific forms as such, rather than in the detailed analysis of the novels (in fact, he has also defended the rather polemical method of "distant reading"), the basic assumption of cultural dependency, unevenness, and diffusion from the center to the periphery is hard to contest and perhaps little surprising.[33] Yet as soon as we look at the novels of the literary peripheries in greater detail, it is indeed the difference, the variation, the specifics of the "compromise formula," that come to light. Moreover, in the context of the nineteenth century, the notion of the "emergence" of the novel is not unproblematic, since the novel is a constantly evolving form that always builds on and transforms previous models, according to the conditions of the local context.[34]

Moretti's use of the term "provincialism" in the quotation above is likewise revealing, since, in contrast, the term "periphery" is potentially much more ambivalent, for as a place of liminality it is associated both with marginality and productiveness. Albrecht Koschorke, drawing on the cultural semiotics of Jurij M. Lotman, has clarified the difference between the two terms: "While the province is customarily associated with the seat of tradition, having become rigid in its conventionalism and which thus forms a 'cold' zone [in the terminology of Lévi-Strauss], 'periphery' refers to the contact zone to other cultural and discursive spaces, where different semiotic conventions collide and disintegrate."[35] In this sense, I would argue that the "peripheral" novels here discussed anticipate not only our current concern with processes of globalization but also our present sense that the "homogenizing force of modernity" is an illusion that has faded in the light of a "plurality of paths toward modernization" and a plurality of temporal worlds.[36]

What is the relationship of the periphery to history? And what is the significance of the (internal) periphery for the self-constitution, or self-understanding, of the nation? The various novels considered here concern themselves with worlds in transformation or with disappearing worlds. The modern sense of nationhood relies on the temporal structure of the novel to imagine its own relation to historical change. I focus deliberately on national case studies that are thought of as peripheral within the context of nineteenth-century (literary) history. While

I will work with the conceptual opposition of center and periphery throughout this study, it is again important to emphasize that these terms are not intended as stable, fixed categories, but that the rapport is always one of relation and perspective, subject to particular views and historical change.[37]

With regard to the corpus of novels discussed here, I argue that a more explicit representation of nationhood occurs during specific moments in time and in particular places, in semiperipheral zones that undergo a process of modernization and thus entertain an ambivalent relation to history. Neither Sicily nor Portugal is peripheral per se, but the question of their cultural and political "backwardness" has become a part of their own self-understanding. Methodologically, this means that I will read novels in terms of how their plot of a private history (genealogical decadence, familial rivalry, generational change) echoes specific moments of national history and temporal experience. Genealogy is not just a theme or motif but something like a deep structure of the nineteenth-century novel—and, as we will see in the latter part of the book, it reappears in different forms in the novel of the twentieth century.

As indicated above, such questions have been discussed with regard to regional literature, which is often seen as "resisting" the forces of history, but regional spaces might also be seen to dramatize the workings of history, precisely because they are opposing it, and hence maintain an ambivalent relation to a process of modernization.[38] In this sense, I present exemplary readings of novels in terms of a cultural geography where the conditions and contingencies of "place" are subject to the workings of history and where, accordingly, time is spatialized. In a sense, the central part of my study may be seen as an alternative, complementary panorama of the late nineteenth-century novel, bypassing the conventional center in favor of "peripheral" cultures (Italy, Spain, Portugal, Brazil), which culturally are also strongly related to each other. The focus on these specific peripheral literatures entails no judgment about aesthetic value on my part; it simply follows from my interest in processes of cultural adaptation and multiple temporalities. With respect to the question of how the representation of peripheral cultures may, at least in some cases, achieve a literary universality, let me quote Francesco Orlando's suggestive comment about *Il Gattopardo*:

> How can it be that the Sicilian situation is of interest for Finnish, Brazilian, and Japanese readers, if the literary work was not capable to transform this situation into something greater? For it is indeed transformed into a general category, of which the specific reality represents a particular aspect; yet by definition all other, analogous specific realities are also included. [. . .] From the specific peripheral

situation of Sicily toward the universality of all peripheral situations; from *one* periphery (or: province, hinterland, underdeveloped region . . .) toward what tends to become *the* periphery, even if it is strongly individualized.[39]

These individual novels testify to the importance of spatiotemporal coordinates in the history of the modern novel; they all reflect on moments of crisis, transition, and sociohistorical change. Aside from these thematic and historical contexts, I have also sought to address the ways in which literary history, or indeed the authors themselves, have variously reflected upon the peripheral nature of the novelistic genre in their respective countries. Consequently, I have often asked myself whether the texts I have studied here are themselves somehow peripheral in the canon of world literature. In the case of *Waverley* and *Il Gattopardo*, it is readily apparent that the forceful and culturally influential representation of peripheral space is the *reason* for their prominent position in the history of the novel and within world literature. In the case of the other authors I have chosen to discuss, the situation is more difficult to assess. Certainly Galdós, Eça de Queirós, and Machado de Assis are among the most canonical authors of the literary tradition of their respective countries even today, but they remain relatively little known (and translated) outside their native contexts, certainly among a nonspecialist readership. This is most likely due to the fact that these authors' comparatively strong emphasis on national concerns continues to inform the cultural self-understanding of their respective countries, but the same trait, as well as the problem of translation, has likely hindered their traveling abroad.[40] During the nineteenth century, the cultural centers of the realist novel were undoubtedly France, England, and Russia, but, as the historian Jürgen Osterhammel has rightfully pointed out with regard to the example of Eça de Queirós, among others, even novelists from peripheral countries might be exceptionally incisive about the social and historical transformations of their time.[41]

The methodological challenge of my study lies in combining a certain degree of historical specificity with a comparative range that allows for the emergence and variation of specific patterns of both similarity and difference within the cultural space of Europe (and beyond), extending the comparative radar both to hypercanonical and less canonical authors.[42] Therefore, I bring together texts that are normally discussed only *within* the bounds of their respective national contexts and disciplines. I see the task of comparative literature as establishing and making visible the links between national and international, global frames of reference. I hope that my focus on periphery is a contribution to this line of investigation, because as a relational term it brings to the fore the interconnectedness of spatial relations, highlighting the differences as well as the comparable experiences of history within and among nationally constituted spaces.

Overview

The central chapters of this study are dedicated to the nineteenth-century novel, most of which written during the 1880s and 1890s, falling squarely under the influence of a naturalist aesthetic. As a way of introducing the central categories of this study, the second chapter addresses novelistic history at a much earlier stage, at the beginning of the nineteenth century. It is dedicated to the regions of the so-called Celtic Fringe, Ireland and Scotland. This section serves as a sort of general introduction insofar as it seeks to locate the "origin" of the specific spatiotemporal constellation that uses the form of the novel for the interrelation of a historical, geographical, and genealogical consciousness. Maria Edgeworth's short novel *Castle Rackrent* (1800) serves as a convenient point of entry, because it might be seen as the first European genealogical, or "Big House," novel, a tradition that culminates, at least within the confines of my study, with *Il Gattopardo*. The case of Ireland exemplifies my contention that nationhood enters the nineteenth-century novel as a theme to the extent that it is problematical and contested. The novel introduces a sort of historicizing attitude into its depictions of "old" Irish customs, so as to promote the new union between England and Ireland. The form of the national tale adopted by Edgeworth rests on the central image of the house/family as an allegory for the nation, and it is precisely the "absurd" claim of genealogical continuity—contradicted by factual decline and breakdown—that is meant to show that any claims for an independent Irish state are unjustified and must give way to a peaceful union with England. The historicizing impulse in *Castle Rackrent* has influenced Walter Scott's *Waverley* (1814), another novel concerned with descent and familial union, in which the origin of a national union—between England and Scotland—is put more decisively into the historical past. Scott's vastly influential novel provides a paradigm for the interrelation between past and present, political and private history. These novels by Edgeworth and Scott exemplify the historical idea of transition, from an "old" to a "new" form of existence; the question of geography, especially in the sense of the relation between center and periphery; and finally the problem of nationhood. In all of these aspects, these pioneers of the genealogical-historical novel anticipate much of the novelistic production of the nineteenth century, which will then graft realistic/naturalistic premises on this initial chronotopic constellation based on Romantic historiography. The historical background of these early novels is the incorporation of peripheral regions into a larger framework of national and socioeconomic modernity, and hence there is a more or less direct line from here to *Il Gattopardo*, via the various permutations of this constellation throughout the nineteenth century.

In the third chapter, I look at the more immediate predecessors of Lampedusa's novel in the realm of the Italian, specifically the Sicilian, novel. The family novels by Giovanni Verga (*I Malavoglia*, 1881) and Federico De Roberto (*I Viceré*, 1894) are key texts in the belated flowering of the Italian novel toward the end of the nineteenth century. They are representative examples for the European diffusion of the model of literary naturalism, and therefore I will discuss the ways they differ from Émile Zola's novelistic program and its paradoxical relation to narratives of decadence and progress. As novels that are focused largely on the synchronic group of families, they are concerned, respectively, with a rural, regional lifeworld and the lifeworld of the aristocracy. Both novels are grounded in a sceptic or even pessimist view of the recent process of national unification. In the context of an incipient process of economic and political modernization, the two novels illustrate with "objective" modes of representation two tendencies of modernity's historical understanding of its own recent past, insofar as an—admittedly very small—bourgeois readership was confronted with the picture of a peripheral social world that is left behind and transformed by modernity (*I Malavoglia*), as well as a social group that is simultaneously marked by both decline and adaptation (*I Viceré*). The idea that the peripheral island space is marked by a resistance to modernity and historical change indicates a doubt in the evolutionary thinking of the nineteenth century.

In chapters 4 and 5, I examine the crisis of genealogy in the Spanish novel during the Restoration period. The realist/naturalist authors of this period were extremely self-conscious about the peripheral condition of the contemporary Spanish novel/nation, and accordingly the representation of the literary theme of familial crisis and decline serves to reflect allegorically on the state of the nation and its relation to modernization and change. These questions are discussed here with regard to the urban novel, Benito Pérez Galdós's *Fortunata y Jacinta* (1887), as well as the regional novel, Emilia Pardo Bazán's cycle of Galician novels (*Los Pazos de Ulloa*, 1886; *La madre naturaleza*, 1887). While Galdós uses the motif of genealogical decline with regard to processes of social transformation, Pardo Bazán develops a complex (and often unresolved) portrait of the periphery's resistance to the process of "civilization." While Galdós's novel proposes interclass exogamy as a possible solution to familial/national crisis in the context of the urban bourgeoisie, Pardo Bazán's novels focus on endogamous unions and incest as metaphors for a repeated conflict between nature and civilization, exemplified by the decline of the rural aristocracy.

Incest is also the central metaphor for the genealogical crisis represented in the most accomplished nineteenth-century novel in Portugal, *Os Maias* (1888), by Eça de Queirós. In the sixth chapter, I am especially interested in how the idea of social-familial crisis, the sense of an evolutionary end or impasse, affects the form of the realist novel. In this respect, in its relativizing of naturalist claims, its depiction of a generational disillusion, its stylistic hybridity, episodic structure, and a greater subjective focalization, the novel evidences not only general decadent trends of the European novel at the end of the nineteenth century; it also reflects on the ways "modern civilization" is introduced into the Portuguese context. Eça sees the Portuguese adaptation of cultural modernity as ultimately nothing but a surface change, which explains the critical and satirical tendency of his view on society. A similar tendency toward satire and late-realist techniques of representation may also be seen in Eça's Brazilian contemporary Machado de Assis, despite the fact that they disagreed about their uses of realism. Machado's late novel *Esaú e Jacó* (1904) about identical twin brothers, the subject of chapter 7, brings us from internal European peripheries to the self-perception of Brazil, and Latin America generally, as inheritors of the European model of historical progress. In this sense, Machado's novel can be read as an ironic response to the genre of the historical and genealogical novel. More radically and explicitly than in Eça's novel, Machado's work reveals satirically the truncation of the patriarchal family as well as the idea that historical change might be more rhetoric than practice. Taken together, these novels from roughly the latter third of the nineteenth century are variously concerned with the introduction or importation of modernity into peripheral spaces. Implicitly, and as can be gleaned from authorial comments, this also includes a self-reflection on the introduction of the form of the realist/naturalist novel. While many of these peripheral novels interrogate the idea of social and historical change, they provide a more or less panoramic view of their respective families, societies, and nations.

In chapters 8 and 9, I turn to the legacy of the genealogical novel in the first half of the twentieth century, with two representative, symptomatic case studies. In chapter 8, I discuss briefly the phenomenon of the modernist and regionalist "estate novel," where the problem of genealogy and periphery is represented in a specific regional space that is still seen as metonymic for the nation as a whole. My example here is the Faulkner-influenced Brazilian writer Lins do Rego, whose novel *Menino de engenho* (*Plantation Boy*, 1932) registers the economic decline of the sugar mills in Northeastern Brazil through the decadence of the feudal-patriarchal structure underwriting the plantation world. In contrast to the nineteenth-century novel, this type of fictionalized autobiography abandons the classical third-person narrator in favor of a more or less unfiltered representation of individual consciousness. A subjective, memorial impulse also characterizes Tomasi di Lampedusa's *Il Gattopardo* (1958), discussed in chapter 9—although its subjective focus is ingeniously tempered by ironic distancing. In both cases the reconstructed, dying world is shadowed by a mood of elegiac nostalgia, accompanied by the recognition of inevitable loss. This means that these novels, in regressing to a time "before the end," are already and inevitably shaped by the subsequent knowledge of decline, which accounts for the often complex relation among different levels of time. These genealogical novels of the twentieth century, then, rest on a different understanding of history; they emphasize the importance of individual memory in the representation of collective history; and, finally, they show that these narratives of familial decline correspond to the re-evocation of peripheral spaces that is self-conscious about the inevitably past-oriented view of its "aristocratic" perspective. In terms of literary history, the subjective and memorial perspective is mediated here by the examples of Faulkner and Proust, even if the thematic concerns—most obviously in *Il Gattopardo*—demonstrate strong continuities with the nineteenth-century novel. In my epilogue, I provide a short sketch of the way in particular the formal innovations of Faulkner have enabled yet a further transformation of the genealogical novel in the latter half of the European twentieth century, where the destructive forces of family constellations have served to construct radically disordered narratives about the distinctively traumatic remembrance of history in the postwar period.

CHAPTER TWO

Periphery and Genealogical Discontinuity

The Historical Novel of the Celtic Fringe
(Maria Edgeworth and Walter Scott)

The beginning of the nineteenth century witnessed a transformation in the conception of historical time. The gradual emergence of History as a singular container for human actions and its understanding as a dynamic force within the open-ended flow of time was soon accompanied by the idea of an "allochronic" scenario, an internal differentiation, according to which certain spaces might be characterized as lagging behind the universal flow of progressing time.[1] As Reinhart Koselleck writes, "In the horizon of this progression the simultaneity of the non-simultaneous becomes the basic experience of all history."[2] In this context, the emergence of the new evolutionary, postrevolutionary concept of history is concomitant with the narrative of modernity that always carries with it a "phantasm of the pre- or anti-modern, a phantasm that is marked on all levels by clear signs of the creation of difference," as Albrecht Koschorke has put it.[3]

If the form of the modern novel had since the eighteenth century been conceived as the representation of a particular lifeworld firmly situated in both temporal and spatial terms, the historical turn of the early nineteenth-century novel directly addresses the question of the transitional moments through which modernity conceives its own genealogy as leaving behind what is now reconfigured as its own past. Recent studies of English fiction have generally underscored how much the constitution of the British novel was influenced by negotiation with cultural and geographical peripheries, notably the Celtic fringe nations of Ireland and Scotland.[4] In line with the tenets of Scottish Enlightenment historiography, the British peripheries have been symbolically configured as symbolic "chronotopes," whose lifeworlds are related to the present, homogeneous culture as its own temporal past. Maria Edgeworth's *Castle Rackrent* (1800) and Walter Scott's *Waverley* (1814) are two paradigmatic novels that inaugurate the connection among family narratives, historical transition, and spatialized temporality that will continue to characterize many European novels throughout the nineteenth century. I read these texts as a specific type of (anti)genealogical fiction, whereby familial descent is thematized but actually questioned as a form of legitimization. These novels amount to "retrograde fictions," which reconstruct the past in terms of its difference. They are typical fictions of modernity to the extent that the genealogy of the present actually depends on the demotion of the claims of traditional genealogy.

History and Discontinuity in Maria Edgeworth's *Castle Rackrent*

In relation to the other material to be treated in this study, Maria Edgeworth's short novel *Castle Rackrent* (1800) is an extremely early text that in many respects still belongs to the cultural history of the eighteenth century. And yet *Castle Rackrent* has been repeatedly claimed as an inaugural text on several accounts. It is variously said to be one of the first novels to be written in dialect, one of the earliest (and certainly most famous) Irish novels, the first regional novel, the first historical novel, and the first family or Big House novel.[5] Regarding this latter genre, it has also been argued that *Castle Rackrent* began a specifically Irish tradition of literature, "where marital introversion and endangered succession will come to provide a potent theme in Anglo-Irish modernism."[6] This, however, also accounts for the fact that this fascinating text has for a long time received the attention only of specialized scholars dedicated to the study of Anglo-Irish literature. This state of affairs has recently changed somewhat, especially thanks to the work of Katie Trumpener, who has argued that the Irish and Scottish novels of the so-called Celtic Fringe have played an important role in the development of what we call, somewhat paradoxically, the tradition of the English novel, especially the historical novel.[7]

But why Ireland? Why should the origin of genealogical fiction in the European novel take place precisely here? For a long part of its history, the national identity of England or Great Britain has been defined and complicated by its composite nature, an array of internal differences comprising the different territories and traditions of England, as well as Ireland, Wales, and Scotland. As Linda Colley has remarked in her magisterial study of British nationhood, the case of Ireland is even more exceptional than the other peripheries of the empire: "the invention of Britishness was so closely bound up with Protestantism, with war with France and with the acquisition of empire, that Ireland was rarely able or willing to play a satisfactory part in it."[8] Ireland in particular posed a challenge to the identity of England, and throughout the nineteenth century there were numerous discussions about the possibility of its assimilation, the difference or otherness (not to mention the alleged primitivism or barbarity) of the

Celtic element, including the question of whether there existed such a thing as an Irish nationality in its own right. Yet what prevailed and underwrote all of these discussions was a sense of Ireland's marginality with regard to the center of England.

History, Time, Narration

The literary works of Maria Edgeworth (1767–1849), possibly the most highly regarded Anglophone novelist before Scott, are concerned with the problem of the union of England and Ireland during the eighteenth century. Edgeworth's novels are exemplary instances of the genre of the "national tale," a specifically Irish genre that flourished between the Act of Union (1800) and the Catholic Emancipation (1829).[9] The historical significance of the national tale consists in the way it fashions the identity of national communities, as well as international relations. With the partial exception of *Castle Rackrent*, Edgeworth's novels have often been criticized as overly schematic in their moral didacticism. However, as Terry Eagleton has suggested, the antirealist and allegorical bent of nineteenth-century Irish prose fiction might be understood as a correlative of the colonial, pre-urban society of Ireland in which social roles are more deeply entrenched than in the contemporaneous metropolitan society, which was more conducive to the notion of individualism and the illusion of realism.[10] If the question of nationhood emerges first in the work of Maria Edgeworth and her Anglo-Irish near contemporaries, this was no coincidence, Eagleton argues, for the question of national identity becomes an issue for fiction precisely there, where it is beset by anxieties and is not a "natural" given. The metaphor of the family union, central to the work of Edgeworth and her contemporaries, is undoubtedly a key to this dimension of allegorical meaning. In the wake of the union between England and Ireland, the metaphorics of a family union were frequently used in political and literary discourse. In this context, Ireland was variously termed as the "brother," "cousin," "younger sister," "reluctant bride," or the "uneducated son" of England.[11] In this sense the family politics of Edgeworth's novel refer directly to the conflicted international relation between Ireland and England, the creation of a "family" past that may license the situation of the present.

The title of *Castle Rackrent* refers, on the one hand, to the name of the particular family that will be chronicled here over four generations. On the other hand, the practice of "rackrenting" refers to the broader phenomenon of the customary financial exploitation by which mostly absent landlords were extricating money from the local Irish tenant population, by means of resident middlemen, to finance their costly lifestyle abroad. Already the word "Rackrent," then, links together the history of a family and the question of economic property. The image of the house, or "castle," becomes a domestic symbol for a disordered nation and a ruling class in decline.

Using the example of the Rackrent family, the novel depicts in a satirical manner the way of life of the Irish landed aristocracy before 1782. After the reconquest of Ireland in 1649 by Oliver Cromwell, the government had reinforced Protestant settlements in a country with a primarily Catholic population. Although the situation of Catholicism was intermittently strengthened—for example, at the time of the Glorious Revolution (1688–89)—the eighteenth century witnessed the securing of the "Protestant Nation." The Protestant minority controlled the practice of jurisdiction and administration, and Protestant power was further strengthened by a series of penal laws that deprived the Catholic population of its social and civic rights. Ireland had been declared part of the British Empire in 1780, and in 1782 it received a new constitution that guaranteed partial independence from England, and accordingly the aristocracy and gentry aimed to achieve a greater sense of Irish nationhood. Yet the growing sense of discontent among the rural classes paved the way for the legislation leading to the union with England. The year 1800—the year of the publication of *Castle Rackrent*—is the year of the Union, and hence it marks the end of Irish political autonomy. The Union had been preceded by extreme political unrest, including the Wolf Tome rising, a rebellion of Irish nationalists in 1798, which was defeated by the English.[12] Eventually, the Irish Parliament, dominated by Protestant landlords, agreed to vote for the Act of Union, against the will of the Catholic Irish population.

Maria Edgeworth's father, Richard Lowell Edgeworth, was an estate-owning landlord in the county of Longford, in the family's possession since the sixteenth century. In 1782 the Edgeworth family had settled in Ireland, where Richard Lowell dedicated himself to the improvement of the life of his tenants. Maria's father transmitted to her a freethinking spirit and the rational-empirical values of the Enlightenment so that, as her biographer Marilyn Butler puts it, she bore "the intellectual stamp of a generation, or half a generation, earlier than that of her own adulthood."[13] Both father and daughter generally endorsed the pro-Union argument, hoping that it would raise the level of civilization in Ireland.[14] Essentially, their unusually "enlightened" view of the aristocracy's social responsibility was intended to stall the specter of social revolution.[15] The Edgeworths shared a belief in a liberal market economy and were exemplary landlords in the sense that they engaged no middlemen on their Irish estate in Edgeworthstown.[16] From early on, at only fourteen years of age, Maria served her father as an assistant on the estate, and she claimed that many of her novels and tales were inspired by her experiences with the tenants.[17]

The historicizing, documentary intention of *Castle Rackrent* already appears in its complete subtitle: *An Hibernian Tale Taken from Facts and from the Manners of the Irish Squires before the Year 1782.* Both the time and the geographical space of the narrated events are marked by a distance from the perspective of the contemporary English reader. As Franco Moretti has underscored, representations of "other," peripheral spaces habitually conceive of them as historically prior to the cultural or political center.[18] The situation of the impending union leads the author to historicize the representation of Irish manners. This historicization is achieved especially by the complex paratextual material of the short novel, which both authenticates and distances the content of the main narrative for the contemporary reader. Note how the following passage from the preface, sometimes attributed to Richard Lowell Edgeworth, figures the narrative's temporal relation to the event of the Union:

> The Editor hopes his readers will observe, that these are "tales of other times"; that the manners depicted in the following pages are not those of the present age: the race of the Rackrents has long since been extinct in Ireland, and the drunken Sir Patrick, the litigious Sir Murtagh, the fighting Sir Kit, and the slovenly Sir Condy, are characters which could no more be met with at present in Ireland, than Squire Western or Parson Trulliber in England. There is a time when individuals can bear to be rallied for their past follies and absurdities, after they have acquired new habits and a new consciousness. Nations as well as individuals gradually lose attachment to their identity, and the present generation is amused rather than offended by the ridicule that is thrown upon their ancestors. Probably we shall soon have it in our power, in a hundred instances, to verify the truth of these observations.
>
> When Ireland loses her identity by an union with Great Britain, she will look back with a smile of good-humoured complacency on the Sir Kits and Sir Condys of her former existence. (*CR*, 4–5)

This passage projects the time of union into the future, while it simultaneously enacts a vision of a discontinuous past from the prospected view of this future ("will look back"). The passage establishes an implicit parallel between the nation and the family, while the term "generation" appears as the mediating link between the individual and the larger collective. The external narrator of the preface is bent on containing the dubious manners of the main narrative by telling the reader that these customs may no longer be observed in the present. The

novel does ideological work, then, in displacing present contradictions to a diachronic narrative that turns them into signs of the past. The humor produced
by the depiction of these customs is precisely an effect of the historicization of
the old Irish ways and hence of a distinctively Irish character.[19]

The narrative situation is unusually complex and accounts for the special
interest, as well as for the divergent interpretations, of this novel. The author of
the preface and the other paratextual material, the "editor," is to be distinguished
from the narrator of the novel proper, the Irish Catholic and old family steward
Thady Quirk, who tells the entire story with his characteristically rambunctious
and rambling voice, full of indigenous humor and Irish expressions ("in his ver-
nacular idiom," *CR*, 4), as a "plain unvarnished tale" (*CR*, 2) and who relates this
story to the editor of the book. The editor clearly disassociates himself from
Thady, one of those "who without sagacity to discriminate character, without
elegance of style to relieve the tediousness of narrative, without enlargement of
mind to draw any conclusions from the facts they relate, simply pour forth anecdotes and retail conversations, with all the minute prolixity of a gossip in a country town" (*CR*, 3). While the editor takes a conscious distance from the high-flown,
aristocratic style of traditional historiography, he also looks down on what he
regards as the severe limitations of Thady's anecdotal, unordered, and unrefined
style.

Edgeworth, then, has recourse to the convention of an editor, who, as it were,
"translates" the story of the Rackrent family for an English audience. Ingeniously,
the narration of the family history is given over to the voice of Thady, a marginal
figure who is a subordinate part of the narrated world but who reconstitutes
himself as a narrating subject. The servant, as Bakhtin remarked, is the most
"privileged witness to private life."[20] At the same time, the paratextual framing
of the editor (consisting of the preface, notes, and "glossary") has the function
not only to mediate but also to actively contain Thady's discourse.[21]

Most central to the significance of the novel, then, is the fact that the strongly
individualized, flavorful voice of Thady is not allowed to speak directly but is
temporally and culturally framed by the mediating, "objective" voice of the editor. It is precisely this double narrative construction that accounts for the combined features of a regional novel with a colonial perspective in *Castle Rackrent*.[22]
Edgeworth's novel is the product of a particular situation of "internal colonialism," a specific cultural, linguistic, ethnic identity that has been, or will be, suppressed by and coerced into the centralizing logic of a nation-state that seeks to
assimilate its Celtic otherness. While a "regionalist" perspective would look for
the survival and continuity of local traditions, the novel in fact exhibits these

traditions as characteristic of a past that is different from "our" present. The region is domesticated, since its foreignness is both distanced and contained.[23]

Genealogy and Discontinuity

So far, we have seen that Maria Edgeworth, or the editorial voice, is invested in containing Thady's story by consigning it to the past. We need now to have a closer look at the kind of family story Thady tells. The choice of the "old" and "faithful" family retainer as the narrating voice of a multigenerational story is a convenient device to anchor the narrative in a subjective, distanced viewpoint and yet to cover a broad arc of time. Thady's memory encompasses the entire series of four different landlords over half a century, up to the pathetic death of its last representative, and even goes back to what he has heard about the early family history, especially the half-mythic figure of Sir Patrick, from *his* grandfather, who had also been in the service of the family (*CR*, 9):

> The family of the Rackrents is, I am proud to say, one of the most ancient in the kingdom. Everybody knows this is not the old family name, which was O'Shaughlin, related to the Kings of Ireland. . . . The estate came . . . in *the* family, upon one condition, which Sir Patrick O'Shaughlin at the time took sadly to bear, they say, but thought better of it afterwards, seeing how large a stake depended upon it, that he should, by Act of Parliament, take and bear the sirname [*sic*] and arms of Rackrent. (*CR*, 9)

As this passage implies, under the Penal Laws the Irish aristocracy was forced to become Anglo-Irish; the change of name already betrays a distance from their originally Irish identity. It is significant that the reader learns at the beginning that at the ancient Sir Patrick's time the family name was changed from O'Shaughlin to Rackrent—that is, from a Catholic to a Protestant association—as the government's condition for the family to acquire the estate. Thady's simultaneous contention that the Rackrent family is "one of the most ancient in the kingdom" (*CR*, 8) is thus immediately contrasted with a factual discontinuity. Insofar as the feudal genealogy ("related to the kings of Ireland") is replaced with a new entitlement depending on legal-political authority—and the Irish name with an Anglo-Irish one—Thady's assertion of long-standing continuity is revealed as a fictional construct.

Likewise, the succession of four different generations is not matched by a true sense of temporality. On the contrary, the novel is characterized by a narrative disconnection between the different sections and episodes that endows it with a certain static quality. This sense of disconnectedness is the formal equivalent of the novel's implicit moral agenda, namely to critique what is merely a semblance or mockery of genealogical continuity. The first of the Rackrents, Sir Patrick, signifies for Thady's nostalgic vision an image of plenitude and unbounded hospitality. Although Thady had never seen him in life, he says, "I love to look upon his picture, now opposite to me" (*CR*, 10). The image of plenitude, continuity, and social conviviality embodied by Sir Patrick is thus literally the effect of Thady's retrospective imaginings. The narrative of dynastic lineage and decline requires an original, mythic point of original presence. Indeed, the servant's discourse and his transgenerational memory is the only place in the novel where a semblance of genealogical continuity exists and is actively constructed.[24]

As for the different generations of the Rackrent family, they are all examples of a ridiculously irresponsible, self-gratifying squirearchy, giving themselves over to gambling, drinking, sloth, and greed. The succession of the first four Rackrents illustrates their different vices. Sir Patrick has run into debts because of his endless eating and drinking. Sir Murtagh is satirized because of his innumerable lawsuits ("he had a law-suit for every letter in the alphabet," *CR*, 15) and perfects the system of tenant duty labor, while his wife, Lady Murtagh, extracts all kinds of feudal tributes from the tenants (*CR*, 14). Sir Kit imprisons his Jewish wife for seven years because he has no access to her money, and the fourth, Sir Condy, coming from decidedly lowly origins, marries an elegant Jewish woman from London who is appalled at the ruined condition of the estate. Although he is in Thady's view the most sympathetic representative of the Rackrents, Sir Condy displays a similar degree of irresponsibility and remains childless, as well. Indeed, with the exception of Sir Patrick (who bequeaths the estate to his son Murtagh), all of the other Rackrents fail to produce an heir. Instead of a line of patriarchal succession, the inheritance is passed along the fraternal line: "Sir Murtagh, I forgot to notice, had no childer [*sic*], so the Rackrent estate went to his younger brother" (*CR*, 18). Hence, these repeated disruptions of continuity glaringly disprove the dynastic-genealogical claims of Thady's narrative. The question of the Rackrent genealogy is intimately connected to the question of the transmission of property. The men are always marrying with the intent to acquire money or property, the marriages are always unhappy ones, and the women are represented as essentially foreign to the Irish element.

Thady's pathologically loyal account always tries to present the Rackrent family in the best possible light, against the patent facts that he himself reveals to the reader. Thus, about the founder of the Rackrent dynasty, Sir Patrick, we learn merely that he was distinguished in the arts of singing and drinking and that he was the "inventor of raspberry whiskey" (*CR*, 10). Thady's comments on the Rackrents are continuously marked by this ambivalence, where his apparent naïveté is merely a cover for a deeper, implicit social critique. The comic effect and the irony of the text derive precisely from the mismatch between the proclaimed illustriousness of the family and their actual performance. Indeed, it is not difficult to see how Thady's professed pride just barely covers an underlying sense of inarticulate, half-conscious shame. This becomes apparent, for example, when he touches upon the practice of absenteeism, the responsibility for which he displaces to the agent, rather than directly blaming his master (*CR*, 21).

The narrative concerning the history of Sir Condy, taking up the entire second part of the novel, is markedly distinguished from the first part, with its rapid sketches of the merely absurd activities of the first three Rackrent representatives. Since Sir Condy comes from only "a remote branch of the family" (*CR*, 38), Thady tries to instill in him a sense of family tradition (*CR*, 39). Likewise, the peasant neighbors tell Sir Condy that "he was a great likeness of Sir Patrick, which made him first have an ambition to take after him, as far as his fortune should allow" (*CR*, 40). It appears, then, that the semblance of genealogical continuity is literally an effect of narratives, for Thady creates Sir Condy in the image of Sir Patrick. For instance, before Sir Condy dies at the end of the novel, he comes up with the absurd idea to witness his own funeral, whereupon Thady comments, "I did not doubt his honor's would be as great a funeral as ever Sir Patrick O'Shauglin's was" (*CR*, 81). Through Thady's stylization of Sir Condy as a second Sir Patrick, we are thus referred to the early scene of Sir Patrick's "grand" funeral. At the moment of Sir Patrick's funeral lamentations, the editor inserts in the "glossary" a long note about Irish funeral customs, quoting various authorities to the effect that during the Irish funeral the "genealogy, rank, possessions, the virtues and vices of the dead were rehearsed," according to customs deriving themselves "from their Celtic ancestors, the primaeval inhabitants of this isle" (*CR*, 100). The editor takes this occasion to comment on the decadence of these customs in the present: "It is curious to observe how customs and ceremonies degenerate. The present Irish cry or howl cannot boast of much melody, nor is the funeral procession conducted with much dignity" (*CR*, 101). This editorial emphasis on the decline of folkloric tradition, then, might be related to the familial decline of the Rackrents. For, as it turns out, Sir Condy, the last of the Rackrents at the time of his second—actual—death, "had but a very poor funeral, after all" (*CR*, 96). The comments of the "glossary," then, reinforce the sense of decline: a decline of customs, a decline from Sir Patrick to Sir Condy.

Let us return to the question of Thady's viewpoint, which has provoked various critical speculations as to his being naïve, scheming, dissimulating, sycophantic—in short, unreliable. His absolute loyalty to the dissolute family is so persistent that we might indeed ask whether there is not a particular motivation or strategy behind it. If Thady were completely serious about what he was saying, we would have to judge him hopelessly blind in light of the blatant dissolution of the Rackrent estate. But if he were not serious, why then would he adopt a tone that does not betray his critique and insight? Why would he protest so much—since as the loyal servant he is obviously complicit with the malpractices of the family?[25]

The irony of Thady's position is buttressed by the fact that it is his son Jason Quirk who is to take over the family estate after the "race of the Rackrents" has died out, suggesting the emergence of practical, bourgeois thought and a capitalist money economy as a consequence, or cause, of the demise of feudalism and its irresponsible practice of economic waste. Jason might be an unsympathetic figure and a parasite of the feudal system, yet he symbolizes future social change and mobility, an emerging middle class—a characteristic constellation of forces that will recur in many subsequent Big House or genealogical novels (Primitivo in *Los Pazos de Ulloa*, the Snopes clan in Faulkner's Yoknapatawpha cycle, Don Calogero in *Il Gattopardo*, etc.).

While the legal takeover occurs only at the end of the novel, Thady had already mentioned his son at the beginning of the text, bringing into view his clever machinations. Thady sets up a contrast between him and Jason, and the reader is alerted not only to the retrospective nature of Thady's account—the takeover has already taken place at the time of narration—but also to Thady's essential ambivalence (shame? anger? concealed pride?) toward the social success of his son Jason: "you would hardly think 'poor Thady' was the father of attorney Quirk; he is a high gentleman, and never minds what poor Thady says, and having better than 1500 a-year, landed estate, looks down upon honest Thady, but I wash my hands of his doings" (*CR*, 8). Jason has from early on been schooled in practical accounting by the agents, while the absent master was away gambling at Bath. While Sir Condy is entirely oblivious of business matters, or unwilling to deal with them, Jason Quirk, who had helped him already during grammar school, is slowly taking over the financial administration of the estate and is lending money to the heavily indebted Sir Condy, eventually becoming his principle creditor. Faced with Sir Condy's ever-growing dependence on Jason, Thady sings the praises of Sir Condy ("I never seen a man more fair, and honest, and easy in all his dealings," *CR*, 73) and eventually pities him, while he chides his own son for improper dealings: "what will people tink [sic] and say, when they see you living here in Castle Rackrent, and the lawful owner turned out of the seat of his ancestors (*CR*, 77). Thady's ambiguous position between loyalty to the decadent Rackrents and the relation to his ambitious, social-climbing son makes him often speak with an unconscious contradictoriness that might be seen to echo the rhetorical trope of the so-called Irish "bull."[26] As Vera Kreilkamp has remarked, Thady's unstable identity is characteristic for the colonial basis of the Big House: "as in the American ante-bellum South, where the house servant identified himself with an alien class and denied the claims of his own race, Thady exists finally with no identity of his own."[27]

Castle Rackrent, then, is concerned with the problem of upholding the rhetoric of patriarchal continuity in the face of its actual demise, thus addressing obliquely and ironically the question of the transition to a new social and political world around the 1790s. In the context of the impending union between England and Ireland, *Castle Rackrent* presents an often highly contradictory picture in which, depending on the play of perspective, the change is either deplored or welcomed. Yet, in either case, what is emphasized is the inevitable historicity of the recent past and the constructed nature of dynastic identity and property rights.

Domestic and National Descent in Walter Scott's *Waverley*

As is well known, in his postscript to *Waverley* (1814) Scott emphasizes the influence of his friend Maria Edgeworth on his own novel, crediting her with the innovative representation of the "habits, manners, and feelings" (*W*, 493) of the Irish: "it has been my object to describe these persons, not by a caricatured and exaggerated use of the national dialect, but by their habits, manners, and feelings; so as in some distant degree to emulate the admirable Irish portraits drawn by Miss Edgeworth" (*W*, 493).[28] Similarly, in the general preface to a later edition of *Waverley* (1829), Scott asserts that English readers' familiarization with the character of their Irish neighbors has directly contributed to the achievement of the political union and thus his novel strives at something similar for Scotland:

> Without being so presumptuous as to hope to emulate the rich humour, pathetic tenderness, and admirable tact which pervade the works of my accomplished

friend, I felt that something might be attempted for my own country of the same kind with that which Miss Edgeworth so fortunately achieved for Ireland—something which might introduce her natives to those of her sister kingdom in a more favourable light than they had been placed hitherto, and tend to procure sympathy for their virtues and indulgence for their foibles. (*W*, 523)

As these remarks reveal, Scott understands Edgeworth's—and his own—historicizing impulse as pulling into two different directions: narrative fiction is used to generate sympathy for the other, and yet this "understanding" approach to cultural otherness serves the ultimate purpose of assimilation, since these aspects are relegated to the sphere of the past.[29] We will see how *Waverley* dramatizes private and public discontinuities. First, I will consider the ways the novel links the experience of time to the question of a cultural periphery and the idea of a Romanticized space. Second, I will discuss the private and public dimension of ancestry and family, arguing that the notion of dynastic succession is ultimately demoted to the past.

Nation, Periphery, Time

Waverley is a classic example of a text that undertakes the spatialization of time, as it casts the Scottish Highlands as the symbolic past to the present and the future of the Lowlands.[30] In this regard, the protagonist's function as a traveler is crucial in revealing a symbolic topography that is differentiated by history. Therefore, the hero of the Waverley novels generally moves *toward* the periphery, which is equated with a movement back in time.[31] It is precisely the fact that Scott comes from north of the border that enables him to see the nation as a forging together of its different parts. Scott's novels, even as they embrace the mandates of nation and empire, generate a huge amount of empathy for historical, ethnic, and linguistic otherness. The construction of a national past, therefore, is far from a negation of difference.[32] This intersection of different geographical zones with a logic of uneven development is characteristic of Scott's model of the historical novel, which was in turn central for the development of Romantic historicism during the early nineteenth century. The imperial center's relation to the cultural periphery is symbolically equivalent to the relation of present to past, just as the "historiographical operation" of modernity "presupposes a rupture that changes a tradition into a past object."[33]

Consider in this regard the presentation of the race of the Scottish Highlanders. They are not only described as the descendants of ancient forefathers; they appear as the last embodiments of a past that has survived into the present, as becomes clear on the occasion of the Jacobite army's descent into Edinburgh: they "conveyed to the south-country Lowlanders as much surprise as if an inva- sion of African negroes or Esquimeaux Indians had issued forth from the north- ern mountains of their own native country" (*W*, 324). Such a description of the indigeneous population might be seen as protoethnographic, insofar as the novel's protagonist, Edward Waverley, traverses a bounded zone as a participant observer, whereby the space perceived from this inside/outside perspective as- sumes the quality of a specific culture.[34] As Scott himself remarks in his post- script, *Waverley* registers a process of modernization from the time of the novel's action up until the present of narration and publication in 1814. The passage deserves to be quoted at length:

> There is no European nation which, within the course of half a century, or little more, has undergone so complete a change as this kingdom of Scotland. The ef- fects of the insurrection of 1745—the destruction of the patriarchal power of the Highland chiefs—the abolition of the heritable jurisdictions of the Lowland nobility and barons—the total eradication of the Jacobite party, which, averse to intermingle with the English, or adopt their customs, long continued to pride them- selves upon maintaining ancient Scottish manners and customs—commenced this innovation. The gradual influx of wealth, and extension of commerce, have since united to render the present people of Scotland a class of beings as different from their grandfathers as the existing English are from those of Queen Eliza- beth's time; [. . .] the change, though steadily and rapidly progressive, has, never- theless, been gradual; and like those who drift down the stream of a deep and smooth river, we are not aware of the progress we have made until we fix our eye on the now distant point from which we have been drifted.—Such of the present generation as can recollect the last twenty or twenty-five years of the eighteenth century, will be fully sensible of the truth of this statement; especially if their acquaintance and connections lay among those who, in my younger time, were facetiously called "folks of the old leaven," who still cherished a lingering, though hopeless, attachment to the house of Stuart. This race has now almost entirely vanished from the land, and with it, doubtless, much absurd political prejudice— but also many living examples of singular and disinterested attachment to the principles of loyalty which they received from their fathers, and of old Scottish faith, hospitality, worth, and honor. (*W*, 492)

According to this authorial comment, the distant point serves to distinguish past from present. Again, it is through a spatial image that the movement of time and the representation of history can be envisioned. In contrast to the historian's work, though, the task of the novelist consists in the transmission of a quasi-ethnographic experience that appears as a doubly mediated scene of cultural representation that rests on the focus provided by both geographical and temporal distance. Scott himself had still known some people who had personally witnessed the Jacobite risings of 1745, during which the main narrative takes place. As the narrator states in the final chapter:

> It was my accidental lot, though not born a Highlander [. . .] to reside, during my childhood and youth, among persons of the above description; and now, for the purpose of preserving some idea of the ancient manners of which I have witnessed the almost total extinction, I have embodied in imaginary scenes, and as-cribed to fictitious characters, a part of the incidents which I then received from those who were actors in them. (*W*, 492–93)

As the passage shows, the moment of historical passing occurs at the cross-roads of the subject's autobiographical youth ("my childhood") and the object's late time ("ancient manners," "extinction"). The process of historical transformation is glimpsed through the fact of generational change, or through the located perspective of an individual lifetime, upon which the historical events still cast their shadow. In this sense, the " 'Tis Sixty Years Since" of the novel's sub-title refer to the relative proximity of the narrated events, the span of a lifetime, a single generation: "to elder persons it will recall scenes and characters familiar to their youth; and to the rising generation the tale may present some idea of the manners of their forefathers" (*W*, 494). The narrator of *Waverley* is thus the necessary interpretative link between past and present, a critical witness of generational discontinuity, of the lifeworlds of the "last of the race."[35] This emphasis on the idea of generation as a specific age formation is representative for a postrevolutionary, Romantic historiography that developed a more progressive understanding of historical temporality. This new understanding of the concept of generation located historiographical representation in a particular site of enunciation that is defined by precisely this awareness of generational passing.[36] The historiographical procedure of Scott's texts cannot be imagined without this anchoring point of present enunciation that betrays an irrevocably modern self-consciousness that is simultaneously emancipated of and nostalgic for the past. Again, consider in this light the dating of the narrative to a time "Sixty Years before the present 1st November 1805" (*W*, 34). Readers must themselves calculate that this distance from the present brings them to the year 1745, the year of Culloden. The novel is thus not situated in the vague past, say, of Gothic romance (Scott alludes to Radcliff's *Mysteries of Udolpho*), but rather the reader is instructed to understand the past as a precise distance from the historical moment of 1805.

Significantly, Waverley is not only literally a traveler to the Scottish Highlands; he is also a stand-in for the reader, who "travels" with him in both time and space, and thus he serves to bridge and mediate the different spheres, just as the "border-poet" Scott also occupied an authorial position located in a spatial in-between as a Scottish author primarily writing for an English audience.[37] Accordingly, Waverley is described as potentially belonging to a quasi-bourgeois realm that is relatively close to the experiential world of the contemporary English reader.[38] *Waverley* conjoins the bildungsroman of its "wavering" protagonist with the historical process that is shaping the nation. The reader is constantly confronted with a double perspective: first, the "naïve" perspective of Waverley, who is fascinated by Highland life and manners and, second, the posterior perspective of the narrator who always speaks from the vantage point of the "end," Edward's bildungsroman also implies the developmental path from youth to early manhood, a transition that is imagined as a transformation of generic terms: "the romance of his life was ended, and [. . .] its real history had now commenced" (*W*, 415). The hero's infatuation with the idealized figure of Flora is explicitly associated with the romance mode, and although the hero eventually leaves this mode behind, it also testifies to the fact that romance survives within the realist novel, functioning precisely as a sign for modernity's fascination with its own past.[39]

From Genealogy to Community

Walter Scott himself has reflected on the relationship between romance and history as two different modes concerned with narrative representation of social origins. In an article for the *Encyclopaedia Britannica*, Scott figures the relation between romance and history itself in genealogical terms, as a patriarchal relation between father and son. According to this scheme, the transition from father to son marks a decisive turning point in the mythic reconfiguration of a primordial act of foundation, as it concerns the shift from family to nation:

> The father of an isolated family, destined one day to rise into a tribe, and in further progress of time to expand into a nation, may, indeed, narrate to his descendants the circumstances which detached him from the society of his brethren [. . .]. But when the tale of the patriarch is related by his children, and again by his descendants of the third and fourth generation, the facts have assumed a very different aspect.[40]

In fact, the plot of *Waverley* charts the dissolution of genealogical claims in favor of new "familial" and national forms of community. On the levels of both private and political history, the novel questions the claim of genealogy as a principle of natural legitimization. In this sense, *Waverley* prefigures the sense of the bourgeois-realist novel as representing the crisis and end of traditional (aristocratic) genealogy.[41]

The plot of the novel reflects the problem of dynastic restitution of the Stuart monarchy, which had been excluded from the throne since the Glorious Revolution (1688–89). This restitution was the explicit goal of the (failed) Jacobite Rebellion of 1745. The Pretender Charles Edward appears only briefly in the novel. During this scene, his attempt to reclaim the "palace of his ancestors" in Edinburgh, the narrator sheds an ironic light on his dynastic claims by suggesting that genealogical authority is necessarily manufactured retrospectively: "a long, low, and ill-proportioned gallery, hung with pictures, affirmed to be the portraits of kings, who, if they ever flourished at all, lived several hundred years before the invention of painting in oil colours" (*W*, 292). This comment is part of a wider narrative strategy to demonstrate the anachronism and the questionable legitimacy of the Stuart cause as well as the skepticism it encounters even among its Lowland followers.[42]

Private and public history intersect in the figure of Waverley, who is caught up in a complex network of genealogical relations, laid out at the beginning of the novel, that are structured according to a patriarchal model of indebtedness but that also reveal a significant instability at the core of the patriarchal scheme. At the heart of Waverley's family, which he leaves early on in the novel (ch. 6), stands a rivalry between two brothers. Waverley's mother dies early on (*W*, 49), and as a quasi-orphan the protagonist will be exposed to a series of alternative paternal influences. After his father Richard abandons the Stuart cause, pursues a career in the Whig Parliament of George II, and is subsequently disgraced, young Edward grows up in the house of his childless, bookish uncle Everard, whose life of aristocratic self-isolation hinders his founding a family of his own, and yet—or precisely because of this—he is obsessively steeped in "family tradition and genealogical history" (*W*, 51).

While the two brothers frequent each other reluctantly, both father and uncle look upon Edward as the embodiment of their hopes of patriarchal continuity (*W*, 44). Edward is positioned, then, between his foster and his biological father, as well as between George and James, the Hanoverians and the Stuarts. The double familial alliance, therefore, mirrors Waverley's ambivalent, wavering political alliances. When Waverley's "real" father orders his son to serve in Captain

Gardiner's regiment, "the army under the Brunswick dynasty" (*W*, 59), Everard is plunged into a conflict between his own Jacobean loyalties and his simultaneous high esteem for the principle of "paternal authority" (*W*, 59). He eventually submits to the latter and in his parting words to Edward implores him to emulate his ancestors in the military profession: "remember also that you are the last of that race, and the only hope of its revival depends on you" (*W*, 64).

In a sense, Waverley's subsequent temporary venture into the Highland terrain might be understood not only as a desertion from his military duties but also as a way of escaping from these various genealogical and patriarchal claims and to try out other alliances. The leave of absence that he takes from his military camp becomes a larger metaphor for his flight into the land of romance. While never ceasing to be a "true" Waverley, he develops his own doubts against the mandate of patriarchal authority to support the Stuart cause, a cause whose very idea hinges on the notion of dynastic reinstitution. The Stuarts might have "original rights" on their side, but the "united voice of the whole nation" had spoken out against James II's misdeeds (*W*, 222). Edward's individual conscience, then, values the good of the nation above the commandments of his two fathers, whose fraternal rift allegorizes, moreover, the state of the nation plunged into civil war.

To play off the principles of descent and foster parentage, the novel exposes Waverley to a further series of alternative father figures. For instance, the Baron of Bradwardine, a friend of Sir Everard who had once fought for the Stuarts, is presented as an antiquarian whose pompous verbosity and use of legal Latin, as well as pedantic anecdotes about "history and genealogy" (*W*, 108), qualifies him literally as a man of the past. The narrator also juxtaposes the latter's predilection for "prose" to Waverley's preference for imaginative "poetry" (*W*, 109), and thus antiquarian history with history-as-romance. Bradwardine's obsession with the question of patriarchal succession is motivated by his own genealogical anxiety, namely the running out of his own line (*W*, 343). According to the Salic law of feudal custom and its prescription that women may not inherit, he does not bequeath his possessions to his daughter Rose but rather to a decayed branch of the family tree (*W*, 119). While Rose does not initially capture Waverley's Romantic imagination, she will in time become his destined bride, just as Bradwardine will be led to give up his "pride of birth and rank" (*W*, 459). The final "alliance between the houses of Bradwardine and Waverley" (*W*, 459) marks in this way the end of Waverley's exaggerated Romanticism and Bradwardine's old-fashioned dynastic obsessions.

Yet another father figure is the charismatic Highland chief Fergus MacIvor, whom Waverley joins in his last battles against the Hanoverian army. Edward and Fergus are in a sense introduced as parallel characters, since both can claim a long line of ancestors. Even before Fergus appears on the scene, the Baron of Bradwardine has informed Waverley about the "high pedigree" (*W*, 130) of the Highlanders, and the narrator's full introduction of the character of Fergus—another embodiment of the "last of the race"—provides a long genealogical account of his forefathers, reaching back to the fifteenth century (*W*, 155). Yet if both Waverley and Fergus appear to be standing at the endpoint of a patriarchal line, this parallel ultimately serves to underline a significant difference. While Fergus is locked in a moment of the past that cannot be brought into the stream of history (and at the moment of narration he is no longer alive), Edward is the subject of a bildungsroman, growing from youth into maturity. In a final conversation shortly before his death, Fergus enlists Waverley as an "adopted son" of his family and race, while the narrator describes Waverley as his "foster-brother" (*W*, 472). The idea of fostering or adoption creates a new transgenerational bond, precisely as a sign of the healing of the wounds created by warfare motivated by the claims of dynastic lineage.

In contrast, the character of Flora, Fergus's sister and the object of Edward's Romantic infatuation, is entrusted with the performance of dynastic continuity and genealogical loyalty. Sitting at a dramatic waterfall, she sings a battle song that extols the collective and patriarchal ethos of clan and kin (*W*, 179), while she includes an admonition to Edward to remember his loyalty to *his* ancestors. Yet these appeals to ancient tradition are curiously mediated, for Flora is said to translate the song from the Gaelic into English (*W*, 178). As reproduced in the novel, Flora's minstrelsy performance is only a distant echo of the "extraordinary string of names which MacMurrough has tacked together in Gaelic" (*W*, 172), thus emphasizing the remoteness of original Highland customs—and their transmutation into cultural artifact.

Moreover, this scene operates as a self-conscious mise en abyme of Waverley's problematized wish to hear and follow the call of his ancestors, as well as of *Waverley*'s narrative strategy to exhibit its own literary genealogy as growing out of sources that are accessible only through various mediations. In both cases there is an emphasis on tradition, yet tradition has become culture and memory rather than a direct chain of continuity. It is clear that Flora is not only a representative but also an interpreter and translator of Highland culture. This mediating function is underscored by the fact that she is both the product of indigenous nature and of a refined education in Paris (*W*, 169). She and Fergus are indeed orphans who have been brought up by the Stuart prince and princess in French exile (as a result of the failed resurrection of 1715). This establishes again a certain parallel with Waverley, who is not literally an orphan but, as we have seen, a multiple foster son.

While Flora embodies and performs for Waverley the idea of genealogical continuity and dynastic indebtedness, the narrator ironically also assigns to her the role of prophetess of the future. Flora, alongside the narrator himself, is the only character who recognizes early on that Edward's disposition is "exclusively domestic" rather than military (*W*, 369). In this regard, his "abandonment" of Flora for Rose Bradwardine is significant, for Flora is clearly not capable of entering the new domestic sphere of modernity. Like Flora, the narrator has known "all along" that Rose is in fact a much better match for Waverley (*W*, 121). According to the progressive structure of the bildungsroman, Waverley has to pass through and ultimately leave behind these Romantic yearnings—which explains the symbolic equivalence between Waverley's desire for Flora and his fascination with Highland culture.

In predicting Edward's ultimate union with Rose Bradwardine rather than with her, Flora emphasizes the superficiality of his military engagements and thus locates him outside the realm of old-time heroism and romance, which is to say outside the paradigms of his genealogical legacy—and ultimately outside the form of the historical novel itself, in relation to which he already appears as belated (thus approaching the position of the contemporary reader):

> But high and perilous enterprise is not Waverley's forte. He would never have been his celebrated ancestor Sir Nigel, but only Sir Nigel's eulogist and poet. I will tell you where he will be at home, my dear, and in his place,—in the quiet circle of domestic happiness, lettered indolence, and elegant enjoyments, of Waverley-Honour. And he will refit the old library in the most exquisite Gothic taste, and garnish its shelves with the rarest and most valuable volumes; and he will draw plans and landscapes, and write verses, and rear temples, and dig grottoes. (*W*, 370)

If Waverley, then, is really more of a domestic character, it might be asked why he even has to undergo all these outdoor adventures and experiences. One answer might be that the novel, insofar as it is concerned with a historical moment of transition, leads the protagonist through an earlier phase as part of a "successful mourning process."[43] The events and cultural manifestations witnessed by Waverley are already presented as elements of the past, even as they appear "new" to him.

The marriage between Edward and Rose Bradwardine mobilizes the idea of a sexual union as a metaphor for national union, and hence the composite nature of British nationhood, which since the end of the eighteenth century assimilated Scots into the structures of power and administration.[44] The concluding wedding and arrival in the domestic sphere represents the situation of the modern British nation-state, made up of ideally copresent, transindividual affiliations and family units and no longer of locally rooted, clan-like filiations, thus bearing out a notion of progress defended by eighteenth-century Scottish historiography.[45] If the novel charts this larger historical process from a regional to a national orientation, it cannot, however, simply abandon the one for the other. The modern nation-state requires precisely narratives that help to construct a sense of spatial continuity—the integration of the peripheries—and of temporal continuity and development.[46] At the novel's end, the notion of paternity has undergone a transformation. The relation between Waverley and the baron is reinstituted as one of choice, and the baron's sense of dynastic alliance and traditional genealogy is overpowered by spontaneous feeling ("the pride of birth and rank were swept away") when he enthusiastically embraces Waverley as "my son!" (*W*, 459). If this signifies a sort of spontaneous adoption, it brings to mind the previous foster relation between Fergus and Waverley. And indeed the end of the novel dwells on a painting hanging on the wall of Bradwardine's house that shows Fergus and Waverley literally side by side in the pictorial space:

> It was a large and spirited painting, representing Fergus Mac-Ivor and Waverley in their Highland dress; the scene a wild, rocky, and mountainous pass, down which the clan were descending in the background. It was taken from a spirited sketch, drawn while they were in Edinburgh by a young man of high genius, and had been painted on a full-length scale by an eminent London artist. Raeburn himself [. . .] could not have done more justice to the subject; and the ardent, fiery, and impetuous character of the unfortunate Chief of Glennaquoich was finely contrasted with the contemplative, fanciful, and enthusiastic expression of his happier friend. Beside this painting hung the arms which Waverley had borne in the unfortunate civil war. (*W*, 489)

The detailed description of the painting might be taken as an allegorical reference to the novel's own procedures of representation. For one thing, it emphasizes that the image of the past is mediated several times and finally realized through a London perspective—thus marking a movement away from a temporal and spatial point of origin, so that the central capital now becomes the origin for a representation that reaches back to the Highlands by way of the Lowlands (Edinburgh). Furthermore, the description stresses elements of aestheticization ("the scene a wild, rocky, and mountainous pass") and spatialized historicization ("descending in the background"). Finally, the last sentence contains the idea of historical closure and the musealization of the past. A violent past must be exorcized and is remembered in the form of an ornament that signals its inclusion in the present. Obviously, this situation resonates with the broader strategies of retrospective invention during the Romantic period through which original Highland cultural traditions have been first thought up and then integrated into Lowland Scotland—a process in which not only the fashion of tartans and kilts but also Scott's work has actively participated.[47]

Waverley, and the Waverley novels generally, do not simply aim at a representation of history but are constituted by an internal dynamic according to which origins and ancestry are relocated from the realm of politics to the realm of culture. As Ian Duncan has put it, "To locate national distinction in the past, the ideal time of dead ancestors and lost origins, is to divert it from the contentious arena of contemporary politics. Thus national identity is split between a political and economic dimension (imperial Union) and a supplemental cultural one (national distinctiveness)." As we have seen, the novel's hero moves away from his patriarchal obligations to arrive in the scene of the present, where new affective and communal bonds take the place of inherited alliances. It is as if the transitional experience of *romance* liberates the protagonist from his familial ties and presents an exit from the "middle station of life" (*Robinson Crusoe*) so that he may eventually be (re)integrated into the conjugal, domestic family, the metonymy of national community and the correlative of the form of the modern *novel.*[48]

The novels by Edgeworth and Scott establish a pattern whereby the narration of private genealogy is connected to the constitution of the British nation, a modern nation-state that is symbolically unified out of its constituent parts. In both cases, the historicizing effect derives from the specific perspectival presentation of the authorial voice, which constructs the multiple, conflictive origins as a past in relation to the present of the reader. Only if the border between narrated past and the present of narration is clearly demarcated is it possible to transmute the Irish-Scottish difference, the genealogical inheritance of the nation into the mode of humor (Edgeworth) or the picturesque (Scott). It is especially this distancing in both temporal and spatial terms, as well as the discovery of the general discontinuity of the human world, that has been recognized as the distinctive, innovative feature of the historical novel, which has profoundly influenced the subsequent development of the nineteenth-century novel, including the notion that genealogical narratives become a privileged means to represent the transformation of society.[49]

CHAPTER THREE

Progress and Pessimism

The Sicilian Novel of *Verismo*
(Giovanni Verga and Federico De Roberto)

After the year 1861 literary-novelistic production in Italy shifted from a single center in the North to multiple centers in different regions of the country, in particular the South and Sicily.[1] Sicily's remarkable re-emergence—after its early importance as a center of poetry in the thirteenth century—as a center of literary activity around the last third of the nineteenth century has to be seen in the context of its reawakened self-consciousness after the landing of Garibaldi's Thousand on its shores (1860), as well as the subsequent development toward national unification. Sicilian authors were initially strongly in favor of political union with the mainland, yet they increasingly registered the ways the central state and the South failed to communicate.[2] Although their parameters are obviously radically different, we might compare the Sicilian novel of this period with the earlier novels set in the Celtic Fringe of Great Britain, to the extent that they all try to account for the moment a centralized nation-state co-opts a region from its cultural and geographical margins.

The Sicilian authors associated with *verismo*, who wanted to depict, in naturalist fashion, the social conditions of their own region, naturally directed attention not at the—largely nonexistent—bourgeoisie but instead at the lower classes (Verga, *I Malavoglia*) or the aristocracy (De Roberto, *I Viceré*). Instead of social-historical development, biology and myth determine the narrative structure of these texts.[3] It is surely no coincidence that the Sicilian school became practically coextensive with the Italian version of novelistic naturalism. Sicily was the paradigmatic geographical periphery with regard to the new unitary state of Italy: it was characterized by the recent reign of the Bourbons and became increasingly associated with socioeconomic backwardness and the persistence of archaic traditions. During the 1870s the "Southern question" brought into focus local corruption and failed efforts at centralization and threw a critical light on the ways unity was imposed after 1860.[4] As Roberto Dainotto has re-cently detailed, Sicily has been read as a prototypical place for the South, a para-digmatic periphery that is central for the definition and self-understanding not only of Italy but even of Europe as a whole.[5]

The literary fashioning of Sicilian backwardness could be achieved only through a characteristic relation of mediation, distance, and otherness, that is to say, through a positioning toward the literary center represented during this time above all by Milan, heavily influenced by French culture. In fact, it is well known that the literary techniques of the *verismo* school are an adaptation and transformation of the model of French naturalism. Sicilian authors aimed not primarily at a Sicilian but at a pan-Italian, or even European, readership, because it was not in Sicily itself—and hardly even in Italy—where a bourgeois readership was to be found.[6] If Sicily, then, was a paradigmatic place of otherness for the bourgeois readers of Central and Northern Italy, the symptomatic significance of the cultural represen-tations of Sicily derived from their ambiguous function as revealing a deeper truth not simply about the geographical margin but indeed about the country as a whole: it was arguably the relation between center and periphery that was (and is) at the heart of the problematic constitution of Italian nationhood. At the time of *verismo*, the insight into this "deeper truth" was achieved precisely through the strategy of distancing, and thus possibly containing, problems that were far from marginal.[7]

Giovanni Verga's *I Malavoglia*: Family, Community, Modernity
Verga, *Verismo*, Versions of Naturalism

The movement of Italian *verismo* was originally associated with a new mode of impressionist painting and was then especially associated with the Sicilian writ-ers Luigi Capuana and Giovanni Verga, as well as Federico De Roberto.[8] The novels of *verismo* may be understood as an Italian version of naturalism, which, in its broadest sense, is a useful matrix for understanding many of the Euro-pean novels from the late nineteenth century. In this broader sense, novelistic naturalism is distinguished by an impersonal, "objective" narrative voice, polyph-ony, a circular construction instead of linear development, and an opening of new social themes.[9] More specifically, naturalism is the explicitly "scientific" approach of French novelists such as Flaubert and especially Zola. Verga's interest in these authors has been dated to the year 1874; in his letters around 1880, he frequently raises questions related to the naturalist ideals of impersonality and objective documentation to his friend Capuana. In their correspondence they agree that a new literary content should be reflected by an appropriate literary form. During this period, then, the modernization of the Italian novel occurs via the reception of French naturalism, especially Zola's *L'assommoir* (1877), an emblematic text about the working-class life of the washer woman Gervaise and her downward spiral to desolation and death, propelled by the vice of alcoholism.[10]

This novel forms part of Zola's cycle of the Rougon-Macquart, comprising a total of twenty novels (1871–93). This gigantic project is built on a new combination of diachronic and synchronic modes of organization as a response to the specific epistemic situation of the late nineteenth century. Its positivistic scientific implications, notably the assumption of a social as well as biological determinism, are laid out in the programmatic text *Le roman expérimental* (1880).[11] On the one hand, the novels of the cycle amount to a synchronic portrait of various social and professional milieus during the Second Empire (1852–70) in France, of which the family of the Rougon-Macquart is representative, according to the full title, Histoire naturelle et sociale d'une famille sous le Second Empire (Natural and Social History of a Family under the Second Empire). On the other hand, this vast synchronic picture is correlated to certain metaphysical and biological assumptions about the diachronic development of this representative family and, by implication, the history of the Second Empire and humankind as such. The correlation of the synchronic description with diachronic laws of development, as stated in Zola's programmatic assertions, is made explicit only in a few of the individual novels. A good example is the symbol of the tree (in *La faute de l'abbé Mouret*), which stands precisely for the double perspective of a synchronically structured organism and a diachronically "rooted" context of hereditary transmission.[12] One of the most intriguing paradoxes of the overarching scheme is Zola's curious philosophy of history, according to which the Second Empire is conceived as a period of decadence and yet is seen as engendering new life, thus resulting in an ultimately optimistic view of historical progress in which social proletarization and capitalist modernization are parts of the same progressive ideology. The individual novels are dedicated to developing biographical aspects of single family members, who, characteristically, are conceived as the results of the double influence of social milieu and hereditary features. Yet, as Hans Ulrich Gumbrecht has pointed out, with the partial exception of the opening and the concluding novels of the cycle (*La fortune des Rougon* and *Le docteur Pascal*), the diachronic aspect remains conspicuously underprivileged both on the level of the individual biographies and the structure of the novelistic cycle as a whole—"the reason why the cycle consists rather in a panorama of different social situations than a continuity of successive developmental phases of the represented decadence of a family."[13]

The Sicilian writers imitated, but also differed, from the French model. Most obviously, Zola's almost exclusive focus on social milieus in an urban context (with significant exceptions such as *La terre*, 1887), is transposed by the Italian writers onto a decidedly provincial scene. In Italy, the social realism of *verismo* is focused on the relation between regional realities and the new unitary nation-state. Furthermore, in contrast to Zola's unresolved coexistence of familial degeneration and historical optimism, these writers are generally more pessimistic and conservative with regard to the question of historical progress.[14] Another important difference concerns precisely the fundamental role of the family. Whereas in Zola—somewhat in contradiction to the cycle's subtitle—the idea of the family ultimately leads to the novelistic isolation of individual family members, who are only conceptually related to each other via a genealogical-biological structure, the authors of *verismo* write family novels in an emphatic sense. Here, the individual is only conceivable as part of a collective entity. The unity of the family, resisting the disintegrating forces of social progress, always remains the ideal horizon for the depiction of characters—even if the narrative emplotment focuses on decadent or otherwise problematic families.[15] The novels by Verga and De Roberto are naturalist in the sense that they are characterized by objectifying modes of presentation, a choral and collective focus that foregrounds transindividual patterns and modes of behavior. Yet from the beginning, in his letters to Capuana, Verga distances himself from the scientific aspirations of Zola and at the same time radicalizes the ideal of observational objectivity, the occultation of the narrator, to such a degree that few contemporary readers were able to appreciate it.[16] In fact, what is decisive here is not the question of heredity and descent but the way certain deep structures of the cultural periphery provide a resistance to what appears as surface change. In this sense, these texts can be read as self-critical explorations of modernity: they are concerned with the clash between a generation-spanning continuity of tradition and the new forces of progress that impinge upon a closely circumscribed space.

In November 1877 Verga moved to Milan, and it is from here that he embarks on this new orientation that marks a radical departure from his previous literary practice, more associated with urban, melodramatic fiction. It is precisely this geographical distance that appears to enable him to frame the Sicilian lifeworld that he left behind and to write about the enclosed world of Aci Trezza, a fishing village in the vicinity of Catania. This distant view on Sicilian reality, the perspective from Italy's most modern city on one of its most backward social formations, resonates with other contemporary attempts to envision Sicilian society, such as an important sociological project from 1876, Sidney Sonnino's *I contadini in Sicilia* (The peasants of Sicily), as well as Leopoldo Franchetti's *Condizioni amministrative e politiche della Sicilia* (Administrative and political conditions in Sicily, 1877). Like these two sociological works on the Southern question, Verga was extremely critical of industrialization and the capitalism embodied by the economy of Northern Italy. Through these works, Verga became convinced that a study of family structure would reveal some of the most fundamental truths of Southern society and, by extension, of the country as a whole.[17]

Verga himself made only few programmatic contributions to the poetics of the naturalistic novel. The famous preface to *I Malavoglia*, where he speaks of the "studio sincero e spassionato" (*MV*, 3) [a sincere and neutral study], resonates with the posture of scientific objectivity similarly adopted by the sociological case studies.[18] In fact, never before had an Italian novel dedicated so much attention to the serious representation of the minute details of an everyday world, something that must have appeared revolutionary in a literary tradition largely dominated by a notion of rhetorical nobility.[19] In a well-known letter to Capuana, Verga expresses his desire to document as faithfully as possible a given social reality, but this inside perspective is complemented and corrected by a conscious stance of distance:

> Avrei desiderato andarmi a rintanare in campagna, sulla riva del mare, fra quei pescatori e coglierli vivi come Dio li ha fatti. Ma forse non sará male dall'altro canto che io li consideri da una certa distanza in mezzo all'attività di una cittá come Milano o Firenze. Non ti pare che per noi l'aspetto di certe cose non ha risalto che visto sotto un dato angolo visuale? E che mai riusciremo ad essere tanto schiettamente ed efficacemente veri che allorquando facciamo un lavoro di ricostruzione intellettuale e sostituiamo la nostra mente ai nostri occhi?[20]

> [I would have liked to go and withdraw to the countryside, on the coast of the sea, between those fishermen, and to apprehend them in their lives, as God has made them. Yet, on the other hand, maybe it will not be bad that I consider them from a certain distance, in the middle of the activity of a city like Milan or Florence. Don't you agree that for us the aspect of certain things would not be evident except when seen under a certain visual angle? And that we never succeed in being so evidently and effectively true unless we undertake a work of intellectual reconstruction and when we substitute our mind for our eyes?]

Verga's "intellectual reconstruction" presupposes a geographical distance that is both hidden and exposed. To a certain extent, the documentary basis and the assumption of a distant perspective makes *I Malavoglia* comparable to the genre of the historical novel. Also here we have a calculated effect of anthropological similitude and exoticism. Yet in contrast to the spatial expansion and evolving subjectivity of a historical-generational narrative such as Ippolito Nievo's novel *Confessioni di un italiano* (*Confessions of an Italian*, 1867), Verga's family saga, in its epic-objective ambition to represent a larger, transindividual, yet concretely situated reality, is distinguished by both spatial contraction and temporal extension.[21] While the historical novel is subject centered, the family novel is choral and without a clear center.

If the disintegration of traditional structures is shown to be the effect of modernity, at the same time these novels question the very category of historical change. The idea that Sicily's archaic, primitive nature may be invigorating to an artistic sensibility weakened by the bourgeois comforts of universal modernity and progress motivated Verga to direct his attention to the poor folks, for centuries forgotten and exploited by the various overlords of the island and now victim to the Italian government. This move would later be repeated by D. H. Lawrence, who turned to Sicily and to Verga (as a translator)—for "the colder heart of the northener [sic] feels a sense of loss haunting his brave new world"—to find the genius loci of a specific, authentic region, a mythic place of origin, the nostalgia of an ancient society of immutable nature.[22] In the opening text of his famous collection of novellas, *Vita dei campi* (1880), entitled *Fantasticheria*, introducing the place of Aci Trezza, Verga writes, "Parmi che le irrequietudini del pensiero vagabondo s'adormenterebbero dolcemente nella pace serena di quei sentimenti miti, semplici, che si succedono calmi e inalterati di generazione in generazione"[23] [It seems to me that the unrest of vagabond thought would sweetly fall to rest in the serene peace of those mild, simple sentiments, which succeed each other from generation to generation]. The novel *I Malavoglia* builds and expands on this sense of timeless continuity. Yet it also presents a world that works not only as a countermeasure to the new world but that is already traversed by its first signals.

Community and Continuity

The famous opening lines of the novel contrast a fabulous time of myth with another time that is already marked by the first signs of disintegration. The present family of the Malavoglia is small in comparison with that of the old times: "un tempo i *Malavoglia* erano stati numerosi come i sassi della strada vecchia di Trezza; ce n'erano persino ad Ognina, e ad Aci Castello, tutti buona e brava gente di mare" (*MV*, 9) [once the *Malavoglia* were as numerous as the stones on the old road of Trezza; some of them were even in Ognina, in Aci Castello, all of them good and brave people of the sea]. The contrast between the former generational continuity ("li avevano sempre conosciuti per Malavoglia, di padre in figlio," *MV*, 9) [they have always known them as Malavoglia, from father toward son] and the present situation is marked by the adverbs "always" and "now" ("adesso a Trezza non rimanevano che i Malavoglia di padron 'Ntoni, quelli della casa del nespolo," *MV*, 10) [now at Trezza remained only the Malavoglia of padron 'Ntoni, those of the house of the medlar tree].

The family of the Malavoglia is metonymically associated with the house ("la casa del nespolo"), and in English the novel is indeed known as *The House by the Medlar Tree*. This metonymical image is typically invoked as the symbol for temporal continuity—and in this sense it contrasts with the other metonymical image of the family, the fishing boat called *Provvidenza*. The following passage links the two symbols and creates an effective contrast between stability and economic/existential crisis: "la casa dei Malavoglia era sempre stata una delle prime a Trezza; ma adesso colla morte di Bastianazzo, e 'Ntoni soldato, e Mena da maritare, [. . .] era una casa che faceva acqua da tutte le parti" (*MV*, 73) [the house of the Malavoglia had always been one of the principal ones in Trezza; yet now with the death of Bastianazzo, and 'Ntoni as soldier, and Mena to marry . . . it was a house that was leaking on all parts]. The fact that Bastianazzo dies early on in the novel (ch. 3) and remains entirely colorless as a character reinforces the paternal function of the "grandfather" 'Ntoni and thus characterizes the Malavoglia as a kind of patriarchal clan that transcends the more restricted bonds of the bourgeois family structure. If in the first chapter a sea storm already announces the destruction of the ironically named *Provvidenza*, it also implies the threat of the dispersion of the family members. And if padron 'Ntoni invokes here the strong simile of the fist as an image for the patriarchal idea of the mutual support of the single fingers, the narrator immediately confirms this idea with the same image: "e la famigliuola di padron 'Ntoni era realmente disposta come le dita della mano" (*MV*, 11) [and the family of padron 'Ntoni was really disposed like the fingers of the hand]. In Verga's novel, the individual is indeed subsumed by what is larger than the individual, be it the family, the community, or nature. And the individual voice is but the reflection and echo of the community's voice.

The radically reduced function of the narrator is a device that Verga approached gradually. Famously, in a metaliterary passage of his novella *L'amante di Gramigna* (included in the collection Vita dei campi, 1880), Verga—or rather the narrator—already formulates a stylistic ideal of the novel, according to which an altogether invisible narrator creates an effect as if the novel and its milieu were "writing themselves."[24] Yet, the novellas that Verga wrote before *I Malavoglia* (*Nedda*, *Fantasticheria*, and even *L'amante di Gramigna* itself), although they are remarkable for the shift toward the rural milieu of Sicily, actually rest on a pronounced opposition between the represented milieu and the distanced perspective of the bourgeois lifeworld shared by narrator and implied reader, and they even retain certain romanticizing elements.[25]

In contrast, in *I Malavoglia* the narrator avoids explicit commentary or interpretation, exploiting only the metaphorical potential of the images. The repeated evocation of how the Malavoglia have been "always," either stated by their own voice or that of others, indicates precisely the crisis of this perpetual condition. Yet the novel's focus on a family in crisis is part and parcel of the portrait of the larger community of the village. In this sense, *I Malavoglia* is not a traditional family novel. Even as the family of the Malavoglia is obviously the central focus, the novel actually presents a multiplicity of viewpoints and individual histories that cover the entire community, including a wide range of social roles and types. The broader social conflicts of Aci Trezza permeate the heart of the family, which—in contrast to representations of the bourgeois ideal of the family—is not an "island of protection against the struggle of existence and survival outside."[26] Characteristically, these multiple viewpoints are not introduced by an omniscient narrator (who is in any case reduced to the role of an anonymous witness), but the technique of free indirect discourse confronts the reader with all kinds of gossip, unexplained references, and judgments, all of which the reader must gradually decipher—without, however, penetrating to a level of interior motivation or ultimate order. In other words, the various voices, including cynical or interested comments about the Malavoglia, are an integral part of the presented milieu and its own characteristic limitations.[27]

As Romano Luperini has noted, the dispersal of narrative perspective, demanding the reader's full attention, is rather unusual in the second half of the nineteenth century.[28] However, this multiplicity of voices is less a narrative polyphony than a "plurivocality," insofar as these various viewpoints do not conflict with each other but are all expressions of a single, unitary worldview, with all characters, including the narrator, appearing to speak in the same way and with the same language.[29] In the course of the novel, a certain rift opens between the community at large and the family of the Malavoglia, whose newly commercial activities, the enterprise with the *lupini* beans, makes them increasingly suspect in the eyes of others. The family's enterprise is perceived as an infraction of the social order, and the ensuing natural disasters create the impression that it has also violated the order of nature.

Through various rhetorical techniques Verga achieves the effect of representing a natural world. One of the most striking techniques to establish maximal authorial distance is the frequent use of popular proverbs, as well as the use of natural metaphors, all employed through Verga's artistry to achieve an effect of static, circular reality, the representation of a world that is closed in upon itself.[30] Padron 'Ntoni, while not the only one to use them, is certainly the figure most characterized by his constant recourse to ever-recurring proverbs ("motti antichi," *MV*, 13), which serve to confirm his conservative worldview. For instance, many of his proverbs evoke images from the animal or natural world and justify the status quo precisely as natural: "ad ogni uccello, suo nido è bello" (ch. 11; *MV*, 231) [every bird likes its own nest]. The dimension of anthropological "truth" is thus complemented by the copious use of proverbs, by way of which the characters comprehend and comment upon particular events, which are aligned with a transtemporal, "eternal" truth, a kind of folk wisdom that categorizes every new occurrence as a confirmation of an already existing system of values and beliefs. These proverbs Verga had found in various books written and compiled by men such as Giuseppe Pitrè or Salomone Marino, proverbs that derive not just from Sicily but from many Italian regions.[31] Moreover, many characters are described with recurring linguistic tics and attributes that serve to assign them a fixed place in the represented cosmos. Stylistically and rhetorically Verga's novel uses a variety of different means—proverbs, epithets, repetitions, modes of speech—to convey an internal portrait of a self-enclosed social world, suggesting authenticity while still being comprehensible for the reader.

As Antonio Candido has written in a masterful analysis of the novel, in contrast to traditional naturalism, the specific social world is conjured up here not through the accumulation of descriptive detail but rather by way of abstraction and symbolic condensation, thus emphasizing an internal perspective that can dispense with the informative and illusionistic function of description: "The indeterminacy and sparseness of descriptive traits contribute to the dissolution of the settings into their social significance. The house is not a decisive and imposing physical reality, [. . .] it is the expression of the family."[32] Verga himself has commented, in a letter to Capuana, on the disorienting effect on the reader: "tutti quei personaggi messivi faccia a faccia senza nessuna presentazione, come li aveste conosciuti sempre, e foste nato e vissuto in mezzo a loro"[33] [all of the characters are presented to you face to face without any introduction, as if you had always known them, and were born and had lived in their midst]. The effects of familiarity and estrangement are thus two sides of the same coin. It is evident that Verga's careful linguistic inventions and simulations are central to generating the novel's reality effect, making us believe that the language and imagery of the Sicilian people provide the material with which they will be represented. The combination of a fishing village with the world of agriculture might seem somewhat incongruous, yet Verga was not interested in a realistic mimesis of an existing village but rather in portraying a Sicilian location in the most typical and general sense, where the culture of sea and land intersect in what has been called a "deliberately artificial model."[34]

The novel proposes padron 'Ntoni as a model for the figure of the small proprietor, whose interests are opposed by a series of characters who live by various forms of parasitic work: most importantly, the predatory lending of zio (uncle) Crocifisso, the fraudulent tactics of the administrator don Silvestro, the exploitative power of Fortunato Cipolla. Despite the oppositions among the characters, they never cease to be part of the same social and natural cosmos, and, even as they express different opinions, they have recourse to the same undifferentiated language, including proverbs, commonplaces, and so forth. As Candido notes, these modes of expression are precisely characteristic of nonindividualistic, transgenerational, collective speech, resistant to temporal change. Specifically, the proverbs are expressions of an "eternalized linguistic norm."[35] The originality of Verga's novel consists in the way this linguistically rendered static world absorbs, and conflicts with, the forces of change.

Change, Time, Modernity

The preface of the novel articulates not only the objectivist-positivist agenda of its author; it also links this agenda to what it conceives as an almost mythical point of origin for the apparently innate human tendency to strive for change and the improvement of one's state:

Questo racconto è lo studio sincero e spassionato del come probabilmente devono nascere e svilupparsi nelle più umili condizoni, le prime irrequietudini pel benessere; e quale perturbazione debba arrecare in una famigliuola vissuta sino allora relativamente felice, la vaga bramosia dell'ignoto, l'accorgersi che non si sta bene, o che si potrebbe star meglio. (*MV*, 3)

[This story is the sincere and dispassionate study of how the first anxious desires for material well-being will likely be born and develop themselves in the most humble conditions; and of the perturbation caused in a family which had until then lived in relative happiness, by the vague yearning for the unknown and by the realization that they are not so well off, or that they could be better off.]

It is from this primordial human activity, observed in its most simple conditions, that "the stream of progress" (*MV*, 3) [la fiumana del progresso] originates. Verga envisions this progress as a continuous, gradually more forceful and complex movement that, after humankind's striving for basic material benefits, will then also encompass the bourgeoisie and the aristocracy. This socially ascending movement of universal progress is thus echoed by the prospected continuation of Verga's novelistic cycle, from the fishing family in *I Malavoglia* to the eponymous bourgeois social climber in *Mastro-don Gesualdo* (1888/1889), to the aristocracy in *Duchessa de Leyra* (which he never completed).[36] In the preface, this movement is also described as one toward greater individualization, including an "enrichment" of the language. The development toward greater material wealth and spiritual complexity is seen, on the one hand, as a "fatal, incessant march" (*MV*, 5) [il cammino fatale, incessante] that, on the other hand, observed from a distance and in its ideal totality, rather than absorbed in the often painful particular details, produces a "grand" and "glorious" picture. This generally serene scenery, however, does not prevent the author from immersing himself in the drama of the "struggle for life" and focusing on single individuals, all "those defeated [vinti] whom the stream has deposited on the shore" (*MV*, 6).

Although the novel depicts a relatively large arc of time, covering the years from 1863 to 1878, it is a historical novel only in a rather peculiar way. The cosmos of the Malavoglia resists the model of the historical novel, for the state and national history enter this microcosm only in the most attenuated form. In the self-enclosed world of the Malavoglia, time is largely undetermined and mostly characterized by ritual, religious, cyclical, agricultural, or natural events ("the year of the earthquake," *MV*, 40). While the first part of the novel (chs. 1–4) covers a short period of time, only four consecutive days, the central part (5–9) covers a much longer period of several months, during the years 1865–66, and the last chapter several years, until 1874.[37] This change in temporal coverage is accompanied by a gradual transition in frequency of use of verb tense of imperfect to the perfect (*passato remoto*). The latter part of the novel, by signaling a distancing from the habitual and the ritual and by shifting the focus to the more "eventful" character of 'Ntoni (10) through an increasing concentration on a series of concrete events, becomes less ethnological and more historical in nature.

If the world of the Malavoglia is generally distinguished by ethnological and natural time, there are a few significant references to the time and space of the nation: 1862, the year of 'Ntoni's military recruitment, as well as more general allusions to the draft and military service; the indirect reference to the battle of Lissa, in 1866; or the outbreak of the cholera in 1867 (responsible for the death

of La Longa).[38] There are also a number of allusions to the problem of unification and references to the National Guard and to Garibaldi. These historical
references are complemented by various allusions to technological modernity,
whereby the closed space is opened up to chronological time: the construction
of the railway line in the south of Catania (*MV*, 46), the appearance of the new
steam boats on the coastline (*MV*, 122), and the introduction of the telegraph
line (*MV*, 72). If these means of transport serve to convey objects and messages,
the villagers' sense of incomprehension and ignorance reveals that they cannot
make sense of the things and events that reach them from afar (*MV*, 15).

Furthermore, it is also characteristic that these significant national-historical
events are exclusively envisioned from the utterly restricted, often deforming
viewpoint of the characters. For instance, the battle of Lissa reaches the village
in the form of rather confused rumors: "il giorno dopo cominciò a correre la voce
che nel mare verso Trieste ci era stato un combattimento tra i bastimenti nostri
e quelli dei nemici, che nessuno sapeva nemmeno chi fossero, ed era morta
molta gente; chi raccontava la cosa in un modo e chi in un altro, a pezzi e bocconi,
masticando le parole" (*MV*, 174–75; cf. 170) [the day after, there ran rumors that
in the sea near Trieste there had been a battle between our ships and those of
the enemies, that no one knew who they were, and that many people had died;
some recounted the event in this way, some in another, in pieces and bites, chew-
ing the words]. Note also that this passage is characteristically hybrid in its perspective, insofar as the third-person viewpoint is interspersed with the inclusive
pronoun "our." All these more or less indirect references to the making of the Republic, then, reproduce the villagers' sense of incomprehension, illustrating the
narrator's attempt to disappear into the interior perspective of the natives.

In fact, if the striving for material betterment and economic surplus is presented as a kind of original human sin, it is significant that even the apparently
unchanging padron 'Ntoni is tempted to give in to commercial interests, as illustrated by his decision to enter the fateful business with the *lupini* beans, buy-
ing them on credit from the money lender Crocifisso so that his son Bastianazzo
could sell them to a ship anchored in the region. Yet clearly padron 'Ntoni's
decision points not to any questioning of the natural order; it is simply the
consequence of exterior economic circumstances—concretely, the necessity to
make ends meet after young 'Ntoni was conscripted into the military. By contrast,
the negative figures of the novel are associated with abusing the new power of the
state for personal gain, such as don Michele, who represents one of the most resented features of the new state, the fiscus (the revenues it collected from the various regions); or don Silvestro, who uses the codified law to his own advantage.

The passage from ethnological to historical time is embodied by the generational sequence from grandfather to nephew. Whereas the first part of the novel is more or less concentrated on the figure of padron 'Ntoni, the latter part of the novel focusses on the individual drama of the nephew 'Ntoni (the last five chapters, 11–15). He is the character in the novel most attracted to modernity and its promises of material wealth, with which he has come into contact after his military service in the city (*MV*, 100, 242–46). Thereafter he refuses to return to the life of a hard-working fisherman in Aci Trezza: instead, he makes money by contraband and ends up in prison. In contrast to the age-old family sentiments, young 'Ntoni stands for the new egotism of an incipient bourgeois society. Within the novel's symbolic intergenerational opposition between grandfather and nephew, the latter embodies the breaking of the eternal cycle of generational continuity and transmission. In contrast to the immobile, monological, and epic figure of padron 'Ntoni, young 'Ntoni may be seen as the quintessentially problematic hero of the modern novel, who questions his own condition and undergoes a certain evolution.[39] He is a figure standing between two worlds: he first dreams of the city, goes there, and then comes back to the village with his knowledge of the city, his disapproval of village life reinforced. This move into the unknown is far from being represented as a liberation from constraining bonds, and the family members reproach him for his egotism and pseudorevolutionary rhetoric. Yet from an external perspective 'Ntoni's complaint about the uncritical acceptance of the way things have always been appears indeed as a justified social critique: "Ma voi altri ve la passate forse meglio di me a lavorare, e ad affannarvi per nulla? [. . .] Sapete per chi lavorate, dal lunedì al sabato, e vi siete ridotto a quel modo che non vi vorreberro neanche all'ospedale?" (*MV*, 298) ["But are you others perhaps better off than I am? (. . .) Do you know for whom you work, from Monday to Saturday, and that you are reduced to such a state that you will not even be admitted to the hospital."]

Although 'Ntoni becomes the novel's central character, it is important to note that his attitude of revolt leads him not to any real alternative but rather to an easy life of pleasure and vice, whereby he becomes associated with the marginal character of the drunkard Rocco Spatu—to whom the last sentence of the novel is dedicated. After being separated from his love interest, Santuzza, 'Ntoni's perdition is sealed when he violently attacks the customs officer don Michele (ch. 13) and is sentenced to prison. This is not the only tragedy the family suffers: his brother Luca dies in the battle of Lissa, and his sister Lia ends up prostituting herself. Counteracting all these tragedies, the youngest Malavoglia son, Alessi, finally reacquires the family house and thus has the opportunity to start the cycle again. However, the re-establishment of the family by the union of Alessi and Nunziata is altogether different from the still-traditional model presented at the beginning of the novel. In fact, this young couple, embodying a new type of mononuclear family, is also distinguished from the often farcical marriage negotiations typical of the old patriarchal world. Regardless, the idea of cyclicality is contradicted by the fact that the reacquisition of the house, which has cost the Malavoglia so much work and suffering, is now accorded a relatively minor importance. The opposite tendency, the dispersion of the family, appears much more consequential. The clearest sign that a time has come to an end is the death of padron 'Ntoni. It is no coincidence that his death is described with the conventional metaphor of the final journey: "padron 'Ntoni aveva fatto quel viaggio lontano, piú lontano di Trieste e d'Allessandria d'Egitto, dal quale non si ritorna piú" (*MV*, 366) [padron 'Ntoni had made that long voyage, longer than Trieste or Alexandria in Egypt, from which one never returns]. Not only is this passage connected to other moments that mark events of departure, the dispersion of the Malavoglia, and the impossibility of return (*MV*, 346, 360), but the novel generally figures spatial distance with temporal change.

Significantly, in the last chapter when the young 'Ntoni refuses Alessi's final offer and says his last farewell to the world of Aci Trezza, he nostalgically invokes the circle of the family as coextensive with the community of the village:

> No! rispose 'Ntoni. Io devo andarmene. Là c'era il letto della mamma, che lei inzuppava tutto di lagrime quando voleva andarmene. Ti rammenti le belle chiacchierate che si facevano la sera, mentre si salavano le acciughe? E la Nunziata che spiegava gli indovinelli? e la mamma, e la Lia, tutti lì, al chiaro di luna, che si sentiva chiacchierare per tutto il paese, come fossimo tutti una famiglia? Anch'io allora non sapevo nulla, e qui non volevo starci, ma ora che so ogni cosa devo andarmene. (*MV*, 371)

> ["No!" answered 'Ntoni. I have to go away. There was the bed of the mamma, which she drowned in tears when I wanted to go away. Do you remember the nice chats we had in the evenings, while one was salting the anchovies? And Nunziata, who was explaining the riddles? And the mama, and Lia, all of them there, in the light of the moon, that one heard the chatting throughout all the village, as if we were all one family? At that time, even I didn't know anything, and here I didn't want to stay, but now that I know everything I have to go.]

'Ntoni affirms rhetorically the religion of the family that he has desacralized, and his voluntary exile clears the way for a possible regeneration. Language itself now receives a nostalgic coloring. 'Ntoni's discourse is pronounced in the imperfect, thus marking a time of duration as recalled by 'Ntoni's memory. As a matter of fact, the entire last chapter is distinguished by an elegiac atmosphere that contrasts the situation of the present with the memory of the past, referring obsessively to "those times" (allora), and where the imperfect signals recurring habits and traditions ("Allora ognuno si conosceva") [then everybody knew / was knowing each other], but also to what was "then" unknown: "allora la gente non si sbandava di qua e di là, e non andava a morire all'ospedale" (*MV*, 363) [in those times people did not disband here and there, and did not go to die in the hospital]. Paradoxically, then, the young 'Ntoni, leaving his home for the prospect and promises of modernity, finds the meaning of life by looking *back* on the peripheral world he has left behind—and the comment also reveals a new contradiction between thought and action.[40] Significantly, the very ending of the novel shows how the choral way of speaking and thinking is now replaced by a more personalized manner of speech, when 'Ntoni says, "Ora è tempo d'andarmene" (*MV*, 373) ["Now it is time for me to go"]. This break in the way of interpreting the world points in the direction of a decadent, if somewhat open, future.[41] When one evening, finally, 'Ntoni returns to visit the house of Alessi, he is so changed that even the dog does not recognize him anymore (*MV*, 368). Faced with the impossibility of return and the paradox of lost innocence, 'Ntoni's famous last words are torn between the remembered duration of the imperfect tense and the present moment in which he consciously leaves this world forever behind. *I Malavoglia* presents a perspective of retrospection typical of the school of *verismo*, where a bourgeois readership is confronted with its own past and exoticized other, and thus experiences a melancholic, yet never idealizing, understanding of modernity's imagined origin.

Federico De Roberto's *I Viceré*: Genealogy and Decadence

De Roberto's novel *I Viceré* (*The Viceroys*, 1894) posits the Sicilian aristocracy similarly as the other of modernity. Yet in contrast to the impression of the tragic, "fateful" dispersion of the Malavoglia, De Roberto's less empathetic tapestry of decline hinges more explicitly on causes related to biology, history, and social politics. Thus, De Roberto writes about the plan for his novel in a letter to a friend: "il primo titolo era *Vecchia razza*: ciò ti dimostri l'intenzione ultima che dovrebbe essere il decadimento fisico e morale di una stirpe esausta"[42] [the first title was *Old Race*: that shows to you the ultimate intention, namely the physical and moral decadence of an exhausted dynasty]. The change of title shows that De Roberto wanted to shift the emphasis from the theme of naturalistic inheritance to the dynamics of social power. The novel is the second and strongest part of a projected (and unfinished) three-part cycle that was meant to trace three generations of the family Uzeda. The protagonists, the viceroys of the title, are the members of the old feudal family of the Uzeda di Francalanza, of Spanish-Sicilian blood, who have for centuries ruled in Catania. The social class of the family clan, the condition of the aristocracy, is symbolically equivalent to the function of the region as the place that is the other of modernity—and as such it becomes comparable to the entirely different social world of *I Malavoglia*.

The historical arc covered by the novel reaches from the Bourbon period to the post-Unification state, from 1854 to 1882. This period is marked by the opening and the final scene in the novel. While the first scene relates the funeral of the old princess and family head Teresa, with all the pomp of the old regime, the end of the novel shows how the young prince Consalvo is elected to the new national Parliament in Rome. Yet this sense of historical transition—from the end of monarchical absolutism to the new parliamentary system—belies a deeper sense of continuity that shows the bourgeois revolution to be a failure. In their transgression of everything measured, their tendency toward extremes, the family of the Uzeda paradoxically symbolizes both decline and persistence. Their common traits—ambition and lust for power—work precisely to turn them against each other, constantly beset by mutual envy, avarice, and malfeasance. To a large extent these familial intrigues are set in motion by Teresa's skirting of the law of primogeniture, when she bequeaths the family wealth to her favorite, Raimondo, and not to the firstborn, Giacomo. The initial impulse for the *decadence*, then, is an economic one, related to the abolition of the institution of the so-called fedecommesso in 1812 (*VR*, 94, 425), precisely the juridical construction designed to guarantee the "eternal" continuity of familial property rights in a strictly defined, time-resistant law of inheritance.[43] Yet at the same time the family members adapt to this and all subsequent historical transformations in such a way as to secure their positions of political and economic power, and thus the continuity of the family is shown to overrule historical disruptions.

Yet what does the identity of the family, the special distinction of being a Uzeda, actually consist of? It is clearly not religion, the family as a center of affective relations (so important to the self-understanding of the Malavoglia), or simply the mechanical determinism of the *fêlure*, as in Zola's cycle, but rather a peculiar, pseudobiological trait that makes them internally divided against themselves and leads to a characteristic bifurcation of types:

> I due fratelli, quantunque avessero la stess'aria di famiglia, non si rassomiglia-
> vano neppure fisicamente: Raimondo era più che bello, Giacomo quasi brutto.
> Nella Galleria dei ritratti si potevano riscontrare i due tipi. Tra i progenitori più
> lontani c'era quella mescolanza di forza e di grazia che formava la bellezza del
> contino; a poco a poco, col passare dei secoli, i lineamenti cominciavano ad alter-
> arsi, i volti s'allungavano, i nasi sporgevano, il colorito diveniva più oscuro; un es-
> trema pinguetudine come quella di don Blasco, o un'estrema magrezza come quella
> di don Eugenio, deturpava i personaggi. (*VR*, 93–94)[44]

> [The two brothers, even though they had the same family air, did not resemble
> each other even physically: Raimondo was more than beautiful, Giacomo almost
> ugly. In the portrait gallery the two types could be encountered. Among the most
> distant ancestors there was that mixture of force and grace that shaped the beauty
> of the young count. Slowly, with the passing of the centuries, the lineaments began
> to change, the faces became elongated, the noses protruded, the coloration became
> darker; the characters were disfigured by an extreme obesity, as in the case of don
> Blasco, or by an extreme slimness, as in the case of don Eugenio.]

Raimondo, then, presents an exception to the general situation of the Uzeda's physical decline, since in him "the old cells of the noble blood" (*VR*, 94) are newly revived. Many pages and one generation later, the case of the unusually beautiful Teresa confirms this pattern according to which the process of biological degen-eration is contradicted by a survival of an original essence of the "race":

> La vecchia razza spagnuola mescolatasi nel corso dei secoli con gli elementi iso-
> lani, mezzo greci, mezzo saracini, era venuta a poco a poco perdendo di purezza e
> di nobiltà corporea: chi avrebbe potuto distinguere, per esempio, don Blasco da
> un fratacchione uscito da lavoratori della gleba, o donna Ferdinanda da una vec-
> chia tessitrice? Ma come, nella generazione precedente, s'era vista l'eccezione del
> conte Raimondo, così adesso anche Teresa pareva fosse venuta fuori da una vec-
> chia cellula intatta del puro sangue castigliano. (*VR*, 503)

> [Over the course of centuries, the old Spanish race had been mixed with elements
> deriving from the island, half-Greek and half-Saracene, and had slowly been los-
> ing its purity and physical nobility: who, for example, could have distinguished
> don Blasco from a descendant of laborers of the earth, or donna Ferdinanda from
> an old weaver? Yet as in the previous generation there manifested itself the excep-

tion of the count Raimondo, so now also Teresa seemed to have come out of an old
cell, intact with the pure Castilian blood.]

Actually, the term "race" (*razza*) is more frequently used in referring to the
Uzedas than "family," which testifies to the fact that at the end of the nineteenth century the idea of the sick family was at the intersection of different
scientific discourses, both sociological and biological.[45] These quasi-genetic
speculations under the sign of degeneration are evidently a heritage of Zola and
French naturalism, specifically the biological-hereditary speculations of Bernard
and Taine.[46] As such the racial bond among the members of the Uzeda differs
markedly from the Malavoglia family continuity, which bears exclusively positive connotations and where the core of identity is not biological but rather spiritual, as when padron 'Ntoni praises Luca or Mena as being a "true," or born,
Malavoglia (*MV*, 89, 121). The mixture of positivist and decadent ideas of inheritance fell on fertile ground in the Italy of the 1890s, when, after a period of fe-
verish speculation and general optimism in the 1880s, the crisis of the parliamentary system and the Bank of Rome (Banca Romana) led to a general mood of
pessimism, distrust in institutions, discussions about endemic political opportunism (*trasformismo*), and growing social disorder, notably the emergence of the
Sicilian Fasci.[47] In the novel, the sense of a physical degeneration achieves its
climax when the Marchesa Chiara has a miscarriage that leads to a bizarre scene
in which the deformed, monstrous embryo is preserved in a glass jar: "the fresh-
est product of the race of the Viceroys" (*VR*, 394) [il prodotto più fresco della
razza dei Viceré]. However, while the novel draws in various ways on the discourse of biological decadence, it is ultimately more interested in exploring aristocratic power as a mechanism of social distinction.

Therefore, let us look at how the image of aristocratic pedigree is explicitly
figured throughout the novel. The notion of genealogical continuity and aristocratic elitism, to which the old and ultrareactionary donna Fernanda, avid reader
of the "Teatro genologico [*sic*] di Sicilia" (*VR*, 105) dedicates herself to the point
of becoming "sick" (*VR*, 104), is itself presented as a thing of the past. At the
same time, Fernanda's genealogical obsession testifies to the fact that the turn
to the family tree is indeed characteristic of historical periods that witness a dissolution or transitional rearrangement of social institutions. While the *Teatro
genealogico di Sicilia* is an actual historical document (by the seventeenth-century
historian Filadelfo Mugnós), another member of the Uzeda, don Eugenio, is the
author of a fictional counterpart, or continuation, entitled *L'araldo sicolo*, whose
subscription is advertised with the promise that the buyer may see his own

pedigree imprinted: "Chi procura sei soscrizioni avrà diritto a pubblicare il proprio albero genealogico. Chi ne procura dodici avrà tuttosì lo stemma colorato"
(*VR*, 490). [Whoever buys six subscriptions will have the right to publish one's
own genealogical tree. Whoever buys twelve, will have his stemma in color.]
Eugenio is hassling every single family member to help him finance and market this book, but they all decline and consider it a ridiculous idea, given the new
bourgeois times that work against the hierarchy of class: "per esser considerati,
bisogna venire dal niente" (*VR*, 500) [to be considered, you have to come from
nowhere]. Yet despite the doubts of the other family members, the multivolume
work actually sells very well, especially since Eugenio "simplifies" the representation of the intra-aristocratic connections in such a way that those families who
happen to bear the same name as the authentic nobles may believe themselves
to be part of the same tree (*VR*, 548). In a further twist, and spurred on by the
publishing success, he prepares a second edition that also includes the "new nobility" (*VR*, 564). The satire here is clear: Eugenio's capitalist marketing of aristocratic pedigree shows that the new rhetoric of liberalism and social equality
actually fosters the pride in family trees, real or imaginary.

In the early scene of the novel where Fernanda is reading the *Teatro genologico*
as if it were a "novel," "her gospel," "the only pleasure of her imagination," she
delights in its "fantastic orthography" (*VR*, 105) [ortografia fantastica], while in
Eugenio's newly assembled book, the new nobility is said to have "more or less
fantastical coats of arms" (*VR*, 564) [stemmi più o meno fantastici]. The two scenes
are hundreds of pages apart, yet both emphasize the imaginary, fantastic, and indeed theatrical aspect of enjoying one's own pedigree. The irony consists in the
fact that the readers of Eugenio's work are precisely those false aristocrats despised by Fernanda, now in turn eager to distinguish themselves from the
masses. Since the scenes describing Eugenio's marketing of the family tree occur in close conjunction with Consalvo's crash course in literary and political
knowledge as a means to further his political career, the novel emphasizes this
instrumental use of history. These ironies imply not only a comment about social
transformation and distinction; they also underscore to what extent the reading
of the family tree is an imaginary desire that helps to comfort the individual
against the homogenizing forces of modernity. In this sense, De Roberto's novel
does not only set up a crazy old family for derision. As the archival research of
Giovanni Grana has shown, De Roberto himself might have identified with a
sense of social dislocation; although he was growing up under social conditions
of the lower bourgeoisie, De Roberto had ancestors who were themselves related
to the actual family of Uzeda.[48]

Adaptation and Historical Pessimism

Despite the choral, collective ambition of the novel, the figure of Consalvo has the special function of articulating the historical and collective consciousness of the Uzeda family in an exemplary manner. The depiction of his inner psychological consciousness and the voluntarism of his ideas also increasingly work against the naturalist doctrine of objectivist determinism, especially in the last quarter of the novel. Consalvo is a representative for those members of the aristocracy, who, to prevent and co-opt the liberalizing tendencies of the new state, do not oppose but seemingly collaborate with this movement. The aristocracy stalls and counteracts its inevitable social decline by adapting itself to the emergent class of the high bourgeoisie under the conditions of the new order (*VR*, 459) [*nuovo ordine*]. This opportunistic strategy of adaptation is directly opposed to the notion of emphatic progress, as advocated by the liberals of the industrial North. This is evidenced, for example, by the witty remark of the Duke of Oragua, the "liberal" uncle of Consalvo, which contains an obvious caricature of the famous pronouncement by Massimo d'Azeglio:

> E certuni bene informati assicuravano che una volta, nei primi tempi del nuovo governo, egli aveva pronunziato una frase molto significativa, rivelatrice dell'ereditaria cupidigia viceregale, della rapacitá degli antichi Uzeda: "Ora che l'Italia è fatta dobbiamo fare i fatti nostri. . . ." Se non aveva pronunziato le parole, aveva certo messo in atto l'idea: per ciò vantava l'eccellenza del nuovo regime, i benefici effetti del nuovo ordine di cose! (*VR*, 459)

> [And some well-informed people insisted that one time, during the first time of the new government, he had pronounced a very significant phrase, revealing of the hereditary viceregal cupidity, the rapacity, of the old Uzedas: "Now that Italy is accomplished, we have to do our own business. . . ." If he had not pronounced these words, he had certainly realized the idea: for this reason he praised the excellence of the new regime, the beneficial effects of the new order of things.]

This comment is reproduced in the context of a longer representation of the uncle's *trasformismo*. What is especially relevant here is the way the narrator communicates a sense of sociopolitical denouncement, without directly using the authorial voice. The self-condemnation of the uncle is said to be reported by informants; yet, we may ask, is it still those informants who think that this phrase is "revelatory" of the Uzeda kind and who exclaim that if the pronouncement has not literally taken place, it would still correspond to his behavior? This is just one of a series of passages in which De Roberto's radically objectivist style, for long parts of the novel relying only on dialogue and indirect free discourse, subtly slides into something resembling an authorial perspective. The example is also typical insofar as these almost imperceptible authorial intrusions often concern precisely the identification of a common family identity. In a scene where the young Consalvo's father angrily reprimands his son for profligate spending, the narrator cannot suppress a comment about his own relation to money: "meglio che tutti gli altri Uzeda, egli era il rappresentante degli ingordi Spagnuoli unicamente intenti ad arrichirsi, incapaci di comprendere una potenza, un valore, una virtù più grande di quella dei quattrini" (*VR*, 463) [more than all the other Uzedas, he was the representative of the Spaniards, only intent to enrich themselves, incapable of understanding a power, a value, a virtue that was bigger than money].

Especially toward the end, the novel approaches the question of how the self-identity of the Uzeda relates to the larger dimension of history and politics. History itself seems to be at a point of dissolution where every change is only apparent, as Consalvo explains to his aunt Fernanda on one of the very last pages of the long novel:

> La storia è una monotona ripetizione; gli uomini sono stati, sono e saranno sempre gli stessi. Le condizioni esteriori mutano; certo, tra la Sicilia di prima del Sessanta, ancora quasi feudale, e questa d'oggi pare ci sia un abisso; ma la differenza è tutta esteriore. Il primo eletto col suffragio quasi universale non è né un popolano, né un borghese, né un democratico: sono io, perché mi chiamo principe di Francalanza. Il prestigio della nobiltà non è e non può essere spento. Ora che tutti parlano di democrazia, sa qual è il libro più cercato alla biblioteca dell'Università, dove io mi reco qualche volta per i miei studi? L'*Araldo sicolo* dello zio don Eugenio, felice memoria. (*VR*, 697)

> [History is monotonous repetition: men have been, are, and will be always the same. The external conditions change. Certainly, an abyss seems to separate today's Sicily from the still almost feudal Sicily that existed before 1870. The difference, however, is completely external. The first one to be elected by an almost universal suffrage is neither one of the populace, nor a bourgeois, nor a democrat: it is I, because I call myself prince of Francalanza. The prestige of the nobility is a fact that will never be extinguished. Now that everybody is talking of democracy, do you know which is the most sought-after book in the library of the university where I sometimes go for my studies? The *Araldo sicolo* of Uncle Eugenio, of happy memory.]

These are surely the most often quoted sentences of the novel, usually taken to embody something like the general moral of the book and view of the author, and it is certainly possible that De Roberto entrusts here his own view to a character. Yet, in a novel as rigorously objectivist as this one, this pronouncement still remains above all the view of the speaker, Consalvo. Accordingly, the antihistoricist, fatalist assumptions of historical immobility and anthropological constancy might as well be a part of the nobility's self-delusional rationalization about the demise of their own class, an ironic possibility that will be richly exploited in Lampedusa's *Il Gattopardo*.

This skeptical view of historical progress is intimately connected to the site of enunciation, the place from which the narrator speaks: the difference of the South, of the Mezzogiorno, that is shown to be "out of line" with the development up north, because of the persistence of tradition and family.[49] On the one hand, the family is meant to illustrate a process of moral and biological decline. On the other hand, everything is supposed "to remain as it was," because the apparent change gives way only to new but essentially identical formations of power. Consalvo, the last descendant of the family tree, despite his antidemocratic convictions, enters the parliamentary elections as a candidate of the Left, explaining to his ultrareactionary aunt that this is actually a means to preserve continuity. At her deathbed, he maintains that the hereditary taint of the family does not threaten its continuity: "no, la nostra razza non è degenerata: è sempre la stessa" (*VR*, 699) ["no, our race is not degenerated: it is always the same"].

While history seems to advance according to a mechanistic law of "progress," this is no longer the outcome of individual, wilful actions, as it has been the case, say, in Ippolito Nievo's *Confessioni di un italiano*.[50] The pathologies that distinguish the Uzeda family characterize their entire environment and symbolize the mood of exasperated individualism of postunitary Italy as a whole. In other words, the story of the Uzeda is intended to reflect the larger history not only of the particular region but of the young Italian nation-state as a whole. With rigorous adherence to the objectivist principles of the naturalist doctrine, De Roberto refuses to center the novel, even momentarily, on any individual's particular perspective, so that the perspective of the narrator may coincide with any of the characters. The reader is rarely allowed to build up identification with any of the numerous characters, and the novel's constant kaleidoscopic change of focus makes it radically decentered. While the text is littered with historical events and allusions, the focus of the narrative remains, with few exceptions, rigorously on the private sphere. The confinement to the house(s) of the Uzeda confirms the sense of being locked in a network of power that is entirely shielded from temporal and spatial movement. In this sense, as a postunification reprise of the genre of the historical novel, the text might be characterized as an ironic inversion of the historical optimism prevalent in the tradition of the Italian historical novel as it was flowering around the time of the Risorgimento.[51]

As a matter of fact, Verga's and De Roberto's novels testify to the fact not simply that Sicilian literature at the end of the nineteenth century is an expression of regional literature but that the peripheral space of Sicily emerges as the most vital literary zone within Italy, in which the representation of a local identity serves to critically investigate and to accompany the process of constituting an Italian nationhood.[52] Although historical and political questions are much more prominent in De Roberto, even Verga's novel shows how the insularity of the represented space aims at, and is envisioned from, the historical self-consciousness of the new nation in the wake of the Risorgimento, after the failure of hopes for democratic integration. Accordingly, the two novels are today considered to be two of the most canonical instantiations of the *Italian* novel during this period. In both of these texts, it is the—decidedly nonbourgeois—institution of the family that marks a frontier of resistance against the process of modernization associated with the North and thus signifies a certain temporal circularity. Yet if Verga's family of the Malavoglia represents the *vinti*, the defeated, that progress and history have relegated to its shores, De Roberto's family of the Uzeda resists progress by pretending to join it.

CHAPTER FOUR

National and Genealogical Crisis

The Spanish Realist Novel (Benito Pérez Galdós)

In his classic study, *Imagined Communities*, Benedict Anderson argues for a connection between the concept of nationhood and the realist novel of the nineteenth century. According to this view, the realist novel is distinguished by a constellation of different, personally focused perspectives, which are all held together by the encompassing, totalizing position of an objective narrator, a position that Anderson sees as formally homologous with the integrative functions of the liberal nation-state.[1]

This basic affinity, however, does not necessarily imply a strong thematic presence of nationhood in the novel—many realist novels offer proof to the contrary. For this reason the correspondence between realist novel and nationhood should not be automatically assumed or posited as a universal fact; rather, it has to be identified and problematized in the context of specific national and literary traditions.[2] In the case of Italy, we have seen paradoxically that the geographically marginal region of Sicily, where the disenchantment with national unification was especially pronounced, played a decisive role in the consolidation of the Italian novel as a modern literary genre. As in Italy, the political and cultural situation in Spain is marked by a general state of belatedness. This explains, for instance, why the new movements of realism and naturalism are adapted to the form of the novel at basically the same time, during the 1880s. I will discuss the work of two authors, Benito Pérez Galdós and Emila Pardo Bazán, who are generally seen as the representative figures for realism (Galdós) and naturalism (Pardo Bazán) in Spain. Yet already the respective publication dates of their signature novels (*Fortunata y Jacinta*, 1887; *Los Pazos de Ulloa*, 1886) shows how the customary sequence of literary historiography is of little help here.[3] Instead I approach the two authors as representative, respectively, of an urban and a regional version of realism/naturalism, corresponding in turn to a bourgeois and an aristocratic perspective. As we will see, in contrast to the novel in France or England, the Spanish novel is distinguished by an explicit *thematization* of the question of national history, which is focalized through familial crises of succession.

Nation, Genealogy, and History in Benito Pérez Galdós's
Fortunata y Jacinta

The novelistic oeuvre of Galdós occupies a special position in the framework of the European novel, not only with regard to its staggering extension but also because it is so incessantly concerned with explicitly national themes in a way that, say, the work of Balzac or Dickens is not (or, at any rate, not directly). Not only in the series of the Episodios nacionales (a special form of the historical novel) but also in the great Novelas españolas contemporáneas, the question of the nation, in its different manifestations, occupies pride of place, and in some cases it takes on the form of a veritable allegory.[4] This, then, might be seen as the specific difference of Spanish realism. The present chapter is dedicated to the most significant and most voluminous text among the series of contemporary novels, *Fortunata y Jacinta* (1886–87), since both its thematic orientation and its formal means constitute an especially complex and resonant realization of the connection between novel and nation. I will show how the formal and structural features of this text might be understood as a literary reaction to a specific view of Spanish society. *Fortunata y Jacinta* enacts the traditional link among realism, nation, and the middle class, but it is also self-consciously problematized. In this regard, the text is markedly different, both formally and ideologically, from the historical optimism and the teleological model of the first series of the Episodios nacionales.[5] This novel represents the problematic unity of the nation, as exemplified and allegorized by the sphere of the private domain. I will especially draw attention to how the figuration of the nation is reflected in the genealogical narrative of the novel, which both presents and ultimately interrogates an organic model of society.

First, based on some of Galdós's own literary criticism, I will discuss the context of novelistic development in nineteenth-century Spain. Second, I will briefly develop the idea how the novel imagines national history in a private mode. Third, I will more specifically argue that the plot of *Fortunata y Jacinta* is based on a crisis of the upper bourgeoisie, an aspect that is reflected and thematized in the form of a genealogical crisis, a crisis of patriarchal succession. Finally, it will become apparent why the female protagonist Fortunata gains her significance precisely by resisting the paradigm of genealogical derivation. The figure of Fortunata constitutes a kind of answer to the question of the novel's genealogical crisis, while she also serves to reveal the limit of the organic-integrative model of society. In this process, the traditionally realist mode of writing increasingly gains a greater openness, perspectivism, and self-reflexivity, which is shown in particular by the meaning of mental representations, the subjective reality of fictions and imaginations, a characteristic that appears to be typical for the specific difference of the realist novel in Spain. Galdós's novel is in many ways typical of the nineteenth century novel in that it shows the tension between the efforts of a third-person narrator to represent the external world objectively and the simultaneous attempt to portray the individual consciousness of a character. Insofar as the history of the realist novel roughly follows a path of increased subjectivity, Galdós's novel might be said to mirror this formal development from the predominance of an omniscient narrator to a more perspectival mode of presentation in the sequential order of its text.

Novel and Nation

In one of his few programmatic writings, *Observaciones sobre la novela contemporánea en España* (Observations on the contemporary novel in Spain, 1870), Galdós grapples with the question of the uncompleted, or belated, modernization as it concerns the establishment of a Spanish tradition of the novel.[6] In this text, the author invokes, on the one hand, the exemplary function of a specifically Spanish tradition of the observation of reality (*observación*), which he links to the names of Velázquez and Cervantes, as well as the picaresque novel, while, on the other hand, he criticizes the flooding of the Spanish book market with melodramatic popular literature from France.[7] It is obvious that Galdós tries here to compensate for Spain's retrograde cultural position with an affirmation of its autochthonous values. This argumentation in favor of a genuine and long-standing Spanish tradition of realism is mobilized not only for the obviously nationalist reasons (i.e., it questions the primacy of France in the field of literary realism). In the Spanish context it is also an argument that serves to legitimize the practice of literary naturalism, a question that was highly contested throughout the 1880s. For instance, in his prologue to Clarín's *La Regenta* (1884) Galdós writes, "[Que de Francia] recibimos [. . .] con mermas y adiciones [. . .] la mercadería que habíamos exportado [. . .] nuestro arte de la naturalidad [. . .] responde mejor que el francés a la verdad humana."[8] [That from France we received, (. . .) with losses and gains (. . .), the merchandise we had exported. (. . .) Our art of nature (. . .) corresponds better than the French one to human truth.] Again, the latter claim is clearly strategic, but the specific difference of Spanish realism might be seen in a blending of materialism and idealism that indeed goes back to the literature of the baroque.

In the text "Observaciones" Galdós links the self-realization of the Spanish novel with the self-affirmation of the bourgeoisie as the central motor for a dynamic development of society ("la clase media [. . .] la base del orden social")[9] [the middle class, (. . .) the foundation of social order], as well as the consolidation of a genuinely Spanish tradition of literature. In the words of Galdós, the task of the novel consists in the production of a "cuerpo multiforme y vario, pero completo, organizado y unico, como la misma sociedad"[10] [a multiform and varied body, yet complete, organized, and one, as society itself]. Both the novel and society are imagined in the metaphor of the organic body, as the structured integration of the multiple. In his analysis Galdós draws a parallel between the comparative weakness of the Spanish novel and the political weakness of the country:

> Somos en todos unos soñadores que no sabemos descender de las regiones del
> más sublime extravío, y en literatura como en política, nos vamos por esas nubes
> montados en nuestros hipógrifos, como si no estuviéramos en el siglo XIX y en
> un rincón de esta vieja Europa, que ya se va aficionando mucho a la realidad.[11]
>
> [We are all dreamers who do not know how to descend from the most sublime regions of exaltation, and in both literature and politics we reach toward these clouds, mounted on our hippogriffs, as if we lived not in the nineteenth century and in a corner of this old Europe, which is already much endearing itself with reality.]

The present dominance of the fanciful, which is apparently an immediate manifestation of the national character (la fantasia andaluza), shall now give way to the observation and representation of reality, of which the Spaniards are well capable (la aptitud existe en nuestra raza)[12] but which has been lying dormant because of the reception and imitation of those French works and fashions whose negative influence on Spanish culture is described with images of colonial occupation, the imposition of foreignness, or an epidemic-like contamination.[13] In this sort of anti-French rhetoric, one might sense the echo of the trauma of the Napoleonic invasion (1808) and the war of independence (the central theme of the first series of Galdós's Episodios nacionales).

Insofar as this text thematizes, at least implicitly, Spain's peripheral position in the field of European literature, as well as its extremely ambivalent position with regard to the dominant model of French modernity, it merits a special consideration of the question of the circulation of literary capital through a cultural geography. Let me briefly repeat here a point already discussed in the introduction. With different orientations, both Franco Moretti and Pascale Casanova have described this phenomenon of structural inequalities in the sphere of an international literary market characterized by the dependence of geographic-cultural peripheries on the paradigms provided by the center (England, France), forced to strive for the legitimacy and distinctive value of their own products.[14] For instance, Casanova emphasizes that the struggle for literary recognition corresponds to the struggle for national self-affirmation, even as the literary agon is not directly dependent on the political one but rather follows its own laws, immanent to its own system of communication.[15] Galdós's (and other Spanish realists') critical adaptation of the French model is accompanied by the thematization of the peripheral situation of Spanish literature in an international context. In this situation of peripheral contestation, the form of the novel takes on a surprisingly modern openness and complexity, as the paradoxical result of the compensation for cultural belatedness.[16]

Galdós's novels substantially contribute to the flowering of the Spanish novel during the last third of the nineteenth century. The novel was ascending to become the principal literary genre, a development that had been prepared by the import of translations from France, which in turn led to the indigenous production of popular novels (*novelas por entregas*).[17] The rapid change of political, social, and economic conditions during these years, emblematized by the September Revolution of 1868, is certainly another important factor that contributed to the increased cachet of the novelistic medium at this time.[18] Because of the comparatively late development of the realist novel in Spain, readers and writers already dispose of a broad set of literary models and conventions, which now may variously be invoked, imitated, or criticized. The distinctive quality of the Spanish novel, which develops against the background of an already established tradition of realism, is often analyzed as a confrontation between an idealist and an anti-idealist worldview, taking on the form of a distance between the protagonists and the world by which they are surrounded, something that ultimately goes back to *Don Quixote* and that is figured, especially in Galdós, as an affinity for idealism and folly (as in the heightened mental states of Fortunata and Maximiliano Rubín).[19] Corresponding to the thoughts in the "Observaciones," Galdós echoes and criticizes, especially in the novel *La desheredada* (*The Disinherited Lady*, 1881), the genre of the novel-*folletín* (namely via the protagonist's *bovarysme*) and thus shows an ambivalent view of mass and popular culture, especially in the form of female consumerism.[20]

In various passages, *Fortunata y Jacinta* also takes on the character of a metaliterary novel, as when the narrator or the characters make allusions to popular genres (*folletín*, melodrama, *novela*), which are both inscribed in the novel as well as criticized as illusionary from a realist perspective. During some moments, the characters even have to insist on the reality of their feelings against the recognition that they are themselves living the life of a type in a popular novel or play.[21]

The principal narrative of *Fortunata y Jacinta* follows one of the standardized plots of the nineteenth century novel, the triangular situation of adultery, especially characteristic of novels that center on women (*Madame Bovary, Anna Karenina, La Regenta, Effi Briest*)—paradoxically, because, as Fredric Jameson puts it, "the role of the adulteress becomes the negative or privative one of showing that there is no place for them in that bourgeois society whose representation was to have been the object of the novel in the first place."[22] The juxtaposition of Jacinta as the legitimate wife and Fortunata as the lover of Juanito de Santa Cruz also introduces the class opposition of the higher bourgeoisie and the lower classes, the "fourth estate." Juanito, the male protagonist, after having had an affair with Fortunata, marries his cousin Jacinta, thus renewing an endogamous alliance between the two families of the upper mercantile bourgeoisie. Fortunata, however, intermittently sinking into prostitution, eventually marries the pharmacy student Maximiliano Rubín, who is distinguished by a fragile bodily constitution and whose family belongs to the lower-middle class. However, before she enters this marriage, she has to follow the authoritative instructions of Nicolás Rubín, Maxi's clerical brother, to undergo a—scarcely successful—moral-religious "correction" in a pedagogical institution for "fallen" women, Las Micaelas. Both Juanito and Fortunata are unhappy in their respective marriages and are thus predisposed to—repeatedly—betray their partners. This simple pattern of the plot of adultery is subjected by Galdós to a series of different permutations (Fortunata, for instance, is allied with a different man in each of the four parts of the novel), which allow him to portray different strata of society and their milieus, families, and urban regions from different perspectives. Especially during the first part, the urban space of Madrid takes on a central role, "este Madrid, que entonces era futuro" (*FJ*, 1.2.5.154) [this Madrid, which then was the future]. The space of the city and the historicizing markers of the novel are part of a national and temporal continuum. The interlocking of different histories, including the question of History, is central to the conception of a novel that presents itself as a representation of the nation.

History and Privacy

The subtitle of the novel, *Dos historias de casadas*, is already significant in emblematically referring to Galdós's intention to combine private history with the official history of the nation. The self-characterization of the narrator as a "historiador" (*FJ*, 2.7.8.636) is typical for the realist novel, which in this way shows its dependence on history as a symptomatic, paradigmatic discourse of nineteenth-century culture. It is well known that the decisive innovation in the genre of the novel derives from Balzac, who transformed the historical novel after the model of Walter Scott into a novel of modern society that was no longer concerned with some temporally remote event of national history but rather with an aspect of contemporary social history and that developed specific techniques of representation to create an "illusion of historicity."[23] In this context, critics of Galdós's work often mention the anecdote of his discovery of Balzac, his first revelatory encounter with *Eugénie Grandet* (1834), a text he says he read "for breakfast" during his stay in Paris at the time of the world exhibition.[24]

Balzac does constantly appeal to a historical horizon of meaning, although within the *histoire* he rather rarely has recourse to concrete events of the "great," official history. In striking contrast, Galdós introduces into his novel a wealth of explicit historical references and symbolic allusions. The reader of today may not be familiar with the numerous historical names and events to which he refers and thus is in need of an explanatory commentary. This potential for confusion and hypertrophy of facts, however, is not only due to the obvious fact of the historical distance but is also a result of the nature of the political events in question. After all, Spanish history of the nineteenth century is distinguished by a series of military coups (the *pronunciamentos*), as well as disputes of royal succession, wars, and finally by the failed revolution of the year 1868. The restoration of the Bourbon dynasty introduces into this chaotic period a relative stability, even as it signifies the failure of liberal hopes (very much so for Galdós).

The narrator of the novel tells the story from the perspective of 1886–87 and refers to events that mostly take place between 1869 and April 1876, from the abdication of Isabella II to the First Republic, the military coups, and finally the Bourbon Restoration. In the first part of the novel, the narrative tracks back to a time long before the revolutionary year of 1868. During this year a comparatively liberal coalition under the leadership of Prime Minister Juan Prim took the place of Queen Isabella and thus cleared the way for the establishment of a constitutional monarchy. The Savoyard Amadeo was crowned in 1871 and could occupy the throne only until 1873. A republic of rather short duration (1873–74) was swept away by a military coup, whereupon the Bourbon dynasty was restored to the throne with Alfonso II, Isabella's son.

Lilian Furst has pointed out that in the realist novel historical references have the function of a strategic code, which serves to communicate the text's aspiration toward the status of factual truth: "As an actuality of the recent past becomes the present of the narrative, an 'air of reality' is lent to the fiction. When

history merges into fiction, fiction legitimizes itself as history."[25] Historicization as a strategy of self-legitimization of the realist text is certainly at work in
Galdós's novel, although here the allegorical-metonymic dimension takes on a
much greater significance. For instance, the instability and the constant change
of the political conditions is mirrored by the volubility of Juanito, the "hombre
del siglo," who, in contrast to his father, randomly changes his political convictions and easily turns from Republican to monarchist: "porque Juan era la in-
consecuencia misma" (*FJ*, 1.7.2.287) [for Juan was inconsequence personified].
Already his first appearance in the novel illustrates his scarce political credibil-
ity. With his fellow students he takes part in the tumultuous events of the Noche
de San Daniel (April 10, 1865), triggered by the protest of the dismissal of a university professor, an event that became a symbolic rallying point for the Liberal
movement in Spain. Juanito's participation in this event is entirely inconsequential, and the narrator's (and, later, Jacinta's) ironic characterization of him as a
"revolutionary" and "anarchist" underscores from the beginning the dichotomy
of reality and appearance.

Insofar as Juanito is put forward as a figure who embodies an entire epoch or
generation, we can see a typical example of the metonymic nature of Galdós's
understanding of realism.[26] This becomes especially apparent at the beginning
of the third volume. In the chapter "La Restauración vencedora" (3.2), the national events of the political restoration—namely the instauration of King
Alfonso XII on January 14, 1875—coincide with the restoration of Jacinta and Juanito's marriage. Fortunata, rejected by Juanito, also returns to her husband.[27] Don
Baldomero, Juanito's father, as well as his family circle, happily welcome the political restoration. Yet when at this moment Jacinta finally learns of her husband's
unfaithfulness, his renewal of relations with Fortunata, her subjective condition
is actually not in tune with, but rather opposed to, the perception of the event of
national history, a fact emphasized by the narrator with a metaphorical parallel-
ism: "Jacinta tenía que entusiasmarse también, a pesar de aquella *procesión* que
por dentro le andaba, y poner cara de pascua a todos los que entraron felicitán-
dose del suceso" (*FJ*, 50; italics mine) [Jacinta also had to show her enthusiasm,
in spite of that *procession* taking place *inside* her; she had to put up a happy face
for all those who entered congratulating themselves on the success].

The contrast engendered by the metaphoric parallel thus promotes the interior psychological state of the character at the expense of the exterior events,
especially given the fact that the exterior event is not even properly described. At
the same time, D. Baldomero and his son Juanito argue about a political difference regarding the military nature of the Restoration, as well as its possibly

transitory state, which leads D. Baldomero to utter a commentary, which, in the context of the preceding signals, clearly refers not only to the evaluation of the national character but also of the character of Juanito:

> En la sociedad española no se puede nunca fiar tan largo. Lo único que sabemos es que nuestro país padece alternativas o fiebres intermitentes de revolución y de paz. En ciertos periodos todos deseamos que haya mucha autoridad. (*FJ*; 3.2.1.53)

> [In the Spanish society you can only trust so long. The only thing we know is that our country suffers from alterations or intermittent fevers of revolution and peace. In certain periods we all crave for much authority.]

The title of this chapter, "La Restauración vencedora," then, refers to the parallel of the political restoration and the restoration of Juanito's marriage and hence the—temporary—rejection of his extramarital relation with Fortunata: "en realidad no era aquello virtud, sino cansancio del pecado; no era el sentimiento puro y regular del orden, sino el hastío de la revolución" (*FJ*, 3.2.2.56) [in reality this was not virtue, but rather the tiring of sin; it was not the pure and regular feeling of order, but the weariness of revolution].

The public and the private restoration thus mutually illumine each other, for Juanito's "flexible ingenio" (*FJ*, 3.2.3.63) [flexible character] corresponds to the political instability of the nation. This somewhat forced political allegorization was apparently so important to Galdós that he does not seem to mind that Juanito's rather questionable relation with Fortunata thus becomes associated with the term "revolution." The names and events of national history are briefly invoked to contrast it with the narrative as a history of domestic, private life. From the vantage point of the present—the epoch of the Restoration, which is mostly represented in static terms—the contemporary reader learns to apprehend history as something that is already a part of the past. In other words, the principle of historicizing realism is still present but has already been historicized.

The End of Genealogy: Juanito

In this regard it is remarkable how the first part of the novel represents history in metonymic-allegorical fashion, in the form of a private genealogy of family. This occurs, above all, in the second chapter, entitled "Santa Cruz y Arnaiz: Vista histórico sobre el comercio matritense" (*FJ*, 1.2; "Santa Cruz and Arnaiz: A Historical View on Commerce in Madrid"). Through a comparatively strong compression of narrated time, the first part of the novel tells of the period of consolidation of the liberal-conservative upper bourgeoisie during the absolutist reign of Fernando VII and the liberal phase of the first half of the nineteenth century. It thus provides the historical basis for the actual narrative plot of the novel, falling into the epoch of the *sexenio revolucionario*, from the September Revolution of 1868 to the return of the Bourbons in 1874. The genealogical theme of the second chapter constitutes a kind of historical excursus within a text that is otherwise mostly concerned with the representation of the most recent past. Strictly speaking, this means that there are *two* moments of the present from which the past is being taken into view.

The narrator subjects the self-understanding of the family to irony when he describes the forefathers of the male protagonist Juanito Santa Cruz in the style of monarchical succession (Baldomero I, Baldomero II). This quasi-aristocratic characterization of the high-bourgeois family has to be understood as pointing to the uncertain standing of the bourgeoisie at this time. It is precisely during a time of the dissolution of traditional structures of society when, paradoxically, the legitimizing model of dynastic-genealogical derivation is mobilized.[28] For instance, it is telling that Galdós's urban novel *La desheredada* (1881), the first novel of the series Novelas contemporáneas, features just such a search for an aristocratic origin in the context of a rapidly modernizing world. The heroine, Isidora Rufete, is obsessed by her wish to claim the lineage of a noble family, while being simultaneously encouraged and blocked by a new sense of social equality: "ya todos somos iguales" [we are already all equals]; "la desaparición de las clases" [the disappearance of the classes].[29] The female protagonist of Clarín's novel *Su único hijo* (1891), Emma Valcárcel, in contrast, a descendant of a declining noble family, tries to compensate for her marriage to a socially inferior husband by indulging in amorous fantasies about the historical founder of her own family.[30]

The bourgeoisie, marginalized during the Restoration, follows the social norms of the aristocracy.[31] The irony of this relation becomes fully clear in the frequently mentioned nickname of Juanito, el Delfín, that is, the French title of the prince heir (le Dauphin). From the perspective of the period of the Restoration, when the liberal hopes of the bourgeoisie were arrested, an earlier time comes into view: the economic success story of the textile company owned by Baldomero I and II, which has provided the material basis for Juanito's comfortable yet unproductive position. As Stephen Gilman has stressed, the extended discussions not only of the genealogical details but also of the sociological, topographical, and economic aspects of the first part are not really justified in terms of the narrative plot. Also, the initial descriptive density is not maintained in the following parts of the novel, which raises the question of the function of these passages, which are likely to irritate the reader.[32] It is not surprising, then, that this apparent disproportion in the construction of the novel has been variously criticized and that only a few studies have ventured an interpretation of the genealogical excursus with regard to the meaning of the novel as a whole.[33] Let us have a closer look at the beginning of the second chapter:

> Don Baldomero Santa Cruz era hijo de otro D. Baldomero Santa Cruz que en el siglo pasado tuvo ya tienda de paños del Reino en la calle de la Sal. [. . .] Había empezado el padre por la humilde jerarquía commercial. Y a fuerza de trabajo, constancia y orden, el hortera de 1769 tenía, por los años 10 al 15, uno de los más reputados establecimientos de la Corte en pañeria nacional y extranjera. (*FJ*, 1.2.1.118–19).

> [Don Baldomero Santa Cruz was the son of another D. Baldomero Santa Cruz who in the past century already owned a drapery store in the street de la Sal. (. . .) The father had begun within the humble commercial hierarchy. Through the force of work, constancy, and order, the shop assistant of 1769 possessed, between the years 10 and 15, one of the most well-regarded establishments for national and foreign draperies in the Court.]

The ascent of the mercantile family, brought about by a work ethic and the continuity of tradition, is a symptomatic of the dynamism of a socially and economically mobile society—precisely in the sense of Galdós's reflections in the "Observaciones," discussed above. Several times the narrator insists on the fact that in Madrid the process of familial and professional ramification may always be reduced to a common origin: "y escudriñando los troncos de estos linajes matritenses, sería facil encontrar que los Arnaiz y los Santa Cruz tenían en sus diferentes ramas una savia común, la savia de los Trujillos" (*FJ*, 2.1.2.125) [and by scrutinizing the trunks of those Madrilenian lineages, it will be easy to find that the Arnaiz and Santa Cruz families had in their different branches a common sap, the sap of the Trujillos]. Consider the following example: "Las familias de Santa Cruz y Arnaiz se trataban con amistad casi íntima, y además tenían vinculos de parentesco con los Trujillos. La mujer de don Baldomero I y la del defunto Arnaiz eran primas segundas, floridas ramas de aquel nudoso tronco" (*FJ*, 2.1.2.136). [The families of Santa Cruz and Arnaiz treated each other with almost intimate friendship, and moreover they had parental links with the Trujillos. The wife of Don Baldomero I and the one of the deceased Arnaiz were first cousins, flowery branches of that knotty trunk.] It is apparent, then, that the blending of the families of the Santa Cruz and the Arnaiz, which both stem from the branch of the Trujillos ("Todos somos unos!" *FJ*, 1.2.1.125) [We are all one!] is potentially incestuous. The reader thus comes to realize that the panorama of the extensive genealogical ramification ultimately rests on a single root and an endogamous structure. After the marriage of Don Baldomero and Barbarita, Juanito's parents (a union praised by the narrator in the highest tones: "para eterna ejemplaridad de las generaciones futuras," *FJ*, 1.2.4.141) [as an eternal ex-emplum for the future generations], however, have to wait ten years for the birth of their son, "como los judíos al Mesías" (*FJ*, 1.2.4.142) [as the Jews for the Messiah] in 1845. The reproductive problems of the Santa Cruz family might symbol-ize a crisis of the continuity of the higher bourgeoisie, whose standing was due to the long tradition of commerce but falters in the face of the forces of moder-nity. The genealogical narrative of the Santa Cruz family thus appears like an abbreviated anticipation, a sort of Iberian version of the *Buddenbrooks*.[34]

Thereupon, the reader learns that Barbarita plans the marriage of her son with his cousin Jacinta Arnaiz, who in this way comes to occupy the structural place once occupied by her aunt. In striking contrast to the sterility of the Santa Cruz family, Isabel de Cordero de Arnaiz, Jacinta's mother, is blessed with an abundance of children (which corresponds in turn to the fertility of Queen Isa-bella II). As soon appears, this contrasts with the complete childlessness of Jacinta and Juanito's marriage, which is also reflected by the oedipal relation-ship of Juanito to his mother. This constellation provides the central motivation for the plot of the novel, the problem of the production of a—male—heir and hence the continuation of the apparently decadent family line. In fact, Galdós's novel needs to be situated within the larger context of European naturalism, where the unity of the family becomes the privileged site for the interference of the biological with the social, nature with nurture, inheritance with environ-ment.[35] As the historian Eric Hobsbawm also reminds us, the problem of eco-nomic and biological self-perpetuation was one that was characteristic of the European bourgeoisie as a whole, and a figure like the idle Juanito is indicative precisely of the contradiction between effort and enjoyment identified by Hobsbawm with regard to the latter part of the nineteenth century: "the bour-geois class found enormous difficulty in combining getting and spending in a morally satisfactory manner, just as it failed to solve the equivalent material problem, how to secure a succession of equally dynamic and capable business-men within the same family, a fact which increased the role of daughters, who could introduce new blood into the business complex."[36]

As appears from the "Observaciones," originally Galdós might have had hopes for the productive-dynamic energy of the bourgeoisie. The present form of the novel, however, where the flowering of the bourgeoisie is only apparent in the historical retrospection of the first part ("Vistazo histórico"), makes clear that for Galdós a renewal of the self-estranged bourgeoisie might be possible only via its combination with the *pueblo*, the true guarantor, as it were, of national identity. In other words, the genealogical crisis, which, on the level of narrative, motivates the plot of adultery (as a "breaking away" from sterility), illustrates the diagnosis of a social and national decadence, as became apparent during the period of the Restoration.

It is not at all a coincidence that these symptomatic families of the Madrid bourgeoisie, the Santa Cruz and the Arnaiz, are involved precisely in the commerce of textiles. For it was textile production that from very early on embodied the principle of the capitalist circulation of goods and thus introduced into economics a net of relationships that connected individual persons far beyond the circle of the city, with international trade and world-political events. Galdós uses this economic context to thematize the problem of Spanish modernization. First, the flowering of the trade company is accompanied by the introduction of the Free Trade Laws in 1849 (extended in the Unión Liberal of 1858) and a free circulation of goods, which is especially associated with women's fashion textiles (in contrast to the former trade in military uniforms). Fashion, especially women's fashion, signals in emblematic form the principle of economic dynamism and of social change:

> Lo más interesante de tal imperio está en el vestir de las señoras, origen de energías poderosas, que de la vida privada salen a la pública y determinan hechos grandes. ¡Los trapos, ay! ¿Qien no ve en ellos una de las principales energías de la época presente, tal vez una causa generadora de movimiento y vida? (*FJ*, 1.2.5.153)[37]

> [The most interesting aspect of that empire consists in the dressing of the women, the origin of powerful energies, which rise from the private toward the public life and determine great deeds. The dresses, ah! Who does not see in them one of the principal energies of the present epoch, maybe a generative cause of movement and life?]

The voice of the narrator does not neglect to mention that the import of foreign—mostly French—fashion leads to a corruption of the original, natural Spanish character, which is attested to, above all, by the falling out of fashion of the *mantón de Manila* (*FJ*, 1.2.2.127), a symbol of the Spanish national character, whose name, of course, already betrays its colonial character: "esta prenda, esta nacional obra de arte, tan nuestra como las panderetas o los toros, no es nuestra en realidad más que por el uso" (*FJ*, 1.2.2.128) [this garment, this national work of art, so much ours as the tambourines or the bullfights, is in reality not ours if not by use]. The *decadencia* of this emblematic shawl as a result of its substitution by "gray" fashion from the North makes clear that this phenomenon is also related to the decadence of the Spanish colonial empire in an international context of political power, and hence the problem of the increasing isolation and backwardness of Spain in relation to Europe:[38]

> Las galeras aceleradas iban trayendo a Madrid cada día con más presteza las novedades parisienses, y se apuntaba *la invasion* lenta y tiránica de los medios colores, que pretenden ser signo de cultura. La sociedad española empezaba a presumir de seria, es decir, a vestirse lúgubremente, y el alegre *imperio* de los colorines se derrumbaba de un modo indudable. [. . .] Aquel incanto de los ojos, aquel prodigio de color, remedo de la naturaleza sonriente [. . .], empezó a perder terreno, dunque el pueblo, con instinto de colorista y poeta, defendía la prenda española como defendió el parque de Monteleón y los reductos de Zaragoza. (*FJ*, 1.2.2.150; italics mine)

> [With more speed every day, the swift galleys were bringing to Madrid the novelties from Paris, and one could observe the slow and tyrannical *invasion* of the half colors that pretended to be signs of culture. The Spanish society began to give itself airs of seriousness, that is, to dress itself in a lugubrious manner, and the happy *empire* of the bright colors was undoubtedly collapsing. (. . .) That enchantment of the eyes, that wonder of color, the mirror of smiling nature, (. . .) began to lose ground, while the people, with the instinct of a colorist and a poet, defended the Spanish dress, as it had defended the park of Monteleón and the redoubts of Zaragoza.]

The narrator here takes a clear position with regard to contemporary debates about the necessity of economic protectionism, as was especially the case with textile production. Yet what is remarkable about this passage is how the import of French fashion is associated with the political-military rhetoric of invasion and occupation and that the people, *el pueblo*, are fighting against both the Napoleonic troops and French textiles. The pan-European process of modernization leads to a situation where Spain itself comes into the position of a "colonized," "subaltern," or "dependent" country, a question that Galdós has also discussed on another occasion.[39] Yet also in the novel itself the narrator describes the economic dependency in terms of a colonial power relation, one that subjects the country in the name of progress:

Las comunicaciones rápidas nos trajeron mensajeros de la potente industria belga, francesa e inglesa, que necesitaban mercados. Todavía no era moda ir a buscarlos al Africa, y los venían a buscar aquí, cambiando cuentas de vidrio por pepitas de oro; es decir, lanillas, cretonas y merinos, por dinero contante o por obras de arte. (*FJ*, 1.2.5.151)

[The rapid means of communication were brought to us by the messengers of the powerful Belgian, French, and English industries, which were in need of markets. It was not yet the fashion to look for them in Africa, and hence they came looking here, exchanging glass beads for nuggets of gold; which is to say, flannel, *cretonne*, and merino wool, for ready cash or works of art.]

This openly autarchist position of the narrator, then, shows a clear parallel to the anti-French polemic in the "Observaciones," which is to say that the affirmation of Spanish culture is part of a larger mobilization of the national economy. From this nationalist perspective, the people appear as the true essence of Spanish nationhood. Accordingly, it is no coincidence that in these passages the narrator repeatedly employs the first person plural: "estamos bajo la influencia del Norte de Europa, y ese maldito Norte nos impone los grises que toma de su ahumado cielo" (*FJ*, 1.2.5.151) [we are under the influence of Northern Europe, and this cursed North imposes upon us the grey tones taken from its smoky sky]. The import of fashion from the North is associated, moreover, with modern methods of production and transport (especially the train system), social modernization, the ascent of a mercantile class, and the rapidly increased transformation of Madrid into a modern metropolis, "de aldeota indecente a la de capital civilizada" (*FJ*, 1.2.5.154) [from an indecent village to a civilized capital]. By way of the decadence of the once suddenly wealthy bourgeoisie, embodied by Juanito, the narrator ultimately criticizes naïve belief in progress during that time ("la idea madre de aquellos tiempos, el progreso," *FJ*, 1.2.4.144) [the mother idea of those times: progress]. When D. Baldomero refuses to instill in his son the traditional work ethic and instead follows modern ideas of liberal education according to which his son might follow his own instincts, he uses language that is clearly reminiscent of the contemporary debate on Free Trade: "*laissez aller, laissez passer*" (*FJ*, 1.2.4.144). Through such signals the narrator articulates a critique of national decadence brought about by "progress," a decadence especially of the social class that had originally been responsible for Spain's first ascent as a modern nation-state and that is represented in the novel by the history of the Santa Cruz family.

The theme of family genealogy, however, does not only determine the formal structure of the novel, for in subsequent parts of the text the image of the family tree also becomes a symbolic motif.[40] The image of the family tree refers in a literal sense to the genealogical and social context of the Santa Cruz family, but it also becomes a metaphor for the narrative embedding, or "ramification," of special lifeworlds, in the sense of the organic mimesis of reality that is claimed by the aesthetic of realism. For instance, significant turning points of the novel are motivated by what appear to be purely chance meetings of characters within the space of the city.[41] Insofar as the urban space concerned is Madrid, there might also be an implicit reference here to the arboreal emblem of Madrid, the *madroño*. At the end of the novel, the death of Moreno-Isla, a friend of the Santa Cruz family, is explicitly linked with the idea of the tree of life, which helps to establish a loose but resonant continuity with the image of the family tree in the first part: "Se desprendió de la humanidad, cayó del gran árbol la hoja completamente seca, solo sostenida por fibra imperceptible. El árbol no sintió nada en sus inmensas ramas" (*FJ*, 4.3.6.363). [He detached himself from humanity, and from the great tree fell the leaf that was entirely dry, only sustained by an imperceptible fiber. The tree felt nothing in its enormous branches.] The image of the family tree, then, aims at the organic unity of family and society.[42] It can be seen as an instance of the common strategy in which realist novels employ metaphors of organic cohesion—think of the web metaphor in George Eliot's *Middlemarch*—to signal their aspiration of total, exhaustive representation.

This imagery, as it is developed especially in the second chapter, is highly significant for the genealogical theme of the novel. One might think here also of the central function of the *arbre généalogique* in Zola's Rougon-Macquart cycle, which in fact reveals how Galdós's use of the image of the family tree *differs* from the naturalist paradigm. In contrast to the model of naturalism— which, originally "imported" from France, had a modernizing function in the Spanish context[43]—it is important to note that the principle Spanish novelists of the 1880s (Galdós, Clarín, Pardo Bazán) did increasingly distance themselves from the idea of a biological and sociological determinism and hence were able to introduce a greater openness into the relations between individual and environment.[44]

Although the sons of the Rubín family are marked by a hereditary defect, very much in the sense of Zola's *fêlure*, the decadent pattern of the genealogical constellation in Galdós's text also signifies the diminishment of the genealogical model of explanation itself—and not, as in Zola, its ratification. The *gran árbol* of humankind takes over the role of the dying family tree. This organic image of society motivates the narrative of an attempt at integration—the civilizing and domestication of Fortunata. Accordingly, the entirety of the nation appears as a single "big family," where social and class differences are transcended by a "happy confusion":

> Es curioso observar cómo nuestra edad, por otros conceptos infeliz, nos presenta una dichosa confusión de todas las clases, mejor dicho, la Concordia y reconciliación de todas ellas [. . .] Aquí se ha resuelto el problema sencilla y pacíficamente, gracias al temple democrático de las españoles y a la escasa vehemencia de las preocupaciones nobiliarias [. . .] han salido amigos el noble tornado y el plebeyo ensoberbecido por un título universitario; y de amigos, pronto han pasado a parientes. Esta confusión es un bien, y gracias a ella no nos aterra el contagio de la guerra social, porque tenemos ya en la masa de la sangre un socialismo atenuado y inofensivo. (*FJ*, 1.6.1.240)

> [It is curious to observe how our time, in other respects so unfortunate, presents to us a happy confusion of all classes, or better, the concord and reconciliation of them all. (. . .) Here the problem has been solved in a simple and peaceful manner, and thanks to the democratic temper of the Spaniards and the weak influence of aristocratic preoccupations. (. . .) The new aristocrat and the plebeian emboldened by a university degree have become friends, and from friends they have become relatives. This confusion is a good, for thanks to it we are not afflicted by the contagion of social warfare, because already in the substance of our blood we possess an attenuated and inoffensive socialism.]

The ideal of a mixing of classes as a means of doing away with class differences is easily recognized as the view of the narrator (or Galdós) and as an ideological myth. Here we can identify a significant difference between Galdós and the French model of realism. For, whereas Balzac describes the social dynamics of the world of early capitalism while simultaneously expressing his nostalgia for the order of the ancien régime, Galdós presents himself as sympathizing with a process of social democratization, which he even understands as being rooted in an ethnic-biological principle ("en la masa de la sangre").

This interpenetration of private and public, however, is also presented as problematic. Of special significance in this regard is the first chapter of the third book, "Costumbres turcas," where already the title announces its affinity with *costumbrismo*, the literary movement of the 1830s and 1840s, which, before the proper emergence of the realist novel in Spain, had precisely the function of achieving a self-portrait of the middle classes and the national community.[45] The chapter serves to characterize Juan Pablo Rubín, the politicizing brother of Maxi who passes a good part of his life in the *tertulias* of the coffee houses in Madrid. In a *costumbrista*-realist manner the narrator emphasizes the continuity between the character and his material surroundings:

> Proporcionábale el café las sensaciones íntimas que son propias del hogar doméstico, y al entrar le sonreían todos los objetos como si fueran suyos. Las personas que allí vieran constantemente, los mozos y el encargado, ciertos parroquianos fijos, se le representaban como unidos estrechamente a él por lazos de familia. (*FJ*, 3.1.1.12)

> [The café provided to him the intimate sensations typical of the domestic hearth, and on entering all the objects smiled to him as if they were his. He thought of the people who were constantly coming here, the young lads and the commissioners, certain habitual clients, as intimately bound to him through family bonds.]

This identification with the milieu prefigures Juan Pablo's adoption of the most different ideological positions (Carlism, atheism, socialism, etc.), which in turn refers to the brotherly relations among the coffee-house politicians and, allegorically, to the nation as a whole:

> Allí brillaba espléndidamente esa fraternidad española en cuyo seno se dan mano de amigo el carlista y el republicano, el progresista de cabeza dura y el moderado implacable. [. . .] Esto de que todo el mundo sea amigo particular de todo el mundo es síntoma de que las ideas van siendo tan solo un pretexto para conquistar o defender el pan. (*FJ*, 3.1.1.15)

> [There shone splendidly that sense of Spanish fraternity in whose bosom the Carlist and the Republican extend to each other their hands in friendship, as well as the hard-headed liberal and the implacable moderate. (. . .) This habit of everybody being the special friend of everybody else is a symptom for the fact that the ideas are only going to be a pretext for winning or defending bread.]

Directly following this passage, the narrator—again assuming now the first person plural ("nosotros") of the national community—speaks rather generally of a change in leadership, a "turno en el dominio." For the contemporary readers this must have been a clear allusion to the so-called *turno pacífico*, that is, the only seemingly democratic power arrangement of the epoch of Restoration (1874–97), according to which Conservatives and Liberals took turns in exercising political power.[46] The narrator's critique of the contemporary present, then, is relocated around twelve years back, to a time directly before the Restoration, by associating it with the development of the national character ("esa fraternidad española") [this Spanish brotherhood] that manifests itself in a cultural ritual.[47]

Whereas Galdós (or the narrator) has, on the one hand, a vision of the "happy confusion of all classes," in the sense of an organic view of society, on the other hand, he also formulates a critique (via the satirical figure of Juan Pablo) of the random adoption of different political positions. The nation is represented by the image of the family, yet an exaggerated familiarity in politics amounts to a problematic privatization of public structures. The image of family bonds ("lazos de familia") aims at the idea of an organic (national) community, which, however, also appears as insufficiently modern insofar as the spheres of private and public are insufficiently differentiated. Indeed, rather than pointing in the direction of bourgeois individualism, Juanito's genealogical background calls up an older model of feudalism.[48] This ideological contradiction is fundamental to the structure of the novel, and it illustrates Galdós's ambivalent stance toward modernity. The genealogical narrative, then, combines a history of social-economic progress (the ascent of the bourgeoisie) with a plot of social-reproductive decadence or crisis (sterility).

Realism and Perspective: Fortunata

The extended representation of the genealogical history of Juanito's family is contrasted not only with his own rather insignificant position but also with the representation of Fortunata, whose family origin as an orphan lies more or less in the dark and hence cannot be narrated in a genealogical, and therefore historically significant, form.[49] The striking contrast in the depiction of Juanito and Jacinta, then, is programmatic. On the one hand, the novel, in an almost polemical move, directs its focus to a female perspective; on the other hand, it changes from a historical-sociological model to a more psychological interest. At the same time, the unrooted figure of the orphan, which this text shares with a number of nineteenth-century novels, serves to maximize the effect of the individual's confrontation with (social) reality. Even in her capacity as a representative of the people, Fortunata is more an allegorical symbol than the socially determined subject of naturalism.

Significantly, the two central female names (Fortunata and Jacinta) are always mentioned without the *apellido*, in marked contrast to the two strategically and symmetrically located chapters, "Juanito Santa Cruz" (1.1.1) and "Maximiliano Rubín" (2.1.1), which introduce a male representative of the higher and lower bourgeoisie, respectively. Moreover, the contrast signifies above all a social opposition. The class of the high bourgeoisie, seemingly come to the end of its social function, is contrasted with the emergence of a member of the fourth estate. In this regard, it is highly significant that Fortunata's first entrance in the novel, when Juanito encounters her dramatically on the steps at the Cava de San Miguel, seems literally an appearance out of nowhere. At this encounter, Fortunata, standing in the middle of a chicken farm, drinks a raw egg, and in the following scenes Fortunata is frequently associated with chicken or generally with birds. In this scene, even her clothes make her resemble a chicken ("cierta semejanza con una gallina," *FJ*, 1.2.4.182). Such an obviously symbolic accumulation of motifs shows that Galdós's conception of realism aims to give the reader specific directions for the constitution of meaning, in this case Fortunata's association with nature, which Juanito, through whom the reader experiences this scene, finds both fascinating and repulsive.

The radical opposition that appears in the characterization of the two protagonists is complemented by a formal turn in the structure of the novel, as well as in Galdós's literary oeuvre as a whole. As we have already mentioned, during this time Galdós distances himself from the naturalistic notions of environment and inheritance, as he had still mobilized it, under the influence of Zola, for his earlier novels *La desheredada* (1881) and *Lo prohibido* (1884–85).[50] Moreover, the change of perspective is also motivated by the fact that Galdós abandoned his original plan to write a novel about the Spanish bourgeoisie in favor of a more critical perspective that ended up granting redemptive powers to the people.[51] Also in this regard the structure of the plot is highly conventional. The egoistical seduction of a woman in a lower social position by a man in a relatively high social position is, at this general level, a long-standing literary topos, driving the logic of a great many domestic dramas or *bürgerliche Trauerspiele*. This aspect of self-conscious literary conventionality is surely implied by the name Juanito, with its allusion to the specifically Spanish myth of Don Juan. While in this literary tradition the status difference refers above all to the distinction between aristocracy and bourgeoisie, in Galdós the functional "place" of the aristocracy is filled by the upper bourgeoisie.[52]

In this sense, various critics have rightfully pointed to the fact that a major interest of the novel lies in representing Fortunata's emergence as a complex character with a subjective consciousness. This emergence is reflected in the novel's very structure and form, given that the narrative perspective zooms in on her only in the second, and then ever more in the third and fourth, part.[53] Consequently, one of the innovations of *Fortunata y Jacinta* in the tradition of the Spanish novel consists in its elevation of a simple, illiterate woman of the people to the role of protagonist, akin to the naturalist strategy of widening the social inclusiveness of the novel, what the brothers Goncourt have called *le droit au roman*. The representation of Fortunata as figure and symbol of the fourth estate is characteristic of the generally democratic inclusiveness of the realist novel, with its double tendency toward social expansiveness and psychological investigation. As Alex Woloch has shown, this "asymmetric structure of characterization," typical for literary realism, has the unavoidable consequence that the aspiration toward social expansiveness cannot avoid imbalances in the narrative focalization, which in turn correspond to the social and economic inequalities of a democratic society.[54] In this context the special significance of *Fortunata y Jacinta* lies in the fact that here the attention is directed principally, if not exclusively, at the figure of Fortunata, the personification of the people, in comparison with whom the bourgeois protagonist, Juanito, appears as a rather flat and almost exclusively negative character.

At the same time, it should not be forgotten that the peripheral first-person narrator, even as he remains fully on the margins, is clearly socially situated as a member of the higher bourgeoisie. In part, he repeatedly appears as a direct acquaintance of the characters ("me ha contado Jacinta," *FJ*, 3.2.1.49) [Jacinta has told me]. This first-person narrator, however, becomes less visible and finally disappears the more the narrative turns its focus to Fortunata in such a way that an external, objectifying perspective (peripheral first-person narrator, auctorial narrator) is increasingly substituted by a more subjectivist, internal perspective (interior monologue, indirect free discourse) in the case of Fortunata but also of other characters, such as Maxi. The position of the objective narrator is never fully abandoned, but the balance between these two modes of narration has clearly been shifted.

If the realist novel had always sought to combine the investigation of the social world with the representation of psychological inwardness, this novel presents a crisis and hence an increasing problematization of such a balanced relation. This means that the extended descriptions of milieu no longer have a clearly determinative function. Conversely, the psychological developments, which are mostly presented as specific, perspective-bound interpretations of reality through the interior worlds of the characters, take on an important, plot-controlling function. The internalization of Fortunata in the religious house of betterment, Las Micaelas, is an example. The two chapters ("Las Micaelas por fuera" and "Las Micaelas por dentro," 2.5 and 2.6) signify already at the level of their title, as if in a concentrated form, as a mise en abyme, a movement from exterior description of external milieu to the level of personal consciousness as it manifests itself, here and elsewhere, especially by dreams and the realm of individual thought. This tendency toward the dissolution of the exterior world also becomes apparent in Fortunata's final hour: "pero mientras la personalidad física se extinguía, la moral, concentrándose en una sola idea, se determinaba con desusado vigor y fortaleza" *(FJ,* 4.6.13.519) [yet while the physical person expired, morality, concentrated in a single idea, was resolving itself with unusual vigor and forcefulness].

Already in the course of the novel, the two principal female characters have been brought together by the plot, although there was hardly an actual encounter between them. Through this mutual identification each realizes that the fault for her misery lies not with her rival but only with Juanito. In the end, a final, ideal alliance is reached between the two female protagonists, while Juanito has again been unfaithful to his wife. Thinking of her son, Fortunata even imagines a utopian, purely female family, according to which she would be "la mama primera," complemented by Jacinta and Guillermina Pacheco *(FJ,* 4.6.12.489).

In many respects this ending is left open and ambivalent. On the one hand, the birth of a son apparently guarantees the patriarchal pattern of inheritance; on the other hand, the alliance between the two women is precisely also an alliance *against* Juanito. If the birth of the son, as the fulfillment of the initial motivation of the plot, projects a hope for the future, Fortunata's lonely death at the end of the novel signifies simultaneously the failure, or the limit, of the attempt at social integration. Toward the end, Maxi, who becomes increasingly mad, is consigned to the mental asylum of Leganés. At the end of the novel both he and Fortunata appear more than ever to be shut out of bourgeois society.

However, the position of Fortunata's son as illegitimate also signifies the productive amalgamation of social classes, insofar as the sterility of Jacinta—and hence of the bourgeoisie as a whole—is counteracted by the fertility of Fortunata. The fertility and primordial nature of Fortunata, and of the *pueblo* for whom she serves as a synecdoche, is mentioned, implicitly and explicitly, in many passages of the novel: "¡Pueblo!, eso es—observó Juan [. . .]: lo esencial de la humanidad, la materia prima, porque quando la civilización deja perder los grandes sentimientos, las ideas matrices, hay que ir a buscarlos al bloque, a la cantera del pueblo" *(FJ,* 2.7.6.690). [The people! As Juan observed, they are the essence of humanity, the prime matter; for when civilization witnesses the loss of great sentiments and fertile ideas, you have to look for them in the block, in the quarry of the people.] Therefore, the fourth estate is capable of fertilizing a bourgeoisie that has been rendered sterile by incest. While Fortunata recognizes the higher social—and possibly also moral—standing of her rival Jacinta, her "pícara idéa" ("sly, roguish idea," a term that is repeatedly employed) is based on the fact that it is she alone who is able to give birth to Juanito's son and inheritor.

The figure of Fortunata, who is repeatedly termed a "salvaje," is an embodiment of the other with regard to the premises and conventions of the realist novel.[55] Fortunata signifies both the object and the limit of integration. It is not only Juanito who sees Fortunata as the embodiment of the healthy character of the people; the narrator also repeatedly and explicitly comments that the people are associated with vital energy, even as they are in need of civilization as long as they are left to its "raw" state:

> Así era la verdad, porque el pueblo, en nuestras sociedades, conserva las ideas y los sentimientos elementales en su tosca plenitud, como la cantera contiene el mármol, material de la forma. El pueblo posee las verdades grandes y en bloque, y a él acude la civilización conforme se le van gastando las menudas de que vive. (*FJ*, 3.7.3.251)

> [This was the truth, because in our society the people preserve the ideas and the elementary sentiments in their rough fullness, as the quarry contains the marble, the material of form. The people possess the truth fully and en bloc, and civilization turns to it when its life-sustaining means run out.]

Many of the minor characters, both male and female (especially Doña Lupe, Guillermina), both from the lower and the higher bourgeoisie, want to form Fortunata according to their own image and hence make her socially acceptable. The text implicitly alludes to the myth of Pygmalion and thus to the process of artistic creation. Indeed, Fortunata is not only the object of the projection of different phantasies of integration and civilization (socially, linguistically, religiously), but she is also a symbolic figure created by the narrator, only vaguely characterized in sociological terms.

In this regard, a comparatively positive role is played by the figure of Don Evaristo Feijoo, who is intermittently Fortunata's secret elderly lover and advisor before she reconciles herself again with her husband Maxi only to be seduced once more by Juanito.[56] Feijoo's pragmatic instructions aim to influence Fortunata in such a way that she erects a civil façade for society to protect herself. Fortunata, argues Feijoo, can only be free if she maintains appearances by remaining in her marriage with Maxi, even if it is without happiness: "hay que guardar en todo caso las santas apariencias, y tributar a la sociedad ese culto externo sin el cual volveríamos al estado salvaje" (*FJ*, 3.4.10.144) [in any case you have to observe holy appearances, and to give to society this external worship without which we would return to a primitive state]. Yet his well-meaning admonitions are not crowned by success. Against Fortunata's own aspirations to social recognition ("ser honrada"), her natural instinct and her vital character always gain the upper hand.

The motif of being uncivilized or wild, as it appears here as an attribute of Fortunata, plays an important role as well in the chapter programmatically entitled "Una visita al quarto estado" (*FJ*, 9.1.9; "A Visit to the Fourth Estate"), where Jacinta, accompanied by Guillermina Pacheco, an obsessive Catholic philantropist, moves through a lower-class area of the city in search of the "Pitusín," who is said to be Fortunata's child and who apparently also shows a likeness to his father, Juanito. Jacinta, yearning for a child of her own, wants to adopt him. This entire scenario is a fabrication of Fortunata's uncle Ido, and the very conventional, genre-like story of the foundling primarily has the function of prefiguring the end of the novel, namely the gift of a son from Fortunata to Jacinta, as well as of introducing Jacinta to a socially marginal world that is populated by "dirty," "savage" people. Significantly, the small children hidden in the capes of their mothers are called the "ciudadanos del porvenir" (*FJ*, 1.9.1.318) [citizens of the future], and as such they will first have to undergo a process of civilization. The children playing in the dirt are variously referred to as "salvajes," "puercos," "marranos" and "caníbales," some of the mothers are even called "lobas" (324–25) [wild, swine, dirty, cannibal, female wolves]: these terms occur both in the discourse of the narrator and in Jacinta's inner monologue.

At another moment, the motif of the lack of civilization is explicitly connected with the condition of Spain, even though this occurs with regard to the very caricature-like figure of Moreno-Isla, who embodies the type of the anglophile "antipatriota" (*FJ*, 4.2.1.333): "¡Que pueblo, válgame Dios, qué raza! [. . .], han de pasar siglos antes de que esta nación sea presentable. A no ser que venga el cruzamiento con alguna casta del Norte, trayendo aquí madres sajonas" (*FJ*, 4.2.1.332). ["What a country, God help me, what a race! (. . .) Centuries will have to pass before this nation will be presentable; unless it comes to a cross-fertilization with some race of the North, which brings here Saxon mothers."] Thus, while Moreno-Isla laments Spain's lack of modernity, the narrator has earlier represented the destruction of popular-traditional fashion by free trade as a threat to its cultural identity. Behind such different evaluations lies an ambivalent stance toward modernity. The narrator admits different views of what is responsible for the nation's decadence, depending on whether the problem is seen as underdevelopment, that is, a lack of modernity, or an exhaustion of the process of civilization, which is to say, an excess of modernity.[57] Seen from this perspective, it also becomes clear why both Juanito and Fortunata are constructed as allegorical representations of the nation. They embody Spain's insecure position in a process of accelerated yet unfinished modernization, whereby the extreme positions are coded as male and female, civilized and primitive, bourgeois and popular.

Insofar as the act of adultery implies also a break from one's own class, it will ultimately be productive for the continued existence of the bourgeois, patriarchal line, which means that the fated death of Fortunata almost acquires the quality of martyrdom. The end of the novel implies a significant ambivalence: on the one hand, the birth of Fortunata's son affirms the ideal of class amalgamation, as it is advocated by the narrator; on the other hand, Fortunata's almost simultaneous death, as well as her entire history of suffering, show, as it were, the human costs of this process.[58] The birth of an heir provides a thematic link between the end of the novel and its beginning, namely the genealogical narrative of the second chapter. This establishes a both formal and thematic unity, insofar as the generative event (birth, the beginning of life) is the end from which the beginning of the narration appears to be retrospectively determined.

The reader realizes the problematic nature and openness of the ending especially through the scene in which two marginal characters, Ponce and Ballester, debate on the occasion of Fortunata's funeral the question of why and how Fortunata's "story" (history) has to be represented. Since the reader is in fact now nearing the end of precisely this story, the metanarrative thematization foregrounds once again the very possibility of narrative, that is to say, the difference between history/story (*histoire*) and narration (*discours*), between the claim to truth and aesthetic form:

> Segismundo contó al buen Ponce todo lo que sabía de la historia de Fortunata, que no era poco [. . .]; a lo que dijo el eximio sentenciador de obras literarias, que había allí elementos para un drama o novela, aunque, a su parecer, el tejido artístico no resultaría vistoso sino introduciendo ciertas urdimbres de todo punto necesarias para que la vulgaridad de la vida pudiese convertirse en materia estética. [. . .] Segismundo no participaba de tal opinion, y estuvieron discutiendo sobre estos con selectas razones de una y otra parte, quedándose cada qual con sus ideas y su convicción, y resultando al fin que la fruta cruda bien madura es cosa muy buena, y que también lo son las compotas. (*FJ*, 4.6.16.535)

> [Segismundo told the good Ponce everything that he knew about the history of Fortunata, which was not a little; (. . .) to which the distinguished judge of literary works replied that here there were elements for a drama or a novel, although in his opinion the artistic fabric is not attractive unless one introduces certain schemes that are absolutely necessary for the transformation of the vulgarity of

life into aesthetic material. (. . .) Segismundo did not share that opinion, and they were debating these points with excellent arguments from both sides, both of them remaining with their respective ideas and conviction, with the final result that the raw, well-matured fruit is a good thing, and so are the compotes.]

This often-quoted metaliterary passage is symptomatic of the self-reflexive perspectivism of Galdós's understanding of realism, which is situated between direct representation and artistic presentation, or between authentic nature and civilization. In any event, the novel appears as a product, a *composite* artifact. Seen against the background of the birth of Fortunata's son, the literary text itself becomes the first and the last point in a genealogical-generative process.

As we have seen, the novel represents the program of literary realism in a downright prototypical manner, especially through the thematic motifs of genealogy and history. However, and especially in the second half of the novel, the reference to reality is systematically refracted by the representation of interior worlds and self-referential comments. Such an interior tension, where the exposition of the principle of mimesis is simultaneously accompanied by a problematization of this same principle, where referentiality and textuality are constantly related to each other, is indeed characteristic of the tradition of literary realism as a whole, yet it appears to be especially prominent in the Spanish tradition, which might be seen as a comparatively late—and hence especially self-conscious— manifestation of the form.[59] As one of the central Spanish novels of the Restoration period, *Fortunata y Jacinta* formulates an especially complex commentary on the Spanish nation's attempts at integration. It is a text that constantly interrogates its own assumptions, especially with regard to the leading role of the bourgeoisie.

CHAPTER FIVE

Nature, Nation, and De-/Regeneration

The Spanish Regional Novel (Emilia Pardo Bazán)

While Galdós's novels explore the question of the peripheral nature of Spanish nationhood from an exclusively urban (and exclusively Madrilenian) perspective, the various contemporary examples of the regional novel are concerned with the question of Spain's internal peripheries. As a matter of fact, the implied contrast between center and periphery, between city and country, but also between Europe and Spain, might be said to be "a basic narrative opposition typical of the period."[1] Indeed, this spatial opposition structures many examples of the nineteenth-century novel generally, be it that a highly idealizing vision of the countryside emerges out of the squalor of the modern metropolitan city (in Dickens, *Oliver Twist*) or that the periphery becomes the scene of cultural atavism or the sign of a disappearing world (in Thomas Hardy, *The Return of the Native*). Yet arguably the opposition between city and country is especially pronounced in the Spanish case, given that regional identities and the conditions of geographical isolation were there preserved for a longer time and that processes of modernization occurred on a lower, less conclusive scale. We might say that economic underdevelopment is thus the objective correlative for the cultural significance of the regional novel.[2]

Roberto Dainotto has characterized regional literature as a kind of last stronghold of authentic nationalism, since it can be said to represent the national values of an "imagined community" in a more "natural" form than the centralized nation-state at large. As a consequence, the true meaning of the region would not be its otherness but rather its function as a symbolic resource of national authenticity, as well as fantasies of an original, healthy sense of place:

As a spatial metaphor, the binary region/center proposes naïve polarizations between nature and culture, rustic and industrial life, authentic and imagined communities, marginalized region and marginalizing center. It is in this reevaluation

of notions of authenticity, of natural and organic community, that I see regionalism as an attempt to revive some peculiarly nationalist ideals by passing them off
as "new" regionalist ones.[3]

Dainotto's characterization certainly holds true for a broad stream of regionalist
narratives, and it is especially insightful for its insistence on the intimate, "dis-
placed" connections between the region and the nation. Yet, by assigning to regionalism a simplistic bipolar logic, it tends to gloss over the internal differences
occurring *within* regionalism itself. In fact, critics of nineteenth-century Spanish
literature conventionally divide the different representatives of the regional
novel into two different tendencies: one being conservative and traditional, pro-
moting the restorative and genuinely, symbolically "national" character of the
regional periphery as a *patria chica* (Fernán Caballero, Valera, Pereda); the other
being "liberal" and more pessimist in its assessment of the social reality of the
region's backwardness (Clarín, Pardo Bazán). Even though this twofold model
of the Spanish regional novel might still be rather schematic, it already cautions
us against Dainotto's too one-sided understanding of regionalism, according to
which "the region suggests the utopian possibility of a community considered as
an undivided whole."[4] In this regard, one might also consider the different connotations of region and province as specific *chronotopes* of the novel. While the
idea of the region proposes the model of a self-sufficient and idyllic community,
the province cannot be conceived without its necessarily negative relation to and
difference from the center.[5]

   Emilia Pardo Bazán's novelistic cycle, composed of *Los Pazos de Ulloa* (1886)
and *La madre naturaleza* (1887), set in her native region of Galicia, has often
been read as kind of regional literature. First, I would maintain that it is indeed
the relation *between* region and nation that is the key to a historicized understanding of these novels. Second, I would speak here of a form of *critical* regionalism, for the significance and richness of these texts derives precisely from the
fact that Pardo Bazán no longer operates with a clear-cut, "naïve" opposition
between corrupt center and healthy periphery—or barbarous province and civilized city, for that matter. Finally, and comparable to the contemporary regional
novels by Thomas Hardy, the novels of the Pazos are concerned with a period of
historical transition that is measured, as it were, by the timelessness of the provincial space. If regional difference is distinguished by endogamic unions and
the unaltered continuity of tradition, the symptom of a genealogical crisis is a
measure of the region's contact with modernity. While in the previous section
we have seen that in Galdós's urban novel interclass exogamy has a potential of

regeneration, in the regional novel of Pardo Bazán a sexual union that bridges city and country leads to tragedy. In any event, the plot of *Los Pazos* shares with other Spanish novels of the time (aside from *Fortunata y Jacinta*, I think of Clarín, *Su único hijo*, 1891) the motif of the need to produce an heir, which is indicative of a genealogical crisis and is related to a broader scene of political and social upheaval.

The two novels explore alternatively the provincial and the regional connotations of the periphery. Insofar as they are concerned with a genealogical crisis on the level of plot, the predominantly provincial world of *Los Pazos de Ulloa* tends in the direction of degeneration, while the predominantly idyllic world of *La madre naturaleza* portrays a failed project of regeneration. The cyclical relation between the two novels implies a genealogical continuity among the characters—we are taken from an earlier to the next generation—yet this temporal approximation of the time of writing is presented as neither straight progress nor as decadence but rather as a sort of cyclical repetition. The peripheral space continues to resist, adapt, and distort the influence of modernity, and in this way it functions as an allegory for the incorporation of heterogeneous spaces into the nation-state. It is a *critical* regionalism, because nature can no longer be represented as an original, idyllic space of innocence. Hence, we also find in Pardo Bazán the tendency to integrate the depiction of regional realities with at least some of the characteristics of naturalism.[6]

If these ambiguities account for the complexity of Pardo Bazán's novels, we may now begin by first observing the similarly ambivalent and contradictory nature of her adaptation of French naturalism, which she was the first to introduce into Spain. The first Spanish translations of Zola date from 1880–81, and they are accompanied by the broader reception of positivist theories from Northern Europe.[7] Pardo Bazán's most substantial volume of literary criticism, *La cuestión palpitante* (The burning question, 1882–83) is an extraordinary historical document, not least because it concerns a problem of literary geography: What happens when the naturalist program moves to another national and geographical space? What kind of variation does the periphery introduce into a model associated with the literary center?[8]

It should first be noted that the importation and adaptation of French naturalism into the Spanish literature of the 1880s (next to Pardo Bazán, especially Clarín and Galdós [*La desheredada*, 1881]) has a specific symbolic function as a generational phenomenon, a kind of rupture within the national literary space, opening it up to the time of modernity. At the same time, the Spanish authors introduce this model not without changing it, and they insist on differences from the work of Zola.[9] Pardo Bazán's attempt to fashion a form of "Catholic naturalism" illustrates the ideological contradictions that arise from the combination of her genuinely conservative worldview and her—qualified—adherence to a literary school whose very name was a synonym for modernity and the self-conscious group identity of a "young," "new" generation that claimed the authority of scientific objectivity for the literary portrayal of one of its favorite themes, familial decline and degeneration.[10] Émile Zola himself would think of such a combination as an oxymoron and was indeed rather surprised to see himself defended in Spain by a militant Catholic countess: "no puedo ocultar que me extraña una cosa, y es que la señora Pardo Bazán sea católica convencida, batalladora y al mismo tiempo naturalista"[11] [I cannot hide my bewilderment about one thing, namely the fact that Señora Pardo Bazán is a convinced, militant Catholic, and at the same time a naturalist]. As a matter of fact, Pardo Bazán was both an outspoken critic of naturalism and the most visible of its representatives in Spain.[12]

In *La cuestión palpitante*, Pardo Bazán comments on the fact that naturalism in Spain presents a moment of literary modernism, since it is perceived as "the most recent novelty" (como última novedad),[13] and not without ambivalence: "y por muchos burletas y donaires que los gacetilleros disparen a Zola con motivo de su famoso árbol genealógico y sus alardes de fisiólogo y médico, no impedirán que la generación nueva se vaya tras sus obras"[14] [and despite the many mockeries and witticisms that the gossip columnists fire at Zola on account of his famous genealogical tree and his displays of being a physiologist and medical doctor, they will not prevent that the new generation takes its cue from his works].

Although Pardo Bazán initially recommends the work of Zola to her contemporaries, she ultimately renounces determinist, materialist explanations in favor of spiritual solutions, where "determination" is redefined as the condition of fallen man in a world without grace.[15] Based on St. Augustine's theory of the free will, she argues that human nature is always open to different influences: "sólo la caída de una naturaleza originariamente pura y libre puede dar la clave de esta mezcla de nobles aspiraciones y bajos instintos"[16] [only the fall of a nature originally pure and free can provide the key for this mixture of noble aspirations and base instincts]. This quote reveals how central the term "nature" is in combining and differentiating spiritual and material meanings. The strategy of Pardo Bazán's literary work is generally to translate naturalist motifs onto a theological framework, as when she comments on Zola's use of hereditary transmission in the Rougon-Macquart series: "No cabe negar la fuerza de la transmisión hereditaria. Todos la comprobamos a cada momento, y la Escritura, en su enérgico lenguaje, nos dice que los padres comieron el agraz y a los hijos les rechinaron los dientes."[17] [There is no denying the force of hereditary transmission. We all experience it at every moment, and Scripture, in its forceful language, tells us that the fathers ate the sour grapes and that the children's teeth were set on edge.] Given what she sees as the "exaggerations" of French naturalism, Pardo Bazán argues for a more comprehensive understanding and defense of literary realism that will be able to reconcile the natural and the ideal in accordance with the Catholic Church and the conciliatory ideology of philosophical Krausismo:

> Si es real cuanto tiene existencia verdadera y efectiva, el *realismo* en el arte nos ofrece una teoría más ancha, completa y perfecta que el *naturalismo*. Comprende y abarca lo natural y lo espiritual, el cuerpo y el alma, y concilia y reduce a unidad la oposición del naturalismo racional.[18]

> [If the real is what has a true and effective existence, *realism* in art offers us a theory that is broader, more complete and perfect than *naturalism*; it contains and includes the natural and the spiritual, body and soul, it brings together and unifies the oppositions of rational naturalism.]

The conclusion of the long essay surprisingly affirms the scientific paradigm that she found first so objectionable in Zola, even as she rejects a wholesale adaptation of naturalism because of the fundamental differences between the social situations of France and Spain:

> Así el realismo, que es un instrumento de comprobación exacta, da en cada país la medida del estado moral, bien como el esfigmógrafo registra la pulsación normal de un sano y el tumultuoso latir del pulso de un febricante.[19]

> [In this way Realism, which is an instrument of exact demonstration, provides in every country the measure of the moral situation, just as the pulsimeter registers the normal pulse of a healthy person and the tumultuous beat of a feverish one.]

In the course of the essay, she tries to show that Spanish literature has indeed always departed from a strong sense of realism. In what amounts to a kind of nationalist argument, Pardo Bazán effectively contests the chronological priority of French naturalism/realism.[20] However, she also defends the legitimacy of literary imitation, and hence she implicitly questions the notion of the necessarily hierarchical relation inherent in the model that associates literary innovation with the center and backwardness with the periphery.[21] The question of the Spanish novel's dependence on French models and the complex interrelations of French-Spanish influences were already vital issues during the first half of the century (as Elisa Martí-López has recently shown in great detail), yet Pardo Bazán's accommodations of the naturalist program in *La cuestión palpitante* present a new, sophisticated response to the different temporalities of a historical and contemporary literary geography.[22] The text's various contradictions and accommodations are symptomatic of Pardo Bazán's attempt to navigate between the conflicting claims of her own political and religious convictions, her understanding of literature, and the moral and doctrinal coordinates of Spanish society.[23]

Therefore, it should come as no surprise that her novels feature similar ideological inconsistencies and ambivalences. As a matter of fact, the novels are typically structured around the opposition between culture and nature, city and country, but they do not come down easily in favor of one or the other (as is the case, the author points out in *La cuestión palpitante*, in the respective novels of Galdós and Pereda).[24] As a result, the ideological contradictoriness of her novels— conservative on some matters (religion, social class), liberal on others (science, the role of women)—is the expression of her mixed response to literary naturalism. This might also be conditioned by the specific situation of her native Galicia, where both the center and the periphery are shown to be defective: the lack of culture in the periphery corresponds to the loss of nature in the center.[25] The harsh, mountainous landscape of Galicia provides a different geographical background for literary regionalism than the more picturesque connotations of Andalucía, a traditional setting for many regionalist novels.[26] Read together, Pardo Bazán's two novels about the Pazos dramatize, especially also by way of their sequence (moving from a predominantly Gothic toward a predominantly idyllic representation of nature), a dialectical investigation of the regional periphery as alternatively the flip side and the remedy of civilization.

Los Pazos de Ulloa: Nature, Culture, Decadence

Let us now see how the conflict between spiritual and material perspectives is worked out in the novels. What a great number of regional novels have in common, despite their different ideological visions, is a narrative construction according to which an outsider figure, equipped with a measure of civilized knowledge, serves as the perspectival focus for the perception of a foreign, backward world.[27] In *Los Pazos de Ulloa* the outsider/observer role is embodied by the figure of the young priest Julián Alvarez. Yet already, at the moment of his first appearance in the first chapter, as a traveler on his way to the feudal estate of Los Pazos in Galicia, which is symbolically located in an "infernal valley" (*LPU*, 131) [allá en el fondo del valle], he encounters a series of ominous signs, such as a wooden cross that appears to mark a scene of "violent death" (*LPU*, 130) or a huntsman who is described as the epitome of wilderness ("de astucia salvaje, más propria de un piel roja que de un europeo," *LPU*, 132) [of savage astuteness, more typical of a redskin than a European]—and who will later turn out to be the aptly named Primitivo, the sinister *mayordomo* of the estate.[28] The third-person narrator distances the figure of Julián through an ironic portrayal that stresses, in typically naturalist fashion, his physical inadequacy in relation to the rough, untamed environment that he sets out to confront:

> Iba el jinete colorado, no como un pimiento, sino como una fresa, encendimiento propio de personas linfáticas. Por ser joven y de miembros delicados, y por no tener pelo de barba, pareciera un niño, a no desmentir la presunción sus trazas sacerdotales. (*LPU*, 127)

> [The horseman turned full of color, not like red pepper, but rather like a strawberry, an intensity characteristic of lymphatic persons. Since he was young and his limbs were delicate, and he did not have a single hair of beard, he seemed like a child, if this impression hadn't been disproved by his sacramental clothes.]

Julián's physiological traits are frequently stressed and repeated throughout the novel—"su temperamento linfático-nervioso, puramente femenino" (*LPU*, 146) [his lymphatic-nervous temperament, entirely feminine]; "el curita barbilindo, con cara de niña" (*LPU*, 134) [the dapper priest, with the face of a child]—and contrasted with the virile exterior and "despotic" (*LPU*, 134) bearing of the marquis Don Pedro, the embodiment of patriarchal authority at the Pazos. As an outside visitor, coming from the city of Santiago, Julián's stunned confrontation with the world of the Ulloa estate immediately comes to stand for the larger confrontation between nature and culture that structures the novel as a whole:

> Julián abría mucho los ojos, deseando que por ellos le entrase de sopetón toda la ciencia rústica, a fin de entender bien las explicaciones relativas a la calidad del terreno o el desarrollo del arbolado: pero, acostumbrado a la vida claustral del Seminario y de la metrópoli compostelana, la naturaleza le parecía difícil de comprender, y casi le infundía temor por la vital impetuosidad que sentía palpitar en ella, en el espesor de los matorrales, en el áspero vigor de los troncos, en la fertilidad de los frutales, en la picante pureza del aire libre. (*LPU*, 150–51)

> [Julián opened his eyes wide, desiring that there would enter in one movement all the rustic science, to understand well the explanations pertaining to the quality of the earth and the development of the woodland; yet, accustomed as he was to the secluded life of the seminary and the metropolis of Santiago, it seemed difficult to

him to understand nature, and it almost installed in him terror because of the vital forcefulness that he sensed working in it, in the density of the thickets, in the rough vigor of the tree trunks, in the fertility of the fruit trees, in the sharp purity of the free air.]

As these passages already indicate, the first scene of the novel, set in the autumn of 1866, combines the individual perspective of Julián as an outside observer with the omniscient narrator's observation of the observer, thus doubly distancing the narrated events from the reader. Consider also the following example, where the visibly untrained horseman, on his way from Santiago to Orense, comes first into the view of the narrator: "bien se advertía que el traje del mozo era de paño negro liso, [. . .] leíase en su rostro tanto miedo" (*LPU*, 127–28) [it was easy to observe that the boy's dress was of smooth black cloth, (. . .) you could read great fear in his face]. Shortly thereafter, the narrative perspective shuttles back and forth between Julián's subjective perceptions and thoughts, on the one hand, and an outside knowledge and assessment of his character, on the other:

—¡Estamos frescos!—*pensó* el viajero [. . .]. *Experimentaba* el jinete indefinible malestar, disculpable en quien, nacido y criado en un pueblo tranquilo y soñoliento se halla por vez primera frente a frente con la ruda y majestuosa soledad de la naturaleza, y *recuerda* historias de viajeros robados, de gentes asesinadas en sitios desiertos.

—¡Qué país de lobos!—dijo para sí, tétricamente impresionado. (*LPU*, 130; italics mine).

["What is this?" *thought* the traveler. (. . .) The horseman *experienced* an undefinable discomfort, understandable in someone who, born and raised in a tranquil and sleepy town, finds himself for the first time face to face with the rough and majestic loneliness of nature and who *recalls* the histories of robbed travelers, of people killed in abandoned places.

"What a godforsaken place!" he said to himself, with an apprehension of gloom.]

The unstable or multiple perspective of this scene, the back and forth between interior and exterior observation, between subjective psychology and objective causes, is characteristic of this novel, in which Pardo Bazán always adduces multiple causes, where neither the human imagination nor materialist circumstances provide a single explanation of events.[29] By way of this qualified focalization, the author combines the naturalist emphasis on milieu with a strong subjective element. As Thomas Pavel has aptly remarked, the dissociation of the individual from the surrounding world, as well as the mixture of the reader's distance and empathy, are typical of the Spanish novel of this period, in what amounts to a compromise solution to the established paradigms of the European novel.[30]

We soon learn that Julián has been sent to the Ulloa estate on the recommendation of the owner's uncle, with the purpose of assisting the old abbot in the management of the parish, as well as the less explicit intention of exerting a civilizing influence upon the noble, yet utterly corrupted and savage, lord of the estate, Don Pedro Moscoso de Cabreira y Pardo de la Lage, the marquis. Don Pedro appears to be dependent on Primitivo, since he lives in concubinage with Primitivo's daughter, the lusty house servant Sabel. Julián's shock and inexperience is stressed when he realizes—long after the reader, in fact—that the neglected young boy Perucho is indeed the offspring of this undignified liaison.

The plot of the novel might be equated with Julián's various, ultimately unsuccessful, attempts to civilize the world of the Pazos, starting with the early scene in which he reprimands Don Pedro for making Perucho drunk (*LPU*, 139–40). In a context of rural atavism, Julián acts as the sole motor of change. Yet while he is the bearer of civilized knowledge, he is simultaneously distinguished by his fatal inexperience and naïveté in the face of life and nature. This specific narrative situation reflects the allegorical dimension of the novel. While Julián's subjective viewpoint (rendered by interior monologue) serves to highlight the "barbarous" isolation and almost gothic atmosphere of the estate, the third-person narrator provides a more comprehensive perspective that aims to show the inherent blindness and inadequacy of Julián's thoughts and actions. It is this narrative constellation that reflects the novel's unique dialectical confrontation between barbarism and civilization, according to which decadence is both inherent and inimical to nature.

If the novel develops out of the motifs of decadence and genealogical crisis, it turns into what we might call a genealogical tragedy. At the moment of his first appearance, Don Pedro is designated as the last representative of the noble family of Ulloa, which is also reflected by the ruination and disorder of the feudal estate: "por entre estos residuos de pasada grandeza andaba el último vástago de los Ulloas" (*LPU*, 150) [between these remnants of past greatness walked the last representative of the Ulloas]. From the beginning, the decadence embodied by the marquis is attributed to the influence of the rough conditions of the provincial environment. Tellingly, this view is uttered by Pedro's urban uncle Manuel de la Lage, whose warning comment is remembered by Julián during his first day on the estate: "Encontrará usted a mi sobrino bastante adocenado. . . . La aldea, cuando se cría uno en ella y no sale de allí jamás, envilece, empobrece y embrutece" (*LPU*, 144). ["You will find my nephew rather ordinary. . . . When people are bred in the countryside and never leave it, they become degraded, degenerate, and brutalized.] Since the uncle does *not* reside in the countryside, we may assume that he stands on the side of civilization—and hence we are immediately alerted to the fact that such a difference occurs within a single family and is conditioned by the specific environment.

The idea of the *historical* decadence of the aristocratic family is primarily shown by the scene in which Julián is asked to bring order to the family archive of the Ulloas (ch. 4). While Julián is studying the disordered and moth-eaten documents of the estate, it is the narrator who steps in to provide a history of Don Pedro's family and the economic background of the estate. While Pardo Bazán thus again complements (somewhat awkwardly in technical terms, it must be said) a subjective with an objective perspective, this scene in particular serves to provide a historical *flashback* to the situation of the present, including the passing of generations:[31]

> La verdad era que el archivo había producido en el alma de Julián la misma impresión que todo la casa: la de una ruina, ruina vasta y amenazadora, que representaba algo grande en lo pasado, pero en la actualidad se desmoronaba a toda prisa. Era esto en Julián aprensión no razonada, que se transformaría en convicción, si conociese bien algunos antecedentes de familia del marqués. (*LPU*, 158)

> [The truth was that the archive had produced in Julián's soul the same impression as the entire house: it was a ruin, a vast and threatening ruin, which represented something great in the past, but which in the present rapidly disintegrated. In Julián this was a spontaneous apprehension that would change into conviction if he knew well some of the familial antecedents of the marquis.]

This is a scene that resonates with what Bakhtin has called "the historicity of castle time" and has associated with the genre of the Gothic novel, distinguished by the spatial, architectural, or archival condensation of the past.[32] It is a convenient device to introduce the diachronic dimension of the family history of the Ulloas, which the novel itself otherwise shows only through the fact of Don Pedro being its "last representative."[33] There are a few other scenes that also stress this diachronic dimension, such as the cleaning of the uncle's attic by his daughters, where various discarded objects recall the history of the feudal past (*LPU*, 227),[34] or the later visit of the married couple (Pedro and Nucha) to the neighboring, ruined aristocratic estate of Limioso (*LPU*, 269). These scenes are clearly meant to suggest that the sad figure of Don Pedro is just one example of a broader social phenomenon.

More specifically, the novel's visit to the archive has the function of clarifying the socioeconomic changes that have led to the deplorable state of the manor house and thus again to complement Julián's apprehensions of decline with objective knowledge. For instance, we are informed by the narrator that the region of Galicia was characterized by the problem of subdividing land into so many "handkerchief" plots and among a number of heirs, the custom of *minifundismo*: "dada la complicación de la red, la subdivisión atomística que caracteriza a la propiedad gallega, un poco de descuido o mala administración basta para minar los cimientos de la más importante fortuna territorial" (*LPU*, 161) [given the complication of the system, the atomistic subdivision that characterizes Galician property, a little bit of carelessness or bad administration is enough to undermine the foundations of the most important territorial possessions]. Since the narrator also mentions the common practice of absenteeism, we are reminded of the central significance of this problem in the novels of Maria Edgeworth, and indeed the historian Raymond Carr has for this reason referred to Galicia as the "Ireland of Spain."[35]

Finally, we are also informed that the present marquis of Ulloa represents only a collateral branch of the family ("rama colateral," *LPU*, 162), since the noble title properly belongs to a member of the family in Madrid as a result of a "rigurosa agnación" (*LPU*, 163) [rigorous agnation], the patriarchal law of male-descent only. These economic and genealogical clarifications alert the reader to the fact that Don Pedro's power is largely symbolic. While the country peasants continue to refer to him with the title of marquis, this vestige of aristocratic distinction is dissociated from both legitimate nobility and material, monetary wealth. According to Jo Labanyi's detailed historical reconstruction of the novel's legal and economic context, Don Pedro's position is characterized by a complex intersection of ancient feudal rights with a new market economy typical of modernity, where the ancient squirearchy retained only nominal ownership and factual land rights had passed to the members of a new middle class—all of which is the result of a process of centralizing state legislation (namely, the midcentury disentailment laws), causing a transformation from an economy based on inherent value to one based on nominal value.[36]

While the specific reasons for social and economic decline might be subordinated to the psychologically and dramatically concentrated development of the novel, Pardo Bazán herself has characterized her work (in the *Apuntes autobiográficos*, released as a preface to the novel when it was first published in 1886) as a study "of the mountainous region of Galicia, *caciquismo*, and the decadence of a noble estate" [la montaña gallega, el *caciquismo* y la decadencia de un noble solar].[37] Although some critics have claimed that this characterization somehow misrepresents her novel, I find it more relevant to consider how the social and the psychological are brought together in this work.[38] In fact, if we see *Los Pazos* not necessarily as a social, but rather as a genealogical, novel, it becomes clear that the oblique, mediated, and subjective presentation of aristocratic, familial decline (think, say, of Thady in *Castle Rackrent*) amounts to a complex, multiperspectival way of representing a situation of social crisis. As we have repeatedly pointed out above, the combination of subjective and objective elements is entirely characteristic for Pardo Bazán's interpretation of naturalism.

On the level of novelistic plot, an attempted solution to this "crisis of the aristocracy" consists in Don Pedro's attempt to engender a legitimate male heir. Outraged with Don Pedro's more or less open relationship with Sabel and the scandal of the bastard Perucho, all flying in the face of the dignity of the marquis's social class, Julián persuades Don Pedro to go with him to Santiago in search of an appropriate bride. The novel, then, reverses the outside perspective of Julián (chs. 10–13) and is thus temporarily brought out of the orbit of the barbarous province. Significantly, when Don Pedro is "disappointed" about the life conditions in the provincial city, the narrator points out that this is due to the "exaggerated ideas" resulting from his provincial perspective but also agrees with Don Pedro on the less than magnificent aspect of Santiago, hardly living up to the expectations of a "modern city" (*LPU*, 315) [una ciudad moderna]. While the city, then, is not seen as entirely positive, the change of milieu is important, because it also serves to reveal a more affable, playful, and human side of Don Pedro. Hence, his removal from the world of the Pazos reinforces the impression that the true root of evil there is Primitivo. Most significantly, the importance of milieu is stressed by the contrast between Don Pedro and his city-dwelling uncle, Manuel Pardo de la Lage, who is distinguished by strikingly identical hereditary physical traits:

> Viéndoles juntos, se observaba extraordinario parecido entre el señor de la Lage y su sobrino carnal: la misma estatura prócer, las mismas proporciones amplias, la misma abundancia de hueso y fibra, la misma barba fuerte y copiosa; pero lo que en el sobrino era armonía de complexión titánica, fortalecida por el aire libre e los ejercicios corporales, en el tío era exuberancia y plétora: condenado a una vida sedentaria, se advertía que le sobraba sangre y carne, de la cual no sabía qué hacer. (*LPU*, 207)

[Seeing them next to each other, one observed an extraordinary likeness between the señor de la Lage and his biological nephew: the same imposing stature, the same broad proportions, the same abundance of bone and fiber, the same strong and copious beard. Yet what in the nephew was the harmony of a titanic complexion, fortified by the open air and bodily exercise, was in the uncle exuberance and abundance: condemned to a sedentary life, one could see that he had blood and flesh in excess with which he did not know what to do.]

While uncle and nephew clearly display their biological kinship, in the case of the uncle the "sedentary life" of the city and the absence of "fresh air" results in the fat of degeneration and the congestion of blood, in contrast to the healthy virility of his nephew:

> Magnífico ejemplar de una raza apta para la vida guerrera y montés de las épocas feudales, se consumía miserablemente en el vil ocio de los pueblos, donde el que nada produce, nada enseña, ni nada aprende, de nada sirve y nada hace. ¡Oh dolor! Aquel castizo Pardo de la Lage, naciendo en el siglo XV, hubiera dado en qué entender a los arqueólogos e historiadores del XIX. (*LPU*, 207)

> [A magnificent exemplar of a race apt for the warlike and mountainous life of the feudal period, he now miserably consumed himself in the vile idleness of the villages where the person who does neither produce, teach, or learn anything, serves for nothing and doesn't do anything. What a pain! That purebred Pardo de la Lage, originating in the fifteenth century, would have been a revealing object of study for the archeologists and historians of the nineteenth century.]

This passage reveals that the fact of biological degeneration is not only associated with the problem of milieu (explaining the difference between uncle and nephew) but that it is also related to the longtime historical decline of a class. For after all the decadence works in both directions, since it concerns both the aristocracy of the land and that of the city. However, when the contrast between uncle and nephew is continued in a later chapter (13), Manuel is explicitly associated with a superior status of education, attributed to the long residence in an urban environment, as well as the civilizing influence of the female company of his wife and daughters. His occasional longing for the countryside is not so much due to a residue of atavistic desires ("instintos selváticos," *LPU*, 247) but rather to the genuinely modern need for (domesticated) nature as spiritual recreation: "le solicitaban aficiones más delicadas, de origen moderno: el deseo de tener un jardín, de cultivar frutales" (*LPU*, 247) [he was attracted by more delicate fancies of modern origin: the desire to have a garden, to cultivate fruits].

The physiological degeneration of the uncle is thus contrasted with his simultaneous embodiment of the results of the process of civilization and progress in an inverse relation to the generational sequence: "he aquí por qué el suegro, a pesar de encontrarse cronológicamente una generación más atrás que su yerno, estaba moralmente bastantes años delante" (*LPU*, 247) [this is why the father-in-law, although in chronological terms he was one generation more remote than his son-in-law, was in moral terms much more advanced in years]. The fact that the older relative is more advanced underlines the decisive role of culture. While in this episode Pardo Bazán obviously harps on the naturalist discourse of decadence and heredity, the ambivalences that result from nature's interaction with culture contradict the conventions of a more orthodox, scientific naturalism, according to which "heredity is the invisible, deific force which provides a pattern of necessity revealed, of law unfolded."[39]

Again, the interconnection of culture and nature is also shown by the more complex personality of Don Pedro as it surfaces during these scenes. On one occasion (when he sends Julián back to the Pazos and his conscience tells him to warn Julián of Primitivo's evil ways), the narrator comments explicitly on Don Pedro's latent capabilities and natural wisdom, which, however, have not had occasion to fully develop under the conditions in which he has led his life:

No era esta la única vez que don Pedro manifestaba sagacidad en el conocimiento de caracteres y personas, don esterilizado por la falta de nociones de cultura moral y delicadeza de esas que hoy exige la sociedad a quien, mediante el nacimiento, la riqueza o el poder, ocupa en ella lugar preeminente. (*LPU*, 239)

[This was not the only time when Don Pedro showed sagacity in the knowledge of characters and persons, a gift that was sterilized because of the lack of notions of moral culture and that kind of delicacy that society today requires of everybody who, by virtue of birth, wealth or power, occupies in it a place of pre-eminence.]

This rather positive evaluation of Don Pedro not only sets up an implicit contrast with the unexperienced character of Julián; it also contains an explicit appeal to the social-ethical responsibilities of a naturally constituted, privileged ruling class.[40] Characteristically, Don Pedro's well-meaning warnings are soon revealed to be *also* motivated by his tendency to derive pleasure from Julián's fear: "en la índole de don Pedro había un fondo de crueldad, sostenido por su vida grosera" (*LPU*, 240) [in the character of Don Pedro there was a disposition toward cruelty, which was supported by his coarse life]. One and the same act, the warning of Julián, then, reveals the distorting influence of the provincial life on Don Pedro's inmost qualities—a cause that is seen as overriding any possible hereditary features. While Don Pedro's good character traits ("don") lie largely dormant, his bad inclinations ("fondo") gain the upper hand.

As for the development of Don Pedro's and Julián's plan to find Don Pedro a suitable wife, Don Pedro's inclinations and the vested interest of Don Manuel conspire to identify the bride-to-be precisely among the daughters of the uncle. The venturing out into the city introduces Don Pedro to another environment, but ultimately he remains within the endogamous confines of his own class and family. Among the four daughters of his uncle, it is the oldest, Rita, who appears to provide the most "natural" mate for Don Pedro, who is instinctively attracted to her lively character and generous figure. The instinctive sexual attraction is further confirmed by Don Pedro's "rational" reflections (again, rendered here in typical free indirect style) on Rita's procreative faculties—a biological insurance against imminent genealogical decline:

> Lo que más cautivaba a su primo, en Rita, no era tanto la belleza del rostro, como la cumplida proporción del tronco y miembros, la amplitud y redondez de la cadera, el desarrollo del seno, todo cuanto en las valientes y armónicas curvas de su briosa persona prometía la madre fecunda y la nodriza inexhausta. ¡Soberbio vaso en verdad para encerrar un Moscoso legítimo, magnífico patrón donde injertar el heredero, el continuador del nombre! El marqués presentía en tan arrogante hembra, no el placer de los sentidos, sino la numerosa y masculina prole que debía rendir. (*LPU*, 211–12; cf. 218)

> [What most enthralled her cousin with Rita was not so much the beauty of her face or the perfect proportion of her trunk and limbs, the fullness and roundness of her hip, the growth of her breast, everything which in the fine and harmonious curves of her spirited person promised the fertile mother or the inexhaustible wet nurse. Truly a great vessel to enclose a legitimate Moscoso, a magnificent stock on which to graft the heir, the one who continues the name! The marquis sensed in that proud female not the pleasure of the senses, but the numerous and masculine offspring that it will yield.]

However, after having carefully listened to the small-town gossip about Rita's reputation, Don Pedro discusses the different daughters' respective (dis)advantages with Julián and comes to the conclusion that Rita's reputation as a flirt disqualifies her for the position of an honorable wife. Instead, following the suggestions of Julián, he decides that the religious piety and strict morality of the less striking Nucha are to be preferred, and she will also bring a substantial financial inheritance into the marriage. While Manuel finally cedes to the un-expected choice of his nephew (he had hoped to marry off Rita first), the whole discussion between the uncle and nephew emphasizes the economic and class considerations involved in the patriarchal system of marriage transaction, in which the woman concerned, Nucha, has no say whatsoever.

We realize that the counterintuitive choice of the feeble Nucha is the result above all of Julián's suppressed and subconscious desires, a choice that soon turns out to be a fatal, tragic mistake, when the newlywed couple returns to the Pazos. Nucha, as a result of her city-bred constitution, is wholly inappropriate for life in the rural world. For the third time (after Julián's initial confrontation with the world of the Pazos and Don Pedro's sojourn in the city), the novel stages the conflict between a character and an environment that is essentially alien to his or her upbringing, thus traversing the boundaries between city and country, center and periphery.[41] Although Nucha bears Don Pedro a child—to his disappointment it is a daughter, Manuela—her fragile constitution is put to a severe test. Since Pedro also re-establishes his old bonds with Sabel, Julián's project of regeneration has dramatically failed.

The mismatch of Pedro and Nucha is contrasted in the novel with the ideal-istic alliance of Nucha and Julián, who assumes toward her the role of a protec-tor and spiritual brother as soon as Pedro has abandoned any care for his wife. Given Julián's sexual inexperience, the reader further realizes that subconscious sexual desires must be at work (significantly, they are articulated on the sym-bolical level of dreams)—a variation on the common naturalist plot of the young priest in love (Zola, *La faute de l'abbé Mouret*; Clarín, *La Regenta*; Eça de Queirós, *O primo Basílio*).[42] Furthermore, given the fact that Julián is consistently described as a feminine character who also shares with Nucha the "lympho-pathological" condition (which was traditionally associated with women in nineteenth-century medical science), the relation between the two characters has overtones of a same-sex alliance, or, if we take seriously their designation as ideal siblings, of an in-cestuous one. Since Julián's and Nucha's relation would be incestuous on such a symbolic level, it provides a mirror image to the different, biological incest of the union between Pedro and Nucha. Obviously, these pathological meanings are not made explicit in the text, but they inhabit a space of hidden secrets and dark revelations that is constitutive of the Gothic genre with which *Los Pazos de Ulloa* is related in more than one account.[43]

Insofar as the novel remains largely focused on the perspective of Julián, his relation with Nucha is rationalized and sublimated by its stylization as an ex-ample of the Holy Family, the Christian myth of a sexual union that is not one, since the Virgin Mary is a paradoxical image of asexual motherhood, a virgin mother.[44] In Julian's words, Nucha is designated as a symbol of transcendent purity, she is "el tipo de la bíblica Esposa" (*LPU*, 257) [the ideal type of the biblical bride], "viva imagen de Nuestra Señora" (*LPU*, 274) [the vivid image of our Lady], an "angel" (*LPU*, 302), and so on. Julián's attempt to institute an example of the Holy family in the Pazos has not only failed but has been perverted through his own involvement:

> Una penosa idea le acudía de vez en cuando. Acordábase de que había soñado con instituir en aquella casa el matrimonio cristiano cortado por el patrón de la Sacra Familia. Pues bien, el santo grupo estaba disuelto: allí faltaba San José o lo sustituía un clérigo, que era peor. (*LPU*, 303)

> [A distressing thought came to him from time to time. He remembered that he had dreamed to institute in that house Christian marriage minus the master of the Holy Family. Well, then, the holy group was dissolved: here St. Josef was missing and he was substituted by a cleric, which was worse.]

These theological and martyrological fantasies are a paradoxical "solution" to Julián's necessary celibacy as a priest ("se había propuesto renunciar a toda familia y todo hogar en la tierra entrando en el sacerdocio," *LPU*, 302) [he had resolved to renounce all idea of family and home when entering the priesthood]. Again, the fact that he finds himself now as the metaphorical father (or second "mother") of such an imaginary, nonbiological family, provides an ironic contrast with the somewhat opposite situation of Don Pedro, who refuses to consider his biological, legitimate daughter Manuela as a proper heir. The imaginary and the biological family are shown as equally pathological and as complementary sides of the same tragic constellation.

Moreover, the highly idealizing and spiritualizing view of Julián is contrasted with the perspective of Juncal, the medical doctor from Cebre, an avid reader of Darwin (*LPU*, 299), who sees the "decadent" Nucha as deprived of the forces of nature as a consequence of her "antihygienic," "sedentary life" (*LPU*, 278) [vida sedentaria]. To raise her child, she has to rely on the services of a wet nurse from the neighboring village, designated as "gran vaca," "vaca humana" (*LPU*, 280) [great cow, human cow]. As the narrator points out, Juncál's scientific-materialist view of nature might distinguish him from Don Pedro, yet they concur in their view of the proper function of femininity: "también el hidalgo rancio pensaba que la mujer debe ser principalmente muy apta para la propagación de la especie" (*LPU*, 279) [also the old nobleman thought the woman must principally be suitable for the propagation of the species]. And as in the case of Julián's spiritual sublimations, in this case the narrator leaves no doubt about the critical distance from this view, for after all Juncal does not even follow his own hygienic prescriptions. Nucha's peculiar sexuality is thus interpreted by two conflicting discourses, theological on the one side, physiological on the other. Both discourses are shown to be problematic, and the potential conflict between them is not resolved in either direction.[45]

The twenty-eighth chapter is unusual in that it moves the perspective of narration to the boy Perucho. When he is tempted by a coin on Primitivo's table, the narrative voice captures his moral conflict in the form of an interior monologue. Although Perucho will ultimately give way to his capitalist impulse (his fondness for money is repeatedly stressed), his moral hesitations lead the narrator to reflect on the question of whether that "very embryo of conscience" (*LPU*, 393) [aquel mismo embrión de conciencia] is the result of biological inheritance or rather of civilizing education. In other words, the conflict between nature and culture is here applied to the question of whether there is such a thing as inborn nobility:

> ¿Fue una gota de la sangre de Moscoso, que realmente corría por sus venas y que, con la misteriosa energía de la transmisión hereditaria, le siguió la voluntad como por medio de una rienda? ¿fue temprano fruto de las lecciones de Julián y Nucha?
> (*LPU*, 393)

> [Was it a drop of Moscoso blood that was really running through his veins and that, with the mysterious energy of hereditary transmission, halted his will as with a rein? Or was it an early fruit of the teachings of Julián and Nucha?]

This is one of the few moments when the novel makes explicit reference to the problem of biological heredity—and it is in the form of a question. Otherwise, as we have repeatedly seen, the moral and physical features of the characters are mostly explained through the circumstances of upbringing and environment.[46] In this way Pardo Bazán cites the discourse of naturalism but disassociates it from the doctrine of deterministic inheritance. If the novel combines a narrative of familial crisis with the ambivalent factors of nature and culture, we need to look closer now at the function of historical and local context as it is inscribed in the novel itself.

The Politics of the Periphery

We have seen above that the opposition between city and country is reflected in the contrast between Manuel de la Lage and Don Pedro. The narrative furthers this contrast by associating the two relatives with opposed political orientations. Yet here again Pardo Bazán confounds the conventional logic of oppositions. While Manuel is a moderate conservative, his nephew, motivated by the spirit of contradiction, defends the liberal Revolution and the exile of Queen Isabella.[47] When the uncle accuses him of not having arrived at this idea through his own reflection—that he merely repeats the antimonarchical pronouncements found in the daily press, as would be typical from within the narrow, uneducated village perspective—the narrator in turn qualifies Manuel's view as "nonsense" (*LPU*, 249) [este tremendo disparate] repeated from some leading article. In this way, we might say that the narrator turns Manuel's judgment of Don Pedro's political incompetence against him, thus showing the deficiencies of both the urban and the provincial perspective. A further irony of Pedro's pseudorevolutionary rhetoric appears just a few lines later, when his unease in the university city of Santiago makes him long for his position of authority back in the country, "su amor propio de monarca indiscutible en los Pazos de Ulloa" (*LPU*, 249) [his self-gratification as the undisputable monarch of the Pazos de Ulloa]. And, in fact, shortly after the heated discussion with his uncle, Don Pedro prepares to leave the city, not least because urban life rests on a measure of social equality that contradicts his own sense of autonomous power and aristocratic entitlement: "No podía sufrir la nivelación social que impone la vida urbana; no se habituaba a contarse como número par en un pueblo, habiendo estado siempre de nones en su residencia feudal. ¿Quién era él en Santiago?" (*LPU*, 250). [He could not suffer the social leveling imposed by urban life; he could not get used to see himself as an equal number in a town, since he is always been of a special position in his feudal residence. Who was he in Santiago?] And, as if to confirm this unease, there is also an old "chronicler" / "genealogist" in Santiago who is eager to disprove Don Pedro's right to the title of Ulloa (*LPU*, 250).

As may be seen in the (pseudo)political dispute between uncle and nephew, Pardo Bazán, similar to Galdós, introduces into the novel a correlation between a private, fictional plot and the public, historical context of national politics. The references to contemporary politics may at first appear somewhat extraneous to the concerns of the novel (as some critics have complained), but on closer inspection they reveal a structural correlation between center and periphery that serves to explain their ambiguous relation to the signs of decline and progress, barbarism and civilization.[48] Specifically, the context of politics refers to the incorporation of the regional periphery into the modern state.[49] The political context gains particular importance toward the end of the novel (chs. 24–26), culminating in the election scene in which Don Pedro himself appears as a political candidate, now of the Conservative Party, and who loses because of the manipulations of the Liberal Party. The fact that Don Pedro has easily exchanged his political persuasion for its opposite again shows that it is only the preservation of power that motivates his actions—and it might refer to the system of *turnismo* that distinguished the constitutional monarchy of the Bourbon Restoration (which also motivated the allegorical allusions in *Fortunata y Jacinta*).

Taking its cue from the historical introduction of universal male suffrage in 1869, the narrative leaves no doubt that politics in the periphery amounts merely to a personal struggle for power ("la política, si tal nombre merece el enredijo de intrigas y miserias que en las aldeas lo recibe," *LPU*, 343) [politics, if the entanglement of intrigues and miseries merits the name, which it indeed receives in the villages]. The situation of national revolution is related to the fight between the two local caciques, Barbacana (representing the "moderate," Conservative side) and Trampeta (standing for the Liberal side and now gaining the upper hand). The narrator is explicit in indicting the completely superficial nature of the pseudopolitical constellation, entirely bereft of convictions and ideas:

> Conviene saber que ninguno de los dos adversarios tenía ideas políticas, dándoseles un bledo de cuanto entonces se debatía en España; mas, por necesidad estratégica, representaba y encarnaba cada cual una tendencia y un partido. (*LPU*, 345)

> [One should know that none of the adversaries possessed political ideas, not caring a bit about what was then discussed in Spain; yet, out of strategic necessity everybody represented and embodied a tendency and a party.][50]

In fact, Pardo Bazán was a very outspoken critic of the practice of *caciquismo*, which she saw as one of the key problems of the contemporary Spanish malaise.[51] The term refers to the excessive power of a local administrative figure, and it was especially associated with the manipulation of suffrage.[52] The whole system was neofeudalist in nature, as it linked the power elites in Madrid to the oligarchies in the peripheries. Aside from the issue of illicit practices such as bribery and intimidation, the system is typical of a backward society in which the political modernization of the state has insufficiently penetrated into the interior periphery. In other words, despite its archaic or even criminal outlook, the practice of *caciquismo* originally had a certain practical function in linking the city to the country and hence forging a sense of nationhood. However, after 1887, during the period of the Restoration, it grew to its greatest power and degenerated into a practice of systematized violence, for the formerly stable world of agrarian economy and local families that sustained it was now in a state of dissolution.[53] In other words, the malpractice of *caciquismo* was a somewhat more virulent problem in 1886, the publication date of the novel, than during the time in which the novel was set. Clearly, Pardo Bazán appears to comment here on a very contemporary problem and not merely a historical issue.

At the same time, the novel chronicles the transition to a new economic order based on the economy of money and symbolically embodied by the figure of Primitivo, which ultimately contributes to the fall of the house of Ulloa, based as it is on the notion of aristocratic entitlement. Although he figures more clearly as an embodiment of evil, Primitivo occupies the typical structural position of the middleman and self-made capitalist who profits directly from the decline of the aristocracy—and thus he would be comparable with the figures of the "new man" Jason Quirk in *Castle Rackrent* or Don Calogero in *Il Gattopardo*. It is Primitivo who lends money to Pedro to finance his election campaign, money that he had stolen from Pedro in the first place to derive interest from it (*LPU*, 357). Yet, clearly Primitivo remains a wholly negative figure, who at the end is killed off by the opposing political party.

Pardo Bazán, an aristocrat herself (upon her father's death in 1890 she inherited the title of countess), was certainly very critical of this new order. Her political position was essentially conservative, so that her critique of the aristocracy is aimed not at the idea of class privilege as such but rather at the degenerate practice of a "natural" right.[54] The fact that the new order is symbolically represented as "barbaric" and "primitive" goes to show that modernity and backwardness might in fact combine or even reinforce each other in the space of the periphery. However, the end of the novel insists in fact on the opposition between periphery and modernity. After the intimacy between Julián and Nucha has been discovered by Primitivo—they have been embarking on a plan of escape—Julián is exiled from the estate, and Nucha dies of desperation and as a result of her weak physical constitution. Now Julián resigns himself to the cyclical time of natural and agricultural life ("entrando en el ritmo acompasado, narcótico y perenne de la vida agrícola," *LPU*, 408) [and he enters the monotonous, sleepy, endlessly recurring agricultural cycle]. The last chapter of the novel (30) relates how he visits the estate after ten years, and it begins with an explicit invocation of historical time and the parallel between individual and public or national development. However, the idea of historical change is introduced only to assert that the situation of the Pazos expresses a resistance to it:

Diez años son una etapa, no sólo en la vida del individuo, sino en la de las naciones. Diez años comprenden un período de renovación: diez años rara vez corren en balde, y el que mira hacia atrás suele sorprenderse del camino que se anda en una década. Mas así como hay personas, hay lugares para los cuales es insensible el paso de una décima parte de siglo. Ahí están los Pazos de Ulloa, que no me dejarán mentir. La gran huronera desafiando al tiempo, permanece tan pesada, tan sombría, tan adusta como siempre. Ninguna innovación útil o bella se nota en su moblaje, en su huerto, en sus tierras de cultivo. Los lobos del escudo de armas no se han amansado; el pino no echa renuevos; las mismas ondas simétricas de agua petrificada bañan los estribos de la puente señorial. (*LPU*, 410)

[Ten years are a great step not only in the life of an individual, but in the life of nations. Ten years encompass a period of renovation: rarely do ten years run by in vain, and the person who looks back usually is surprised about the way taken in a decade. But just as with people, there are also places for which the step of a tenth part of a century is not noticeable. There stand the Pazos of Ulloa, which will not prove me wrong. The great lair challenging the flux of time, remained as heavy, as gloomy, as austere as always. One can see no practical or aesthetic change in its furniture, in its garden, in its fields. The wolves of the coat of arms have not become tame; the pine tree does not have any new shoots; the same symmetrical waves of petrified water bathe the steps of the feudal fountain.]

The ten years referred to here are 1870–80, thus approaching the time of writing (1886) up to a distance of six years. While the Pazos remain impervious to change, surviving the effects of the 1868 Revolution, the neighboring town of Cebre has entered into the orbit of national time where the forces of reaction and progress fight it out and where progress appears to win the upper hand in the person of the Liberal politician Trampeta ("encarnación viviente de las ideas avanzadas y de la nueva edad," *LPU*, 411) [the living embodiment of advanced ideas and of the new time]. In this way the Pazos become a metonym for the periphery's resistance to historical, national time. At the same time, as we have seen, the strategies of resistance testify to the fact that the region suffers the influence of modernity.

Genesis and Nature in *La madre naturaleza*

The last scene of *Los Pazos de Ulloa* prepares the transition to the second novel. It ends with two children, Nucha's daughter (Manuela) and Sabel's son (Perucho), the legitimate heiress and the bastard, playing together on the overgrown ruins of a graveyard, suggesting to the observer Julián an image of natural abundance that is somehow opposed and indifferent to the higher values of human spirituality ("parecía que era sustancia humana [. . .] la que nutria y hacía brotar con tan

enérgica pujanza y savia tan copiosa aquella flora lúgubre por su misma loza-
nía," *LPU*, 413) [it seemed like a human substance (. . .) which nurtured and
made bud with so much energetic vigor and so much copious sap, that flora,
ghastly for its very lushness]. Since the cemetery contains Nucha's grave (indicated by a white butterfly), the image suggests the life of a new generation literally arising out of the death of the previous one.

In this characterization of nature as a vital, haphazardly evolving force, Pardo
Bazán takes up the contemporary discourse of Darwinism—echoing here, in
particular, the last sentence of the *Origin of Species* (1859), with its emphasis on
"endless forms most beautiful and most wonderful" (a work that is also read by
the medical doctor Máximo Juncal in *Los Pazos de Ulloa*, 299).[55] The scene also
recalls the opening passage of Zola's novel *La fortune des Rougon* (1871), which
similarly links images of life and death at the site of a gravestone.[56] Clearly, such
an intertextual echo with the opening piece of Zola's cycle of novels unmistakably calls up the context of naturalist genealogy, that is, the understanding of
heredity as a material process. The emergence of the two children at the end of
the novel suggests a cyclical model according to which the tragic process of decline gives way to a new cycle of life. And indeed the sequel novel puts the emphasis on the *chronotope* of the idyll, which appears to abandon the historical
dimension of the first novel in favor of the more static question of nature, an
impression confirmed by the paucity of specific indications of time throughout
the novel, except for the generic fact that it is summertime and that the action
takes place during the span of only six days.

La madre naturaleza begins with a recounting of Genesis, in a mythical and
highly literary style that differs markedly from the social and psychological realism in *Los Pazos*. In the opening scene we see a generic couple ("la pareja,"
LMN, 84) taking shelter under a "protective" tree during a storm and emerging
under a rainbow like a second, postdiluvian Adam and Eve.[57] While they are of
course Manuela and Perucho, the narrator refers to them with a literary allusion (the novel *Paul et Virginie*, by Bernardin de Saint-Pierre, 1787) that heightens their symbolic, classical, and pastoral connotations: "realizando el simpático
y tierno grupo de Pablo y Virginia, que parece anticipado y atrevido símbolo del
amor satisfecho" (*LMN*, 85) [they represented the likeable and tender group of
Paul and Virginie, which appears to be an anticipatory and daring symbol of
fulfilled love].

The tree, however, is described as "árbol patriarcal, de esos que ven con in-
diferencia desdeñosa sucederse generaciones de chinches, pulgones, hormigas
y larvas, y les dan cuna y sepulcro en los senos de su rajada corteza" (*LMN*, 84)

[a patriarchal tree, one of those that looks with disdainful indifference on the change of generations of bugs, lice, ants, and larvae and are to them cradle and grave, in the womb of their cracked bark]. The symbol of the tree refers to the biblical scene of the fall, from which it derives its double significance as sign for both life and knowledge, as well as its status as an epistemological icon for the genealogical differentiation of species.[58] Insofar as the novel is centrally concerned with incest and nature, it might be said to explore all of these different meanings of the biblical tree.

Moreover, the image is remarkable not only because it assimilates human and (low) animal life but also because as a symbol of nature it is profoundly ambivalent, signifying simultaneously protection and indifference, birth and death: "parecía que la naturaleza se revelaba allí más potente y lasciva que nunca, ostentando sus fuerzas genesíacas con libre impudor" (*LMN*, 90) [it seemed that here nature revealed itself as more powerful and lascivious than ever, showing its generative powers with an uninhibited shamelessness]. It is apparent how Pardo Bazán combines traditional biblical imagery with allusions to the more disturbing vision of a biocentric universe that dethrones humans from their privileged position, thus again invoking the contrast between spiritual and material views.[59]

Máximo Juncal, the medical doctor, clearly functions as a signifier for the paradigm of naturalism in the novel, yet his exaggerated Darwinian philosophy and anticlerical pronouncements are obviously cast in a parodistic-satirical light, although the events of the novel do not necessarily prove him wrong. The figure of Antón, the local bonesetter (*algebrista*), also contributes to such a Darwinian view by insisting that there is no fundamental difference between animals and humans and that he cures all of them alike. As he observes a group of pigs and their possibly incestuous relations, he comes to the following conclusion: "Yo no sé qué diferentes son de los marranos los hombres, carraspo. [. . .] Tras de lo mismo andan; el comer, el beber, las mozas. . . . Al fin, de una masa somos todos" (*LMN*, 381). ["I don't know how men are different from hogs. (. . .) They chase after the same things: food, drink, and women. In short, we're all made of the same stuff."] The novel cites these Darwinian ideas to ultimately question the determinist axioms of orthodox naturalism, insofar as they pose a challenge to humankind's distinctive spiritual destiny.

While *La madre naturaleza* presents itself as a sequel to the first novel, its formal and stylistic features turn it into a somewhat different experiment in literary technique. The relation between the two novels, then, is marked by both continuity and discontinuity. On the level of style, the second novel was perceived, at the moment of its first appearance, as one of the most orthodox examples of the fashion of Spanish naturalism. Indeed, as we have indicated, the novel frequently cites naturalist topoi and discourses, but it also features many impressionist passages, anticipating the aesthetic of turn-of-the-century decadence.[60]

Generation and Nation

On the level of plot, the novel shifts the perspective of the characters and continues the narrative, as it were, from another angle. For instance, Nucha's younger brother Gabriel, confined to a marginal role in the first novel, emerges as a central character in the second. Significantly, at the beginning of the eleventh chapter, he sets out on horseback to the Pazos de Ulloa, thus setting up an immediate parallel to the opening scene of the first novel. Both Julián and Gabriel appear in the role of the focalizing outside observer who travels from the civilized world of the city to the world of the Pazos, a synonym for barbarity in the first novel and for nature in the second. Both are on a civilizing mission. The parallel structures of the two novels show that traveling between culture and nature is subject to a process of repetition, which is indicative of the fatal inconsequentiality of the attempts to civilize the space of nonculture.[61] On his way from Santiago to Cebre, an imaginary place in the region of Orense (ch. 5), Gabriel becomes involved in a coach accident and is kindly sheltered by the medical doctor Máximo Juncal. It is during this time of recovery that the narrative abandons its initial distanced, third-person presentation of Gabriel as one of the several passengers in the coach ("un viajero," finally identified by name, *LMN*, 141) in favor of a long interior monologue that establishes him as the principal focalizer of the novel. This occurs in the longest chapter of the novel (8), which stands out for its almost unique, explicit concern with the problem of nationhood and is hence key for the suggested allegorical meaning of this novel (which is generally close to the idea of a "thesis novel").

Starting with his childhood, Gabriel's reminiscences recapitulate a whole period of Spanish history, going back to the September Revolution in 1868—during which time *Los Pazos* was set—to the Carlist war of 1873, the Restoration (1875), and so on. Initially, during his time as a member of the military academy (Colégio de Artillería de Segovia), he is staunchly Conservative, lamenting that the Revolution has led to the loss of his idea of a glorious Spain ("una España épica y gloriosa, compuesta de grandes capitanes y monarcas invictos," *LMN*, 159) [an epic and glorious Spain, composed of great captains and undefeated monarchs]; later he becomes a radical Liberal. Gabriel's ideological reversals and fickleness in political orientation allegorize the contemporary national situation, namely the event of the second Carlist wars, which were essentially a civil war: "No veía flotar la sagrada bandera de la patria contra el odiado pabellón extranjero. Aquellas aldeas en que entraba vencedor eran españolas; aquellas gentes a quienes combatía, españolas también. Se llamaban carlistas y él amadeísta: única diferencia" (*LMN*, 159). [He did not see the sacred flag of the fatherland fluttering against the hated foreign tent. Those villages he entered as a victor were Spanish; those people against whom he fought, Spanish, as well. They were called Carlists and he was an "Amadeist": the only difference.]

Gabriel's "determination to save Spain" (*LMN*, 167) [determinado a salvar a España] and subsequent disillusionment (*LMN*, 168) regarding these reformist and "civilizationist" hopes ("a fin de civilizarlo," "el gran reformador," *LMN*, 172) [in order to civilize it, the great reformer] function as an ideological analogue to the regenerative plot of the novel. If the last chapter of *Los Pazos* evokes the difference between regional and national development, *La madre naturaleza* applies the problem of arrested development more explicitly to the relation between Spain and Europe, thus moving from the case of an internal periphery (Galicia) to Spain as a periphery of Europe and hence also suggesting the novel's allegorical relation to the notorious theme of the decadence of Spain.

It is suggested that Gabriel's own period of individual formation ("años de peregrinación y aprendizaje," *LMN*, 177) [years of pilgrimage and learning], including readings in Rousseau and Krausist and Kantian philosophy (*LMN*, 165–66) and travels to "civilized" European countries, not only characterizes his own tendency toward idealism but might also be read allegorically as a (negative) bildungsroman of the Spanish nation itself, namely its intellectual and political trajectories. When he travels to England, France, and Germany, the "civilized" countries turn out to be one great disillusion, yet his return to Spain suddenly deflates his patriotic sentiments when he realizes its precarious link to modern civilization:

Echó de menos el oxigenado aire francés, y le pareció entrar en una casa venida a menos, en una comarca semisalvaje, donde era postiza y exótica y prestada la exigua cultura, los adelantos y la forma del vivir moderno, donde el tren corría más triste y lánguido, donde la gente echaba de sí tufo de grosería y miseria. (*LMN*, 171)

[He missed the oxygenated French air, and it seemed to him as if he was entering a dilapidated house, a half-barbarous region, where the meager state of civilization, the advancements of modern life, were artificial, exotic, and borrowed; where the train was running more sadly and languidly, where the people were emanating the smells of coarseness and misery.]

On the day Gabriel visits the house of his deceased father, Manuel Pardo, the narrator comments on the antipathy that reigned between them: "pertenecían a dos generaciones muy diversas" (*LMN*, 173) [they belonged to two very different generations]. The insistence on the generational gap is surely important in light of the preceding autobiographical account ("recuerdos autobiográficos," *LMN*, 173) that showed Gabriel as a representative figure of the young generation. Yet, the visit to the old family home triggers not the memory of the father but rather of his sister Marcelina (Nucha), "*la mamita*, la única mujer que con desinteresado amor le había querido" (*LMN*, 174) [*the mommy*, the only woman who had loved him in a selfless manner]. Stirred by this idealized remembrance of this sister/"mother," Gabriel's earlier plans to "civilize" (*LMN*, 172) the nation finally give way to a more small-scale project, to found a family, a "natural" route to the goal of regeneration: "la esposa, el hijo, la familia; arca santa donde se salva del diluvio toda fe; Jordán en que se regenera y purifica el alma" (*LMN*, 175) [the wife, son, the family: the sacred ark where all faith is saved from the flood; the Jordan in which the soul regenerates and purifies itself]. This conservative, socially normative, and highly idealized vision of family is presented as the regressive answer to a "postdiluvian" problem of generational vacuity: "todo individuo sano e inteligente, con mediano caudal, buena carrera e hidalgo nombre, está muy obligado a *crear una familia*, ayudando a preparar así la nueva generación que ha de sustituir a ésta tan exhausta, tan sin conciencia ni generosos propósitos" (*LMN*, 176; italics in original) [every sane and intelligent individual, with average means, a good career, and hidalgo name, is very much obliged *to create a family*, thus helping to prepare a new generation that will substitute the present one, which is so much exhausted, so much devoid of conscience and generous intentions].

Significantly, in this passage, when the category of generation is invoked, the narrative voice briefly and suddenly switches from the first person singular into the first person plural: "Yo soy víctima de mi época y del estado de mi nación, ni más ni menos. Y nuestro destino corre parejas. Los mismos desencantos hemos sufrido; iguales caminos hemos emprendido, y las mismas esperanzas quiméricas nos han agitado. ¿Fue estéril todo?" (*LMN*, 176).[62] [I am a victim of my period and of the state of my nation, not more, not less. Our destiny is a common one. We have suffered the same disillusions; we have undertaken similar paths, and we have been moved by the same chimerical hopes. Has everything been sterile?] At the end of the following chapter (9) is a brief reference to the political events of the year 1885, whereby the contemporary reader understands that the novel's action immediately precedes the time of its first publication in 1887: "[el] porvenir de la regencia y posible advenimiento de la Republica" (*LMN*, 202) [the coming of the Regency and the possible advent of the Republic]. From this reference we may infer that the historical moment depicted in the novel is one of transition and uncertainty. Gabriel's own vacillation between different ideas and ideologies characterizes this condition not only as characteristic of modernity but as a specifically generational phenomenon, in turn characterized by a typically decadent predisposition for mental instability and neurasthenia as a result of the "over-stimulation of the brain by modern city life."[63] It is not clear to what extent the figure of Gabriel might be seen as a mouthpiece for the author and her own experience,[64] but his insistent concern with national decadence and the possibilities of regeneration can be understood as anticipating the preoccupations of the generation of 1898 and is characteristic of the discourse of decadence at the end of the nineteenth century.[65]

Regeneration and Degeneration

The special significance of Gabriel's plan to found a family lies in the fact that he intends to marry not just any woman but the daughter of his dead sister Nucha, Manuela, his niece. Gabriel develops this plan even before he has met her, motivated by Nucha's letter to their dead father, which he reads as a command to take "paternal" care of the daughter, just as Nucha had been to him a "protective sister" (*LMN*, 154, 178) [la hermana protectora]. Although she might be equipped with a better physiological constitution than was Nucha, it is repeatedly stressed that Manuela is the living image of her dead mother ("el retrato de su difunta madre," *LMN*, 187; cf. 213), and, as she is continuously referred to as "mamita," the dimension of symbolic incest becomes unmistakably clear. Just as his sister took care of him as a boy, so Gabriel's intent now is to take care of his niece, in turn repeatedly characterized as his figurative "mother" and "sister." This "programmatically" incestuous attraction on Gabriel's part can be seen as a paradoxical attempt to return to a point of natural origin, as a remedy for his hypernervous, neurasthenic sensibilities. From Gabriel's perspective, such an (incestuous) union would indicate the path to a spiritual regeneration.

The inconsistencies and ambivalences surrounding the question of what is natural are part of Pardo Bazán's general intent to suspend judgment on the issue of nature versus nurture. As he gets to know Manuela, Gabriel is constantly wavering between his adoration of her as an ideal child of nature and the notion that she is urgently in need of civilization and his guidance ("educándola, formándola, iniciándola en los goces y bienes de la civilización," *LMN*, 198). This ambivalence is echoed by his understanding of nature as autonomous evolution ("la evolución es fatal," *LMN*, 304) *and* as an agonistic, Darwinian battlefield that requires social correction: "La evolución sin lucha. . . . Sin lucha, es una utopía. Quizás la lucha misma, el combate de todos contra todos, es la única clave del misterio" (*LMN*, 304). [Evolution without battle. . . . Without battle, is a utopia. Maybe battle itself, the fight of all against all, is the only key to the mystery.] Read in conjunction with the earlier novel, we notice another reversal here. While in *Los Pazos* Don Pedro traveled to the city to be redeemed by an urban woman (Nucha), in *La madre naturaleza* the city-bred Gabriel sets out to the countryside to be redeemed by the nature child Manuela (while she refuses to play this role).

The central conflict of the novel stems from the fact that the unnaturalness of Gabriel's incestuous intentions is contrasted with another kind of incestuous union, the one between Manuela and Perucho. As children of the hidalgo, they are both the offspring of a barbarous (Perucho) and an unnatural (Manuela) union. Yet paradoxically this young generation comes to stand for an original state of nature that seems to leave behind their problematic biological origin. When Gabriel first sees them at the Pazos, his eyes encounter them (and they seem so also to the narrator) as the crowning image of a highly wrought pastoral-georgic idyll, sitting on top of a hay cart: "Una mocita y un mancebo risueños, morenos, vertiendo vida y salud [. . .]. Y venía tan íntima y arrimada la pareja, que más que carro de mies, parecía aquello el nido amoroso que la naturaleza brinda liberalmente (*LMN*, 210). [A laughing girl and boy, full of life and health (. . .). And the couple was so intimate and close that, more than a hay cart, it seemed a love nest liberally offered by nature.] The stylization of Manuela and Perucho as children of nature who are identical with their natural environment and almost mythical figures of physical strength (Perucho is frequently described in hypervirile, classicizing terms) is clearly a serious proposition of the narrator. Through metaphor and rhetorical emphasis, numerous passages reinforce their vital and immediate connection to the natural environment and to animal life. For instance, while they drink fresh cow's milk in the mountains, the narrator employs a characteristic rhetoric of biological vitalism: "Manuela [. . .] bebía aquella gloria de leche, aquella sangre blanca, que traía en su temperatura la vida del animal, el calor orgánico a ningún otro comparable" (*LMN*, 273) [Manuela (. . .) was drinking from that glorious milk, that white blood, which carried in its temperature the life of the animal, the incomparable organic warmth].

As Gabriel's apprehensions grow, the novel moves toward a scene that suggests an instinctual consummation of brotherly love between Manuela and Perucho (ch. 11), embodying a state of being that is out of time and history altogether, a moment of absolute presence ("sólo el momento presente, con su

solemnidad, su intensidad, su peso decisivo en la balanza de nuestro destino,"
LMN, 299) [only the present moment, with its solemnity, its intensity, its decisive weight in the balance of our destiny]. Manuela and Perucho have left the
world of the Pazos far behind and are now in the heights of the Galician wilderness, the two mountaintops called Castros, which contain, as the narrator points
out, pre-Christian Roman fortifications built to secure regional independence,
a site of heroic military resistance (*LMN*, 291; 295). The ruined remains of "remote times" (297) [épocas lejanas] seem to illustrate the ultimate victory of nature
over human-made constructions, yet as the symbolic site of incest they also
throw an ambivalent light on the problem of regional, in this case Galician, autonomy. For Manuela and Perucho the collateral attraction founders on the pro-
hibition of incest; yet the incestuous disturbance of the patrilineal succession,
with its threat to continuity and authority, is also associated with an atmosphere
of myth and counterhistorical time, a conjunction of motifs that will be richly
exploited by the genealogical novel of the twentieth century.[66]

The realization of the incest taboo marks, as Lévi-Strauss has put it, the transition from nature to culture.[67] Yet, paradoxically, for Gabriel Manuela's cultural
education can best be achieved by an endogamous union with him. The whole
idea of an incestuous union might appear especially strange in a context where
Gabriel confronts the idea of marital union only as an entirely rational response
to the diagnosis of familial and national decadence. In *Fortunata y Jacinta* it was
precisely the idea of exogamy that presented itself as a response to decadence
following from too much social inbreeding; in Eça de Queirós's novel *Os Maias*
(1888), incest between brother and sister is modeled on the paradigm of classical tragedy. All of these realist novels from the Iberian Peninsula written around
the 1880s use the disturbance of the familial and sexual order as the privileged motif to comment and reflect upon the perceived decadence of the nation
vis-à-vis the progressive countries of Northern Europe.[68] While Manuela and
Perucho are not conscious of their parental relation, Gabriel identifies their
union with the scandal of incest. This is, to say the least, a rather contradictory
standpoint on his part, but it serves to underline Gabriel's double role as the
bearer of civilization and the decadent urbanite in need of natural regeneration.
Again, Gabriel sees the seemingly hackneyed plan to marry his niece as perfectly rational and natural, while he angrily resents the fact that Manuela and
Perucho are living in an "unnatural" and "monstrous" relation of incest. This
fault is rationalized with the argument of their class difference, most directly in
the late scene where Gabriel directly confronts his rival, Perucho, eliding the
question of who his real father is:

¿Y siendo sus padres de usted . . . un mayordomo y una criada . . . , cómo se ha atrevido usted . . . a poner los ojos en mi sobrina? ¿Cómo se ha atrevido usted [. . .] a levantarse hasta donde usted no puede ni debe subir? (*LMN*, 351)

[And your parents being . . . a *mayordomo* and a servant . . . , how could you dare . . . to put your eyes on my niece? How could you dare (. . .) to lift yourself to a position to which you cannot and should not rise?]

When at a somewhat later point Perucho ("el bastardo de Ulloa," *LMN*, 358) finally learns of his biological relation to Manuela, he is completely shocked and cannot believe what he hears. He recoils in shame and renounces his status as a son and heir to his father ("que se cisca en lo que le deje por testamento, y que no quiere de él ni la hostia," *LMN*, 368) [that he may soil himself in what he leaves to him as a testament and that he wouldn't take the host from him]. Even after the tragic revelation, however, Gabriel is still ready to assume for Manuela the role of a tutor and endogamous superfamily: "a ser para ella cuanto le negó la suerte hasta el día: padre, madre, hermano, protector, esposo amantísimo" (*LMN*, 394) [to be for her what she had been denied by fate until this day: a father, mother, brother, protector, most loving husband]. Yet while Perucho, following Gabriel's "suggestions," leaves for the city, Manuela becomes sick and finally resolves to go into a monastery in Santiago.

Where in *Los Pazos* the figure of Julián served, especially at the beginning, as a civilized entry point into a world of self-enclosed barbarity and atavism, the parallel figure of Gabriel in the second novel is confronted primarily with the spectacle of nature, as embodied by the two half siblings. Gabriel's various plans to educate and civilize his niece, to shape her according to literary and idealizing models, is shown to be a ridiculous pretension, indeed a symptom of the sickness of the modern self. This impression is reinforced by the passages devoted to Gallo, the husband of Sabel and successor of Primitivo in the role of the estate's *mayordomo*. Through the figure of Gallo, who eagerly learns to read and write and to decorate his rooms with the signs of culture (in bad, imitative taste), the narrator caricatures and openly ridicules the cultural and social pretensions of those members of the inferior classes who have succeeded in their social ascent ("el falso bienestar y el lujo de similor que hoy penetra hasta en las aldeas," *LMN*, 224) [the false well-being and the fake luxury that today penetrates even into the villages].

It is easy to see in the narrator's comments an echo of the conservative, aristocratic class-consciousness of Pardo Bazán herself: "por eso hay quien se ríe oyendo que para civilizar al pueblo conviene que todos sepan escritura y lectura;

pues el pueblo no sabe leer ni escribir jamás, aunque lo aprenda" (*LMN*, 218)
[therefore there are men who laugh when they hear that to civilize the people it
is advisable that all know how to write and read; for the people never know how
to write or read, even if they should learn it]. If Primitivo's reign over the Pazos
had already marked him as a kind of parasite in material terms, his successor
Gallo might be called a social parasite, because he predates on and envies the
distinction conferred by the nobility:

> (. . .), Su sueño dorado fue subir como la espuma, no tanto en caudal cuanto en
> posición y decoro; y se propuso, ya casado con Sabel, convertirse en *señor* y a ella
> en *señora*, y a Perucho en señorito verdadero. [. . .] Era de tal índole la vanidad del
> buen Gallo, que dejándose tratar de papá por Perucho y sin razón alguna para re-
> gatearle el título de hijo, la idea de que por las venas del mozo pudiese circular
> más hidalga sangre, le ponía tan esponjado, tan hueco, tan fuera de sí de orgullo,
> que no había anchura bastante para él en toda el área de los Pazos. Lo pasado, el ayer
> de Sabel en aquella casa, lejos de indignarle o disgustarle, era el verdadero atractivo
> que aún poseía a sus ojos una mujer marchita y cuadragenaria. (*LMN*, 220–21).

> [His golden dream was to rise like foam, not so much in fortune as in position and
> honor; and he resolved, after he was married to Sabel, to convert himself into a
> señor and her into a señora, and Perucho into a true señorito. (. . .) The vanity of
> the good Gallo was of such a kind that he let himself be called daddy by Perucho,
> for no other reason but to be able to give him the title of son, because the idea that
> in the veins of the boy might circulate more noble blood turned him so, so proud,
> that there was no sufficient width (space) for him in the entire area of the Pazos.
> Sabel's past in that house was far from displeasing to him, was in his eyes the real
> attraction that a faded woman in her forties still possessed.]

Both Gallo's self-civilizing, bourgeois mission and Gabriel's idea to civilize his
niece appear thus as misguided attempts to go against the rule of nature. On
the other side, Don Pedro at least momentarily still appears as the representative of an old feudal order in the strongly ritualized demonstration of physical
strength in the hay threshing scene at the end of the harvest. However, when
suddenly his physical strength fails him, he calls out for Perucho. When he refers to Perucho as his effective "príncipe heredero," he underlines the idea of
aristocratic, blood-based succession (and the factual disowning of his legitimate
daughter Manuela): "llamarle a que majase la camada en lugar del hidalgo, era
lo mismo que decirle ya sin rodeos ni tapujos:—Ulloa eres, y Ulloa quien te en-
gendró" (*LMN*, 319) [to call him to the effect that he would pound the bundle of

hay in the place of the nobleman was the same as telling him right out: "You are a Ulloa, and a Ulloa is the one who engendered you"]. However, given the fact of Perucho's illegitimacy, it is clear that the theatrical display and the rhetoric of feudal entitlement covers over the factual disintegration of the noble class, which is already in the process of being overtaken by the less spectacular, more invisible dynamics of bourgeois power.[69]

Given Spain's peripheral situation in the context of nineteenth-century Europe, it is remarkable that precisely this marginality enabled Pardo Bazán to arrive at a differentiated position on the question of modern civilization. In the two novels discussed here, Julián and Gabriel, as representatives of civilization or modernity, move to a peripheral space with a project of regeneration, the attempt to establish an alternative family, that is ultimately doomed to fail. In *La madre naturaleza*, Gabriel's last words are also the last of the novel: "Naturaleza, te llaman madre. . . . Más bien deberían llamarte madrasta" (*LMN*, 405). [Nature, they call you mother. . . . They ought to call you a cruel stepmother.] Julián, for his part, true to his theological perspective, invokes a higher power than nature: "la ley de naturaleza, aislada, sola, invóquenla las bestias: nosotros invocamos otra más alta" (*LMN*, 401) ["by itself, the law of nature is only invoked by the beasts: we invoke another, higher law"]. The civilizational outsiders are shown with all their deficiencies and self-delusions, but nature is revealed to be both idyllic and indifferent to higher spiritual principles. If the first novel was concerned with the relation between modernity and barbarism—the resistance of the province to education and progress, the failed attempt to regenerate the countryside—the second novel problematizes the colonizing gesture of culture toward "mother" nature, the failed attempt to regenerate oneself in the countryside. If the first text may be qualified as a genealogical tragedy, the second contrasts the reformist aspirations of a specific generation with the self-enclosed, mythical, and ahistorical sphere of an ambivalently natural world.

CHAPTER SIX

Dissolution and Disillusion

The Novel of Portuguese Decline (Eça de Queirós)

If the depiction of social decline in the Spanish and Italian novel resonated generally with the idea of a decadent South, the same is true for Portugal, and the quintessential, canonical novel in this regard is *Os Maias* (*The Maias*, 1888) by Eça de Queirós, the leading novelist of late nineteenth-century Portugal. *Os Maias* not only represents a narrative of decline, but it also pushes the envelope of the realist novel, so much so that we can speak here of a dissolution of the framework of realism. This is all the more significant because Eça de Queirós is credited with having introduced literary realism to Portugal. How, then, can we explain the fact that this author is responsible for both establishing, and then dissolving, the idea of literary realism? And why is in this case the theme of social-familial decline related to the possible decline of the realist aesthetic?

Alluding to the enormous size, as well as the extended period of gestation of *Os Maias*, Eça himself famously referred to his most famous novel as "this vast machine" [essa vasta machine].[1] The novel's combination of a minimal familial— and familiar—plot with a proliferation of conversational set scenes might in some respects be compared with the late novels of Theodor Fontane, notably *Der Stechlin* (1897). Broadly speaking, both of these late realist novels propose a reconception of the novel form, no longer imagined as the re-modeling of a more or less coherent, grounded view of reality. It is conceived, rather, as a situation where the hypertrophy of social conversation, as rendered by extensive scenes of dialogue, is indicative of a disintegration of traditional reality, with often satirical character portraits that involve, if not all aspects of society, its most elevated parts, those belonging to the sphere of politics, government, finance, the aristocracy, and the world of artists and literati.

At the beginning, *Os Maias* appears to chart the fate of the Maias, a rich, aristocratic Lisbon family, over three generations. The motive for the disturbance of the familial order is used to comment on the perceived fin de siècle crisis and decadence of the nation in comparison to the progressive countries of Northern Europe, notably France and England. If the theme of familial decline is hardly original, the specificity of *Os Maias* lies in its peculiar formal makeup, the fact that the familial plot appears as an almost conventional justification for the dramatization of a vast panorama of cosmopolitan Lisbon society, with long parts given to dialogues and individual set scenes. Moreover, even as the novel invokes the conventional pattern of familial decline, it does not present the picture of a clear historical transition whereby a certain social formation is marked as belonging to the past and thus gives way to something new. *Os Maias* combines and overwrites the pattern of decline with the idea of an essential historical immobility deemed characteristic of the national psyche. Furthermore, the peculiar treatment of the theme of familial decline is linked to the question of how this version of late realism escapes the determinist and strictly causal logic of doctrinal naturalism. The literary interest of *Os Maias* consists precisely in this transitional quality, in the attempt to transcend the constraints of naturalism.

Eça de Queirós was part of the generation of 1870, whose members diagnosed a Portuguese decadence, an enfeeblement of the national sense of adventure and enterprise, in contrast to their ideas of political regeneration (although Eça turned out to be far more pessimistic with regard to this latter aspect). The reformist concept of regeneration as a response to what was perceived as the decadent state of the nation is a recurrent phenomenon in Portuguese literary history and testifies to the strong connection between programs of literary and national renewal from the middle of the nineteenth until the first decades of the twentieth century.[2] The generation of 1870 was composed of literary writers and historians (notably Antero de Quental, Ramalho Ortigão, and Oliveira Martins), who convened in the small university town of Coimbra to deliver a series of public lectures on social and cultural reform, causing a major stir throughout the small intellectual world of the nation. As in the case of France, where Zola was soon followed (and then criticized) by a group of fellow writers, in Portugal the naturalist movement was associated with the self-affirming gesture of a specific generation. The modernizing influence of literary naturalism in Portugal, started by Eça in 1871, is generally comparable to the situation in Spain, where it will develop some years later, spurred on only by the influence of Zola's phenomenal success *L'assommoir*, published in 1877.[3]

Yet one of the most powerful and typical formulations of the 1870 generation's general outlook comes from the writer Antero de Quental, who, influenced by the biblical criticism of Renan and the socialism of Proudhon, was soon consecrated as the intellectual leader of the Coimbra group. In a text significantly entitled "Causas da decadência dos povos peninsulares nos últimos três séculos" ("Causes of the Decline of the Peninsular Peoples in the Last Three Centuries," 1870), he faults post-Tridentine Catholicism, political absolutism, and the Portuguese fixation on the past for the inhibition of modern thought and freedom, and he urges his countrymen to re-enter the "community of cultured Europe" and to "reacquire our place within civilization," to respect the "deeds of our grandfathers" but "not to imitate them."[4] As this short quote indicates, the 1870 generation was obsessed with the question of the nation's relation to and difference from the past, as well as its difference from and inclusion in Europe. Although the 1870 generation's obsession with the problem of decadence was evidently related to the specific case of Portugal and its self-perception as a cultural periphery, it is important to remember that at the end of the nineteenth century the discourse of decadence functioned in Europe generally as a "generative metaphor," that is, as a mode of rational explanation for commonly perceived problems of decay and social crisis.[5]

I will discuss how the novel's form reflects and reacts to this paradoxical perception of a specifically generational Portuguese identity at the end of the nineteenth century. Not only does the novel represent a crisis of familial and national continuity, I will argue, but the very form of the novel articulates and embodies a crisis of realist/naturalist representation, and in the process it reflects on the problem of modernity in the cultural periphery.

Genealogy and Generation

In its opening pages, *Os Maias* unmistakably invokes the genre of the family novel: "os Maias eram uma antiga família da Beira, sempre pouco numerosa, sem linhas colaterais, sem parentelas—e agora reduzida a dois varões, o senhor da casa, Afonso da Maia, um velho já, quase um antepassado, mais idoso que o século, e seu neto Carlos que estudava medicina em Coimbra" (*OM*, 6)[6] [the Maias were an old and never numerous Beira family, with few relatives and no collateral branches, in fact, they were now down to the last two males, the master of the house, Afonso da Maia, who was an old man, almost a patriarch, older than the century, and his grandson, Carlos, who was studying medicine at Coimbra University; *TM*, 2]. The first two chapters provide an extensive, analeptic account of family history, covering a period from circa 1820 to 1875. The reader is introduced to three male representatives of the Maia family, who stand for three consecutive generations, which in turn refer to distinct periods of Portuguese history in the nineteenth century: from the liberal struggles (Afonso da Maia) to late Romanticism (Pedro da Maia) to the so-called period of decadence and Regeneration (Carlos Eduardo da Maia). It is Carlos Eduardo who represents the current and third generation of the patriarchal line.[7] The bulk of the novel is set in the year 1875–76, with an epilogue set in 1886 (ch. 18).

Insofar as Carlos will become the focal point of a narrative of aristocratic decline, he functions not only as a sign of decadence but also as a potentially positive figure for the reader to identify with, insofar as he stands for a modern condition of the new, the undefined—in short, the transitional. In fact, Carlos becomes partly unmoored from the continuity of a patriarchal line and thus turns into the emblem of a specific generation in Portuguese history, which contemporary readers would have equated precisely with the generation of 1870. The very term "generation," in its specific postrevolutionary meaning, associates a distinctive mode of temporal acceleration with the deeds and sentiments of a *young* generation. In this context, the term does not refer only to a specific age group but rather to the idea of a group of individuals who have been formed by a common experience of history, an "Erfahrungsraum," "shaped by the same 'great events' into a homogeneous whole."[8] In this sense, Carlos, along with his companion João de Ega—a dandyish figure in which Eça has satirized himself— come to represent in the novel a specific generational experience. This is borne out by the focus of the novel, which, after the first two chapters, zooms in almost entirely on Carlos. While the third chapter is dedicated to Carlos's education in Santa Olávia, the subsequent fourteen chapters—the bulk of the novel—is concerned with his perspective on the societal life in Lisbon since his arrival there in 1887. The last chapter, an epilogue, takes place ten years later, when Carlos is observed for a few hours on his brief return from Paris. This is to say that the principal part of the novel largely confronts the reader with the particular viewpoint of Carlos and his generation.

In *Os Maias*, genealogical history appears thus above all as a function of Carlos's personal history, that is, his relation specifically to his *male* forebears. In contrast to a more generationally patterned naturalist novel such as, say, *Buddenbrooks*, the reader gets the sense of family not as a collective, transindividual entity but rather of isolated male representatives whose wives (prematurely dead, in the case of Afonso; quickly disappearing in the case of Pedro) do not seem to matter greatly. Rather typically for Eça's novelistic universe (one thinks also of the posthumously published novels *A cidade e as serras* and *A ilustre casa de Ramires*), the two central representatives of the Maia family, Afonso and Carlos, appear as eternal bachelors—figures that in literature are often associated with a characteristic ambivalence of freedom and solitude and that are simultaneously positioned inside and outside genealogy and familial order.[9] Family sentiments are thus largely reduced to the feelings between these two men. In fact, for Carlos, who was entirely brought up by men, all sense of family is conjoined and collapsed in the figure of his grandfather: "o papa, a mama, os seres amados, estavam ali todos—no avô" (*OM*, 184) [father, mother, and loved ones were all contained in his grandfather; *TM*, 159].

Let us now look at the ways the novel appears to locate the origin of the patriarchal decline but at the same time gives us subtle hints that precisely this question of origins and the fable of decline are not without problems. The familial decline would seem to have begun with Afonso's son, that is, Carlos's father, the sensualist and dissolute Pedro, who abducted an "improper" woman not worthy of the good Maia family name, Maria Monforte, the daughter of a greedy slave trader. In this sense, it appears that the narrator singles out Pedro— and by implication, his generation—as the one who is originally responsible for the subsequent decline of family and nation, which becomes visible in the torpor and inertia that characterizes Carlos and *his* generation.[10] Yet, curiously, Afonso perceives a similarity between Pedro and his own wife's grandfather, insofar as family legend knows that the latter went mad and committed suicide (*TM*, 16). The novel thus suggests that the biological origin of such nervous crises goes back to an older generation, even if not from the Maia side. Certainly to Carlos and the members of his generation Afonso looks like the model of age-old heroism and traditional patriarchal values. Yet the novel reveals this as more of a subjective impression than a literal truth. In fact, it is Afonso himself who points out how much this heroic quality resides above all in the eyes of the beholder:

> Afonso era um pouco baixo, maciço, de ombros quadrados e fortes: e com a sua face larga de nariz aquilino, a pele corada, quase vermelha, o cabelo branco todo cortado à escovinha, e a barba de neve aguda e longa—lembrava, como dizia Carlos, um varão esforçado das idades heróicas, um D. Duarte de Meneses ou um Afonso de Albuquerque. E isto fazia sorrir o velho, recordar ao neto, gracejando, quanto as aparências iludem! Não, não era Meneses, nem Albuquerque, apenas um antepassado bonacheirão que amava os seus livros, o conchego da sua poltrona, o seu *whist* ao canto do fogão. (*OM*, 12)

> [Afonso was quite short and stocky, with strong square shoulders; and, with his broad face, aquiline nose and ruddy complexion, his close-cropped white hair and long snow-white beard, he had the look, as Carlos put it, of a courageous man from an age of heroes, a Dom Duarte de Meneses perhaps, or an Afonso de Albuquerque. This always made the old man smile, and he would jokingly remind his

grandson how deceptive appearances can be! No, he was no Meneses or Albuquerque, he was merely a good-natured old man who loved his books, the comfort of
his armchair, and a game of whist by the fireside. *TM*, 7]

By casting the venerable and good-natured rentier Afonso in such a light, the
novel shows the reader that the Portuguese aristocracy is no longer the bearer of
a historical mission and of a colonial empire (for which the historical figure of
Afonso de Albuquerque stands) but rather an image of bourgeois self-enclosure
and harmless domesticity. Moreover, Afonso's role as a traditional patriarch,
who at first appears "rigid and inexorable, the very embodiment of domestic
honor" (*TM*, 23) [rígido e inexorável como a encarnação mesma da honra do-
méstica; *OM*, 30], is shadowed by his own history of rebellion against his ultra-
conservative father Caetano (as analeptically recounted on the beginning pages
of the first chapter), who, a symbol of the last phase of the traditional period of
absolutism (Carlota Joaquinha and Dom Miguel), denounced his son as a radical Jacobin devoted to the reading of Rousseau and Voltaire and even labeled
him a "bastard" (*TM*, 8), thus prefiguring, as it were, the "bastard child" produced
by the feeble, effeminate Pedro (*TM*, 15). The person of Afonso, then, illustrates a
temporal process whereby the bearer of liberal-revolutionary ideas will give in to
conservative impulses, thus illustrating the repetitive and futile nature of the
reformist impulse. Moreover, his youthful "revolutionary" enthusiasm is, except
in the view of his father, entirely innocuous. And as soon as he is exiled to
England—like many other liberal-minded Portuguese men in the wake of the
first Portuguese revolution of 1820—the narrator sarcastically reveals the fri-
volity and superficiality of his rebellious stance, since he quickly forgets about
his ideals:

> Bem depressa esqueceu seu ódio aos sorumbáticos padres da Congregação, as
> horas ardentes passadas no café dos Remolares a recitar Mirabeau, e a república
> que quisera fundar, clássica e voltairiana [. . .]. Durante os dias da *Abrilada* es-
> tava ele nas corridas de Epsom, no alto de uma sege de posta, com um grande
> nariz postiço, dando hurras medonhos—bem indiferente aos seus irmãos de Ma-
> çonaria, que a essas horas o senhor infante espicaçava a chuço, pelas vielas do
> Bairro Alto. (*OM*, 14–15)

> [He soon forgot about his hatred of the grumpy priests of the congregation and
> about the ardent hours spent in the Café dos Remolares reciting Mirabeau, as well
> as the republic he had hoped to found on classical Voltairian lines [. . .]. During
> the 1824 uprising in Portugal, Afonso was to be found at the Epsom races, riding

in a gig, wearing a large false nose and uttering fearsome war whoops, utterly indifferent to the fate of his brother masons, who were, at that very moment, being
driven along the alleyways of the Bairro Alto in Lisbon by the Infante Dom
Miguel. *TM*, 9]

True to the historical fact that the exiled Portuguese associated with liberalism
and Romanticism were absorbing in England the values of a new bourgeois and
Protestant culture and later tried to introduce these values into their home
country, *Os Maias* shows through the figure of Afonso that this was indeed the
first generation prone to believe that the nation had to be civilized by way of
foreign means and methods. All of this serves to demonstrate that the generational difference and apparent opposition between grandfather and grandson is
actually bridged by a sense of continuity and similarity.[11]

That even the anglophile Afonso is far from embodying the pragmatic virtues of the British nobility is underscored by the fact that his entire economic
and household affairs are run by the conservative administrator Vilaça, whose
son, Vilaça Jr., will in turn serve Carlos. Again, this dependence on the figure of
the practical, devoted, and patriotic administrator strengthens the sense of
continuity between Afonso and Carlos. The sequence of the male representatives of the Maias illustrates not so much the gradual decline of a patriarchal
line but rather a repetition of infringements on and restitutions of the patriarchal code. If the stately family house, called Ramalhete, is the conventional symbol
of generational continuity—and is invoked as such in the novel—it is also important to point out that the novel begins with Afonso and Carlos *moving* (back)
into this building. Moreover, Carlos's refitting of the house with the help of an
English architect/decorator in a wildly eclectic style indicates that this house serves
above all as a façade for the *idea* of familial tradition. Afonso indeed says that he
likes to live in "a house that has a long family connection" (*TM*, 3) in response to
Vilaça's ominous warning that this house had always been fatal to the Maias.

As the novel initially goes back in time from this present moment of moving
into the old Lisbon house, the reader begins to understand that this reconstruction—
Vilaça does not fail to mention "the vast amount of renovation work" (*TM*, 3)
that will be necessary—might well be a sort of attempt to undo the earlier disruption of the family line by Afonso's son. Indeed, Pedro's filial revolt is presented as a kind of oedipal revolt against Afonso's conservative, patriarchal values, as it is put by Maria Monforte herself: "para lhe mostrar bem que nada
valiam genealogias, avós godos, brios de família—diante dos seus braços nus"
(*OM*, 33) [to show him that genealogies, a long ancestral line, and family honor

were as nothing compared with her bare white arms; TM, 26]. The opposition between Afonso and Maria is one between a patriarchy of noble lineage—despised by Maria—and of a newly and unethically acquired wealth, despised by Afonso and Lisbon society, who shun Maria and label her a "slaver's daughter" (*TM*, 23). Later, Maria runs off to Paris with Pedro's good friend Tancredo, an Italian "Romantic," which then leads the disgraced Pedro, now pathetically regretful of having contradicted his father's authority, to commit suicide and hence leave his son Carlos an orphan. While Maria's antiaristocratic stance would seem to associate her with bourgeois modernity, her irresponsible impulsiveness points to the cultural past, an unbridled Romanticism.[12] Pedro and Maria's daughter, Maria Eduarda, is (mistakenly) believed to have died as a child.

The novel's plot hinges on the fact that Carlos is ignorant of this entire prehistory of his "Romantic" parents. Six chapters into the novel, Carlos abandons his rather superficial adulterous trysts with a socialite and falls passionately in love with a mysterious woman, Maria—who eventually, after the reader has long suspected it, turns out to be his own sister. Thus, the novel deploys the motif of incest as its central trope for the disturbance and involution of genealogical linearity. As a matter of fact, Carlos is said to encounter "his own image" (*TM*, 175) in the person of his sister, thus marking the unconscious incestuous attraction as a symptom of narcissism. Critics of the novel have often understood this in allegorical terms, that incest points to the sterility, immobility, and self-specularity of Portugal's social elite.[13] It is in any case highly significant that Eça has moved from the classically realist theme of adultery in his earlier novels (*O crimen do padre Amaro*, 1876; *O primo Basílio*, 1878) to the threat of incest and genealogical sterility as another, more decadent way of figuring the disturbance of the familial order and "the demise of paternal authority."[14]

Eça uses the incest plot in yet other ways to test the limits of the realist novel. The fact that Maria Eduarda upon her first appearance comes literally out of nowhere (somewhat similar to the mysterious provenance of her mother, Maria Monforte), free of all genealogical baggage, turns her into the perfect object for projections of a Romantic ideal.[15] She is repeatedly described as "divine" and compared to goddesses like Juno or Diana, just as her mother had earlier been compared with a goddess or a being from another world (*OM*, 22, 23). Moreover, like Carlos, she also seems to partly transcend the debased context of Lisbon society. Therefore, the idealist undertone that characterizes the relation between Carlos and Maria forms a stark contrast with the other adulterous affairs in the novel (such as the frivolous trysts between Ega and Raquel Cohen or between Carlos and Mrs. Gouvarinho). Most crucially, Maria appears to Carlos as both excitingly different and strangely familiar, with her strangely Maia-like eyes and her similar-sounding name. The incestuous attraction, therefore, rests on an essentially *uncanny* sense of familiarity that presupposes Carlos's partial ignorance of his own family history, namely a secret of a previous generation that comes to *haunt* the character in the present.[16] Again, in *Os Maias* this is not just a motif or psychic complex; it deeply affects the formal structure of the novel as a whole, whose only plot device consists precisely in the unveiling of this secret. Toward the end of the novel, a written document by Maria Monforte finally reveals Maria Eduarda's family history. Yet, for Carlos's relation with her it is obviously decisive that her past is unknown—she appears as a "literary" character that is endlessly malleable, contradictory (an adulteress, a single mother, goddess), and escapes any clear sense of identification (*TM*, 176). Eventually Carlos's Romantic infatuation with Maria is shown to be an illusion, when her "husband" Castro Gomes reveals her dark past, her "true" identity as Mrs. Mac Gren, a woman who is merely receiving money from him. The peculiar nature of this incestuous relationship is crucial to Eça's novel since it signifies both the weight of the past and the desire to be free of accumulated customs and traditions.

The decisive scene of anagnorisis between the two siblings, taken together with all the previous allusions to the "fateful" family house, the "fateful" encounter with Maria, and so on, seems to call up the genre of tragedy and, by implication, a sense of predetermination. Yet it is really more akin to a quotation of tragic motives. For instance, when Carlos eventually comes to learn the history of his parents and Afonso gives in to tell him the "whole wretched tale" (*TM*, 158), Carlos decides that this revelation of dark family secrets does not really disturb him too much: "He could feel for that tragedy only a vague, almost literary interest. It had all taken place twenty or so years before, in a now more or less vanished world. It was like an historical episode from some old family chronicle" (*TM*, 158–59). [Nem lhe era possível sentir por essa tragédia senão um interesse vago e como literário. Isto passara-se havia vinte e tantos anos, numa sociedade quase desaparecida. Era como o episódio histórico de uma velha crónica de familia; *OM*, 183–84.] In other words, Carlos sees himself as distinguished by his liberty from history and the parental bond. And even when it is revealed—again, through a constellation of coincidences—that Maria Eduarda is his sister, this revelation has no *real* tragic consequences, for, at the end of the novel, Carlos merely relinquishes all hopes of founding a family and producing an heir and resigns himself to a life of luxury and idleness in Paris.

If the novel had initially invoked the ingredients of a family saga, the decidedly nontragic, but still resigned, ending of *Os Maias* not only points to the
possible end of the Maia line; it highlights the fact that the various ambitious
projects of the two friends (Carlos's medical career, Ega's novel about an atom
and his plan to found a cultural magazine) have all come to null. In this way,
Os Maias appears to comment allegorically on the shattered hopes of an entire
generation and its regenerative hopes—in this it is comparable to a certain
variety of the bildungsroman, especially Gustave Flaubert's *L'éducation sen-
timentale* (1869), one of the most representative trends of the nineteenth-century
novel.[17]

The Dissolution of Naturalism

This structural-thematic proximity to Flaubert's novel is echoed on the level of
novelistic form, insofar as the shattering of the individual's hopes and a skepticism toward historical progress is reflected in a plot structure that is centered
not so much on an evolving action or confrontation as on the retrospective revelation of an underlying truth, as well as by the fact that the individual perceives
reality as only the sum total of a conversational flow made up of stereotypes.[18]
Therefore, *Os Maias*, with its abortive approach to the genealogical model, is a
particularly revealing case for general transformations of the realist novel at the
end of the nineteenth century. It is representative of the decadent inflection of
realist literature around the year 1890, when many novels combined techniques
of traditional realism with variations of realism.[19]

To understand the novel's transitional position in literary history, it is necessary to briefly address its relation to the movement of realism in Portugal. During the 1870s and 1880s, realism/naturalism possessed a polemical and sym-
bolical value as a force of modernity in Southern Europe. It was usually associated
with France and, concomitantly, with a new level of technical and political modernity. As part of the programmatic events of the 1870 generation, Eça himself
delivered the Casino lecture on June 12, 1871, entitled "A nova literatura: O realismo como nova expressão da arte" (The new literature: Realism as the new expression of art), where the iconic names of Flaubert and Courbet served as sign-
posts for the new realist aesthetic in art. The title of the lecture (which does not
survive in written form, only in a fragmentary transcription by an anonymous
witness) underlines the "newness" of the enterprise, which is indicative of the
cultural delay where the terms "realism" and "naturalism"—as in Spain, these
terms operate largely interchangeably—are seen as a reaction against the prevailing tendency of late Romanticism. According to this modernizing, realism

is here understood as a revision of customary modes of representation that are no longer deemed adequate for a new conception of reality.[20]

As we have seen above, *Os Maias* is at least in part a novel typical of naturalism, insofar as it charts a course of generational disintegration that results in sterility and decadence. It is important to note that this naturalist strain has not a comprehensive but rather a local, restricted relevance. Yet, curiously, the naturalist agenda cohabits here with what it has set out to replace, namely the spirit of Romanticism. This is clear already from the novel's subtitle, which reads *Episodes from Romantic Life (Episódios da vida romântica)*, and in fact the decadent relation between the lovers may also be seen as a kind of perfect love, a Romantic ideal that cannot endure the pressures of reality.[21] The peculiar structure and reading experience of the novel derive from the dissonance between a tragic-Romantic story about incest, on the one hand, and a satirical, often highly comedic chronicle of social mores, on the other. Of course, this apparent conflict may be understood as a realist satire of a certain vulgar Romanticism, yet it may also be argued that *Os Maias* is in fact contemporaneous with the emergence of decadence as a period style during the late 1880s, which remobilized aestheticizing Romantic motifs for a critique of pragmatic rationality.[22] Insofar as decadence involves a relation between the present and the past, it expresses above all dissatisfaction with present realities and an opposition to progress. Given this unstable, conflictive stance toward its own temporal moment, decadence is by definition conceived as a movement of transition, and, in the artistic realm, it is thus perceived as an innovative transitional moment on the way to modernism.[23] As a literary style and period, decadence also embraces central features of realism, such as the coherent development of character and plot, with a representation of everyday lifeworlds that reinforces the *critical* view of social reality. It is highly significant that *Os Maias* tilts the realist balance between description and dialogue toward the latter, as it generally increases the satirical mode of presentation and simultaneously diminishes the authority lodged in an omniscient narrator.[24] The coexistence of naturalist and antinaturalist elements, a characteristic stylistic eclecticism involving at turns national allegory, tragic motifs, and romantic and melodramatic elements, is one of the most fascinating aspects of *Os Maias*. The transitional mode of realism is also shared by Eça's Spanish contemporaries Clarín and Galdós; yet while these writers push the boundaries of realism in the direction of an increased psycho-narration, in Eça the relative sparseness of description is combined above all with dialogue and satire.

The novel, then, is typical of this transitional period in literary history, yet it marks also a poetological turning point in Eça's literary career, prefigured by the crisis of the naturalist aesthetic evidenced by his various rewritings of *O crime do padre Amaro*.[25] The fact that *Os Maias* reflects this reorientation is likely to be due, at least in part, to the long period of gestation, almost ten years, during which Eça wrote and revised the novel. When Eça set out to write the novel in 1880, he still believed in the precepts of naturalism, but this had changed by 1888 when the book was published—at this time, in France, Zola had pretty much become the sole practitioner of naturalism (*La terre* was published in 1877). For instance, *Os Maias* diverges from Eça's earlier novels (*O crime do padre Amaro*, *O primo Basílio*), where the characters are fully explained as consequences of their specific milieus and hereditary traits.

Significantly, as several critics have pointed out, in *Os Maias* this naturalist topos is still in evidence in the figure of Pedro, Carlos's suicidal father, who is generally portrayed as a weak, effeminate character, given to sudden passionate impulses.[26] Pedro's psychosomatic, temperamental, and hereditary traits ("nervoso," "fraco," "crises de melancolía negra," *OM* 20) ["nervous," "weak," "crises of black melancholy"] draw parallels to his mother, Maria Monforte—and decidedly not to the Maias, whose race is here still associated with a distinctive virile force. He is under the possessive influence of his mother and is brought up with a stifling Catholic religiosity. In this sense, he is clearly presented as the product of a specific education. The figure of Pedro illustrates the naturalist idea of education as a determining influence: while his father Afonso is exiled to England, Pedro receives an imported, typically Portuguese form of education, distant from nature and heavy on religious morality.

His son, Carlos, receives a British education in Portugal (in Santa Olávia), the inverse image of the father's education. The importance of this theme is underscored by the fact that the entire third chapter is dedicated to it. The young boy Carlos's education is programmatically distinguished from that of his playmate and generational companion Eusebiozinho, who grows up under bookish and feminine, which is to say traditionally Portuguese, influences, while Carlos is brought up by his grandfather with the rigid, "virile" principles of a modern, English education. Aside from this initial episode, however, Carlos, as well as the principle characters of the novel generally (Ega, Maria Eduarda, Afonso), appears not to be delimited by milieu and education or framed by the definitive judgment of a narrator and therefore would seem to transcend the framework of naturalism. In the case of Carlos, the specific nature of his education does not really lead to any decisive difference from the other members of his generation, a generation seen as marked by incapacity and passivity—although his dispersive, dilettante activities appear to underline the fact that he is *not* determined by environmental factors. One might in fact argue for naturalism in the novel precisely because the principles of a different, supposedly modern education appear to crumble under the decisive, determinative nature of heredity and unchangeable national character, namely the pathological passion of his father Pedro, as well as the "nature" of the Portuguese "soul." This is illustrated early on, when Carlos seeks to establish a medical practice in the capital, which soon comes to nothing because of his luxurious and dilettantish tendencies. This career might be seen as standing symbolically for modern science, rationality, and progress and hence also for the more general aspirations of Carlos's generation, including the values of "a democratic revolution based on ability, and not on financial, spiritual, or familial heritage."[27] In fact, Afonso has educated his grandson precisely with the intent that he be useful to his country, "whose main occupation is being ill" (*TM*, 74) [num país em que a ocupação geral é estar doente; *OM*, 89]. The semantics of sickness and health (deftly employed in the first chapters of the novel) generally suggest an allegorical relation to the body of the nation.[28] Yet Carlos fits out his city office more like a decadent salon, complete with piano and lavish furniture, where he treats his very few patients for free (*TM*, 83). Carlos's medical ambition finally gives way to the "poison of dilettantism" (*TM*, 76). In fact, Carlos and his friends form a circle of dilettantes who discuss "Democracy, Art, Positivism, Realism, the Papacy, Bismarck, Love, Hugo, and Evolution" (*TM*, 75). In other words, these preoccupations are clearly reminiscent of the generation of 1870, and the obvious, contradictory eclecticism in the satirical enumeration underlines the arbitrary, inconsequential, and derivative nature of these discussions. Yet, in contrast to Eça's own earnest pronouncements at the time of the Coimbra "revolution," these concerns appear now tainted by the ironic light of dilettantism: "these metaphysical discussions and even revolutionary certainties tasted more exquisite still in the presence of the liveried valet uncorking the beer or serving croquettes" (*TM*, 76). In the same vein, Ega's radical atheism and social-revolutionary rhetoric is countered by the narrator with the comment that "deep down, he was a romantic, always falling in love with fifteen-year-old girls" (*TM*, 78). In other words, in contrast to the "experimental" studies of conventional naturalism, the narrator has here a satirical view of the characters.

The depiction of Carlos's point of view (to the detriment of an omniscient perspective) also maintains an ambiguous relation with naturalist precepts because the narrator refrains from detailed physiological or psychological descriptions of his character.[29] Despite his association with modern, "naturalist" medicine, Carlos is also the representative of a generation still marked by the experience of Romanticism. If the figure of Carlos exhibits a certain ambiguity with regard to the precepts of naturalism, this is also true for his "tragic" alliance with Maria Eduarda. Although Carlos and Maria are fatally attracted by their "spiritual and even genealogical similarities," they are decisively not influenced or determined by the forces of economy and milieu, as orthodox naturalism would have it.[30] Instead, they are drawn to each other by an almost tragic fate, "as if, in the midst of all these barbarians, he had finally found a civilized being" (*TM*, 177) [como desobrindo enfim entre os bárbaros um ser de linha civilizada; *OM*, 204], a supposition that turns out to be a self-deception. And yet there appears to be a certain sense of (pre)determination: Carlos's Romantic infatuation with Maria Eduarda looks like a repetition of Pedro's fateful passion for Maria Monforte. Notice how in Maria's first appearances on the scene she is repeatedly described as if she were a "goddess," a harbinger of a superior civilization—and how the specific wording here, "um ser de *linha* civilizada," "a deusa *descendo* das nuvens de oiro" (*OM*, 204; italics mine) [a being of a civilized *line*, a goddess *descending* from the clouds of gold], not only articulates Pedro's Romantic effusiveness but subtly, and unbeknownst to him, provides an ironic allusion to their common genealogical descent. Yet another aspect of this weakening of the naturalist paradigm is the fact that the decisive discovery of the incest is entirely due to chance, the encounter between Ega and Guimarães: it is, in other words, not determined, as the doctrine of naturalism would have it.[31] Furthermore, Eça uses a subjective form of realism whereby a given social space is observed and experienced by an individual (Carlos) who is implicated in it yet also (because of his foreign education) has a certain critical distance from it.

Finally, every discussion of the novel's relation to naturalism must mention the notorious supper scene at the Hotel Central, where the characters themselves engage in a discussion of literary aesthetics. Against the "official" position of naturalism, voiced by Ega, stands a stereotypical accusation, as uttered here by the Romantic Tomas de Alencar, who, as a former friend of Carlos's father Pedro, represents the outmoded literary ideals of an earlier generation and who abhors the current fashion of naturalism, typified by Zola's *Assommoir*, as nothing but "excrement" (*OM*, 162). These opposing visions of Romanticism and naturalism are both clearly exaggerated, thus satirically exposing the cultural limitations of the Portuguese scene,[32] yet they may also be read as a parodic self-portrait of Eça himself, looking back on beliefs—namely, the belief in

scientific objectivism voiced in the Casino lecture—that he had partly abandoned by 1888.[33] At the same time, it is Carlos who intervenes in this debate
with a more balanced judgment that likely coincides with Eça's own position as
a "reformed realist" during this time:

> Do outro lado Carlos declarou que o mais intolerável no realismo eram os seus
> grandes ares científicos, a sua pretensiosa estética deduzida de uma filosofia al-
> heia, e a invocação de Claude Bernard, do experimentalismo, do positivismo, de
> Stuart Mill e de Darwin, a propósito de uma lavadeira que dorme com um carpin-
> teiro! (*OM*, 164)

> [Carlos declared that what most offended him about realism were its scientific
> pretensions, its much-vaunted aesthetic based on someone else's philosophy, and
> the unnecessary invocation of Claude Bernard, experimentalism, positivism,
> John Stuart Mill and of Darwin, when all the author was doing was describing a
> laundress going to bed with a carpenter! *TM*, 140–41]

Yet the debate between the two must be considered in light of the fact that Ega on
other occasions professes the Romanticism of Victor Hugo or, at the end of the
scene, appreciates Alencar as a genuine representative of the Portuguese spirit.

Peripheral Modernity: Imitation and Immobility

We learn that Carlos's mother chose his name (rather than Afonso, the name of
his grandfather) because she has read about the romantic adventures of the Pretender Charles Edward in a Scottish novel: "such a name seemed to her to contain a whole destiny of love and heroic deeds" (*TM*, 30) [um tal nome parecia-lhe
conter todo um destino de amores e façanhas; *OM*, 38]. The title of this novel is
never mentioned, but it is not unlikely that it was *Waverley*. The fact that Carlos's name is thus associated with Britain and the "last of the Stuart," a "valiant
Walter Scott gentleman" (*TM*, 58) [o último Stuart, um valoroso cavaleiro de
Walter Scott; *OM* 38, 69] is indeed key to understanding the novel; for Carlos's
infatuation with all things British and his entirely British education is seen as a
caricature and allegory of Portugal's problematic relationship with the British
Empire, the symbol of advanced capitalism and colonial power, with whom Portugal was repeatedly allied over the centuries.[34] The culture of the periphery is
seen as dependent on the center—and the satirical criticism of his own country
is complicated by the fact that Eça served for many years as a consul in England,
from where he challenged the insufficient modernity of Portugal. After all, *Os
Maias* is a novel written in England.

Apparently quite in line with the British precepts of his education, Carlos embarks, as we have seen, upon a career as a medical doctor. The fact that, despite singular bouts of activity and initiative, ultimately Carlos's modern education does not prevent him from falling back to the habits of the Portuguese leisure class shows to what extent *Os Maias* does indeed cling to a certain idea of determinacy. Just as Carlos soon abandons his medical career, Ega's plans to write a monumental literary work entitled *The History of an Atom* will be much talked about—but never completed. The obsessive concern with Portuguese nationhood in *Os Maias* occurs in a context where the perceived failure to live up to modernity is thematized by a constant comparison between Portugal and the "civilized" countries of Northern Europe, especially France and England. This is to say that the peripheral desire to be modern is embedded in a conflict between heteronomy and autonomy that figures traits of national identity primarily as signs of deficiency.[35] Significantly, at the beginning of the novel Carlos restores the family house, the Ramalhete, with the help of an *English* architect, leading to an utterly eclectic mixture of styles that are divorced from their original milieu. As we will see, the end of the novel tries to gesture toward a sense of the nationally authentic as a way of escaping the problem of being insufficiently modern. Practically all of the many characters of *Os Maias* are engaged in striving for the mirage of civilization, a goal that is always self-ironically located elsewhere. If something is of cultural worth, it must be imported (*OM*, 109). This idea is voiced by Ega, in a way that has a certain postcolonial ring:

> Aqui importa-se tudo. Leis, ideias, filosofias, teorias, asuntos, estéticas, ciências, estilo, indústrias, modas, maneiras, pilherías, tudo nos vem em caixotes pelo paquete. [. . .] Nós julgamo-nos civilizados como os negros de São Tomé se supõem cavalheiros, se supõem mesmo *brancos*, por usarem com a tanga uma casaca velha do patrão. (*OM*, 109–10)

> [Here we import everything. Ideas, laws, philosophies, theories, plots, aesthetics, sciences, style, industries, fashions, manners, jokes, everything arrives in crates by steamship. [. . .] We imagine that we are civilized in just the same way as the blacks in São Tomé imagine that they're gentlemen, or even that they are white, merely because they wear the boss's old tailcoat over their loincloth. *TM*, 93]

In the final chapter of the novel, Ega takes a pair of shoes modeled on foreign fashion to symbolize the derivative, imitative condition of Portugal and concludes that it inevitably leads to deformation, to caricature: "somente, como lhe falta o sentimento da proporção, e ao mesmo tempo o domina a impaciência de parecer muito moderno e muito civilizado—exagera o modelo, deforma-o, es-traga-o até à caricatura" (*OM*, 703) [however, since it had no sense of proportion, and was, at the same time, dominated by an impatient desire to appear very modern and very civilized, all these models were immediately exaggerated and twisted and distorted into caricatures; *TM*, 612]. Whether it is shoes or a French style of writing, everything is imitated and in the process distorted from its original essence. Even though Carlos and Ega often appear as explicit critics of national decadence and bad taste, they are often portrayed as cultural imitators, thus illustrating the self-criticism of Portuguese modernity. As Alan Freeland has shown, this kind of cultural dependency leads to a hierarchy of imitators, where the imitators themselves are seen as paragons of style and cultural au-thority.[36] For instance, Carlos is imitated by his friend Damâso, a representative of the new bourgeoisie, who, always with the word "chic" on his lips, collects bric-a-brac antiquities and who styles his beard and chooses his shoes on the model of Carlos (*TM*, 165)—and he ends up literally copying academic articles that presumably are intended as material for Carlos's never-to-be-finished book on matters of modern medicine: "considerava Carlos um tipo supremo de chique, um Brummel, um d'Orsay, um Morny—'uma destas coisas que só se vêem lá fora,' como ele dizia arregalando os olhos" (*OM*, 190) [he considered Carlos to be the epitome of chic—his beloved chic—a Beau Brummel, a Count d'Orsay, a Duc de Morny, "the kind of marvelous thing one sees only outside of Portugal," as he put it, wide eyed; *TM*,152]. Even Carlos's dandyism, therefore, does not escape the law of imitation, nor does Ega's, whose Villa Balzac and project for a Portuguese version of the *Revue des Deux Mondes* all too clearly signals his de-pendence on French models. Insofar as Damâso is first introduced to Carlos as the "son of a usurer" (*TM*, 162), a "friend of the Cohens" who has invented his surname, an implicit parallel is established with Maria Monforte ("the daughter of a slave trader"), and the figure is anti-Semitically associated with moneylend-ing, new money, and inauthenticity. Damâso, with his characteristic mixture of pride and servility, is evidently a satire of the social type of the *nouveau riche*, what with his personal emblem "Sou forte" (I am strong), and is thus linked to the upstart nature of the economically successful Monfortes. We will encounter this type again in the figure of Don Calogero in *Il Gattopardo*. Another famous set piece of the novel, quite unnecessary for the development of the plot as such, is the tenth chapter, concerned with the social event of the *corridas* in the hip-podrome in Belém, where the narrator exposes Lisbon's fake cosmopolitanism, its desperate, provincial attempt to live up to the model of the foreign. In this sense, the novel is obsessively concerned with the "typically" Portuguese habit of denationalizing national customs and the broader phenomenon of the dissolution of national boundaries in the context of an incipient globalization.[37]

The discussion within the novel itself of the national vice of bad imitation evidently also has a metaliterary implication with regard to the creation of original literature under conditions of peripheral modernity. For instance, the emerging discipline of literary historiography grappled with the supposed problem, inherited from the Romantic philosophy of history and geography of culture (according to which literary systems were either organic and national or inorganic and imitative), that Portuguese literature was constitutively an imitative literature in comparison with the more original production of literature in the countries of the European North. Characteristically, the generation of 1870 took this literary diagnosis as supreme evidence for the decadent state of the nation as a whole—and the project of a regeneration was thus conceived, since the Romantic generation, with a return to uncorrupted origins.[38] The idea of the unoriginal nature of Portuguese literature was a dominant notion in literary discourse until 1880. Yet if the earlier Romantic generation especially condemned the manifestations of a Portuguese classicism, this later period was concerned with the strong dominance of French literature, which, paradoxically, had itself been relegated to the status of unoriginal in the Romantic conception of literary systems.[39]

This satirical presentation of the national inferiority complex also resonates with the specific position of Portuguese realism in the general European system of literature. As a matter of fact, Eça's signature realist novels, *O primo Basílio* (1878) and *O crime do padre Amaro* (1875/1876/1880) were judged by early critics to be nothing but imitations of French models, namely Flaubert's *Madame Bovary* and Zola's *La faute de l'abbé Mouret*, respectively. Seen from today, such an accusation, a supposed lack of originality, does not take into account these novels' self-conscious departure from protagonists whose moral code or amorous desire is mediated by their readings of literary texts. In this sense, not only does the mimetic desire of the characters, such as the *bovarysme* of Luísa (in *O primo Basílio*), indicate the imitation of a model (Flaubert), but the reiteration opens up a dimension of difference, a "transgression created by a *new* use of the model taken from the dominant culture."[40] Still, the contemporary discussion focused on the question of literary imitation in the more immediate sense. For instance, the most famous contemporary criticism comes from the Brazilian writer Machado de Assis, who deemed his Portuguese colleague a "stubborn disciple of the realism propagated by the author of *Assommoir*."[41] While acknowledging Eça's evident talents, he roundly condemned him for imitating the French school of realism (instead of clinging to a supposedly Portuguese tradition of realism), whose vulgarity he rejects as "amoral." This is not the place to detail Eça's response through his revision of the novel *O crime do padre Amaro*.[42] Instead, I want to insist on Eça's characteristically ambivalent response to the accusation of imitation. For instance, when Eça was accused, by one Fialho de Almeida, that *Os Maias* only features characters that are copies of each other, Eça replies by arguing that an immobile country does not allow for vivid, original characters in a novel that sets out to realistically portray the current society. If a vigorous civilization such as that of London or Paris certainly makes for strong individual characters ("a possante e destacante pessoalidade"), people in Lisbon can barely be distinguished from each other, writes Eça.[43] To achieve "une copie exacte et minutieuse de la vie"[44] [an exact and detailed copy of life], the realist novelist must also face the flatness of character. Thus, toward the end of his life, in 1889, he counters this accusation with a vivid account of how his entire generation had lived and worked under the influence of French culture, in a text entitled "O Francesismo":

> Tenho sido acusado com azedume, nos periódicos, ou naqueles bocados de papel impressos, que em Portugal passam por periódicos, de ser *estrangeirado, afrancesado*, e de concorrer, pela pena e pelo exemplo, para *desportuguesar Portugal*. Pois é um desses erros de salão, em que tão fertil é a frivolidade meridional. Em lugar de ser culpado da nossa desnacionalização, eu fui uma das melancólicas obras dela. Apenas nasci, apenas dei os primeiros passos, ainda com sapatinhos de croché, eu comecei a respirar a França. Em torno de mim só havia a França.[45]

> [I have been accused with acrimony of being a *foreigner* or an *afrancesado* in periodicals or in those chunks of printed paper that pass for periodicals in Portugal. And I have been accused of conspiring, by pen and by example, to *deportugalize Portugal*. Well, this is one of those salon errors in which Southern frivolity is so abundant. Instead of being guilty or aiding in the destruction of national characteristics, I was one of the melancholy results of this destruction. No sooner was I born, no sooner did I take my first steps, still in my crochet slippers, than I began to breathe France. Around me there was only France.]

Eça writes here that not only his own schooling and intellectual upbringing but his entire generation ("toda a minha geração") has fatally turned French, abandoning all Portuguese essence and in turn transforming the Portuguese state institutions into a "bad and gross copy of France" [uma cópia da França, malfeita e grossera], leading to his notorious witticism "that Portugal was a country translated from the French" [que Portugal era um país traduzido do francês].[46] Thus, Eça maintains that in contrast to the Danish imitation of German culture and the Belgian imitation of French culture, Portugal's adherence to the French model appears especially misguided and parasitical because of what he sees as essential differences in national character, particularly the opposition between France as a nation of "intelligence" and Portugal as one of "imagination."[47] The question of imitation, as well as of characteristic national differences, has haunted Portuguese literature and literary history for a long time.[48]

We have yet to address how Eça's novel presents the aporias of Portuguese modernity as a form of a specific generational experience and its relation to history and time. Even as the ending of *Os Maias* invokes with the death of the patriarch the end of a certain image of the past, it also conveys a more general sense of historical immobility and eternal stagnation of the nation. Crucial to this sense is the novel's representation of time: the fact that the reader has witnessed the numerous characters, with their individualized tics and obsessions, over the course of many chapters.[49] Not surprisingly, the place that most symbolically encapsulates the passing of time is the family house of Ramalhete. In the final scene, the dust has settled on the various material objects that have become signs of the remembered past, and in Ega's view Afonso's death coincides with the abandoned state of the house, together signifying the end of an epoch: "ao entrar no Ramalhete, Ega sentia uma longa saudade pensando no lar feliz que ali houvera e que para sempre se apagara" (*OM*, 680) [as they entered Ramalhete, Ega felt a great wave of nostalgia, thinking of the happy loving home it once had been and never would be again; *TM*, 591].

At the end, Ega voices a critical self-assessment of his generation's failure to embody a form of historical modernity: "Que temos nós sido, desde o colégio, desde o exame de latim? Românticos: isto é, individuos inferiores que se governam na vida pelo sentimento, e não pela razão" (*OM*, 714). [What have we been since we were at school, since we were sitting for our Latin exam? Romantics, which is to say, inferior individuals ruled in life be feelings and not by reason; *TM*, 622.] If Ega articulates a sense of generational disillusion, the allusion to the French Republican Gambetta—who is repeatedly named as an "intimate friend" of Guimarães—likely serves as a symbol for the corruption of democratic ideals in the political realm, the deterioration of democratic ideals into Caesarist ideology. In this way Eça connects the figure responsible for the revelation of the family secret, itself belonging to an earlier generation, with the idea of generational and national disillusion not only in Portugal but in the very center of European politics.[50]

Yet the idea of the end, of the closing of a family tradition, is contradicted by a more general sense of historical-national stagnation and *immobility*. In fact, when Carlos returns to Lisbon in 1887, after a period of ten years living and traveling abroad, he observes that the traditional lethargic customs and social type remain unchanged and that his generation's efforts have not altered a thing. In this sense, what appears as the definitive end of the family line does not open up new possibilities, as Michel de Certeau has characterized the historicizing function of writing: "To 'mark' a past is to make a place for the dead, but also to redistribute the space of possibility, to determine negatively what *must be done*, and consequently to use the narrativity that buries the dead as a way of establishing a place for the living."[51] The passing of chronological time has not affected the sense of a national, collective suspension of time, as Carlos observes while standing in the center of the city, at the Largo de Loreto: "Nada mudara. A mesmo sentinela sonolenta rondava em torno à estátua triste de Camões. Os mesmos reposteiros vermelhos, com brasões eclesiásticos, pendiam nas portas das duas igrejas. O Hotel Aliança conservava o mesmo ar mudo e deserto" (*OM*, 697). [Nothing had changed. The same guard patrolled sleepily round and round the sad statue of Camões. The same red curtains, bearing ecclesiastical arms, hung in the doorways of the two churches. The Hotel Aliança had the same silent deserted air; *TM*, 607.][52] The melancholic evocation of the statue of Portugal's greatest poet invokes the traditional topos of the contrast between a glorious national past and a decadent present, which is the other face of a new civilization entirely dependent on the importation of foreign models, a sort of parody of modernity. By way of free indirect discourse, the narrator conveys Ega's opinion that this secondhand version of modernity that manifests itself on all levels of society and culture is really grotesque: "it was exactly what happens with the blacks in colonial Africa who see Europeans wearing spectacles and imagine that this is what it means to be civilized and white" (*TM*, 613).

Faced with this problem of immobility, Carlos, standing high on the hills of the city among the *castelo* and old ecclesiastical buildings and feudal palaces, envisions the return to original, patriotic values. In *Os Maias*, Eça adopts a topical narrative of familial decadence, yet the themes and precepts of naturalism survive here only in a fragmentary form. Moreover, in contrast to his earlier novels and the social diagnosis of the 1870 generation, the underlying narrative of decadence is no longer the flip side of an inherently progressive, regenerative view of society. In other words, the curtailing of the genealogical paradigm—even on a decadent arc—is related to this more skeptical outlook on society and evolutionary history—where the progress of history does not affect what appears to be an unchangeable nature. The ending of *Os Maias* gestures toward the possibility that original values may be retrieved. It is Ega who appears now to become a spokesperson for the narrator, when he revalues the formerly ridiculed Romanticism of the poet Alencar as something "authentic" and fitting with the Portuguese bent for emotionality (*TM*, 622), when he contrasts "old little Lisbon" with the frenetic modernity of Paris. In fact, this idea of a possible revitalization by way of a return to national values and origins would become a major theme in Eça's quasi-posthumous novels, *A ilustre casa de Ramires* (1900) and *A cidade e as serras* (1901), where the male protagonists are the last descendants of aristocratic families and who, with at least a certain measure of success, reconnect to the vital force of their ancestors.[53] Yet, although this is the direction Eça's views on the national problem would finally take, in *Os Maias* the ending is much more ambivalent: the narrator tells us that "the old Lisbon nobility [. . .] dragged out its last days," (*TM*, 613) and Ega and Carlos concur that their idealistic plans have failed.

CHAPTER SEVEN

Surface Change

A Brazilian Novel and the Problem of Historical Representation (Machado de Assis)

In the previous chapters I have discussed the ways various nineteenth-century novels figure problems of genealogy and sociohistorical change in geographical places that can be characterized as internal European peripheries. I turn now to a work by the most important Latin American novelist of the turn of the century, Machado de Assis (1839–1908). We will see how this Brazilian author reflected on the self-perceived peripheral status of his country vis-à-vis modern Europe. Machado's contribution to the history of the novel must be evaluated not as mere imitation of the cultural forms of the European center but as their adaptation to a different context.[1] As briefly mentioned in the previous chapter, Machado debated with his Lusophone contemporary Eca de Queirós the question of literary realism. Here I am interested in the way Machado also, and more radically, pushed the boundaries of the realist novel to express a similar, if more explicit, skepticism of the possibiliy of historical change in a peripheral context.

Novel and Nation

Before we discuss Machado's penultimate novel, let me briefly comment on the relation between novel and nationhood in Brazil.[2] If Benedict Anderson has argued that the nation as an imagined community can emerge only through the widespread availability and general circulation of narratives (newspapers, novels) in the horizon of an empty and homogeneous time, then it must be said that this space is comparatively underdeveloped in nineteenth-century Brazil. In fact, much of Brazilian literary historiography is concerned precisely with this problem of the belated emergence of a literary system, with overcoming a low status of literary capital, as Pascale Casanova would have it.[3] I am referring here to the specific material and social conditions of literary circulation and readership in nineteenth-century Brazil, distinguished by a very high rate of illiteracy, a scarcity of books, and the confinement of reading to a very small intellectual and social elite.[4] As a matter of fact, these circumstances have been a traditional staple of the discourse of literary historiography throughout the nineteenth century.[5]

For instance, contemporaries lamented that the proportion of the reading public was even worse than in the least-developed countries of Western Europe, such as Spain and Italy. The critical discourse about the circumstances of literary distribution became especially intense after the publication of the very sobering literacy statistics made available by the first national census in 1872. In that year, only 18.6 percent of the free population was able to read (15.7 percent of the total population, including slaves). In 1892, the number actually dropped to 14.8 percent. The shock produced by these figures among the literary intelligentsia revealed as largely self-delusional the idea that literature is an important, if not the most important, expression of national consciousness, an idea that had been the driving force of the entire movement of Brazilian Romanticism. Although the latter third of the nineteenth century saw marked progress in establishing a publishing system, the main problem, that of scarce readership, persisted.

Based on Machado's own responses to these sobering statistics, Hélio de Seixas Guimarães has convincingly argued that this situation is at least in part responsible for the peculiarities and the stylistic-formal achievements of Machado's second phase of novelistic production.[6] During this time, around 1875, Machado's view of national politics is increasingly marked by a skeptical distance and disillusionment that starkly contrasts with the contemporary belief in positivism and evolutionism. *Esaú e Jacó*, for example, reflects on Brazil's dependency on foreign, European models, such as liberalism and modernity, and treats ironically the contemporary belief in social and historical change, as embodied by abolition (1888) and the advent of the Republic (1889).

Machado's critical view of national literature may be gleaned from his well-known essay, "Notícia da atual literatura brasileira: Instinto da nacionalidade" (Notice about current Brazilian literature: Instinct of nationality, 1873), where he asserts that literature's concern with national matters need not occur on the overt level of theme and local color but may manifest itself more subtly on the level of literary form, as an "intimate feeling" (certo sentimento íntimo).[7] In the essay, a precocious reflection on the inevitability of young literary nations to create literature in the immediate service of national aspirations, literature is explicitly designated as a project parallel to that of political independence but also in some sense opposed to it.[8] The criterion of difference that is required to ensure the independence of the newly developing Brazilian literature cannot be equated with the notion of local color (certa côr local).[9] According to Machado, the true autonomy of Brazilian literature cannot be achieved if universality and local specificity are seen as a self-evident opposition:

> Devo acrescentar que neste ponto manifesta-se às vezes uma opinião, que tenho por errônea: é a que só reconhece espírito nacional nas obras que tratam de assunto local, doutrina que a ser exata, limitaria muito as cabedais da nova literatura.[10]
>
> [I must add that on this point often an opinion is upheld that I hold to be wrong: namely the opinion that recognizes a national spirit only in those works that deal with some local topic, a doctrine that, taken seriously, would severely limit the means of the new literature.]

By recognizing the rhetoric of nationalism as a trait of his own time and by emphasizing, in contrast, the continuities between the literatures of the colony with that of the European center, Machado shows that a literature's self-affirmation should be based on its universal reach. If Machado's essay already constitutes a critical intervention with regard to the question of literary nationalism, his novel *Esaú e Jacó* continues and deepens this critical stance, reaching the point of a veritable crisis of the relation between novel and nationhood.

At the beginning of the twentieth century, Machado de Assis's late novel *Esaú e Jacó* (1904) presents an extreme case of the impossibility, or negation, of the realist narration of nationhood in favor of a more directly allegorical mode of representation—or in any case a mode where realist and allegorical elements coexist, a characteristic feature of Machado's prose insisted upon by John Gledson.[11] While this novel shares a number of stylistic and thematic features with the other novels of Machado's second, mature phase (after 1880), arguably this is the one that more than any other is concerned with history. Of course, an influential tradition of criticism has insisted on the historical referentiality of practically all of his major novels, yet by and large this has referred to the question of how the novel's characters (or narrators) may reflect the structure of paternalistic Brazilian society during the Second Empire, especially in the case of *Memórias póstumas de Brás Cubas* (1881).[12] *Esaú e Jacó*, I maintain, holds a special place because it is concerned not only with socially symbolic satire and critique but also with the question of historical representation *as such*. In fact, it might be understood as a sort of metanarrative, metahistoriographic inquiry into the possibility of writing a historical novel as well as questioning the realist representation of nationhood through a private, family history. The novel undertakes a critical investigation of both national/historical and novelistic representation.

Similar to the argument by Seixas Guimarães, Roberto Schwarz's view is that the ironic, digressive, antirealist prose of the late Machado might be understood as a kind of allegorical commentary on "the position of modern culture within the countries of the periphery."[13] If the novels of the mature Machado achieve their effects by representing generic and formal negativity according to the standard conventions of the realist novel, in Schwarz's argument this divergence from literary realism paradoxically corresponds with the reality of the social elite of the Second Empire. In this view, Machado's fiction indirectly corresponds with the world from which it emerges as a kind of superior realism, a second-degree realism.[14] I am obviously indebted to Schwarz's well-known line of argumentation that the novel's critique of representation echoes a broader social and political situation, as well as the works of critics such as John Gledson and Sidney Chalhoub, who, partly building on his insights, have variously stressed the levels of historical, referential allusiveness or a correspondence between Machado's literary characters and the general structures of the sociopolitical reality of Machado's time.

Yet in my view *Esaú e Jacó* is an interesting limit case for this idea of historical correspondence (however oblique). For this novel's skeptical interrogation of the conventions of realism advances a general inquiry of representation that plays with but also questions the idea that the fictional text reflects or stands for a specific aspect of (historical) reality. This metahistoriographical component of the novel has been partly recognized by Gledson, when he remarks that the "very superficiality of its historical approach" [a própria superficialidade da abordagem histórica] is itself indicative of a particular historical period, roughly the years between 1871 and 1894.[15] Less concentrated on literary form, exploring instead the possibilities of historical correspondence in great detail, Gledson thus produces his own version of Schwarz's general argument about a paradoxical parallel between Machado's fiction and a specific historical situation.

My own approach, while partly building on this interpretative tradition, reflects my aim to foreground another, related paradox, namely the fact that Machado's "most historical"—and ironically, least realist—novel has not only a historical index but in fact a universal dimension that consists precisely in its general exploration and problematizing of the notion of fiction as historically specific allegory. Moreover, I also tend to concur with Alfredo Bosi, who has criticized Schwarz's "reductionist" and "totalizing" assumptions regarding the correspondence between literary form and the socioeconomic conditions and ideologies of a particular class, for the universalist appeal of Machado can be explained only by taking into account how his work "surpasses the geographical limits of the periphery."[16] In this sense, *Esaú e Jacó* is particularly revealing of a general problem that has occupied and divided Machadian criticism: the question of whether Machado's fictions are necessarily tied to or transcend a specific historical context.[17]

Esaú e Jacó is conceived as a kind of antihistorical novel that refuses to subscribe to the difference between the present and the past, the discourse of difference and development that is otherwise characteristic of nineteenth-century historicism. This critical reorientation of novelistic form might be explained by the absence of the common ground of a national community. Indeed, the absence of a sense of true nationhood is a central feature of the critical discourses about nineteenth-century Brazilian society and politics. I will first discuss the novel's fable-like plot that negotiates the boundaries between allegory and myth and its possible connection with the historical situation of the time. Specifically, I will briefly explain how the novel's antirealist strategies might be related to the perceived failure of representational politics as it was associated with the establishment of the Republican regime. Then, I will analyze concretely how the novel's skeptical vision of history and historical representation is echoed in its distinctive formal features, such as the position of the narrator and the insistent concern with the nature of time and narration. Finally, I will comment on how the novel is distinguished by antigenealogical motifs, thus giving a further dimension to the problem of (dis)continuity. On these various thematic and formal levels, the text subverts conventional associations of nationhood, novel, history, and family in the nineteenth century, yet it also may be seen as implicitly commenting upon our critical desire to inscribe this text into history.

Allegory and History

Published in 1904, *Esaú e Jacó* is set in the Rio de Janeiro of 1869–94, during the transition from monarchy to Republic. It is concerned with two families of the higher bourgeoisie. On the one hand, there is the couple Santos and Natividade, parents of identical twin sons, Paulo and Pedro. On the other hand, there is Batista and Dona Cláudia, parents of Flora, the common love interest of the twins. The basic idea of the plot consists in the fact that Paulo and Pedro are of exactly contrary political persuasions, that they are destined to be locked in an eternal rivalry, and that Flora is existentially unable to choose either of them. The novel is almost completely devoid of any signs of psychological development, and its basic conflict is "resolved" only to the extent that Flora dies in the last chapters of the novel. The entire story is told from the viewpoint of the

"Counselor" Aires, an old, retired diplomat and friend of the families, yet his perspective is in turn refracted through an external narrator.

From the very beginning of the novel, the possibility of an allegorical reading of the problem of nationhood appears to be strongly encouraged. Thus, the first image is of Natividade and her sister Perpétua consulting a wise prophesying woman, a *cabocla*, on the future of her two newborn sons. Significantly, this scene takes place at the Morro do Castelo, the historical origin of the city. The fortress marks the site of the first Portuguese settlement: it was from here that the French were driven in 1581 and here that Manuel de Nóbrega founded the Jesuit College, where Anchieta, one of the founding fathers of (colonial) Brazilian literature, had taught. Against the background of this historically connotative landscape, the narrative, departing from the implicit analogy of historical birth and biological birth (consider the name of Natividade, "Nativity"), lays out a series of ironic traces. For instance, the two women encounter a lay brother begging for alms in Purgatory. His name is Nóbrega, thus recalling the historical figure mentioned above and contributing to the atmosphere of historical allegory. These and other allegorical references have been patiently detailed by John Gledson.[18] An allegorical interpretation seems indeed to be suggested by the novel itself, which, alluding to the fourfold sense of biblical interpretation, explicitly proposes to the reader the presence of a hidden meaning: "o leitor atento, verdadeiramente ruminante, tem quatro estômagos no cérebro, e por eles faz passar e repassar os atos e fatos, até que deduz a verdade, que estava, ou parecia estar escondida" (*EJ*, 134) [the attentive, truly ruminative reader has four stomachs in his brain, and through these he passes and repasses the actions and events, until he deduces the truth which was, or seemed to be, hidden; HC, 142].[19]

Gledson, then, is obviously right about the importance of allegory, yet it is far from clear how this level of symbolical reference functions. The passage cited above announces a "hidden truth" in an obviously ironic way, undermining the stability of allegorical reference, and indeed the novel puts pressure on the assumption that characters "stand for" and "embody" ideas.[20] Also, the allegorical dimension of the text pulls in two opposite directions: on the one hand, a propensity for a maximum of abstraction and "mythic" universality, as indicated by the novel's title; on the other, a pointed, specific referentiality. The reader is constantly asked to "uncover" a possible level of reference, yet this search for correspondence is also frustrated.

This is most clear in the case of the two brothers, who are introduced as standing for different political orientations: Pedro is a representative of the monarchy, or generally of the conservative tendency; Paulo is an adherent of the

Republic, or the progressive tendency. At the same time, as twin brothers, they belie any notion of chronological or generational difference that would map these differences on the plane of diachronic change. As I would like to suggest, it is precisely the paradox of nondifference that marks the novel as deliberately conceived as antihistorical. The novel's polemical intent consists in the fact that it unmasks an epochal event—the transformation from monarchy into Republic—as a nontransition. Given the metaphorical analogy between nation and family, the function of the twin motif is precisely to illustrate a situation of rivalry and reversibility, where differences are only apparent and an essential sameness is revealed. From the beginning, the two brothers' adherence to different forms of government is satirized for its basic fetishism, the adoration of signs of identification/differentiation, which are moreover easily recognizable as "ideas out of place," to adopt Roberto Schwarz's well-known phrase [idéias fora do lugar], that is to say, inadequate, hasty, or superficial assimilations of norms and values that have been dislodged from their original European context.[21] The equidistance of the narrator, Aires, from both Pedro and Paulo illustrates the problem that the apparent difference rests on a fundamental sameness (*EJ*, 67). The problem of a lack of differentiation is also the reason the love triangle stalls: Flora's inability to choose between the brothers, who are both courting her. Eventually she even blends and confuses them in a state of hallucination that abolishes their individuality (*EJ*, 180) and turns them into two versions of one person.

The ideological rivalry between the brothers is exposed as a crisis of differentiation, which is underscored by the perfect and frequently absurd symmetry of their actions and thoughts. For instance, the narrator notes that Pedro is absent from the ball that commemorates the recently installed Republic (ch. 48). Conversely, Paulo does not go to the ball on the Ilha Fiscal, a small island in the Bay of Guanabara (November 9, 1889), a celebration given on the occasion of a visit from Chilean diplomats. In fact, the event went down in Brazilian history as symbolic of the very last days of the fading monarchy, as the "last dance" of the empire.[22] Again, the point is not only that an event is seen differently from individual perspectives but that it might not be perceived as politically significant at all: "não é que só fossem liberais ao baile, também iriam conservadores, e aqui cabia bem o aforismo de D. Cláudia que não é preciso ter as mesmas idéias para dançar a mesma quadrilha" (*EJ*, 113) [it was not that there would be only liberals at the ball, there would also be conservatives, and here is where Dona Claudia's aphorism fits in nicely: It is not necessary to have the same ideas to dance the same quadrille; HC, 118]. The "Republican" ball thus becomes an emblem for the Brazilian subordination of differences to the idea of a "cordial society," where private relations substitute for the deficiencies of the public sphere.[23] The twins' ideological differences are presented in a thoroughly schematic way that does not emphasize the causes or developments of their respective "convictions" but rather plays up the logic of symmetry and the ironic reversal of perspective. From Paulo's Republican perspective, the date of their birth, April 7, 1870 (in the year of the Republican Manifesto), signals the end of the monarchy (the renunciation of Pedro I), while from Pedro's monarchist perspective the event stands for the impending inception of Pedro II's reign (*EJ*, 66). Insofar as the same date gives rise to such different interpretations, the novel's mock allegorical plot calls into question the presumed objectivity of historical events—and by implication also the stable ground of the possibility of allegorical decoding, for the reader realizes that a single event may signify in different ways.

If the brothers' arbitrary leanings and pointless differentiations make them (deliberately) unconvincing as realistic characters, something similar is true for the figure of Flora, their amorous, vaporous ideal, who throughout the novel appears only as the projection of others. In 1889, the year of the regime change, Flora turns eighteen years old. This again suggests an allegorical interpretation for Flora, who would thus stand for Brazil achieving maturity with the young Republic. Accordingly, Flora's premature death, on April 10, 1892, coincides with the (premature) crisis during the first days of the government of Marshal Floriano Peixoto and the military siege of the city of Rio de Janeiro (ch. 107) and might be interpreted as the death of an idealized Republic. Flora (whose name may therefore suggest an allusion to Floriano Peixoto, the first vice president and then the second president of Brazil from 1891 to 1894), might be seen as a symbol of the Republican ideal, of the period of emancipation and national fraternity.

In fact, numerous contemporary illustrations figured a young woman surrounded by, or adorned with flowers as an allegorical representation of the Republic.[24] This was obviously based on European, especially French, classical imagery of Republicanism.[25] In the propaganda that preceded November 15, Republican messianic ideology frequently used the figure of a holy, pure woman, or goddess, which was also helped by the Brazilian cult of Mariolatry.[26] If the death of Flora, then, is linked to the decline of idealizing images of the Republic, other characters of the novel allude to more mundane phenomena of the changing times. The figure of Agostinho Santos, for instance, embodies the type of the capitalist nouveau riche, a member of an arriviste class, who recently received the title of baron from the emperor (ch. 20) and suddenly became wealthy during the time of the *encilhamento*, the period of dramatic turbulence in the bourse, from boom to crash, during the years 1890–91—his obsession with card games (voltarete) clearly has to be seen in this context.

The proclamation of the Republic, resulting from the confluence of the interests of radical members of the military, coffee planters from São Paulo, and Republican politicians, led to a sudden opening of the market to foreign capital and a new market centered in the bourse. The result was an uncontrolled influx of English and North American capital, as well as frenetic and fraudulent speculation. This led to the ruin of many established capital owners and the emergence of a class of "new men," having rapidly acquired riches by the game of speculation during the first years of the Republic.[27] The economic destabilization and social mobility caused by the *encilhamento* are considered an essential factor for Brazil's entry into modernity.[28] Machado seems to have associated the evils of financial speculation with the period of the Republic, which he perceived as generally opposed to the stability of the monarchy.[29] This might be confirmed by another series of historical sources that also document the rapid deterioration of the reputation of the Republic, even among its erstwhile supporters.[30]

These Brazilian realities are seen as a game in which the oligarchies exchange positions in government among themselves—a practice that is not specific to the Republic but already characterized the paternalist system of the parliamentary monarchy during the period of the Conciliação.[31] This can also be seen in the character of Dona Cláudia, Flora's mother, whose behavior illustrates the political opportunism and relativism of the times. On the occasion of the liberal seizure of power, repeatedly referred to as a sort of Lady Macbeth (117), she tries to manipulatively convince her husband, Batista, an unsuccessful conservative politician, that he had always been on the side of the Liberals; she instigates his adaptation to the change from an old conservative order to the new liberal era (*EJ*, 117). When Santos, however, fears that the establishment of the Republic will disrupt his business activities, it is Aires who will comfort him with the prospect of continuity:

Nada se mudaria; o regímen, sim, era possível, mas também se muda de roupa sem trocar de pele. Comércio é preciso. Os bancos são indispensáveis. No sábado, ou quando muito na segunda-feira, tudo voltaria ao que era na véspera, menos a constituição. [. . .] O povo mudaria de governo, sem tocar nas pessoas. (*EJ*, 153–54)

[Nothing would change; the administration yes, it was possible, but one can also change one's clothes without changing one's skin. Business is a necessity. Banks are indispensable. By Saturday, or at the latest by Monday, everything would return to what it was the day before, minus the Constitution. [. . .] The people would change governments without hurting anyone. HC, 165]

Aires's ostensibly untroubled, stoic view in the face of an epochal event resonates with the very similar words voiced by the prince in Tomasi di Lampedusa's *Il Gattopardo* (1956): the argument that revolutionary change is a fiction and that, after some surface adjustments, things will essentially remain the same—a characteristic view of the "futility thesis" of the "rhetoric of reaction," according to which "change is, was, or will be largely surface, façade, cosmetic, hence illusory, as the 'deep' structures of society remain wholly untouched."[32] These examples all go to show that the apparent discontinuity of political regimes is built on an underlying continuity, a point, we have seen, that is symbolically refracted through the figures of the twins and their nondifference. *Il Gattopardo*, a novel also concerned with "new men" and the alleged immobility of the Sicilian condition likewise represents the failure to incorporate a cultural periphery into the sphere of modernity.

This idea of the inherent superficiality of political difference and change is epitomized by what is probably the most well-known episode of the novel, the scene concerning the *tabuleta da Confeitaria* (chs. 62–63). Aires has known the owner of the Confeitaria do Império, the pastry shop of the Empire, for a long time. The shop belongs to and symbolizes the old world of central Rio, a world dear to Aires, who thinks that this world is immortal and will never change. The signboard (*tabuleta*) of the "imperial" shop has been getting old, and so the owner has commissioned a painter to restore it, when suddenly the Republic is established. The shop owner tells the painter to stop right in the middle of painting the name ("pare no d") ["stop on the *d*"; HC, 158] and together with Aires he runs through a gamut of alternative names that would be inoffensive to the new, or in fact any, regime. According to Aires's suggestion, they finally settle on the proper name of the owner (Confeitaria do Custódio), because in this way the shop would not be compromised under any circumstances (*EJ*, 152). The pastry shop owner's sign thus escapes commitment; it does not signify beyond itself.

This highly satirical scene is obviously intended to persuade the reader that the epochal change of governments amounts to nothing but a simple change of names. The custodian, while avoiding reference and extricating himself from history, unwittingly becomes an "allegory" for the type of (Brazilian) citizen who simply accommodates himself to the reigning power or goes with the changing times. This scene is of central significance to the novel not only as an ironic comment on contemporary politics but also because it exemplifies the larger problem of decision. As in the case of Flora's nondecision for one of the twins, Custódio's dilemma is also that he cannot commit to a name, for every possible name is a choice and thus presents a potential risk. Both the spheres of love and politics are distinguished by the absence, the impossibility, of decision. The satirical thrust of Machado's novel, where the announcement of a political Revolution (ch. 60) is soon followed by Aires reading Xenophone's lines about the ephemeral nature of political revolutions (61), might be held against contemporary comments on the establishment of the Republic, such as the following editorial in the newspaper *O Diário de Notícias* by the statesman Rui Barbosa: "o Brasil acaba de passar por uma trasformação política radical e, entretanto, tudo continua como estava, secretamente, sem haver a mínima perturbação da ordem pública"[33] ["Brazil has just undergone a radical political transformation, yet, actually, silently, everything continues as it was, without the minimal disruption of public order"]. Insofar as the novel depends on a level of national allegory, it signifies the superficiality and reversibility of political factions. More specifically, Pedro and Paulo's crisis of differentiation corresponds to what is only a surface difference in the arena of national politics.

Political Representation

Let me say a few more words about the historical context, as called up by the numerous allusions to the central events of the time. The fall of the empire and the proclamation of the Republic on November 15, 1889, is a symbolic moment extensively discussed in Brazilian historiography. After more than sixty years, Brazil ceased to be a constitutional monarchy and now had its first president as a republic, Deodoro Fonseca. Normally, a confluence of causes is adduced for this transformation, such as the exponential increase of European immigration, the abolition of slavery (formally introduced in 1888), and the war with Paraguay (1864–70), as well as the need for a federalist system, backed up by politicians with more firm roots in the regional hinterland. The opinion of the intellectual and political elite was divided. The Republicans argued that since the time of the Inconfidência Revolt, the Republic had always been an aspiration of the nation. The Republican Manifesto of 1870 similarly declared that the monarchical form of government is an anomaly and has no roots in Latin America.[34] On the other side, many monarchists maintained that the Republic had not come about as the result of a political-social movement but was merely the result of the disaffection of a certain segment of the military class.[35] As the Republican deputy Aristides Lobo declared in a notorious phrase, the people assisted at the proclamation of the Republic "like beasts [*bestializado*], surprised, not knowing what it signified."[36] The statesman Joaquim Nabuco perhaps most eloquently voiced the mind-set of the monarchists: "They idealized the past, and with pessimistic eyes they observed the present, which appeared to them as an epoch of disorder and confusion."[37]

The monarchists were certainly correct in observing a gap, a contradiction, between the rhetoric of the "people," essential for the Republic's strategy of self-legitimization, and the fundamental lack of actual structures of citizenship. At the moment of the Republic's proclamation, manifestations of popular support were hastily arranged at the last minute. A contemporary French observer and resident of Rio de Janeiro, Louis Couty, went as far as to say, "Brazil does not have a people."[38] The historian José Murilo de Carvalho has studied the various means of political participation, or lack thereof, in the Republican capital and observes, "The city [of Rio de Janeiro] was not a community in the political sense, it did not have the sense of belonging to a collective entity."[39] Although many citizens were involved in questions of national relevance for the first time during these years, the number of active participants in the electoral process during the Republic was only 2 percent of the total population. In the first direct elections for president in 1894, only 7 percent of the potential electorate voted, which amounts to 1.3 percent of the population. When the regime continued to obstruct any enlargement of the right to citizenship, the initial wave of enthusiastic support among many liberal intellectuals rapidly vanished.[40]

Like his longtime friend Nabuco, Machado lamented the insufficiency of Brazilian nationhood. Nabuco corroborated Machado's vision that political parties are an abstraction in the context of the Segundo Reinado, insofar as they do not reflect distinctive ideas.[41] It was during this period that Brazil witnessed the emergence of a generation of autonomous intellectuals that was distinguished by its constitutive distance from the established Brazilian social formation.[42] For both Nabuco and Machado, this situation leads to a melancholic, skeptical stance of withdrawal from active engagement in politics (although Nabuco would later work as a diplomat for the Republic). We know that Machado was conspicuously immune to Republican propaganda. While he favored liberal positions in his beginnings as a journalist, throughout his life and work he never took a public position with regard to the decision between monarchy and Republic and generally abstained from taking positions on party politics. Clearly, the observer figure of Aires in *Esaú e Jacó* (he reappears in Machado's last novel, *Memorial de Aires*) embodies to some degree the political and philosophical skepticism of its author.

Literary Representation and Time

Let us now see how the novel's peculiar narrative makeup signifies a crisis of not only political but also novelistic representation. The evidently bizarre plot of *Esaú e Jacó* can be understood as Machado's conscious, parodic reworking of the genre of the historical novel, or, more specifically, the historicized modes of representation of nineteenth-century Brazil that were primarily interested in the narrative construction of origins, foundations, and roots.[43] What kind of historical vision does the novel purport to represent, and how is this related to the question of time, arguably the most sustained "theme" of the text? *Esaú e Jacó* is a historical novel that is skeptical of the possibility of historical narrative. The novel does not represent a given historical period (the government of Pedro II) in a realist sense. Instead, it uses certain historical and political signifiers to show the ephemeral nature of political activity and historical change.[44] In fact, it has already been argued that one of its salient differences from the classical historical novel consists in the absence of the characteristically omniscient narrator and, more broadly, in the ironic stance toward the objectifying modes of nineteenth-century historicism.[45]

In contrast to traditional modes of historical representation, here the narrator is both distant and implicated. The author/narrator says in the preface that he has found among the papers of the deceased Aires the manuscript of a diary, "Memorial," as well as a manuscript entitled "Último," a "narrative" that is now appearing under the title *Esaú e Jacó*. This traditional device of the found manuscript forces the reader to realize the difference between the narrator and Aires as a character as well as a "private" narrator. The narrator distinguishes, then, between himself (as author) and Aires as a character, thus emphasizing the difference between narrator and author, as well as the difference between material book and narrative.[46] Accordingly, readers are confronted with a highly paradoxical text. They cannot take it as the objective account of an omniscient narrator—because Aires is the "ultimate" source—nor can they take it as Aires's subjective, autobiographical account, because his views and words are always mediated by an editor.

The "dear old man" [querido velho] and "counselor" Aires is conceived as the quintessentially detached observer, and he is conspicuously disengaged from politics and public life. The chapter that introduces him as a character of the story (ch. 12) portrays Aires immediately as a man attached to the past, which implicitly sets him in opposition to the corruption of the present time (*EJ*, 47). Aires does not possess any specific political affiliation, and even his most private feelings are distinguished by indifference, if not cynicism (*EJ*, 48). Both in private and in political matters Aires adopts a skeptical position of indifference, which is also reflected in his spirit of neutrality and mediation (*EJ*, 49.) Aires comments constantly on the connections between, and the causes of, events, even though he cannot clarify all secrets and meanings. Hence the very level of narrative enunciation is constantly emphasized, so that the act of storytelling is privileged over the story and the characters themselves.[47] How does this uncertain narrator refer to the dimension of history? In talking about the figure of Santos, the narrator distinguishes between Santos's limited view and his own retrospective and "historicizing" perspective:

> Ia pensando [. . .] na lei Rio Branca, *então* discutida na Câmara dos Deputados; [. . .]
> Ao passar pelo palácio Nova-Friburgo, levantou os olhos para ele com o desejo do
> costume, uma cobiça de possuí-lo, sem prever os altos destinos que o palácio viria
> a ter na República; mas quem *então* previa nada? Quem prevê cousa nenhuma?
> (*EJ*, 42; italics mine)

> [He was riding along, thinking of [. . .] the Rio Branco law of *free birth* then being
> discussed in the Chamber of Deputies [. . .]. As he passed the palace of the Count
> of Nova-Friburgo, he raised his eyes toward it with the customary desire, a greedy
> desire to possess it, without ever foreseeing the high destiny the palace would
> attain under the Republic—but who then foresaw anything? Who foresaw any-
> thing at all? HC, 31]

Negative Genealogy

We have seen that the Machadian narrator denies generic expectations and conventions on several accounts. Insofar as *Esaú e Jacó* can also be understood as the story of two families, Machado parodies the conventions of the naturalist novel, such as the notion of genealogical (dis)continuity and inheritance.[48] The importance of this theme may be related to the novel's preface, where the editor mentions Aires's manuscript with the title "Último." "Último" was indeed the title Machado had originally intended for this novel (according to a note written to his publisher, Garnier), for at this point he thought of it as his last. In her introduction to the English edition, Helen Caldwell speculates that the original title belongs to a network of biblical and Dantean allusions, especially dense at the beginning of the novel, according to which the term *último* might refer to the "last generation" of the Brazilian Empire (vi–viii). Caldwell refers to a line from Matthew 12:45, alluded to by Aires: "The last state of that man is worse than the first. Even so shall it be also for this most wicked generation" (xii).

While Caldwell's biblical explanation of the novel's original title remains necessarily speculative, I want to take seriously her suggestion that the novel is about
a last generation, that it presents the end of a period marked by genealogical
discontinuity, "that this society which forms the subject matter of the novel is
not the child of the previous generation, and that it is predestined by its nature
not to fulfill its destiny."[49] Thus, the novel's sense of historical nontransition, of
historical immobility, is counteracted by the idea that an epoch *has* come to
an end.

At the beginning of the novel, Natividade's maternity is described with strong
echoes of biblical language, and Santos is designated as a "patriarch" whose only
purpose in life is to get rich and "establish a dynasty" (*EJ*, 33–34). In contrast to
such dynastic hopes, the novel stresses the truncation of family lines or replaces
natural with imaginary bonds. Aires's sister Rita, for instance, insists that she
is his "last relative" [sua última parente; *EJ*, 84], and the widower Aires himself
is childless. When Natividade mentions to Aires that she might join her sons on
a voyage abroad, Aires, who does not want her to go, responds that he might also
be seen as a kind of son of hers: "Mas eu também sou seu filho. Não acha que o
costume, o bom rosto, a graça, a afeição e todas as prendas grisalhas que a
adornam compõem uma espécie de maternidade? Eu confesso-lhe que ficaria
órfão" (*EJ*, 95). ["But I too (. . .) am your son. Don't you think that habit, kind-
ness, indulgence, affection, and all the other homely virtues that adorn you,
constitute a kind of motherhood? I tell you, I would be an orphan"; HC, 95.] This
kind of logic is also apparent in the scene where his "retrospective desire" [dese-
jos retrospectivos; *EJ*, 102] makes Aires fantasize that he would be the "spiritual
father" [pai espiritual; *EJ*, 106] of twins. While in chapter 16 the narrator/Aires
speaks of the "old religion" of "parenthoodism" (HC, 48) [paternalismo; *EJ*, 56]
dear to the Santos family, in the next chapter he characterizes the twins as "my
children" [meus meninos; *EJ*, 57].

Insofar as the novel is concerned with the notion of family, then, it repeatedly
stresses the primacy of affective and hypothetical over nominal and biological
bonds, and thus it continues the implicit critique of patriarchal-genealogical
ideas advanced in *Brás Cubas*.[50] An inverse image to Aires's hypothetical parentage with Natividade appears in the scene that discusses Flora's relation to her
parents. After Batista and Dona Cláudia are introduced by the narrator, he comments on the literary convention that the description of the parents always precedes the presentation of the children, only to then question this convention, on
both literary and scientific terms:

Nem sempre os filhos reproduzem os pais. Camões afirmou que de certo pai só se podia esperar tal filho, e a ciência confirma esta regra poética. Pela minha parte creio na ciência como na poesia, mas há exceções, amigo. Sucede, às vezes, que a natureza faz outra cousa, e nem por isso as plantas deixam de crescer e as estrelas de luzir. (*EJ*, 77)

[Children do not always reproduce their parents. (Camões) claimed that from a certain father one could only expect a son of the same sort, and science confirms this poetic rule. For my part I believe in science as in poetry, but there are exceptions, my friend. It happens at times that nature does something quite different, and (nevertheless the plants do not stop growing and the stars shining). HC, 73, translation modified]

Flora betrays her parents' hopes for "dynastic consolation" [consolação dinástica; *EJ*, 81]; she turns out not to follow her parents but to be their exact opposite ("tudo o contrário deles," *EJ*, 81). Flora's foreignness, her distance from her parents, is described with a rhetoric that parodies and actually denies the naturalist discourse of the "law" of inheritance ("lei da hereditariedade," *EJ*, 181). Therefore the narrator insists that Flora's affective instability should not be understood as a derivative of her mother's political instability. Compare the comment by the narrator, when Paulo comes up with a catchy phrase in a political discussion about abolition and his mother wonders where it may come from: "as próprias idéias nem sempre conservam o nome do pai; muitas aparecem órfãs, nascidas de nada e de ninguém" (*EJ*, 93) [even ideas do not always keep the name of their father; many appear to be orphans, born of nothing and begotten by no one; HC, 92]. This statement also invokes the age-old topos of paternity and authorship— and indeed the undecidability of Aires's or the narrator's responsibility also posits a narrative "problem of paternity."[51] The question of childlessness, of a genealogical deficiency, is a recurrent theme in Machado, which also resonates with the author's own biography (Machado and his wife Carolina did not have any children): we find it stressed at the end of *Brás Cubas*, and it is central in the tenuous plot of *Memorial de Aires* (1908).[52] The factual and existential sterility of the characters in *Esaú e Jacó* signifies the aborted genealogy of the nation, the lack of historical continuity and national coherence. Machado's novel engages in a parodic view of national formation, where the unit of the patriarchal family no longer serves as a metaphor for national unity and where ideological differences hide an essential exchangeability of ideas and show politics to be the realm of frivolous ambitions and vanities.

Set against the background of a period of national transition, Machado's novel not only addresses the ideas of historical and genealogical transition in terms of a crisis, but it questions the very notions of linear time and allegorical correspondence underwriting these processes of symbolic representation, thus formulating an ironic commentary on the genre of the historical novel and putting an effective end to the representational conventions of the nineteenth century according to which socially placed characters reflect a specific condition of the nation-state. As we have seen, the fact that the two brothers illustrate the collapse and contingency of political (and even psychological) identity may be seen as referring to this historically specific index. Yet as an (anti)historical novel *Esaú e Jacó* also problematizes and pushes to the limits the conventions of historical representation in fiction. Its mythical transfiguration of Brazilian reality, informed by a prerealist, moralistic style,[53] makes it a unique fable about fiction's ability to embody and transcend its own time.

CHAPTER EIGHT

The Last of the Line

Foretold Decline in the Twentieth-Century Estate Novel (José Lins do Rego)

If the family line has been traditionally seen as the homologous expression and correlate of linear time, twentieth-century narrative breaks with this linearity and thus stages a "revolt against the genealogical imperative."[1] In the modern novel, genealogical time is interiorized and fragmented, order is turned into, or confronted with, disorder. If this tendency toward genealogical discontinuity and crisis was already apparent in the nineteenth-century novel, the modernist novel also reflects the disintegration of linearity and temporal progression more radically at the level of its form, moving "from the homogeneous public time to the varieties of private time."[2] In what I would like to refer to as the modernist estate novel of the twentieth century, the narrative depiction of a dying world is shot through with the retrospective, individual consciousness of the narrator, who typically coincides with the position of a descendant or survivor of a lost world.

In the specific case of the estate novel, the text frames the genealogical motif as a story of foretold decadence, where the making present of the past attests to the future knowledge of the narrating voice. The estate novel may be understood as the modernist update to the regionalist or provincial novel, which, according to Mikhail Bakhtin, is concerned with the imminent destruction of what he calls the idyllic chronotope, a world determined by cyclicality, often featuring "a hero who has broken away from the wholeness of his locale."[3] Literary regionalism, as we have already seen with regard to Verga and Pardo Bazán, has always had a connection to the principles of naturalism and thus with the question of generational (dis)continuity and heredity. As Antonio Candido has argued, literary regionalism appears to be especially germane to, and justified by, economic underdevelopment, which explains the particular significance of the Americas in this regard, while in the European center it will only be "a secondary and generally provincial form alongside other, richer forms."[4] Of course, American regionalism is itself a re-elaboration of motifs that form an especially significant thread in the tradition of the English novel, from Gaskell and Eliot to Hardy and Law-rence. Therefore, I would maintain that underdevelopment is no more a cause for regionalism than the rapid change and economic development breaking into the closed lifeworld of rural communities. Both American and European region-alism, therefore, need to be understood as narratives coping with the dying out of long-established, transgenerational lifeworlds, locating them not only in space but in a specific time of transition. The estate novel of American regionalism is exemplified by the sort of plantation saga novel made famous by William Faulkner. Faulkner's novelistic model has been, via its French translations, an enormous, powerfully enabling influence in various peripheral spaces of world literature, not least in Latin America during the 1930s.[5] I will exemplify this phenomenon with a short novel by the Brazilian writer José Lins do Rego. Both his and Faulkner's work is dedicated to the literary exploration of a given geographical region (the American Deep South, the Brazilian Northeast) that appears under the sign of the crisis experienced by the members of the slaveholding ruling class, especially its repercussions on their descendants. In both cases, the rulers of the land are representatives of an aristocratic mentality, consolidated through the values of tradition and heredity, who vainly try to resist the onset of a new economic order that signifies the end of their power and the decline of the patri-archal family.[6] Furthermore, and beyond the question of literary influence, it is important to remember the broader confluence of literary tendencies that char-acterized the somewhat parallel epochs of the golden age of second-generation modernist fiction in Brazil (1930–45) and the so-called second Renaissance in American literature, both characterized by the combination of sociopolitical themes with innovations in narrative technique.[7]

Generally speaking, these twentieth-century novels can be said to take up and develop a theme that had been established as early as Maria Edgeworth's *Castle Rackrent* (1800): a social and historical transformation that leads to the demarcation of an old from a new order, reflected in the process of economic discontinuity and familial, generational decline. But while in Edgeworth a whole country, Ireland, had been designated as a cultural periphery, these modern texts are concerned with the historical characteristics of a region that can be seen as embodying some of the nation's deepest, most fundamental problems, even though it nominally lies at its geographical and cultural margins. In this sense, the region of the modernist novel is geographically in the periphery, but it is a key to understanding the country as a whole. The crisis of family and tra-ditional economies refers to a fundamental phenomenon of the early decades of the twentieth century: the process of accelerated modernization through which local communities increasingly felt the pressure of not only national but international developments.[8]

While nineteenth-century novels generally try to explain the historical genesis of the present or, at the end of the century, to interrogate the very ideas of historical change and "progress," modernist novels are historical to the extent that they refract the past through the medium of memory. This explains the stronger presence of a subjective or focalizing perspective of an individual consciousness—and hence, as the case may be, a greater proximity or solidarity between the author/narrator and the (single or collective) protagonist. In contrast to earlier ways of representing history in the novel, the modernist text is built on the dissociation between public and private history, between the objective/exterior and a subjective/interior configuration of time.[9] Consequently, these modern narratives are marked by a sense of nostalgia and irretrievable loss.

The Patriarchal Family in Brazil

While visiting Brazil William Faulkner came into contact with the work of the famous Brazilian socio-anthropologist Gilberto Freyre.[10] Freyre in turn has commented on the similarity between the specific regional economies in the American Deep South and the Brazilian Northeast, where the system of slavery was most deeply entrenched even after its official abolishment:

> . . . o chamado "deep South." Região onde o regime patriarcal de economia criou quase o mesmo tipo de aristocrata e de casa-grande, quase o mesmo tipo de escravo e de senzala que no norte do Brasil [. . .]. As mesmas influências de técnica de produção e de trabalho—a monocultura e a escravidão—uniram-se [. . .] para produzir resultados sociais semelhantes aos que se verificam entre nós.[11]

> [The so-called "deep South," a region where a patriarchal economy created almost the same type of aristocrat and Big House, almost the same type of slave and of slave quarters, as in the north of Brazil [. . .]. The same influences deriving from the technique of production and of labor—that is to say, the one-crop system and slavery—have combined here [. . .] to produce social results similar to those that are to be observed in our country.][12]

In February 1926 Freyre convened the First Northeastern Regionalist Conference in Recife (Primeiro Congresso Regionalista do Nordeste), where the famous *Manifesto regionalista* was issued (it was published, however, only in 1952).[13] In this text, Freyre insisted on the symbolic significance of the Brazilian Northeast, arguing that the emphasis on regionalist consciousness had nothing to do with provincial or separatist tendencies but rather was a key strategy in bolstering a genuinely national consciousness. The regionalist movement advocated in this manifesto is explicitly seen as a work of recuperation and preservation, for the cultural values of the Northeast are threatened by extinction. Freyre himself characterized the movement of regionalism as a sort of modernist traditionalism. With regard to the aspect of literature, it is noteworthy that in the manifesto Freyre insists on the potentially global dimension and positive value of regionalist literature, even if he does not specify what precisely makes a literary text regional.[14] Freyre's view of the old, patriarchal plantation estates is distinguished by a somewhat nostalgic conservatism, despite his acknowledgment of an incipient modernity. The ambivalence of Freyre's view consists in the fact that he appears to want to preserve the spirit of the old patriarchal ideology, even as he is severely critical of the plantation-based, slaveholding, and monocultural economic practice on which the *engenhos* depended. As Alfredo Cesar Melo puts it in a recent article commenting on the "dynamic" and "modern" nature of Freyre's conservatism, "Gilberto Freyre could take on airs like the prince of Salina, the character from Lampedusa's *Gattopardo*, in order to say that everything had to change in order that everything would remain the same."[15] In his masterwork, *Casa Grande & Senzala* (*The Masters and the Slaves*, 1933) Freyre singles out the system of the patriarchal family as the most important center of economic activity since colonial times and insists on its function as a privileged, representative site of national memory:

> A história social da casa-grande é a história íntima de quase todo brasileiro: da sua vida doméstica, conjugal, sob o patriarcalismo escravorata e polígamo; da sua vida de menino; do seu cristianismo reduzido à religião de família e influenciado pelas crendices da senzala. O estudo da história íntima de um povo tem alguma coisa de introspecção proustiana.[16]

> [The social history of the Big House is the intimate history of practically every Brazilian: the history of his domestic and conjugal life under a slaveholding and polygamous patriarchal regime; the history of his Christianity, reduced to the form of a family religion and influenced by the superstitions of the slave hut. The study of the intimate history of a people has in it something of Proustian introspection.[17]

For Freyre, the study of the "domestic life of our ancestors" exerts a strong influence on the formation of the national character until the present, for it is an "expression of social continuity." In his discussion of the possible sources for such a scholarly enterprise, Freyre explicitly mentions the usefulness of autobiographical texts and novels.[18] Accordingly, Lins do Rego's autobiographical novel, *Menino de engenho* (*Plantation Boy*, 1932), is included in his general bibliography and quoted from at least three times. Indeed, Freyre's conjunction of the critical analysis of society with a subjective stance of nostalgia, modernism, and conservatism, also appears in the work of Lins do Rego. When Lins do Rego (1901–57) first met Freyre in 1923 (after the latter returned from the United States), he was profoundly impressed and remembered it as an incisive day for the development of his literary career and the beginning of a lifelong friendship. It is not surprising, then, that both the writer and the anthropologist from Pernambuco have frequently been accused of class bias, which would mar the objectivity of their analysis of the fate of an oligarchy to which they themselves belonged by birth.

Freyre's study *Casa-grande & senzala* was profoundly influential not only for Lins do Rego but for a whole generation of Brazilian intellectuals, and it has become a canonical example for the Brazilian national essay. The various activities Freyre initiated led to a cultural and sociological appreciation of the Northeast, not least through the medium of the novel, which would subsequently become constitutive of a discourse of *national* identity, insofar as the world of the Northeastern mansions is seen as expressing fundamental truths about the Brazilian family and hence about the connection between national character and racial identity.[19] As Freyre puts it, "It is in the Big House where, down to this day, the Brazilian character has found its best expression."[20]

Lins do Rego's first novel might be taken as representative not only of his own literary oeuvre but of the symptomatic topos of the decadence of the grand landed estate, or "Big House," in the Brazilian fiction of this period.[21] As Roberto Ventura has shown, this issue, emblematic of the crisis of traditional values, was of a lasting concern to the circle of reformist intellectuals associated with the School of Recife (Escola do Recife) within the Faculty of Law of the local university. Members of this illustrious generation of statesmen and intellectuals, including Tobias Barreto, Joaquim Nabuco, and Sílvio Romero, all descendants of a class that has undergone social impoverishment, spoke in their autobiographies about their nostalgic and idealizing relation to the former world of the slaveholding mansions, whose fall they perceived as a sort of expulsion from Paradise and rupture with the world of childhood. Like Lins do Rego, they were all "plantation boys," sons or nephews of *senhores*, in search of careers that might compensate for their loss of social status.[22] In fact, in Lins do Rego's work the semiautobiographical dimension is especially important: it is clear that the novels depend to some degree on a fictionalization of the author's own childhood

memories of growing up on a sugar plantation in Paraíba. While the short novel
Menino de engenho constitutes the first part of the Sugar cane cycle, the Ciclo
da cana-de-açucar (a total of five novels), his tenth novel, *Fogo morto* (Dead fire,
1943), written in a period already beyond the second phase of modernism and
commonly regarded as his most accomplished work, might be regarded as a kind
of postscript to it.[23] Lins do Rego's work as a whole is concerned with the decline
of the rural *aristocracia canaviera*, the patriarchal landholding class of the sugar
economy in the Northeast at the beginning of the twentieth century. Their social decline is directly related to a process of economic transformation and modernization, where the old mercantile and manual economy was replaced by the
emergence of capital-based industry in the form of the sugar refinery (*usina*). In
literary terms, Lins do Rego's novels mold a realm of psychological interiority
that serves as the echo chamber for the remembrance of things past. This mixture of nostalgic evocation (reinforced by the iterative structure of the novelistic
cycle) and the contemplation of inevitable decline is not peculiar to Lins do
Rego, but as Mikhail Bakhtin reminds us, the destruction of the idyllic chronotope has been a fundamental theme of the novel since the nineteenth century:
"The idyllic aspect is the decisive one in the novel of generations (Thackeray, Frey-
tag, Galsworthy, Thomas Mann). But more often than not, the dominant theme
in such novels is the destruction of the idyll, and of the idyllic-type family or
patriarchal relationships."[24] Again, what seems characteristic of the twentieth
century is not the fact of destruction per se but rather the representation of this
fact through the retrospective memory of an individual consciousness.

Plantation Boy: Time, Memory, Narration

Menino de engenho follows the childhood memories of the narrator, Carlos de
Melo, who relates his search for a lost time in the first person, so that the narrated subject becomes the figure of the child Carlinhos, whose life is depicted
from his fourth to his twelfth year. As a matter of fact, we learn that his name is
Carlinhos only toward the end of the novel (*ME*, 126).[25] Insofar as the novel often speaks generically about its protagonist as the "boy," the representative nature of the para-autobiographical account is enhanced: the narrating subject is
speaking not just for himself but for an entire generation.

The narrative of *Menino de engenho* is not so much characterized by a consecutive emplotment of events, but rather it is made up of a series of relatively
self-contained tableaux, centered on the evocation of single events, persons, or
themes (the river Paraíba, religion, travels, visits, etc.) The narrative voice speaks
predominantly in the time of duration, in the imperfect tense, by inserting into

the general mode of existing certain nonsequential temporal marks, such as "one day," "some days," "sometimes," "during holidays," "one time," and so forth (*ME*, 68; 71). Characteristically, the last sentence of an individual section does not provide a transition to what follows but rather a sense of closure, as it often is a kind of general statement or observation. For instance, section 17, concerned with the topic of religion, ends like this: "era assim a religião do engenho onde me criei" (*ME*, 71) [this was what religion was like in the mansion where I grew up]. The structure of the novel, then, evokes a sense of permanence and belonging, of a self-enclosed time.

The chronological time frame underlying this first part of a Brazilian bildungsroman is only lightly suggested by the two train rides that mark the boy's entry into and the exit from the circumscribed world of the sugar plantation. The first train is taking him to the "new world" of the *engenho* [mundo novo; *ME*, 37], the second marks his entry into college and hence the beginning of a new life ("uma outra vida ia começar para mim," *ME*, 146 [a new life was beginning for me]; "vida nova," 147). Even before he has set foot there, his mother's narrations have already predetermined his affective relation to the "new world" of the estate, associated with images of paradise and fairy tales: "Que me acostumei a imaginar o engenho como qualquer coisa de um conto de fadas, de um reino fabuloso [. . .]. Minha imaginação vivia assim a criar esse mundo maravilhoso que eu não conhecia" (*ME*, 38, 41). [I accustomed myself to imagine the estate like something out of a fairy tale, of a fable-like kingdom (. . .). My imagination thus lived in creating this marvelous world that I did not know.] In other words, both before and after his stay, the world of the plantation is present only insofar as it is nostalgically evoked in memory. The association of the *engenho* with the idea of wonder and fable is underscored during the scene in which the boy fondly remembers the itinerant storyteller, the old woman Totonha, whose fairy tales in turn are permeated by the "local color" [a cor local] of the Northeastern plantations: "quando ela queria pintar um reino era como se estivesse falando dum engenho fabuloso" (*ME*, 80) [when she wished to represent a kingdom it was as if she was talking of a fable-like estate]. This scene might be read as a sort of metaliterary allusion to the narrator's own affiliation with a style of oral communication, and he thus presents himself as another storyteller seeking to impersonate a variety of personages ("falar em nome de todos os personagens," *ME*, 79) [to talk in the name of all the characters]. Also in section 9, when the boy is taught reading by his aunt Maria, his resistance to the written language is countered with the "liberty" of oral story-telling (*ME*, 47).[26]

The nostalgic voice of the narrator corresponds to the implied decadence of the social order embodied by the *engenho* of Santa Rosa that can only be resurrected through memory. Given the title of the novel, *Menino de engenho*, the boy is ostensibly part and product of the world of the plantation, which is in turn an allegory for the boy's childhood. What is most remarkable, however, is not only that the coextensive structure of plantation and family presents an image of wholeness and continuity but that it is fractured by internal rifts that give the lie to the idea of organic wholeness, which the novel otherwise aims at through its constant use of metonymical imagery. The boy's original loss of family, his position as an orphan, conditions the narrator's subsequent attempts to create a world of origin and belonging, even as he cannot conceal that he has only been fostered and adopted there. This peculiar situation is also important because it allows for a sense of unbridgeable distance. While the narrator is (or was) ostensibly a part of the world he narrates, his stance of observation is fundamentally distinguished by the experience of loss.

Carlinhos's childhood is initially marked by the terrible trauma of his mother's murder by his pathologically jealous father, which occurred when the boy was four, as is announced by the first sentence of the novel: "Eu tinha uns quatro anos no dia em que minha mãe morreu" (*ME*, 33) [I was about four years old on the day when my mother died]. This terrible event, even as it is recalled now in the present of narration, is primarily recalled as an event that was *represented* to the boy: when the boy woke up from his morning nap, bystanders were looking at the bloodstained body of his mother as if at a "painting" or "spectacle" (*ME*, 33); soon the newspapers reproduce the "portraits" [retratos; *ME*, 34] of his parents, and the events are transformed and distanced as if they were not of immediate concern to the boy: "pareciam-me tão longe, já, os fatos da manhã, que aquela narrativa me interessava como se não fossem os meus pais os protagonistas" (*ME*, 34) [the events of the morning already seemed to me so distant, so that the story aroused my interest as if the protagonists were not my own parents]. Only when he goes to sleep again at the end of the day does he realize the meaning of the events and truly experience the loss of his mother. This early scene already suggests something about the ambivalent relationship between immediate experience and later representation. The same is true for Carlinhos' image of his father, on the subject of which the narrator contrasts the naivety of childhood with his later knowledge:

> Eu o amava porque o que eu queria fazer, ele consentia, e brincava comigo no chão como um menino de minha idade. *Depois* é que vim a saber muita coisa a

seu respeito: que era um temperamento excitado, um nervoso, para quem a vida
só tivera o seu lado amargo. (*ME*, 35; italics mine)

[I loved him because he consented to whatever I liked to do; he played with me on
the floor like a child of my own age. It was *later* that I came to know many things
with regard to him: that he had an excitable, nervous character, for whom life had
only its bitter side.]

If the narrator claims that his memory withstands the destructions of time ("a
minha memória ainda guarda detalhes bem vivos que o tempo não conseguiu
destruir," *ME* 36) [my memory still keeps very vivid details which time did not
manage to destroy], he also asserts that this memorial image—in this case, of
his mother—is the result of a later reconstructive effort that seeks to prolong
existence into the present: "horas inteiras eu fico a pintar o retrato dessa mãe an-
gélica, com as cores que tiro da imaginação, e vejo-a assim, ainda tomando conta
de mim, dando-me banhos e me vestindo" (*ME*, 36) [entire hours I was painting
the portrait of this angelic mother with the colors of my imagination, and I see
her like this, still taking care of me, bathing and dressing me]. Both in the case
of his dead mother and his deranged father, the boy registers the fact of loss
only to then circle back to the present tense ("o vejo" / "vejo-a," *ME*, 35/36) [I see / I
see her]. What I want to suggest is that this opening scene about the violent
death of his mother tells us something about the general representational procedure of the novel, namely its paradoxical tendency to create an image (a "portrait")
of an eternal present that is at the same time knowledgeable and innocent of the
fact of its later loss.

Lins do Rego's "complicit" narrator tends to identify with the system of patriarchy. For instance, he assumes no distance from the authoritative position embodied by the grandfather, who conceives of his land possessions in organic, absolutist terms; he portrays José Paulino as an old, benevolent "feudal lord" whose
dependents, "more than four thousand souls," are said to hardly resent their condition of servitude (*ME*, 103–4). The master is represented throughout as an in-
trinsically sympathetic human person, who unlike other lords refuses to protect
criminality (*ME*, 93) and who is generally presented as a benign exception to the
rule of the "true" lord as a figure of authoritative power (*ME*, 100). However, even
as the adult narrator seeks to capture the affective link with the world of his
childhood and his grandfather, there are a few passages where we clearly feel the
increased consciousness of the adult narrator, who is now able to evaluate his
past—although he represses explicit judgment in favor of memorial reconstruction. It is characteristic of this early work that the subordinated social classes

come into view only through a perspective of the narrator's voice that adopts the position of the dominating class (*ME*, 29, 104). However, the posterior perspective of the narrative first person cannot but dissociate itself from this "innocent" view of the cruelties of the social order. Hence, the double perspective of a self that is split into protagonist and narrator produces the characteristic coexistence of nostalgia and social conscience—reminiscent of the similar ambivalence articulated by Gilberto Freyre.

The universe of the plantation is repeatedly presented as the embodiment of an organic wholeness and continuity, as when the boy is enchanted by the mechanics of the sugar refinery on the side of the mansion, an image that becomes itself an allegory of continuity and slowness, of movement-as-repetition: "quando vieram me chamar para o almoço, ainda me encontraram encantado diante da roda preguiçosa, que mal se arrastava, e as duas bolas alvoroçadas, que não queriam parar" (*ME*, 43) [when they came to call me for breakfast, they still found me enchanted in front of the leisurely wheel, moving ever so slowly, and the two restless balls that did not want to stop]. The boy's fascination in front of the machinery, his unwillingness to detach himself, becomes expressive of his resistance to leave a dream world of "liberty" for the responsibilities of adulthood. Characteristically, this time of duration is related in the imperfect tense, and often the boy's idleness is the mirror image of the sound of unceasing work, in the contemplation of which the boy is immersed.

While the succession of self-contained narrative units follows an implied chronological order, from the beginning the reader understands that the "child's" first-person narrative is shot through with the retrospective consciousness and acquired knowledge of an older self, so that the immediate and interior perspective is complemented by a more distancing view, thus creating a continuous movement between a former and a later self. Numerous other examples might be cited where the adverb *depois* (later) similarly points to a time that lies in a future beyond the narrated events (*ME*, 35, 47, 77, 78) or where an explicit appeal to the faculty of memory or the time of the present ("ainda hoje") [still today] similarly alludes to the time that has elapsed since the events have occurred (*ME*, 36, 46, 63, 69) but also preserves these events and images in an eternal present: "I see it still," "I see them still." The final section of the novel harps on the boy's premature ageing ("era adiantado nos anos," *ME*, 149) [I was advanced in years], the mismatch between his ignorance and his knowledge, between body and soul, bodily development and sexual experience. This is to say that the peculiar mood of nostalgia pervading the novel derives not only from the juxtaposition of two different temporal situations of the autobiographical self (then/now) but also from the sense that the loss of childhood has already occurred during the time that now is remembered. The present of narration wants to reclaim what has been lost, yet the time of the past is not so much an original paradise as the attempt to cover up a series of losses through stories and imagination.

The deepest tension of this narrative derives from the remembering voice enveloping the reader in a vision of a time-suspended present, the eternal moment of childhood, while simultaneously the perspective of the author betrays an awareness of the passing of time. Although the mode of subjectivist, pseudo-autobiographical memory and narrative immediacy in *Menino de engenho* effectively contains and diminishes references to a larger perspective, Lins do Rego's later novel *Fogo morto* (1943) develops the same setting and motifs into a full-fledged estate novel that presents such a microcosm as the symbol for an entire world and society on the wane. While the earlier novel evokes the past through the subsequent knowledge of loss, the later novel puts more emphasis on the manifest signs of decline in a historical present as well as the "objective" and long-term reasons for this decline.

Broadly speaking, Lins do Rego's novels about regional and social decadence are clearly tied to a specific generational experience. In accordance with the work of Freyre, they portray the decline of the patriarchal, slaveholding society through the mythic image of the extended family structure, thus proposing a national allegory built on notions of confraternity, racial plasticity, and conciliation. Paradoxically, the disintegration of a regional system of hierarchical power relations is thus proposed through individual nostalgic re-evocation or sociological reconstruction, respectively, as a metaphor for the self-understanding of the nation as a whole.

CHAPTER NINE

Death of a Prince, Birth of a Nation

Time, Place, and Modernity in a Sicilian Historical Novel (G. Tomasi di Lampedusa)

If the novel by Lins do Rego juxtaposes the desire for continuity to a consciousness and an anatomy of decline, a similar conjunction can be observed in Lampedusa's *Il Gattopardo* (1957). In this novel, every image that expresses a desire for
continuity is shot through with a consciousness of decline or the end. In this
sense, *Il Gattopardo* exemplifies the modern novel's characteristic concern with
time and history. In the words of Marthe Robert, the novel "is an art that deals
with the past yet is intent on a present it would overcome; time is the element in
which it bathes, its essence, or at least what it claims to borrow and to repay in
order that its images may come alive."[1] As the last representative of an aristocratic dynasty, Prince Fabrizio is both desirous of everlasting continuity and simultaneously aware of the imminence and inevitability of change. This paradoxical relation between historicity and making-present is reflected in a narrative
perspective that combines subjective, immediate perception with an external,
distant point of observation.

In contrast to Lins do Rego's work, Lampedusa's novel concentrates its picture of aristocratic decline entirely on the last phase of decadence. Obviously, the
novel is concerned with a very different socioeconomic, not to mention historico-
political, situation, yet both texts center on the incorporation of a geographical
and social world traversed by the forces of modernity. Despite the differences
from the Brazilian novel, *Il Gattopardo* similarly depicts the individual consciousness of the "last of the line." At the same time, *Il Gattopardo*'s most salient
difference appears to be that it is more explicitly presented as a historical novel,
since the temporal distance from the presence of the author is certainly much
greater. Giuseppe Tomasi di Lampedusa (1869–1957) looks back to the time of his
great-grandfather, representative of an aristocratic dynasty with connections at
least far back as the sixteenth century. The distance is greater, the narrator is
seemingly omniscient, but even here the author himself is still connected to the

fictional universe through an intergenerational bond. On the surface, *Il Gattopardo* might appear to be a perfectly classical instance of a historical, as well as a genealogical, novel. Yet, behind its deceptively conservative surface, we may detect a deeply modernist concern with the problematization of representing history and linear time.[2]

In novels of the early twentieth century, genealogy becomes a matter of individual memory and hence of materialized, self-contained images of the past. From Thomas Mann's *Buddenbrooks* (1901) and D. H. Lawrence's *The Rainbow* (1915) to Gabriel García Marquez's *Cien años de soledad* (1967), the novel typically reflects genealogical extension in a long arc of narrated time, corresponding to the succession of several generations.[3] In marked contrast to these works, *Il Gattopardo* focuses its narrative upon a few, sometimes almost autonomous, tableaux that reflect the conflict between stasis and change. Instead of a choral and polyphonic picture, as is typical, say, of Faulkner's novels, we find here a nearly exclusive focus on the consciousness of a single protagonist or reflector figure. The genealogical imperative is rooted here in an individual, subjective perspective, at least to a significant degree. This compression of the genealogical motif, along with the simultaneous distancing of the subjective perspective, accounts for the singular elegance of this novel. Accordingly, we are encouraged to read the novel in a paradigmatic (rather than plot-oriented) way, since it is distinguished by the recurrence of symbols, metaphors, and isotopic images.

In striking contrast to the pseudoautobiographical *Menino de engenho*, here the protagonist and remembering subject is not a child but an old man. This also constitutes a significant variation from the Italian historical novel of the nineteenth century, such as Ippolito Nievo's *Confessioni di un italiano* (1867) or Giovanni Rovani's *Cento anni* (1863), where the public history of the Risorgimento is experienced by a *young* protagonist, as refracted by the memory of an old narrator. Lampedusa's protagonist never remembers events of his youth but rather significant events of his adult life, as well as the historical past of his own class. The different generational perspective of *Il Gattopardo*, then, amounts to a different way of recounting the history of the Risorgimento, and it reverses the European novel's traditional focus on the young hero desirous of countering the norms of society.[4] Even more significant for the novel is the implied contrast with the young protagonist of Stendhal's *La chartreuse de Parme* (1839), whose enthusiasm for Napoleon and political liberation descending from the North, just like Carlino's at the beginning of Nievo's *Confessioni*, sharply contrasts with the historical skepticism of the old prince.[5]

Furthermore, in Lampedusa's case the voice of narration is more clearly removed from the narrated world, and the narrator is by no means identical with
the protagonist, even though the early reception of the novel was often marred
by just such a confusion.[6] The prince and his consciousness provide the principal focus for the greatest part of the novel, although there are significant exceptions to this rule, namely the entire fifth part, the "cyclone of love" centering on
Angelica and Tancredi, as well as the eighth part, subsequent to the death of the
prince. By way of this generally subjective perspective, the novel also departs
from previous Sicilian novels concerned with the decline of the aristocracy,
Verga's *Mastro-don Gesualdo* (1889) and De Roberto's *I Viceré*, or Pirandello's *I
vecchi e i giovani* (1909). Lampedusa himself has insisted on the decisive difference of his own novel, the quintessentially internal perspective: "il punto di
vista è del tutto differente: *il Gattopardo* è l'aristocrazia vista dal di dentro
senza compiacimenti ma anche senza le intenzioni libellistiche di De Roberto"[7] [the point of view is entirely different: *Il Gattopardo* is the aristocracy
seen from the inside, without false idealizations, but also without the polemical intentions of De Roberto]. The implications of this subjective perspective
unfold against the implied objective background, involving, first, the representation of time and history; second, the ideological function of the space of the
periphery; and, third, the connection between aristocratic decline and the
problem of social change.

Time and History

The novel narrates a total of eight isolated episodes in the lives of a Sicilian family against the background of an official history that is not actually represented
but is implied to have already occurred. In the first part, it is the landing of
Garibaldi in Sicily; in the third, the plebiscite about Sicily becoming part of the
nation; in the sixth, Garibaldi's capture in Aspromonte; in the eighth, the fiftieth
anniversary of the unification.[8] In this way, the overall historical horizon of the
novel covers a period of fifty years (from 1860 until 1910), but the individual
parts focus on discrete moments of time, not covering more than a single day
(with the exception of the fourth part). The individual parts of the novel thus
constitute quasi-autonomous narrative units, rather than strictly sequential
chapters. While the first six parts are relatively contiguous in time, the two centering on the death of the prince and the symbolic end of his world have the
character of epilogues that are temporally distant from the main narrative, as well
as from each other. In contrast to the traditional historical novel, Lampedusa
uncouples individual experience from the movement of history.

Already the title of the novel, *Il Gattopardo*, puts the focus on the name of a heraldic entity, referring to a single person (in contrast, say, to a bourgeois family novel like the *Buddenbrooks*) and thus indicates the novel's concentration on a single protagonist. The first words of the novel, the words of the rosary ("Nunc et in hora mortis nostrae. Amen." *G*, 23), introduce, now in the first person plural ("nostrae"), the theme of an aristocratic consciousness that is contemplating its own death. Since the same chapter, after the course of twenty-four hours, also ends with words from the same prayer, there emerges an idea of a cyclical time, the time of ritual iteration, a gesture of self-affirmation in the face of death. The first part, then, introduces the reader to a principle of symmetric structures, temporal stasis, and reappearing motives.[9] On the level of both form and content, the novel contrasts the idea of the progression of time (and of history) with the notion of an arrested, halted, and "frozen" time, and thus it may be seen as an example of what Joseph Frank has coined the "spatialization" of time in the modernist novel.[10]

The framing scene of the rosary not only announces the novel's central motif of death; it also creates a picture of the everyday and of traditional, ritual continuity, which is interrupted by the sudden arrival of a letter by Don Fabrizio's brother-in-law Malvica, which reports on the invasion of Garibaldi and his Thousand at Marsala in Sicily (May 11, 1860), an event intended "to redeem Sicilians from centuries of ill-treatment."[11] The arrival of the letter represents literally and symbolically the invasion of history into a world whose privacy and traditionalism mark it as firmly circumscribed in time and place. If the room of the rosary is decorated with mythological images of the Greek gods who bear the blazon of the Salina family, at the end of the day (and the chapter) the figure of Vulcan on the ceiling all of a sudden takes on historical rather than mythological connotations: "notò come il Vulcano del soffitto rassomigliasse un po' alle litografie di Garibaldi che aveva visto a Torino" (*G*, 55) [he (. . .) noticed how the Vulcan on the ceiling was rather like the lithographs of Garibaldi he had seen in Turin; *L*, 61]. The end of the chapter describes a cyclical movement, yet it also intimates that change is in the offing: a historical figure replaces a mythological continuity; upheaval threatens the tranquility of the "Palermitan Olympus"; what appeared to be an image of stability is subjected to change. As is confirmed by the arrival of another letter, this time by Tancredi, letters function in the novel as a sign for what the novel itself calls "the acceleration of history":

La prima lettura di questo straordinario brano di prosa diede un po' di capogiro a Don Fabrizio. Egli notò di nuovo la stupefacente accelerazione della storia: per

esprimersi in termini moderni diremo che egli venne a trovarsi nello stato
d'animo di una persona che credendo, oggi, di essere salito a bordo di uno degli
aerei pacioccioni che fanno il cabotaggio fra Palermo e Napoli si scorge invece di
trovarsi rinchiuso in un apparecchio supersonico e comprenda che sarà alla meta
prima di aver avuto il tempo di farsi il segno della croce. (*G*, 98–99)

[A first reading of this extraordinary composition made Don Fabrizio's head spin:
once again he noted the astounding acceleration of history; put in modern terms,
he could be said to be in the state of mind of someone today who thinks he has
boarded one of the old planes which potter between Palermo and Naples, and suddenly finds himself shut inside a super Jet and realizes he will be at his destina-
tion almost before there will be time to make the sign of the Cross. *L*, 119]

As becomes clear from this passage, Lampedusa uses the explicit reference to
the experience of accelerated time to insist on the difference between the character of Don Fabrizio and the persona of the implied narrator. Furthermore, it is
precisely this indirect appearance of Garibaldi (in the form of a letter) that establishes the novel's strong link to the form of the historical novel in the tradition of Scott, where the great historical events and figures almost never appear
in a direct way. In *Il Gattopardo*, Garibaldi is frequently mentioned and discussed, but he is never directly shown. The historical King Ferdinand and the
plebiscite are evoked only in Don Fabrizio's memories. Another historical event,
the festivities of the fifty-year jubilee of unification, is the topic of gossip between Angelica and Concetta (part 8). Yet if this indirect mode of representing
historical events is a legacy of the classical historical novel, *Il Gattopardo*
goes as far as to rarely present any actions, even fictional ones, directly (say, Angelica and Tancredi's courtship), but everything is presented to the reader, in
intense visual scenes, through recollections, memories, observations, reports,
and conversations.

In fact, the narrator makes explicit the fundamental difference between the
represented time and the time of representation. If, according to Auerbach, the
classical realist novel depicts the present-as-history,[12] *Il Gattopardo* depicts
history-as-present: in particular, the consciousness of the prince is depicted
with distinctively modernist means of representation. Such a modernist form
of realism allows readers an emotional and intellectual identification with the
prince that belies their considerable alterity in terms of social status and historical time.[13]

Moreover, in numerous passages the narrator interrupts the self-contained
world of historicist fiction with glaring references to a later, anachronistic time,

a time that clearly lies outside the possible horizon of the characters of the novel. These striking instances of extradiegetic prolepsis (to adopt Gérard Genette's term) have an important function with regard to the generic conventions of the historical novel. In fact, Scott had already used various signals that helped to distance the represented historical world and simultaneously to break the illusion of historical immersion by making explicit references to the historical present of the contemporary reader. Yet Lampedusa's novel increases the shock effect of the narrator's interventions to such a degree that the reader is not only made fully and unmistakably aware of the historical distance between the past and the present, the pastness of the past, but is made to understand that the experiential world of the narrator, and consequently his means of literary communication, are shaped by the events of a technological, cultural, epistemological, and linguistic modernity. In other words, the narrator is unmistakably a part of a post-nineteenth-century world. In some cases, the narrator has recourse to clearly anachronistic images and references, like an airplane, the word "snob," or the names Freud and Eisenstein (G, 99, 108, 112, 132). In other cases the proleptic commentary is more explicitly conceived as a commentary on the passing of historical time:

> Dall'ultima visita erano passati soltanto cinque giorni, per esser precisi, ma l'intimità fra le due cugine (intimità simile per vicinanza e per sentimenti a quella che pochissimi anni dopo avrebbe stretto italiani ed austriaci nelle contigue trincee), l'intimità era tale che cinque giorni potevano veramente sembrar molti. (G, 238)

> [In fact, only five days had gone by since her last visit, but the intimacy between the two cousins, an intimacy similar in closeness and feeling to that which was to bind Italians and Austrians in their opposing trenches a few years later, was such that five days really could seem a long time. L, 307]

As becomes clear from this example, the narrative anticipation of the future has yet another function: to corroborate and confront the historical skepticism and political stoicism of the prince with the historical hindsight of the narrator/author who is two generations younger. Aside from such references to a time frame outside the limits of the fictional narrative, there are also a number of proleptic allusions internal to the world of the novel. Both kinds of anticipations serve to create a narrative where different levels of time interpenetrate and are thus potentially copresent, creating a symbolic fusion between narrated time and the time of narration.[14] The rendering of events on the level of chronological, linear time is constantly shot through with a consciousness of the end, or *kairos*.[15]

The fragmentation of the narrative into almost autonomous, discrete units and the withdrawal into the interior consciousness of the prince move the novel's representation of time in the direction of an essential immobility and slowing down that belies the nominally historical framework—even if the author had abandoned his earlier plans to depict in this novel "twenty-four hours in the lives of his great-grandfather" (namely the day of Garibaldi's landing, now the focus only of the first part), similar to what Joyce had done in *Ulysses*.[16] Eventually, Lampedusa arrived instead at a tripartite structure: The first six chapters (or parts) are set in a relatively short span of time, from 1860 to 1862; in other words, they zoom in on the historical moment of the Risorgimento. Part 7 is set in 1883, while the eighth and last part moves forward to the year 1910. This procedure obviously has the effect of bringing the narrated events relatively close to the personal memory of the author and hence also to that of the contemporary reader. The net effect of the temporal dates affixed to the individual chapters is not to create the semblance of a continuum but rather to stress the isolation and relative autonomy of certain temporal moments. After all, with the exception of the fourth part, all the other parts of the novel respect the twenty-four hours of the Aristotelian concept of the unity of time.[17] If Lampedusa was interested in representing how a public-historical event was felt as a moment of crisis in the life of a private individual, it is significant that this moment of crisis or transition is not located in a particular time of the narrative, in the sense of before/after, but rather permeates all parts of the novel to the same degree.[18]

Insofar as the novel makes use of techniques of temporal compression and compartmentalization and as it self-consciously reflects on the nature of human existence in time, it resonates with similar techniques Lampedusa especially admired in the high modernist prose of Virginia Woolf and even, to some degree, in Stendhal, one of his most cherished writers of all time.[19] In his "Lectures on English literature," Lampedusa briefly dwells on Woolf's novel *The Years* (1937), which suggests certain parallels with *Il Gattopardo*, for as a transgenerational novel it is concerned, according to Lampedusa, with "detached episodes of four moments in the life of a family, from 1880 until today," with the "mutable identity of the generations."[20] There are also numerous scenes reminiscent of a Proustian form of remembrance, flashbacks that occur within the prince's psyche. Thus, in the first chapter it is the olfactory sensations of the garden that triggers for him the memory of the "nausea" and "sweetish odors" (*L*, 21; *G*, 27) caused by the dead soldier of the King's army, an event that had occurred in the previous month, and the name of the king triggers in turn memories of his past conversations with the Bourbon monarch.

These typically modernist techniques of questioning and playing with the orderliness of temporal sequence have to be related to the novel's explicit, ideological thematization of the possibility of historical change, the idea that "history" is only a surface manifestation.[21] In fact, the novel's most well-known sentence is the motto first pronounced by Tancredi, then adopted by the prince: "se vogliamo che tutto rimanga come è, bisogna che tutto cambi" (*G*, 41) [if we want things to stay as they are, things will have to change; *L*, 40]. At an earlier moment Don Fabrizio had wondered whether the likely substitution of the moribund Bourbon monarchy by Victor Emmanuel II would actually bring about any significant change: "Non sarebbe stato lo stesso? Dialetto torinese invece che napoletano; e basta" (*G*, 31). [Wouldn't things be just the same? Just Torinese instead of Neapolitan dialect; that's all; *L*, 27.] While both the prince and Tancredi adopt the view that change is a mere surface phenomenon masking an underlying continuity, the prince's attitude is much more passive and observational; he continues to perform his role as a stern paterfamilias, as if nothing had, and nothing will, change. When in a conversation with his dependent Russo the subject of change is broached once more, it is significant that the imminent danger is figured both as oedipal revolt and social revolution: "Ho capito benissimo: voi non volete distruggere noi, i vostri 'padri'; volete soltanto prendere il nostro posto" (*G*, 46). [I understand now; you don't want to destroy us, who are your "fathers." You just want to take our places; *L*, 48.] Again, the prince reflects here on the paradoxical relation between a surface change and an underlying continuity, according to which the sense of revolution as radical social upheaval is assimilated to the earlier, astronomical sense of revolution as a recurrence of a body on a circular axis back to its former place.

Already with regard to the novel *Esaú e Jacó* we have addressed the problem that nominal (historical-political) change masks an underlying continuity. In adopting this idea, Lampedusa's novel self-consciously builds on the previous examples of the specifically Sicilian tradition of the naturalist and so-called parliamentary novel (De Roberto), concerned precisely with this problem of unchanging "Southernness."[22] Yet in contrast to his Sicilian predecessors and the novel by Machado de Assis, Lampedusa's historical skepticism also includes the possibility that things *do* change. Tancredi's motto refers to an "unconscious" truth—the persistence of power structures that survive the restructuring of the social and political system—and it might also imply the stoic self-deception of the prince. It is the narrator who understands earlier than the prince that the opposite might also be true, that signs of outward stability can be deceptive because a change has already occurred in less visible forms. Insofar as this narrator is not simply complicit with the nostalgic melancholia and mystifying perspective of the prince, he also reveals, as Robert Dombroski has noted, "the disjunction, the false consciousness, the illusion," through which the aristocratic consciousness is shown as a form of ideology and myth-making.[23] For instance, faced with the inevitable changes of history and the decline of his own position and class, the prince habitually escapes into the world of astronomy, the "stellar realms" (*L*, 44) [quei sereni regni stellari; *G*, 43] and the "sublime routine of the skies" (*L*, 54) [sublime normalità dei cieli; *G*, 50], which are explicitly associated with a spiritual rather than corporeal life ("questa vita dello spirito nei suoi momenti piú astratti, piú simili alla morte," *G*, 51) [this life of the spirit in its most sublimated moments, those moments that are most like death; *L*, 54].

For instance, during the hunting scene the timelessness of the landscape is ironically juxtaposed to the comment on the army of ants processing toward the saliva of Don Ciccio, Don Fabrizio's rustic hunting companion. The ants are described as enthusiastic "colonialists" who are marching toward a "buoyant future" (*L*, 125) [la marcia verso il sicuro avvenire; *G*, 103]. If the narrator muses about the ants' preoccupation with "the ancient glories and future prosperity" of a certain ant hill (*L*, 125) [la gloria secolare e la prosperità futura; *G*, 103], the reader is encouraged to think of the coming Fascist armies, which incidentally also establishes a certain parallel between the Risorgimento and Fascism that, aside from the ideological implications, works against the escapism not only of the prince but of the idea of the historical novel. The sense that the historical events are there yet "far away" (and only for the narrator, not for the prince), is undermined when the ants remind the prince, by "some association of ideas" (*L*, 125) [di alcune associazioni d'idee; *G*, 103] of the recent events of the plebiscite. Since this train of thoughts leads to an extended reflection about the manipulations of the plebiscite and his interrogation of Don Ciccio (who voted no emphatically because of his loyalty to Bourbon rule), it is clear that the whole idea to escape time and history has come to nothing.

This contrast between the desire for continuity and its factual disintegration, even on the level of the prince himself, is also at the center of the ball scene, situated in the city palace of the family Ponteleone. Not only are Angelica and Tancredi here "submerged into their transitory blindness" (*L*, 259) but the entire aristocracy is. When the "dance was nearing its end" (*L*, 271), the signs of exhaustion are only too apparent, and the allegorical-political significance of this self-contained scene is made even more explicit: "through the cracks in the shutters filtered a plebeian light of dawn" (L, 271). Again, the members of the aristocracy are oblivious to the fact that this is their "last dance." As in the scene with the ants, the factuality of historical change is articulated on a metaphorical, symbolical level outside the purview of the characters, thus creating a complicity between the narrator and the reader.

Furthermore, during this scene, the fact that the assembled aristocrats are oblivious to their own fate is allegorized by imagery of enclosure, suddenly made explicit by a striking prolepsis: "Nel soffitto gli Dei, reclini su scanni dorati, guardavano in giú sorridenti [. . .]. Si credevano eterni: una bomba fabbricata a Pittsburgh, Penn. doveva nel 1943 provar loro il contrario (G, 200). [From the ceiling the gods, reclining on gilded couches, gazed down smiling [. . .]. They thought themselves eternal; but a bomb manufactured in Pittsburgh, Pennsylvania, was to prove the contrary in 1943; L, 258.] With this comment, the narrator takes a spectacular distance from the represented world, otherwise rendered in all its realist detail and atmospheric lushness. Moreover, the narrator *also* parallels the movement of the protagonist, who similarly assumes a distance from the place in which he finds himself. For instance, Fabrizio's hallucinations transform the giggly young aristocratic ladies into a band of wild monkeys (G, 198). However, while Don Fabrizio takes his distance through stoic and melancholy withdrawal into his own consciousness, the narrator signifies his distance through historical hindsight and irony. Another example of this double procedure is the middle section of the book ("Cyclone of Love"), which is actually unique in that it moves the attention entirely away from the figure of the prince. During this scene, Tancredi and Angelica explore the hidden recesses of the palace at Donnafugata, a prolonged exploration and flirtation that is compared to a "voyage," a sojourn on an "ocean," an "island" (Cytherea), or a "New World" (L, 181–83; G, 145–46). The two young lovers are located in a world that is entirely removed from their surroundings, literally withdrawn to the secret and hidden spaces of the labyrinthine castle, which are associated both with the past and with a realm outside of time altogether. Significantly, in this case it is only the narrator who is aware, or makes the reader aware, that this is one of those moments of "real life," similar to those remembered later by the dying prince. The narrator's commentary heightens this significance, paradoxically, by his ironic hindsight (referring, for instance, to the couple's later infidelities).

Different as these scenes are, the novel shows here variously how moments of withdrawal, of enclosure, of memorial immersion, of forgetfulness, bracket, ignore, or resist the actual process of time. We might say that the novel contrasts subjective experience with the background of objective time. While through its formal, narrative techniques the novel tends to confirm the legitimacy and inescapability of subjective experience, the episodes as such demonstrate the "external" truth of actual historical change. This would mean that Tancredi's and Fabrizio's view of an essential permanence is "corrected" by the narrator's historical hindsight. Yet the dictum's paradoxical mixture of self-deception and truth also includes the possibility that historical change and modernization are indeed resisted—namely in the particular space of Sicily.

Place and Periphery

The novel's strong link to the place of Sicily has not escaped critical attention. As a matter of fact, *Il Gattopardo* has long and often been seen as, and criticized for, confirming certain clichés and stereotypes about the Mezzogiorno and the "typically Sicilian" tendency toward fatalism.[24] Recent work in Italian cultural studies has called attention to the ways both Italy and Sicily have been historically constructed as cultural others, and these studies may help us to contextualize the geographical rhetoric of the novel. For instance, Nelson Moe has drawn new attention to the ways Italian cultural differences have been perceived by both Italians and by outside observers, especially with regard to the Mezzogiorno but also with regard to Italy itself as "the South of Europe."[25] According to Moe, in the course of the eighteenth century, when Italy became increasingly marginalized in political terms, "North and South become charged moral categories."[26] Therefore, the differences between North and South have already informed the rhetorical formation of Romanticism and the Risorgimento and are thus also a part of the historical scene Lampedusa depicts.

As Roberto Dainotto has further detailed, Sicily has been read as a prototypical place for the South, a paradigmatic, orientalized periphery that is central to the definition and self-understanding of Europe.[27] If the rhetoric of national character goes back at least to Montesquieu and Madame de Staël, Dainotto rightfully emphasizes that it was only with Hegel that the notion of the South was assigned a role in what amounts to a spatially grounded dialectics of history, according to which the Spirit has left the South for the North of Europe. As Dainotto further points out, this exclusion of the South from the Northern-centered theater of world history "meant here the southern inability to cohere into a nation-state."[28] Building on such conceptions, the novel repeatedly characterizes the Sicilian landscape as a mythical one, one that is resistant to the influence of time, history, and the efforts of civilization. This is attributed, first, to the conditions of climate. Throughout the novel the sun, "the true ruler of Sicily" (*L*, 51) [l'autentico sovrano della Sicilia; *G*, 48] is named as one of the principal reasons for Sicily's ontological immobility and resistance to civilization. This rhetoric of the sun as the absolute monarch of the land subordinates politics and human rule as ephemeral and time bound to the eternal governance of climate. In other words, place in the novel is determined by a certain essence, such as climate, that locks the land into a premodern, irrational state, outside the contemporaneity of history.[29]

The interior, the periphery, of this peripheral region of Europe, reveals the true essence of the land, its utter impermeability by the century-long efforts to colonize and civilize it: "nel termine 'campagna' è implicito un senso di terra trasformata dal lavoro: la boscaglia invece, aggrappata alle pendici di un colle, si trovava nell'identico stato d'intrico aromatico nel quale la avevano trovata Fenici, Dori e Ioni quando sbarcarono in Sicilia, quest' America dell'antichità" (*G*, 101) [the term "countryside" implies soil transformed by labor; but the scrub clinging to the slopes was still in the very same state of scented tangle in which it had been found by Phoenicians, Dorians, and Ionians when they disembarked in Sicily, that America of antiquity; *L*, 122]. This description occurs, not coincidentally, in a scene where the prince is hunting with Don Ciccio, an activity earlier described as providing an escape for Don Fabrizio from everyday troubles. The barren landscape is a symbol for the "real Sicily" (*L*, 124) [l'aspetto vero della Sicilia; *G*, 102], shorn of the exterior trappings of culture, a land that is inimical to cultivation and colonization, to the human, to rationality, and that has "petrified" the flux of time (*G*, 102; *L*, 124).

The problem of the land's resistance to history is the explicit topic of the fourth part. This section directly reproduces a dialogue between Fabrizio and Chevalley, who has ventured to the island to recruit the prince as senator for the new kingdom of Italy. As a visitor from the North, the Piedmontese Chevalley is at the same time a representative and a missionary of the new project of an Italian state. The central significance of this ideological confrontation is emphasized by the fact that the dialogue occurs in "real time," which is to say, through a close, "scenic" approximation of narrated time and time of narration. The worldview of the prince, which the reader until now got to know through the detailed representation of his interior consciousness, is now directly confronted by an opponent, and hence it gets articulated in more explicit terms. In this way the two figures become the representatives and mouthpieces of two different worldviews and national characters, which correspond to the North and the South, respectively.[30] Chevalley's involuntary slip of the tongue, when he speaks of the "recent annexation" of Sicily [dopo la felice annessione; *G*, 159], condenses the historical situation of misunderstanding and disillusionment that emerged shortly after the plebiscite (October 1860), when power was handed over from Garibaldi to Count Cavour, the parliamentary leader in Turin. The disillusionment was mutual: the Northern administrators were surprised by the degree of cultural difference (language, clientelism, "ignorance," "filth") and disappointed with what they perceived as ingratitude or even hostility on the part of the Sicilians; the Sicilians themselves resented the wholesale imposition of Piedmontese institutions as a betrayal of their hopes for regional self-government. As the historian Lucy Riall has put it, referring to Garibaldi's successful invasion of the island, "The South played a vital role in the unification of Italy. [. . .] Yet ironically, in the years after unification, the South came to be seen as an obstacle to Italian unity. [. . .] After 1860, what came to be seen as the 'barbarous' conditions prevailing in the South were increasingly juxtaposed to the values and interests underpinning Italian national unity."[31]

The position of the prince is to renounce any direct participation in the construction of the new state. Fabrizio insists that the plan to not only formally integrate Sicily into the Italian state but to connect it to the larger forces of progress, modernity, and history, is certainly well-intentioned but destined to failure. In his characterization of Sicilian nature, the prince dwells on what he believes is the region's eternal desire for the void, for dream and death, thus establishing an implicit parallel with his own character, which, as we have seen, is built on the tendency to withdraw from time and history. In this sense, it is only logical that the prince uses the first person plural to foreground his own representative and metonymic relation to Sicily (ignoring in this case the question of his own otherness):

> Tutte le manifestazioni siciliane sono manifestazioni oniriche, anche le più violente: la nostra sensualità è desiderio di oblio, le schioppettate e le coltellate nostre, desiderio di morte; desiderio di immobilità voluttuosa, cioè ancora di morte, la nostra pigrizia, i nostri sorbetti di scorzonera o di cannella; il nostro aspetto meditativo è quello del nulla che voglia scrutare gli enigmi del nirvana. (*G*, 162)

> [All Sicilian expression, even the most violent, is really wish-fulfillment: our sensuality is a hankering for oblivion, our shooting and knifing a hankering for death; our laziness, our spiced and drugged sherbets, a hankering for voluptuous

immobility, that is, for death again; our meditative air is that of a void wanting to scrutinize the enigmas of nirvana. *L*, 206]

This insistence on the futility of all endeavors and on the unchangeable resistance of the natural milieu and the mentality of its inhabitants can be understood as a characteristic feature of the "rhetoric of reaction." In his classic study of this subject Albert O. Hirschman has commented on the fact that what he calls the "futility thesis" has been adopted especially by Italian and Sicilian sociologists and political scientists.[32] In this respect, it should be noted that the prince's "ideological inferno" is not only an expression of his own consciousness. The thesis of the debilitating role of landscape and climate is actually confirmed by the exterior comments and descriptions of the narrator. During the scene of Chevalley's departure, the narrator dwells on the dirt in the streets, the "smell of sleep," the disease-infected children, the dearth of work, the extremes of "silence" and "hysterical voices" (*L*, 214; *G*, 168). Faced with this situation, between Chevalley's optimism ("this state of things won't last; our lively new modern administration will change it all") [questo stato di cose non durerà; la nostra amministrazione, nuova, agile, moderna cambierà tutto] and the prince's pessimism ("all this shouldn't last; but it will, always," *L*, 214) [tutto questo (. . .) non dovrebbe poter durare; però durerà, sempre; *G*, 168], the narrator obviously sides with the latter. For the concluding passage of the chapter goes on to dwell on the general state of misery, as evidenced by the fact that the carriage has "four wheels the color of vomit" (*L*, 214) [quattro ruote color di vomito; *G*, 168] and by the "immemorial filth on the windows" (*L*, 214) [sudiciume immemoriale del finestrino; *G*, 168], details that are not simply part of realist description but confirmations of Don Fabrizio's pessimistic rationale.

The prince's stance of climatological determinism is a view that results both from his identification with and his critical distance from the Sicilian environment. The contradictory or ambivalent traits in the character of the prince are in fact attributed to different hereditary factors, which are in turn related to national-geographic types. Thus, an early scene in the novel dwells on Don Fabrizio's double genealogical inheritance, with a "rationalistic" Nordic (German) mother and a "sensualist" Southern (Italian) father:

Ma nel sangue di lui fermentavano altre essenze germaniche ben più incommode per quell' aristocratico siciliano nell' anno 1860, di quanto potessero essere attraenti la pelle bianchissima ed i capelli biondi nell' ambiente di olivastri e di corvini: un temperamento autoritario, una certa rigidità morale, una propensione alle idee astratte che nell *habitat* molliccio della società palermitana si erano mutati in prepotenza capricciosa, perpetui scrupoli morali e disprezzo per i suoi parenti e amici che gli sembrava andassero alla deriva nel lento fiume pragmatistico siciliano. (*G*, 25)

[But in his blood also fermented other German strains particularly disturbing to a Sicilian aristocrat in the year 1860, however attractive his fair skin and hair amid all that olive and black: an authoritarian temperament, a certain rigidity in morals, and a propensity for abstract ideas; these, in the relaxing atmosphere of Palermo society, had changed respectively into capricious arrogance, recurring moral scruples, and contempt for his own relatives and friends, all of whom seemed to him mere driftwood in the languid meandering stream of Sicilian pragmatism. *L*, 18]

The passage is highly significant with regard to the mixed genealogical inheritance of the prince, according to which the Southern father embodies "sensuality" and the Northern mother "severity."[33] Moreover, the passage not only makes explicit this contrast and compromise between inherited attributes; it also states that certain hereditary traits associated with the North are *changed*—and this means deformed, debased, contorted—under the different conditions of the Southern environment. Furthermore, the prince's hybrid genetic heritage is adduced for his unique character (he is, as it were, the "first and last" of his kind), which enables him to become not only a representative but also an observer of his own class:

Sollecitato da una parte dall'orgoglio e dall' intellettualismo materno, dall'altra dalla sensualità e facioneria del padre, il povero Principe Fabrizio viveva in perpetuo scontento pur sotto il cipiglio zeusiano e stava a contemplare la rovina del proprio ceto e del proprio patrimonio senza avere nessuna attività ed ancor minor voglia di porvi riparo. (*G*, 26)

[Between the pride and intellectuality of his mother and the sensuality and irresponsibility of his father, poor Prince Fabrizio lived in perpetual discontent under his Jove-like frown, watching the ruin of his own class and his own inheritance without ever making, still less wanting to make, any move toward saving it. *L*, 19]

The passage suggests that Fabrizio's inactivity is part of his paternal heritage (the "immobility" of the South), while the capacity of distanced observation is due to his mother's side (Northern rationality). The predominance of the maternal inheritance means that the prince is represented both as a symbolic representative of his social kind *and* as an exception, an "outsider."[34] The question of the foreignness of the milieu and its resistance to the possibility of cultivation emerges already at the beginning of the novel, where imported flowers from the European North end up degenerating in the Southern climate:

> Le rose *Paul Neyron* le cui piantine aveva egli stesso acquistato a Parigi erano degenerate: eccitate prima e rinfrollite dopo dai succhi vigorosi e indolenti della terra siciliana, arse dai lugli apocalittici, si erano mutate in una sorte di cavoli color carne, osceni, ma che distillavano un denso aroma quasi turpe che nessun allevatore francese avrebbe osato sperare. (*G*, 27)

> [The Paul Neyron roses, whose cuttings he had himself bought in Paris, had degenerated; first stimulated and then enfeebled by the strong if languid pull of Sicilian earth, burned by apocalyptic Julies, they had changed into things like flesh-colored cabbages, obscene and distilling a dense, almost indecent, scent which no French horticulturist would have dared hope for. *L*, 20]

This motif of an object of Northern European civilization that is introduced into the climate of the South and then becomes deformed or grotesque might also be recognized in other scenes of the novel. Take the scene where Don Calogero enters the palace in Donnafugata dressed in a tailcoat that emblematizes, in the eyes of the prince, the revolution brought about by the new times, especially when he himself had thought it fit to dress down in regular evening dress, in deference to his nonaristocratic guests. Yet Don Calogero's ill-fitting tailcoat shows the farcical aspect of Calogero's social mimicry: "il Verbo londinese si era assai malamente incarnato in un artigiano girgentano cui la tenace avarizia di don Calogero si era rivolta" (*G*, 79) [the Word from London had been most inadequately made flesh by a tailor from Girgenti to whom Don Calogero had gone in his tenacious avarice; *L*, 93]. Somewhat later the reader is also made to understand how Angelica's display of civilized manners barely manages to disguise her peasant origins (*G*, 80; *L*, 115). Obviously, in these cases the narrator makes himself complicit with the prince and his aristocratic derision of the quick and superficial adoption of manners by the social climbers. Aside from these examples of more or less ridiculous social mimicry, there are many other passages that emphasize the fact that the very place of Sicily is resistant to cultural forms from abroad or from the Italian mainland.[35] Therefore, such cultural forms often undergo a process of distortion in their adaptation or introduction. Witness, for example, the linguistic deformation of the famous Risorgimento song "La Bella Gigugin": "trasformate in nenie arabe, sorte cui deve soggiacere qualsiasi melodietta vivace che sia cantata in Sicilia" (*G*, 106) [transformed into a kind of Arab wail, a fate to which any gay tune sung in Sicily is bound to succumb; *L*, 128] or the name of a hair product used by the prince ("*lemo-liscio, il Lime-Juice di Atkinson, densa lozione biancastra che gli arrivava a cassette da Londra e che subiva, nel nome, la medesima deformazione etnica delle canzoni,*" *G*, 118) [*lemo-liscio*, Atkinson's lime and glycerine, a dense whitish lotion which arrived in cases from London and whose name suffered the same ethnic changes as songs; *L*, 144].

The prince himself is conscious of the ephemeral role of culture on Sicilian soil, and, in his dialogue with Chevalley, he makes explicit how he is conditioned by the limitations of time and place. Yet Don Fabrizio's self-awareness with regard to the spatial environment is inevitably different from the much wider view of the narrator, who takes to extremes Don Fabrizio's own tendency to withdraw from his immediate environment. Yet, while the prince typically withdraws toward timelessness, the narrator demonstrates his *historical* distance.

Aristocratic Decline and Social Union

Insofar as *Il Gattopardo* is a historical novel that is concerned with the central event of the Risorgimento, both the geographical setting (Sicily) and the chosen social group (the aristocracy) might appear eccentric at first. If we recall that Manzoni's *Promessi sposi* (1827) deliberately depicts the historical process from the perspective of lowly characters and if Nievo's *Confessioni* (1867) are concerned with the emergence of a bourgeois mentality against the fading backdrop of feudal decline, then it becomes clear that Lampedusa's reversal of social perspective is an unusual, even polemical, choice. This is history "from above," yet the irony consists in the fact that the members of the aristocracy are the "losers" of history, and hence the focus on this social class carries with it a paradoxical perspective that goes against the grain of the official historiography of the Risorgimento. Undoubtedly, this aspect was in large measure responsible for the overwhelmingly critical reception at the time of the novel's publication, in a literary scene then dominated by the Italian Left.[36]

It is easy to see that the novel follows in its basic outline, its ever-so-thin plot, a social transformation that is a key to a great number of nineteenth-century novels, namely the replacement of the dying aristocracy by an emerging capitalist middle class, which in this case corresponds to the consolidation of the nation under the rubric of the Risorgimento. Yet if this common narrative is usually presented as modernity's construction of its own past, the reversal of perspective undertaken in this novel puts pressure on the sequencing that usually underwrites the conjunction of social progress and narrative progression. If narratives generally "organize descent" and "administer genealogies," *Il Gattopardo* rescues images of the past to question the logic of before and after characteristic of modernity's conception of time.[37]

It is this idea of transition that is associated with the process of Sicily passing from the absolutist rule of the Bourbons to its integration into the constitutional monarchy of Italy. In the novel, the accompanying social transformation is embodied by the opposition between Don Fabrizio, on the one hand, and Don Calogero Sedara, on the other. However, this constellation of declining aristocracy and newly enriched bourgeoisie is presented not so much as an antagonism but as a kind of osmotic process whereby the two classes approximate each other via a marriage that is meant to rechannel the riches acquired by Don Calogero to its former point of origin. Yet this tactical and practical assimilation actually brings to the fore essential differences. Fabrizio is characterized by a dissimulated form of nobility that disdains the proud manifestations of exterior wealth in favor of a flight from materiality.[38] This would again signify a retreat from historical and social reality: "thus nobility would seem set to lose almost completely its specifically historical, class connotations, and to dissolve itself, or rather resolve itself into nobility of spirit."[39] In contrast, Don Calogero's incongruous, comic nature results precisely from his imitation of the trappings of nobility in purely material and hence superficial terms, as is typical for a nouveau riche. The figure of Don Calogero embodies precisely a social type, as the prince himself observes, who sees "a type realized in all its details" (*L*, 155) [di vedere un tipo realizzarsi in tutti i suoi particolari; *G*, 125], that of the upwardly mobile peasant, whose emergence was fostered by the formal end of feudalism and the revolution of 1860. These "new men" played a crucial role in generating electoral support for the new state, while they exploited its liberal institutions for their own benefit.[40]

The penultimate part of the novel, dedicated entirely to the account of the prince's death, confirms the idea that true nobility consists not so much in the inheritance of blood but rather in something as immaterial as an uncommon, identity-confirming memory. Don Fabrizio's grandson Fabrizietto might be his biological descendant, but not in a way that counts, not in the sense of a living tradition:

Era inutile sforzarsi a credere il contrario, l'ultimo Salina era lui, il gigante sparuto che adesso agonizzava sul balcone di un albergo. Perché il significato di un casato nobile è tutto nelle tradizioni, nei ricordi vitali; e lui era l'ultimo a possedere dei

ricordi inconsueti, distinti da quelli delle altre famiglie. Fabrizietto avrebbe avuto
dei ricordi banali, eguali a quelli dei suoi compagni di ginnasio, ricordi di mer-
ende economiche, di scherzucci malvagetti agli insegnanti. (*G*, 221)

[It was useless to try to avoid the thought, but the last of the Salinas was really he
himself, this gaunt giant now dying on a hotel balcony. For the significance of a
noble family lies entirely in its traditions, that is in its vital memories; and he was
the last to have any unusual memories, anything different from those of other
families. Fabrizietto would only have banal ones like his schoolfellows, of snacks,
of spiteful little jokes against teachers. *L*, 285–86]

Tancredi is the prince's nephew and is seen by him as his ideal "heir," even as
his "real son" (*L*, 41). The fact that Tancredi stems from an impoverished side of
the family underscores the fragile status of the nobility. The prince's relationship to Tancredi is sometimes marked by disgust and even by erotic, Oedipal
rivalry, but he is generally cherished as a son precisely because this allows the
prince to delegate responsibility to the "liberal" next generation, while he sinks
back into his stance of distanced, resigned skepticism (not unlike counselor
Aires in Machado's novel).

The marriage between Tancredi and Angelica, then, is the decisive element
of the "plot" that conjoins private and public, individual and collective, present
and past. It is a union that embodies—even as it masks—the union between
the classes, the collaboration for the unification of Italy. As we have already
seen, only the narrator with his hindsight is aware of the later failure and betrayals of this union—and hence also of the political failure of the promises of
the project of national unification. The narrator leaves no doubt that the representatives of the newly enriched bourgeoisie (Angelica) cannot redeem or re-
embody the uprooted aristocracy (Tancredi). This sense of amorous union as an
allegory for national union is a tried device of the nineteenth century novel, as
we have seen, going back to Scott and the national tale. If in *Il Gattopardo* the
marriage between Tancredi and Angelica allegorizes the compromise of class
in postunification Sicily, another would-be couple of the novel, Cavriaghi and
Concetta, suggests, through the failure of Cavriaghi's courtship, the miscom-
munication or incompatibility between Italians from the North and from the
South (*L*, 192).

Furthermore, the amorous alliance is repeatedly undercut by allusions to the
economic relations involved in the marriage transaction. From the beginning,
the connection between Tancredi and Angelica is seen as a practical arrangement that is dictated by exterior motives. Even before the figure of Angelica has

emerged upon the scene, the prince reflects upon the possible liaison between his daughter Concetta and her cousin Tancredi; he sees Concetta as standing in the way of Tancredi's "great future" (*L*, 87): "Egli avrebbe potuto essere l'alfiere di un contrattacco che la nobiltà, sotto mutate uniformi, poteva portare contro il nuovo ordine politico. Per far questo gli mancava soltanto una cosa: i soldi" (*G*, 75). [He would be the standard bearer of a counterattack which the nobility, under new trappings, could launch against the new social state. To do this he lacked only one thing: money; *L*, 87.] While the theoretical alliance between Concetta and Tancredi stands for the possibility of inbreeding—rather typical for the aristocracy of the time (*L*, 255)—and thus for a closed system of class-bound tradition, the actual union between Angelica and Tancredi denotes a case of exogamy. In fact, this form of class or genetic mixing could best be described as a kind of "grafting," the production of a new, "superior plant" by combining different, "foreign" genetic materials.

This metaphor is suggested by the novel itself, in the scene of the "foreign" peaches, the product of a grafting with "German cuttings," resulting in a luscious texture reminiscent of the cheeks of Chinese girls ("sembravano testoline di cinesine pudiche," *G*, 77). The grafted peaches are explicitly connected with sexual imagery, as the prince explains to Tancredi: "eppure, Tancredi, anche queste pesche sono prodotte da amori, da congiungimenti" (*G*, 77) [and yet, Tancredi, these peaches are also products of love, of coupling; *L*, 90]. This in turn recalls a comment shortly before this scene, when it is that Tancredi "would always find women falling for him like pears" (*L*, 88) [Tancredi poi, davanti al quale le donne sarebbero cadute come pere cotte; *G*, 75]. Since this comment occurs in an interior monologue of the prince, it is made abundantly clear that the prince's "georgic" activity—Tancredi referred to him ironically as "*agricola pius*"—doubles as a metaphor for his strategic plans to ameliorate the stock of his own class through his "stand-in" Tancredi.

Since Angelica is generally described as a flower arising out of dirt (namely, her ancestor Papa 'Mmerda), the narrator alerts us to the fact that the marriage between Tancredi and Angelica is a way to preserve *and* soil the continuity of class. In a scene of indirect free discourse concerning the marriage preparations, the prince himself is disgusted with "all the guile in language and behavior he had been forced to use for some time" (*L*, 116). However, during the scene of the marriage negotiations, the narrator intervenes to suggest that Fabrizio's attempt to prolong the line of the Falconeri by new, unconventional means might ultimately just amount to a self-delusion. Throughout the novel, the reader is not left in doubt regarding the temporary self-deceptions of the prince, and numerous allusions to death emphasize the point of his (and his class's) end, with in-creased frequency toward the end of the novel.

Thus, the city palace of the Ponteleones is surrounded by signs and images associated with death: the dresses of the prince's daughters have arrived in "long black cases like coffins" (L, 246); shortly before his arrival the prince en-counters a priest bearing the last rites (L, 248); and finally, at the end of the chapter, in the early morning hours, a cart is seen in the streets, carrying bleed-ing bulls to the slaughterhouse (L, 272). There is no doubt that the aristocracy's satisfaction with the ball ("Like the old days!" L, 271) is presented as a form of self-deception, while the reader is made to understand that this is actually the "last dance" of the aristocracy. The function of this scene is to dramatize the contrast between the festive self-congratulation of aristocratic society with the interior, death-bound consciousness of the prince. It is significant that the ball is given in honor of Colonel Pallavicino, the man who wounded and thereafter kissed Garibaldi in the historic episode of the battle of Aspromonte (August 20, 1860).[41] The presence of the military general introduces a dimension of history into an environment that is otherwise perfectly isolated from the exterior world. In the view of the host, the encounter on Aspromonte signifies the ratifica-tion of "the compromise so laboriously achieved between the old and the new" (L, 250). Although the prince is completely disgusted by Pallavicino's sentimentalist rhetoric, the notion of a historical compromise echoes his own collaboration with Tancredi's marriage plans. Indeed, the entire scene turns upon the idea that Don Fabrizio, although alienated from his own class, can-not escape being a part of it, for, as he himself comes to realize, "tutte quelle donne bruttine, tutti questi uomini sciocchi, questi due sessi vanagloriosi, erano il sangue del suo sangue, erano lui stesso" (G, 201–2) [all these faded women, all these stupid men, these two vainglorious sexes were part of his blood, part of himself; L, 260].

During the scene in the library, shortly before Angelica asks him to dance with her, the prince contemplates the print of a painting by Jean-Baptiste Greuze (1725–1805), "una buona copia della 'Morte del Giusto'" (G, 202) [a good copy of Greuze's *Death of the Just Man*; L, 260–61]. The title of the painting does not correspond to an actual work by Greuze but rather combines various Greuzian motives of domestic tragedy:

Il vegliardo stava spirando nel suo letto, fra sbuffi di biancheria pulitissima, circondato dai nipoti afflitti e da nipotine che levavano le braccia verso il sof-fitto. Le ragazze erano carine, procaci, il disordine delle loro vesti suggeriva piú il libertinaggio che il dolore; si capiva subito che erano loro il vero soggetto del quadro. (G, 202)

[The old man was expiring on his bed, amid welters of clean linen, surrounded by afflicted grandsons and granddaughters raising arms toward the ceiling. The girls were pretty, provoking, and the disorder of their clothes suggested sex more than sorrow; they, it was obvious at once, were the real subject of the picture. L, 261]

Insofar as this scene is mentioned in criticism of the novel at all, it is mostly just related to the novel's symbolism of death, as yet another memento mori.[42] In fact, the prince relates the painting to his own death: "subito dopo chiese a sé stesso se la propria morte sarebbe stata simile a quella" (G, 202) [immediately afterward he asked himself if his own death would be like that; L, 261]. It is well known that Greuze had been canonized by Diderot, who recognized in his paintings of realist-bourgeois subjects a legitimate form of "tableaux d'histoire."[43] In fact, the motif of the ageing and dying father, a recurrent theme in the paintings of Greuze and the plays of Diderot, is often interpreted as a kind of anticipation of the coming revolution or as an affective education toward national egalitarianism, a "political and cultural regeneration."[44]

Thus, the motif of the dying father is a curiously ambiguous figure, insofar as it is both a figure for identification and empathy and a symbol of anachronism. This, I would argue, may help us to understand the scene of Don Fabrizio in the library. The aristocrat recognizes himself in a painting, as in a mirror, which associates the death of the father with the birth of an autonomous, bourgeois society. It is highly ironic, then, that a copy of such a painting from the last decades of the French ancien régime should hang in the palace of a prototypical representative of yet another ancien régime, although Ponteleone never appears to enter his own library ("Ponteleone non era tipo da perdere il suo tempo lí dentro," G, 202) [Ponteleone was not a type to waste time in there; L, 260], which again reinforces the contrast between the prince and the other members of his class. The bourgeois genre scene of Greuze's painting alludes to the theme of the social demotion of the prince, thus suggesting a parallel of his own fate in the mirror of history—which entails in turn a cyclical understanding of history. Don Fabrizio's comment that the painting is too idealizing, that the bedsheets are too clean, anticipates the scene of his own death, far from the palace, in a dilapidated, dirty hotel room (part 7).[45] In contrast to the other aristocrats, whose obliviousness to their own historical fate is symbolized by their immersion in the festive atmosphere of their "last" ball, the prince is constantly aware of his own historical situation, a situation that is bound up with that of his class and his generation, as he insists, most explicitly, in his conversation with Chevalley, when he declines to take on the post of senator in the new government:

> Sono un rappresentante della vecchia classe, inevitabilmente compromesso col regime borbonico, ed a questo legato dai vincoli della decadenza in mancanza di quelli dell'affetto. Appartengo ad una generazione disgraziata a cavallo fra i vecchi tempi ed i nuovi, e che si trova a disagio in tutti e due. Noi della nostra generazione dobbiamo ritirarci in un cantuccio e stare a guardare i capitomboli e le capriole dei giovani attorno a quest'ornatissimo catafalco. (G, 164)

> [I am a member of the old ruling class, inevitably compromised with the Bourbon regime, and tied to it by chains of decency if not of affection. I belong to an unfortunate generation, swung between the old world and the new, and I find myself ill at ease in both. And we of our generation must draw aside and watch the capers and somersaults of the young around this ornate catafalque. L, 209]

For this reason, Fabrizio cynically proposes Don Calogero as a candidate for the senate. In Lampedusa's novel the idea of the protagonist as the representative of a larger—transitional—generation is part of a wider strategy informed by the narrator's awareness of a historical and genealogical *longue durée*. Thus, commenting on Don Calogero's gradual and partial appreciation of manners, the narrator projects unto him a whole process of class transformation that suggests a dialectical, or cyclical, vision of social evolution, where decline and emergence are different sides of the same coin: "ma fu dal quel momento che si iniziò, per lui ed i suoi, quel costante raffinarsi di una classe che nel corso di tre generazioni trasforma efficienti cafoni in gentiluomini indifesi" (G, 131) [but from that moment there began, for him and his family, that process of continual refining which in the course of three generations transforms innocent peasants into defenseless gentry; L, 162]. This is another instance when the narration of history in the novel is corrected, or supplemented, by the later, ironic perspective of the narrator.

The novel clearly criticizes the manipulation of suffrage, but it also criticizes the Sicilians for failing to accept the offer of modernity.[46] The wavering and essential ambivalence of the prince in this regard are the result of his contradictory relation to both Sicilian-ness and modernity. As a historical novel, *Il Gattopardo* has inherited from *Waverley* the concern with cultural nonsimultaneity and with the way a cultural periphery is brought into the process of history. Even in the twentieth century, the narrative evocation of a declining system of feudal practices and values is, in light of the ascent of a centralizing state power, a significant way to construct a spatiotemporal past of the nation.[47] Yet, in contrast to earlier narratives, and precisely because it is written from a greater distance, *Il Gattopardo* is both realistic and skeptical with regard to the pastness of the past, and thus it questions the official self-understanding of the nation's historical evolution and of modernity's narrative about itself.

CHAPTER TEN

Epilogue

The Perspective from the End

Through my discussion of *Il Gattopardo*, I have shown how a novelistic theme of the nineteenth century is refracted by a subjectivization of time characteristic of literary modernism. Therefore, Lampedusa's novel, with its rather unusual degree of distance between the represented historical period and the present moment of narration, raises the more general question of how the genealogical novel has fared in the second half of the twentieth century.

The peculiar historical viewpoint of *Il Gattopardo*—an elegiac reconstruction of the life of the aristocracy by a late representative of this social class—was partly anticipated by a novel that appeared in 1956, *Bearn o La sala de las muñecas* (*The Doll's Room*), by the Mallorcan author Llorenç Villalonga (1897–1980), who was himself of rather middle class origins. Initially highly controversial because of his political sympathies, Villalonga is today acknowledged as a towering figure of Catalan literature. After a friend of Villalonga, the Falangist writer Luis Santamarina, alerted him to the striking similarities between the two works, he actually decided in 1962 to translate *Il Gattopardo* into Catalan.[1] In the history of the European novel, these two works may now be seen as a unique pair sharing striking similarities, and a brief comparison is useful to highlight how they may exemplify a specific version of "universal regionalism" during the middle of the twentieth century.[2]

First, *Bearn* locates the narrative of aristocratic decline on a Mediterranean island, in this case Mallorca, so that geographical insularity becomes the correlative of social change. Second, the novel's aristocratic protagonist, Don Toni, shares with Lampedusa's prince the ambivalent stance toward his own class, for he combines a fatalistic acceptance of the decline of his class with a passion for the French Enlightenment and all kinds of technological novelties—and at the same time punishes his negligent workers with the whip. This ambivalence of the central figure is complemented by an original frame of narrative perspective:

the entire novel is conceived as a report written by the house cleric and administrator, Juan Mayol, and addressed to his friend, Don Miguel, the secretary of a Spanish cardinal. As we have seen, such an indirect approach to the representation of familial decline was already present in the "origin" of the genealogical novel, *Castle Rackrent*. However, in this case the exterior perspective is intimately blended with an interior one, insofar as Juan has access to and mediates to the reader the worldview and thought processes of Don Toni—who is his constant conversational partner and who has also entrusted to him his "Memorial," the account of his life, shortly before his death.

The multiply mediated access the reader is given to Don Toni's consciousness (his own "Memorial," containing erasures and silences; the fragmentary citations from this text by Juan; Juan's proleptic allusions) makes *Bearn* a novel full of blank spaces that the reader has to fill in. Just as the coherence of perspective and narrative order is thus broken down, the reader also understands that the genealogical order of the aristocratic family line is not only beset by incest (Don Toni is married to his cousin, Maria Antònia, just as Villalonga himself was married to a cousin) but also by illegitimacy. As a matter of fact, the reader gradually comes to understand that Juan is in fact the natural son—one of many—of Don Toni. Since Juan is a Catholic priest, his explicit commentary condemns his "bienhechor" for his licentious behavior and skeptical philosophy, yet he also sympathizes with and admires him, which contributes to a singularly ambivalent portrayal, constantly wavering between irony and identification. For instance, when Juan tells of his master's amorous exploits with his young niece Xima on the occasion of their common trip to the premiere of Gounod's opera *Faust* in Paris (1859), his moral outrage is colored with the resentment of his own repressed sexuality.[3] In some cases Juan even writes about what his master "thought of in his interior mind"—aspects of his consciousness that Juan could not really have known in realistic terms.[4]

As in *Il Gattopardo*, modernity is associated in this novel with the Continent and the European North. Yet in this case it is not so much the island that is traversed by the historical process, but rather it is Don Toni who travels abroad into the Parisian world of modernity. *Il Gattopardo* and *Bearn*, then, are highly characteristic texts for the figuration of an interior European periphery, as well as a socially eccentric, specifically aristocratic viewpoint on the process of social modernization and change.

In both cases, we are led into the aristocratic consciousness of the protagonist, who stoically accepts the historical change, yet we are also given a certain distance from this perspective. In both cases the aristocratic protagonist is associated with an illusory desire for eternity (Don Fabrizio's desire for "the stars") and the suspension of time[5]—which is realized through remembrance yet simultaneously counterbalanced and destroyed by the knowing, proleptic perspective of the temporal end, of subsequent history, "for in this world exists no other paradise than one that is lost."[6] In formal terms, both texts adopt the moderate modernism of a Proustian lineage, which tries to rescue moments of experiential presence from the knowing perspective of the end: the lifeworld of the nineteenth century is told from the perspective and with the narrative tools of the twentieth century. In other words, while the "eccentric" class position helps to throw a different and distant focus on the process of modernization and the master narrative of the "ascent of the bourgeoisie," the modernist means of representation create their own formal distance from the represented world and save the novels from the dangers of nostalgia. Both of these texts are essentially concerned with the aristocracy, the social class most essentially defined by descent. As we have seen, the nineteenth century novel has already not only represented the crisis of the aristocracy (De Roberto, Pardo Bazán), but it has also figured problems of the (higher) bourgeoisie in terms of a genealogical crisis (Galdós, Machado de Assis)—either way, the question of descent has been central to the narrative representation of private histories during, and of, the nineteenth century.

As a way of concluding this book, I want to briefly consider the question of how the twentieth century novel has continued the genealogical legacy of the nineteenth century—but with respect to the more obvious and frequent case of the European history of the twentieth century. I can address here the topic of the (post)modernist family saga, the relation between family and history, only in the most symptomatic and selective terms, suggesting some observations about the possible transformation of the novelistic link between family and national history. While genealogy no longer provides a kind of master trope for the twentieth-century novel as a whole, we may nevertheless point to certain characteristic cases where novelists continue to use the frame of the family to reflect upon a specific situation of national history: the traumatic and violent history of the twentieth century, which has profoundly changed the novel's relation to history.

Postwar Modernism in Europe

In the context of modernism, the genealogical trope of the family persists, but it is now less a question of origins and decadence than of destructive forces inside the dynamics of the modern family, as Stephen Kern has recently observed: "after James, Gide, Freud, and Faulkner, the family would be rather a potential hotbed of child abuse, counterfeit values, Oedipal tensions, and haunting memories."[7] This specifically modernist legacy can still be felt in the work of a number of outstanding postwar European novels by, for example, Claude Simon, Juan Benet, António Lobo Antunes, and Thomas Bernhard, all of which feature prominently familial-genealogical scenarios. With the exception perhaps of Bernhard, all of these authors are strongly influenced by the work of William Faulkner, who, as Pascale Casanova has emphasized, was enormously important for enabling literary innovation in backward or culturally dominated areas throughout the twentieth century—and this dimension of influence, which results in revolutionizing the literary scene of their respective countries, certainly applies to Benet and Antunes.[8] The authors rework Faulkner's legacy of "haunting memories" with respect to both private and national traumas with similar narrative techniques, namely a radically interior focalization, polyphony, and the dissolution of linear temporality.

I will briefly comment on three novels published in the 1980s that may be seen as representative for a wider tendency of the postwar, contemporary European novel, insofar as they address the often traumatic historical experiences and aftereffects of the twentieth century as mirrored by radically destructive constellations of family. In fact, the decisive difference of their works from the novel of the nineteenth century consists not in the fact that familial, or even narrative, unities dissolve (as we have seen, this is already part of the legacy of the realist novel of the nineteenth century) but precisely in that they are informed by and represent a traumatic notion of historical experience, a past that resists disappearance, as is generally characteristic for the literature of the latter half of the twentieth century.[9]

A highly significant author who had pioneered this reconception of the novel's relation to history is Claude Simon, who in various novels, most famously in *La route des Flandres* (*The Flanders Road*, 1959), obsessively returns to aspects of his own family history as well as his traumatic experience of the Second World War. This is formally expressed by frequent motif-like repetitions of phrases, the dissolution of temporal chronology as well as the boundaries of narrative voice (that is, the potential undecidability of perspective), and the labyrinthine circling around an enigma or trauma that substitutes for the sequential unfolding of genealogical decadence. All of this leads, in Faulknerian fashion, to a confusing presentation of interlocking voices and temporal levels, which the patient reader needs to gradually unravel and yet never fully succeeds in penetrating.[10]

Such difficulties are brought to truly exasperating heights in the forbiddingly hermetic novels by the Spanish author Juan Benet. In what is perhaps his most difficult novel, *Saúl ante Samuel* (Saul before Samuel, 1980), as in his earlier landmark work, *Volverás a Región* (*Return to Region*, 1967), he undertakes a deconstruction of national historiography and mythography in relation to the event of the Spanish Civil War. Set in the fantastic and "unreal" landscape of Región (Region), more specifically in an isolated house in this landscape, these novels figure the experience of national catastrophe on a highly symbolic level, namely by way of incoherent, dispersing family constellations. In the earlier novel, this is expressed via the symbol of the orphan, a nameless young boy who lives in the house of the doctor and hopes that his mother will return.[11] As is the case for previous novels of high modernism, Benet uses myth to interrogate the meaning of history, and sequential narrative is replaced by a "spatialization" of time. Benet's novels constitute a radical disorientation with regard to the coordinates of temporal sequence and narrative perspective. The effect is one of temporal simultaneity, where past and present blend into each other, where the traumatic experience of the Spanish Civil War appears to take place in an arrested time that leaves no room for development or hope, and where the reader is put into a "psychoanalytic" position, is confronted with the task of deciphering the traumatic condition of the characters as well as filling in the voids in the fragmentary and elliptical presentation of these "characters" that signify more in symbolic than in psychological terms.[12]

In this sense, the novels taking place in the imaginary, yet concretely rendered, region of Región turn the very idea of a historical novel on its head. The region's self-isolation and ruined condition refers obliquely to a postwar landscape and the conditions of the Franco regime. Benet was inspired by Faulkner, both with regard to the extreme dissolution of narrative continuity and the use of mythical and tragic motives to stage "his political and historical inquiry into Spanish backwardness and resistance to change."[13] *Saúl ante Samuel* uses the literary motif of the two warring brothers, Cain and Abel (which in fact has already been repeatedly employed by the writers of the 1898 generation to represent the confrontation between the "two Spains"), to show how the Civil War is a confrontation that cuts through the "family" of the nation. In fact, Benet's novel demonstrates how the Civil War affects a single family but also how the family constellation serves as an allegory for the war.

The actual narrative present involves probably a very short span of time—the younger brother approaching his family house after an absence of forty years—thus reinforcing the sense that the past of the Civil War overshadows and immobilizes the present, just as the novel is dominated by the continued presence of past events. The reader may gradually piece together a typically tragic story according to which this younger brother, sometimes enigmatically referred to as Martín (most often characters remain unnamed), the family's outsider and dissident, having left his paternal home for the capital, receives a telegram from his father ordering him to join the Republican side and thus to save his older brother, who, as a Nationalist, has been taken prisoner by the Republicans. However, instead of saving his brother, with whom he had a rivalry from childhood on, he has an affair with his brother's wife and eventually fails to intervene in a decisive moment when he could have saved his brother from being killed.

Even more than in *Volverás a Región*, the symbolic center of this novel is constituted by the family house. As David K. Herzberger has written, "The family house itself becomes a central image of sterility and decadence as it exists amid silence and shadows, and eventually its rotting shell serves as a vivid reification of the physical and spiritual dissolution caused by the war."[14] The self-enclosed house also comes to signify the stasis of time, the permanence of the "brotherly" conflict of the Civil War. The narrative itself is entrusted to different voices, including a pseudo-omniscient narrator, the brothers' cousin Simón (who lives on the third floor of the house and functions essentially as a figure of observation) and the prophesying, almost magical figure of the grandmother. Yet, characteristically for Benet, these different voices are very difficult to tell apart. Benet condenses the supposedly ideological confrontation of the Civil War into a private conflict between an older, legitimate and a younger, bastard brother. Furthermore, the "objective" narrator remarks on the familial and generational nature of ideas and ideologies, rather than their actual content.[15] The paradigm of an archetypal family narrative thus serves Benet to show how deeply historical experience penetrates into private worlds, and at the same time he shows how such genealogical deep structures reduce the movements of official national history to mere surface manifestations.

Faulkner's influence can also be felt in the novels of António Lobo Antunes, many of which are concerned with the wounds inflicted on Portuguese society in the wake of traumatic national events, in this case the colonial wars and the Salazar dictatorship. Antunes's novel *Auto dos danados* (Farce of the damned, 1985) is significant because it marks the transition from his early, autobiographically inspired texts to a series of novels centered on decadent families. Consequently, it is also the first novel that, following Faulkner's family narratives, introduces a panorama of multiple internal focalizations.

Auto dos danados circles around the historical moment of the Revolution in April 1974 and its aftermath. The new political reality, including the Communist persecution of the old latifundarian families in the region of Alentejo, leads the children of the old patriarch Diogo to flee across the Spanish border to save their skin. The text is constituted by the interlocking narrative fragments of nine characters, including Diogo's children Leonor, the schizophrenic Gonçalo, and an anonymous "mongoloid" daughter. As a matter of fact, the symbolic parallel between the death of the patriarch in the familial and political realm (that is, the end of the Salazar regime) has been recognized as a distinctive feature of the post-1974 Portuguese novel, including Antunes's *O manual dos inquisidores* (1996, *The Inquisitor's Manual*), as a consequence of the comparatively late abandonment of colonial and latifundarian structures of power in Portugal.[16]

Indeed, the novel culminates with the metaphorically interlinked deaths of Diogo and a bull killed during a village feast from which the doctor is recalled to come to the patriarch's deathbed.[17] In true Faulknerian fashion, this key event is approached by narrative segments that alternate between the present of narration, ten years after the event (coinciding with the publication of the novel in 1985), and the time before and during the event. As in other novels by Antunes, the polyphonic representation of the disintegration of a patriarchal family is emblematic of the problems of a postdictatorial (and postcolonial) society. Antunes also follows Faulkner closely by using the estranged perspective of psychically deranged characters (Gonçalo, his son Francisco).

The layered levels of time are reminiscent of the style of Benet and Simon, yet Antunes increases the narrative polyphony by completely abandoning the integrative position of a third-person narrator. While the reader is challenged to gradually piece together the parental relationships between the different narrators and perspectives, the narrative style, although laden with stark and eccentric metaphors, is generally less impenetrable than the often foreboding styles of Benet and Simon. While the first part of the novel presents the perspective of Nuno, a dentist married to Ana, the niece of Diogo, that is, from a perspective that is relatively distant from the family itself, the second part, entitled "Before the feast," is composed of the complementary reports of Ana and her mother Lurdes, in two sections designated as "Side A" and "Side B," thus suggesting recordings on an audio cassette, as if the two women had made their testimonials orally. The novel might be said to stage the recuperation of fragmented private memories, the gradual revelation of family secrets that constitute a counterpoint to the "official" collective historical discourse—which is in turn a general characteristic of the new historical consciousness of European novels of the last third of the twentieth century.[18] As in many of Antunes's novels, the chronology of events—in this case, a few days before and after the burial of the family patriarch—is subordinated to the achronological order of retrospective monologues.[19]

The actual sociohistorical situation provides only the implicit background for the private revelations in the decaying feudal house in Monsaraz, including the maltreatment of women (by Leonor's husband Rodrigo), schizophrenia, drug abuse, and incest, all of which amounts to a violent demythification of the privilege of social class, a demonstration of the family's moral and material degradation. Toward the end the characters rival for the inheritance of Diogo's supposed riches, to finally discover that he leaves to his descendants nothing but debts, for he had maintained only the exterior appearance of wealth. The original title of the novel alludes to the *auto*, a popular theatrical genre of the sixteenth century on the Iberian Peninsula, in Portugal represented above all by the works of Gil Vicente. The title thus implies a postmodern revisiting of this late medieval / early modern genre, insofar as Antunes's novel is based on dramatic, dialogical narrative and insofar as it amounts to a carnivalesque exposition of human vices and obsessions.

Antunes's radically polyphonic approach to the family novel differs from the work of the Austrian Thomas Bernhard, whose novels often feature a singularly resentful male subject who finds himself confronted with the sinister legacy of a familial and national past, frequently involving the question of inheriting a material estate. Generally regarded as the most accomplished of Bernhard's novels, *Auslöschung (Extinction*, 1986) is conceived as the fictive autobiographical report of the Austrian aristocrat Franz Joseph Murau. The account is divided into two parts, the first ("The Telegram") centering on the protagonist's receipt of a telegram informing him of the death of his parents and older brother in a car accident; the second, entitled "Testament," depicts the preparations leading up to the funeral.[20] While the novel is obviously vastly different from Benet's, it shares with *Saúl ante Samuel* the device of the telegram that recalls the protagonist to his ancestral home from which he had hitherto been exiled, in this case, to a life in Rome. Whereas in Antunes's novel it is Diogo's deathbed that forms the symbolic center of the various family members, Bernhard's protagonist sets out to write his testimony as a response to his parents' deaths. In this sense, the three novels feature a "plot" to the extent that distant or dispersed family members are more or less suddenly brought back to their ancestral home.

Murau's physical return to the family home becomes a figure for the return of the past in a larger sense. The more than six hundred pages of the novel relate no more than three days, but the narrator's interior monologue recalls many episodes related to his family history and what he calls his "Herkunftskomplex," the "descent complex" (which is in turn an obsessive motif of Bernhard's novelistic work), that is, a hate relationship toward his family and country.[21] Murau becomes the sole inheritor of the Wolfsegg family estate, which as a material inheritance symbolically refers to what Bernhard in many of his texts has denounced as the sinister legacy of the specifically Austrian combination of National Socialism and Catholicism. The novel presents itself as a fictional autobiographical account of Murau, who after the funeral decides to donate the estate and all other family wealth to the Jewish community in Vienna. The novel enacts the obliteration of the family and all that it stands for, and it includes even the self-obliteration of the narrator, whose own death in 1983 is briefly announced by the sudden appearance of an external narrator in the last sentence of the text. The figuration of the familial end in this "antiautobiography" is thus literally conjoined with the end of writing, whereby the text of the novel assumes the significance of a posthumous testimony and testament.[22] Characteristically, when the narrator voices his hatred for what he sees as the destructive trait of Austrian society, the "eradication" and "murder" of landscapes, villages, cities, culture, and so on, he uses repeatedly the word *Auslöschung* (extinction, eradication, obliteration).[23] This term, which in German bears strong associations with the Holocaust, goes to show that the narrator's project to extricate himself from the familial and national continuity is strongly affected by what it seeks to negate. In a central passage where the narrator meditates on the burden of descent, he links the project of *Auslöschung* with the obligation to reflect and report on that "from which we are made and originate, and by which we are *formed* during the entire time of our existence."[24]

In all of these novels, the preoccupation with a specific national history is marked by a violent, iconoclastic contradiction. In contrast to the nineteenth century novel, as well as the case of *Il Gattopardo* and *Bearn*, these texts not only register familial decline and the end of a certain historical formation; they also show how this past does *not* go away but persists in memories, individual and collective traumas, and obsessions with the past. All three novels are concerned with the testimonial transcription of familial events. Stylistically and rhetorically—in part even thematically—they continue the tradition of Proust and Faulkner, that is, they render private remembrance as the novelistic mimesis of interior life. Accordingly, all represent only a few days of actual time: the main part of the discourse is taken over by temporally disordered monologues and memories. Despite their radically modernist techniques, they demonstrate a genealogical continuity, mediated by Proust and Faulkner, between the novel of the nineteenth and the twentieth century. While in the twentieth century the coordinates of world literature have changed and it is yet more difficult to speak of centers and peripheries, the case of Benet and Antunes in particular show how the crisis of patriarchy and family continues to signify in a postdictatorial context that we might see as peripheral to the European scene. Indeed, all of these novelists use private memories and the metaphor of familial inheritance to reflect obliquely on the respective experiences of historical catastrophe and its aftermath in the middle of the twentieth century.

Chapter 1 · Introduction

1. For brief suggestions on the epic form of the family saga and its relation to space and modernity, see Moretti, *Opere mondo*, 222–27.

2. Essential contributions include Calabrese, "Cicli, genealogie"; Tobin, *Time and the Novel*; Boheemen-Saaf, *Novel as Family Romance*; Weigel, *Genea-Logik*.

3. The term "nation," of course, deriving from the Latin *natio*, is related to "birth" and "descent." On the concept and history of nationhood, see Schulze, *Staat und Nation*, esp. 112.

4. Koschorke, *Wahrheit und Erfindung*, 261. Unless otherwise noted, all translations are my own.

5. Beizer, *Family Plots*, 10. See also Calabresi, "Cicli, genealogie," 632.

6. Foucault, *Order of Things*, xxii.

7. Gilmartin, *Ancestry and Narrative*, 12: "Often the intricacies of the family tree reveal or become the crises of plot and subplot; problems of inheritance, younger brothers, arranged marriage, adoption, illegitimacy, misalliance, the need for an heir—these become the driving force of plot, and are centred in the family tree and the will to keep the family line going."

8. Tobin, *Time and the Novel*, 7.

9. Koschorke, *Wahrheit und Erfindung*, 263.

10. See also Nelson, "Émile Zola."

11. For an extended argument concerning cases in which the region is portrayed as the "unadulterated version" of the nation, see Dainotto, "All the Regions Do Smilingly Revolt," esp. 493.

12. Gilmartin, *Ancestry and Narrative*, 242.

13. Sarasin, *Darwin und Foucault*, 196–98.

14. Strindberg, *I Havsbandet*.

15. Shideler, *Questioning the Father*; see also idem., "Borg's Lost Children."

16. Moretti, "Evolution, World-Systems, *Weltliteratur*."

17. Anderson, *Imagined Communities*.

18. Ibid., 26.

19. Ibid., 26n39.

20. For an extended discussion of the pluralization of temporal experience in modernity, see Koschorke, *Wahrheit und Erfindung*, 203–11.

21. Bhaba, *Location of Culture*, 143.

22. See Fredric Jameson's much-discussed argument about the necessarily allegorical nature of "peripheral" literature, "Third-World Literature in the Era of Multinational Capitalism."

23. Casanova, *World Republic of Letters*, 85: "The oldest literary fields are therefore the most autonomous as well, which is to say the most exclusively devoted to literature as an activity having no need of justification beyond itself."

24. Thomsen, *Mapping World Literature*, 25.

25. Dainotto, *Europe*, chs. 2 and 4.

26. On the literary geography of the European South, see also Domínguez, "South European Orient."

27. Marramao, *Pasaje a Occidente*, esp. 37–46.

28. Casanova, *World Republic of Letters*, 86.

29. Ibid., 36.

30. Ibid., 87. Casanova addresses the charge of Franco-centrism in the preface to the second, "corrected" French edition: *La république mondiale des lettres*, xiv–xv.

31. Moretti, "Conjectures on World Literature," 152.

32. Moretti, *Atlante del romanzo europeo*, 170. See also idem., "Modern European Literature."

33. Moretti, *La letteratura vista da lontano*, 3–5.

34. On the global diffusion and the local variation of the form, see the excellent discussion by Siskind, "Globalization of the Novel and the Novelization of the Global."

35. Koschorke, *Wahrheit und Erfindung*, 131.

36. Ibid., 205–6.

37. On the conceptual question of center and periphery, and the problem of artistic "backwardness," see the pioneering essay by Enrico Castelnuovo and Carlo Ginzburg, "Zentrum und Peripherie."

38. Dainotto, *Place in Literature*. See also Vecchi, Albertazzi, and Maj, *Periferie della storia*; Klobucka, "Theorizing the European Periphery."

39. Orlando, *L'intimità e la storia*, 121.

40. The difficulties of "smaller" literatures/languages to enter and be translated into the orbit of world literature has been commented upon already by the Danish critic Georg Brandes, in his article "Weltlitteratur" [*sic*], originally published in German in *Das litterarische Echo* 1 (1899). See Brandes, "World Literature."

41. Osterhammel, *Die Verwandlung der Welt*, 48–49.

42. For such an agenda, see Damrosch, "World Literature in a Postcanonical, Hypercanonical Age," 51.

Chapter 2 · Periphery and Genealogical Discontinuity

1. See also the extended discussion of this transformation in Koschorke, *Wahrheit und Erfindung*, 258–66.

2. Koselleck, *Vergangene Zukunft*, 325.

3. Koschorke, *Wahrheit und Erfindung*, 263.

4. Trumpener, *Bardic Nationalism.*

5. Edgeworth, *Castle Rackrent.* All subsequent quotations refer to this edition with page numbers in the text (*CR*). For the claim of Edgeworth as the first Irish novelist, see Flanagan, *Irish Novelists*, 100. See also Schirmer, "Tales from the Big House and Cabin"; and Mortimer, "*Castle Rackrent* and Its Historical Contexts."

6. McCormack, *Ascendancy and Tradition in Anglo-Irish Literary History*, 135.

7. See Trumpener, *Bardic Nationalism.* For variations, or more condensed versions of this argument, see idem., "National Character, National Plots"; and idem., "Cosmopolitismo periferico." Trumpener's argument that cultural innovation takes place in the periphery rather than in the center complements and corrects Moretti's thesis, according to which literary innovation *always* flows from the center to the periphery (215–16).

8. Colley, *Britons*, 8.

9. For an excellent overview, see Burgess, "National Tale and Allied Genres."

10. Eagleton, *Heathcliff and the Great Hunger*, 176.

11. Gilmartin, *Ancestry and Narrative*, 27–28.

12. Egenolf, "Maria Edgeworth in Blackface."

13. Butler, *Maria Edgeworth*, 66.

14. The extent of the Edgeworths' support of the Union is contested. See Butler's introduction to Edgeworth, *Castle Rackrent and Ennui*; Eagleton, *Heathcliff and the Great Hunger*, 161–68; Kiberd, *Irish Classics*, 263–64; Hack, "Inter-Nationalism."

15. See Hurst, *Maria Edgeworth and the Public Scene*, 30–33.

16. On the question of Edgeworth's economic experience, ideology, as well as the complex question of the possible co-authorship with her father, see Gallagher, *Nobody's Story*, 257–327.

17. Butler, *Maria Edgeworth*, 72.

18. Moretti, *Atlante del romanzo europeo*, 42–43.

19. This aspect has been extensively studied by Deane. See, for example, "Fiction and Politics: Irish Nineteenth-Century National Character," in *Writer as Witness*, 90–113. See also Wohlgemut, "Maria Edgeworth and the Question of National Character."

20. Bakhtin, "Forms of Time and of the Chronotope in the Novel."

21. As Perera has written, "the narrative voice of the illiterate Irish peasant, Thady, is [. . .] heavily mediated by the obviously anglicized editor who interrupts and punctuates Thady's story on every page with textual annotations, learned interpolations, and ironic 'folk' anecdotes." *Reaches of Empire*, 15.

22. For the suggestion that the novel "installs key conventions of regional writing," see the remarks by Duncan in *Scott's Shadow*, 73.

23. See Hechter, *Internal Colonialism*, esp. 30–32; Wright, *Ireland, India, and Nationalism in Nineteenth-Century Literature.* More generally, see Dainotto, "All the Regions Do Smilingly Revolt."

24. See also Butler, introduction to Edgeworth, *Castle Rackrent*, 12.

25. On the question of Thady's disingeniousness, see, for example, Newcomer, "*Castle Rackrent*."

26. See also the definition of "bull" in the *Oxford English Dictionary*: "A self-contradictory proposition, [. . .] an expression containing a manifest contradiction in terms involving a ludicrous inconsistency unperceived by the speaker."

27. Kreilkamp, *Anglo-Irish Novel and the Big House*, 41.

28. Scott, *Waverley*. All quotations refer to this edition with page numbers in the text (*W*).

29. However, the sentimentalizing view of the events of Culloden is different from the much more ambivalent perspective on Gaelic-Catholic culture in the wake of the rebellion of the United Irishmen of 1798 and the Union in 1800. It is also important to note that the events of 1745 are the outcome of the Union of England and Scotland in 1707, while the Irish rebellion of 1798 was actually leading to the Union of England and Ireland. In both cases, as well as in the contemporary England of *Waverley* (1805–14) the threat constituted by France, or the French Revolution, played a significant role. For this reason, the case of the colonization of Ireland is an important subtext for the colonization of the Highlands in *Waverley*.

30. For a detailed argument along these lines, see Makdisi, *Romantic Imperialism*, ch. 4, esp. 92.

31. On the motif of journeying in Scott, see Dekker, *Fictions of Romantic Tourism*, 126–41. See also Welsh, *Hero of the Waverley Novels*, 84.

32. Bhaba, *Location of Culture*, 203: "The desire for the national past disavows the differentiae of culture, community and identity. It does not 'repress' the contradictions and incommensurabilities that inhabit these social realities; nor does the nostalgia for the past 'homogenize' histories, cultures, ethnicities, as is often hastily and polemically concluded. [. . .] The disavowing, split posture turns the enunciative 'present' of national discourses on temporality into a rhetorics of peripherality."

33. Certeau, *Writing of History*, 45.

34. See Buzard, *Disorienting Fiction*, 80.

35. On this motif, especially with regard to the voice of the last representative of a culture in Scott's *The Lay of the Last Minstrel* (1805), see Stafford, *Last of the Race*, 164–65.

36. Ferris, "Melancholy, Memory, and the 'narrative situation' of history in post-Enlightenment Scotland," esp. 78–79.

37. On the significance of the border, see Valente, "Upon the Braes."

38. Iser, "Möglichkeiten der Illusion im Historischen Roman."

39. See Fuchs, *Romance*, 100.

40. Scott, "Essay on Romance."

41. As one of the few critics who have studied this problem in greater detail, see Oberhelman, "*Waverley*, Genealogy, History." However, Oberhelman's Foucauldian application of the term "genealogy" is somewhat inconsistent: it sometimes—but not always—means "the disruption of patrilineal authority and teleology" (32). For a discussion of patrilineal time in Scott's novel *Old Mortality*, see also Ferris, *Achievement of Literary Authority*, ch. 6.

42. For Scott's demonstration of the "obsolence of the whole Jacobite party," see Brown, *Walter Scott and the Historical Imagination*, 13.

43. For this idea, see Armstrong, *How Novels Think*, 63.

44. On the various unifying measures, see Colley, *Britons*, ch. 3. Another classical instance for the allegorical representation of national blending is the culmination of *Ivanhoe* in the marriage of Ivanhoe and Rowena. Scott, *Ivanhoe*, 498.

45. This "progression from the tribal origins of human society to its telos in commercial civilization," from the clan to the bourgeois family, from "blood" to a "sense of kinship," is also reflected in the domestic plots of the Scottish national tale, such as, for

example, *Clan-Albin*. Shields, "From Family Roots to the Routes of Empire," 935. On the difference from Scott, see esp. 937.

46. However, the sense of temporal development and movement is assigned only to Waverley, since all the other characters, including such figures as Fergus or Talbot, are locked into a specific place and position.

47. As Trevor-Roper writes, "Before 1745 the Highlanders had been despised as idle predatory barbarians. In 1745 they had been feared as dangerous rebels. But after 1746, when their distinct society crumbled so easily, they combined the romance of a primitive people with the charm of an endangered species." "Invention of Tradition," 25.

48. On the opposition between romance and the domestic family unit, see Celati, *Finzioni Occidentali*, 5–49, esp. 31. On Scott's transfiguration of traditional romance material into a new kind of novel, his "liberation" of *Waverley* from conventional associations and literary predecessors, see Kropf, *Authorship as Alchemy*, 142: "Just as Waverley finds his 'true' fathers by means of the legalized convention of foster-parentage that subverts natural genealogy, so *Waverley* as a multiplicity of textual material finds a foster-father in Scott who brings this multiplicity under control."

49. Early instantiations, such as John Galt's novel *The Entail* (1832), were still directly influenced by Scott. See Duncan, *Scott's Shadow*, 237: "Galt has pioneered the distinctively nineteenth-century kind of novel, the family chronicle or dynastic anatomy of middle class ascendancy, amplified (in British fiction) by Trollope and exhausted by Galsworthy." On Scott's influence on the novel, see Pavel, *La pensée du roman*, 228; and Wolff, "Sir Walter Scott and Dr. Dryasdust," 19.

Chapter 3 · Progress and Pessimism

1. Tellini, *Il romanzo italiano*, 120–21.
2. See Asor Rosa, *Storia europea della letteratura italiana*, 3:82.
3. Meter, *Figur und Erzählauffassung*, 248–49.
4. On the Southern question, see also Duggan, *Force of Destiny*, 265–73.
5. Dainotto, *Europe*, esp. 198–217.
6. See Meter, *Figur und Erzählauffassung*, 9–12. Verga, for instance, actively helped with the translation and promotion of *I Malavoglia* in France, by closely collaborating with the translator.
7. Meter, *Figur und Erzählauffassung*, 7, 228.
8. Pellini, *Naturalismo e verismo*, 10.
9. Ibid., 9. See also Mazzoni, *Teoria del romanzo*, 291–92; Nelson, *Naturalism in the European Novel*.
10. Baldi, *L'artificio della regressione*, 112, 119.
11. For this paragraph, I have much relied on the valuable account in Gumbrecht, *Zola im historischen Kontext*, 57–62.
12. Ibid., 59.
13. Ibid., 62; see also 33.
14. Pellini, *Naturalismo e verismo*, 10.
15. Meter, *Figur und Erzählauffassung*, 10. The emergence of such genealogical cycles in late nineteenth-century Sicily is a truly remarkable fact, yet these novelists are not the only and not the first engaged in such genealogical work. As Stefano Calabrese has shown, the moment Sicily ceases to exist as an autonomous, geocultural entity, around the year

1870, leads to a whole array of folkloric, linguistic, and historiographical activities, which aim to confront the new reality with a demarcation of Sicily's cultural boundaries and the reconstruction of its genesis via "genealogical-taxonomic terms." See "Cicli, genealogie," 634–35.

16. Veglia, "Il 'maestro' e il 'discepolo,'" 23–53. See also Küpper, *Zum italienischen Roman des neunzehnten Jahrhunderts*, 90–92.

17. Augieri, "La struttura della parentela come codice narrativo, in 'Vita dei campi.'" See also Baglio, "*I Malavoglia.*"

18. Verga, *I Malavoglia*. All further quotations refer to this edition with page numbers in the text (*MV*). Originally, Verga planned to publish *I Malavoglia* in Franchetti and Sonnino's weekly publication *Rassegna settimanale*.

19. Luperini, "*I Malavoglia* e la modernità," 333–34.

20. Verga, March 14, 1879, *Lettere a Luigi Capuana*, 114.

21. See Moretti, *Opere mondo*, 223. Frederika Randall's new translation of *Confessions of an Italian* will be published by Penguin Classics in May 2014.

22. Dainotto, *Place in Literature*, 104, 112.

23. Verga, *Tutte le novelle*, 123.

24. "Che la mano dell'artista rimarrà assolutamente invisibile, e il romanzo avrà l'impronta dell'avvenimento reale, e l'opera d'arte sembrerà essersi *fatta da sé*, aver maturato ed esser sorta spontanea come un fatto reale, senza serbare alcun punto di contatto con su autore." "L'amante di Gramigna," Verga, *Tutte le novelle*, 187.

25. Ibid., 90–114, 117–24, 186–93. See Baldi, *L'artificio della regressione*, 112.

26. Koschorke et al., *Vor der Familie*, 21.

27. On the narrative situation, see Tellini, *Il romanzo italiano*, 197; Baldi, *L'artificio della regressione*, 104–5. See also Mazzoni, *Teoria del romanzo*, 301–2.

28. Luperini, *Simbolo e costruzione*, 39.

29. Ibid., 353; Meter, *Figur und Erzählauffassung*, 24.

30. See the classic essay by Leo Spitzer, "L'originalità della narrazione nei *Maravoglia*."

31. Romano Luperini interprets this as a process of abstraction and generalization: "A Verga non interessava tanto rappresentare un preciso paese di mare quanto un ambiente sociale che fosse il piú possibile 'tipico' della condizione siciliana." *Simbolo e costruzione*, 22.

32. Candido, "O Mundo-Provérbio," 84.

33. Verga, *Lettere a Luigi Capuana*, 110.

34. Luperini, *Simbolo e costruzione*, 22–23.

35. Candido, "O Mundo-Provérbio," 96: They are "modes to petrify language, to confine its dynamism in an immutable code, whose principal role is to eliminate surprise, and thus the openness for new experiences."

36. On the upstart and composite nature of Mastro-Don Gesualdo's social position, as evidenced already by his name, see now Moretti, *Bourgeois*, 149–55.

37. Luperini, *Simbolo e costruzione*, 49.

38. For a detailed discussion of the implicit and explicit references to history, see ibid., 15–59.

39. Luperini, "*I Malavoglia* e la modernità," in Moretti, *Il romanzo*, 5:327–46, 337.

40. Ibid., 327–45.

41. This implied movement of decadence appears to go in the opposite direction of Zola, for the latter conceived of the "gradual genesis of a popular community" that would

emerge out of the ashes of the decadent Second Empire. See Meter, *Figur und Erzählauf-fassung*, 56.

42. Federico De Roberto to Ferdinando Di Giorgi, July 16, 1891, quoted in Borri, *Come leggere "I Viceré" di Federico De Roberto*, 34.

43. On the postrevolutionary critique of this legal institution, see Parnes, Vedder, and Willer, *Das Konzept der Generation*, 105–7.

44. De Roberto, *I Viceré*. All quotations refer to this edition with page numbers in the text (*VR*).

45. See Link-Heer, "Über den Anteil der Fiktionalität an der Psychopathologie des 19. Jahrhunderts," 294–95.

46. De Roberto, *Romanzi, novelle e saggi*, 1725. See also Parnes, Vedder, and Willer, *Das Konzept der Generation*, 174–87.

47. Duggan, *Force of Destiny*, 318–19; 340–42.

48. Grana, *"I Viceré" e la patologia del reale*, 175–77.

49. Contarino, "Il Mezzogiorno e la Sicilia," 733: "De Roberto offriva, nel quadro del dominante ottimismo della cultura umbertina, la risposta più lucida dell' 'opposizione meridionale' al cammino del Risorgimento e all'ufficialità continentale. Facendo dell'arretratezza della società siciliana una sorta di lungimiranza visuale, De Roberto poneva il suo romanzo fuori dalle coordinate del progresso a tutti i costi e antecipava la linea di tanti letterati siciliani (da Pirandello a Sciascia), che rifiuteranno i conforti del provvidenzialismo storico."

50. See Meter, *Figur und Erzählauffassung*, 107–13.

51. Against previous interpretations of *I Viceré* that see it more as a social novel with reference to a particular, restricted milieu, Margherita Ganeri argues that it is a historical novel that drives a polemic against the teleological historicism of the Romantic period. *Il romanzo storico in Italia*, 65–80, esp. 70.

52. O'Connell, "Degenerative Genre."

Chapter 4 · National and Genealogical Crisis

1. Anderson, *Imagined Communities*. For a useful discussion of Anderson's main theses, see Lewis, *Modernism, Nationalism, and the Novel*, ch. 1.

2. For an extended critique of universalizing presuppositions (especially in the Anglo-American context) in the discourse on novel and nationhood, see Reiss, "Mapping Identities." For a discussion of the rhetoric of nationhood in different genres and contexts, see Banti, *L'onore della nazione*.

3. Both of these novels have recently become available in English translation from Penguin Classics: Emilia Pardo Bazán, *The House of Ulloa*, trans. Paul O'Prey and Lucia Graves (2013); Benito Pérez Galdós, *Fortunata and Jacinta: Two Stories of Married Women*, rev. trans. (2011).

4. Bly, *Galdós' Novel of the Historical Imagination*.

5. See Hinterhäuser, *Die "Episodios Nacionales" von Benito Pérez Galdós*; Ribbans, "History and Fiction."

6. Galdós, "Observaciones."

7. It is remarkable that Galdós names Cervantes and Velázquez as paradigms for realist observation, since, seen from today's perspective, it is precisely the metafictional, metanarrative dimension of these artists' works that make them comparable to Galdós's

novels. In Emilia Pardo Bazán's well-known essays on the problem of literary natural-ism, *La cuestión palpitante* ("Genealogía," 1882–83), as well as in the preface to her novel *Un viaje de novios*, it is also Cervantes and Velázquez (alongside *La Celestina* and Goya) that are qualified as the founders of a genuinely Spanish realist tradition. This shows not only historically changing perceptions of the term "realism" but also that during the decade of the 1880's the realist-naturalist technique, for all its assumed objectivity, was not free of national or nationalist connotations, especially vis-à-vis the model of the French novel. The argument of a national tradition of realism (*realismo castizo*) also presupposes that a national identity (or aesthetic) predates the birth of the modern nation-state.

8. Galdós, prologue to Clarín [Alás], *La Regenta*, 1:25.

9. Galdós, "Observaciones," 112.

10. Ibid., 113.

11. Ibid., 106.

12. Ibid.

13. "la sustitución de la novela nacional de pura observación, por esa otra convencio-nal y sin carácter, [. . .] peste nacida en Francia, y que se ha difundido con la pasmosa rapidez de todos los males contagiosos" (Galdós, "Observaciones," 107) [the substitution of the national novel of pure observation by this other one, conventional and without character, (. . .) a pest born in France, which has spread itself with the amazing rapidity of all contagious evils]; "inundar la Península de una plaga desastrosa, haciendo esas emisiones de papel impreso, que son hoy la gran conquista del comercio editorial" (108) [to inundate the Peninsula with a disastrous plague, to make these emissions of printed paper, which today constitute the great conquest of the editorial market]; "el afrancesa-mento de nuestra alta sociedad [. . .] la venida de los Borbones, la irrupción de la moda francesa, comenzaron a desnaturalizar nuestra aristocracia" (109) [the Frenchification of our high society (. . .) the coming of the Bourbons, the irruption of French fashion, be-gan to denaturalize our aristocracy].

14. Moretti, "Conjectures on World Literature"; Casanova, *World Republic of Letters*. See also Lambert, "L'éternelle questions des frontiers."

15. Casanova, *World Republic of Letters*, 36: "Literatures are [. . .] not a pure emana-tion of national identity; they are constructed through literary rivalries, which are always denied, and struggles, which are always international."

16. The phenomenon of cultural belatedness and the question of peripheral compen-sation are often discussed with regard to the novel in Latin America. See Castro Rocha, "Machado de Assis," xxvi.

17. On the important precedent of (French) popular literature and its relation to the realist novel, see Martí-López, *Borrowed Words*, ch. 2; Sieburth, *Inventing High and Low*; Walter, "Normierte Wunschwelten und realistischer Diskurs."

18. Jo Labanyi has shown in great detail how this process of consolidation, especially after the restoration of 1874, was accompanied by a series of institutional, juridical, his-toriographical, and cultural initiatives, such as the founding of universities and acade-mies or the development of a national philology, as represented by the publication of the first Spanish literary history, by José Amador de los Rios, during the years 1861–65. See *Gender and Modernization*, 4–12.

19. See Pavel, *La pensée du roman*, 342–50.

20. See Mercer, *Urbanism and Urbanity*, 74–78.

21. For instance, at the beginning of the third part Jacinta confronts her unfaithful husband thus:

> Jacinta tuvo ya en la punta de la lengua el *lo sé todo*; pero se acordó de que noches antes su marido y ella se habían reído mucho de esta frase, observándola repetida en todas las comedias de intriga (Galdós, *FJ*, 3.2.1.54).

> [Jacinta had already on the tip of her tongue the "I know it all"; yet she remembered that some night before she and her husband had laughed much about this phrase, having observed how it was repeated in all comedies of intrigue.]

All quotations refer to this edition with page numbers in the text (*FJ*). Numbers refer to part number (total of four), chapter number, subchapter number, and page number.

22. Jameson, *Antinomies of Realism*, 148.

23. Küpper, *Balzac und der effet de réel*, 24.

24. Galdós, "Memorias de un desmemoriado," *Obras Completas*, 1656b.

25. Furst, *All Is True*, 94.

26. Another typical example for such generational-national allegory is the narrator's introduction of the character M. J. Ramón del Pez in the twelfth chapter of *La desheredada*: "hombre, en fin, que vosotros y yo conocemos como los dedos de nuestra propia mano, porque más que hombre es una generación, y más que personaje es una casta, una tribu, un medio Madrid, cifra y compendio de una media España" (Galdós, *La desheredada*, 169) [a man, after all, that you and I know like the fingers of our own hand, for more than a man it is a generation, and more than a person it is a caste, a tribe, an average Madrid, a cipher and compendium of an average Spain].

27. A reading of the novel as historical allegory is provided by Ribbans, "Contemporary History in the Structure and Characterization of *Fortunata y Jacinta*." For the historical references, see also Francisco Caudet's introduction to Galdós, *Fortunata y Jacinta*, 56–57.

28. In the light of the factual decline of the aristocracy, many members of the higher bourgeoisie were symbolically equipped with a "noble" pedigree. See Del Porto, *La decadencia de la familia aristocratica en la novela española moderna*, 13–15.

29. Galdós, *La desheredada*, 230, 238.

30. Clarín [Alás], *Su único hijo*, 161. The first two chapters of this novel harp on the theme of familial decline, only to then give way to a radical departure from the naturalist paradigm (see esp. 176n26).

31. See Lewis, "*Fortunata y Jacinta*," 326: "The ideological problematic of the Restoration is defined precisely by the absence of an ideological practice capable of giving representational form, and hence, effective political presence to the bourgeoisie *in its own right*."

32. Gilman, *Galdós and the Art of the European Novel*, 229; "The long, Naturalistic ouverture of *Fortunata y Jacinta* may seem out of proportion to some readers" (323).

33. A study by Carmen Menéndez Onrubia provides a useful overview of the genealogical narrative yet does not provide an interpretation of the novel as a whole. See "Historia y familia en *Fortunata y Jacinta*," 105–14. For a mythopoetic interpretation, see Gilman, *Galdós and the Art of the European Novel*, ch. 10.

34. This structural similarity was first pointed out by Uriarte, "El comercio en la obra de Galdós."

35. For the discursive formation of naturalism in the nineteenth century and the literary paradigms of Zola and Ibsen, see Parnes, Vedder, and Willer, *Das Konzept der Generation*, 174–87.

36. Hobsbawm, *Age of Capital*, 237.

37. On the phenomenon of female dress as a sign of urban modernization in the work of Galdós (especially in *La desheredada*), see Parsons, *A Cultural History of Madrid*, 42–47. See also Labanyi, *Gender and Modernization*, 189–91.

38. See Martínez Cuadrado, *La burguesía conservadora*, 523:

La liquidación del imperio colonial y las dificultades en la implantación de la hegemonía liberal hicieron del Estado español un débil heredero de su antigua poderosa influencia internacional. Ello determinó el eclipse de la intervención española fuera de sus restos coloniales ultramarines o de las fricciones internacionales que la ocasionaban precisamente estas posesiones. La decadencia colonial española y la expansión colonial de sus clásicos competidores europeos, Francia e Inglaterra, fueron paralelas. El Estado español representó entre 1874 y 1889 el papel de una nación europea aislada, escasamente influente, alejada de las grandes alianzas o ententes europeas.

39. Galdós, *Obras inéditas*, 6:60–61:

Pero si se ponen de acuerdo [Inglaterra y Alemania] y marchan unidas, pronto veremos que la preponderancia del principio sajón será decisiva en el mundo, y que aún los más autónomos nos veremos insensiblemente arrastrados a una situación dependiente y subalterna, recibiendo leyes de los más fuertes en lo político y en lo comercial. No sólo perderemos poco a poco nuestras colonias, sino que de una manera insensible nos iremos convirtiendo en algo conquistable y colonizable para provecho de ellos.

[Yet if England and Germany come to agree and march together, we will soon see that the preponderance of the Saxon principle will become decisive in the world and that even the most autonomous ones, like ourselves, will see ourselves in an imperceptible way dragged down to a dependent and subaltern position, receiving laws from the strongest ones in the political and commercial sphere. Not only will we slowly come to lose our colonies, but also we will imperceptibly convert ourselves into something to be conquered and colonized for their benefit.]

40. On the family tree as an iconographic and epistemological model, see the contributions in Weigel, *Generation*. See also idem., *Genea-Logik*, 29–37. For the most extended discussion of the metaphor of the family tree in the present novel, see Turner, "Family Ties and Tyrannies."

41. For example: "Si Juanito Santa Cruz no hubiera hecho aquella visita, esta historia no se habría escrito. Se hubiera escrito otra, eso sí, porque por donde quiera que el hombre vaya lleva consigo su novela, pero ésta no" (*FJ*, 1.3.3.181). [If Juanito Santo Cruz had not had that visit, this story would not have been written. To be sure, another one would have been written, for man takes with him his own novel wherever he goes, yet this one, no.]

42. The image of the family tree is also a central metaphor for the discourse of humanism within Krausist philosophy. According to the philosopher Sanz del Río, a representative of the generation of 1868, the tree of mankind or the tree of life stands for the general direction of civilization and history, signifying a socially unifying, continual process of maturation: "no cesará en sus crecimientos este árbol emblemático de la humanidad, hasta que se cubra de hojas y de frutos maduros después de esta laboriosa educación" [this emblematic tree of humankind will not cease growing, until it is covered with leaves and ripe fruits, after this laborious education]. Sanz del Río, *El ideal de la Humanidad para la vida* (1871), quoted in Toscano Liria, *Retórica e ideología de la Generación de 1868 en la obra de Galdós*, 82.

43. Casanova, *World Republic of Letters*, 102.

44. For an extended discussion, see Matzat, "Natur und Gesellschaft bei Clarín und Galdós."

45. On *costumbrismo* and the function of this chapter, see Lewis, "*Fortunata y Jacinta*," 318–20.

46. See Bernecker, *Geschichte Spaniens*, 239–40.

47. Of course, the term *Costumbres turcas* also simply refers to the custom of drinking coffee. At the same time, the adjective *turcas* implies a perspective of estrangement from Spanish customs.

48. On the sociologically ambivalent status of the familial "household" in Galdós's novels, see the perceptive comments in Jameson, *Antinomies of Realism*, 102.

49. See Gilman, *Galdós and the Art of the European Novel*, 308: "In a novelistic world constructed upon genealogies, Fortunata has none; she is thus as unique in her own way as her princely seducer in his. He is determined by his genetic and social background and therefore admired, whereas she, as Galdós emphasizes repeatedly, has no background at all."

50. On the adaptation of naturalism, see Hinterhäuser, "Benito Pérez Galdós."

51. As Friedrich Wolfzettel puts it, "The defender of the historical mission of the bourgeoisie becomes ever more the outspoken critic of the bourgeoisie, who finally will replace the bourgeois protagonists with heroes of the people." *Der spanische Roman*, 181. See also the almost identical comment in Caudet, introduction to Galdós, *Fortunata y Jacinta*, 27. For the problem of representing the people in the novel, see Neuschäfer, *Der Naturalismus in der Romania*, 68; 72. On the problem of cultural representations of the people more generally, see Jonsson, *A Brief History of the Masses*.

52. See Helgerson, *Adulterous Alliances*. Helgerson traces a protodemocratic and protorealist tendency in early modern drama (Lope de Vega, Diderot, etc.), so that it might be perceived as anticipating the modern novel. See also Banti, *L'onore della nazione*, ch. 2. In *La desheredada*, however, it is the aristocracy that serves as the paradigm for social distinction, but it does so, significantly, in the realm of social *fantasy*.

53. Caudet, introduction to Galdós, *Fortunata y Jacinta*: "Pero el personaje Fortunata va progresivamente individualizándose, diferenciándose y tomando características propias. Esto, en un principio, se manifiesta más que quando habla, quando piensa" (71); "La estructura de la novela está en relación directa con el proceso de emergencia de Fortunata a un primer plano narrativo (e histórico). Mas aún: la estructura de la novela está en función de tal emergencia" (80). See also Profeta, "'Realismo,' punto di vista, linguaggio."

54. "In my reading of the realist aesthetic, a dialectical literary form is generated out of the relationship between inequality and democracy. The realist novel is infused with the sense that any character is a potential hero, but simultaneously enchanted with the freestanding individual, defined through his or her interior consciousness." Woloch, *One vs. the Many*, 31.

55. This quasi-colonial aspect has been especially emphasized by Labanyi: "*Fortunata y Jacinta*, in constructing Fortunata as a 'savage' and superior breeder, takes the form of a miscegenation narrative: that is, as a colonially conceived blueprint for the nation based on the 'improvement of the race' through the white man's fertilization of the 'native' female." *Gender and Modernization*, 192. However, it should be noted that in this case the "improvement" derives from the side of the female "native."

56. The name alludes to the prominent Spanish author of the Enlightenment, Benito Jerónimo Feijoo (1676–1764).

57. See Labanyi, *Gender and Modernization*, 201: "The novel suggests that the distinction between civilization and backwardness is breaking down because both are producing degeneration."

58. On the ambivalence of the ending and its different interpretations, see the detailed discussion by Gold, *The Reframing of Realism*, ch. 2.

59. On the self-reflexivity of realism, see Furst, *All Is True*; Downing, *Double Exposures*, 1–23; Jameson, *Antinomies of Realism*, 15–27. For the Spanish context, see especially Labanyi, *Gender and Modernization*; Turner, "The Realist Novel"; Profeta, "'Realismo,' punto di vista."

Chapter 5 · *Nature, Nation, and De-/Regeneration*

1. Gumbrecht, Eine *Geschichte der spanischen Literatur*, 728.

2. This has been argued by Antonio Candido, who assigns generally a secondary and provincial significance to the regional novel in the context of France and England, while he acknowledges that, "in underdeveloped countries such as Greece and Spain, or in countries with underdeveloped areas such as Italy, regionalism can manifest itself as a valid artistic expression that can produce works of first-rate quality." "Literatura e subdesenvolvimento," 190.

3. Dainotto, "All the Regions Do Smilingly Revolt," 488.

4. Ibid., 489.

5. Moretti, *La letteratura vista da lontano*, 69. On the chronotope of the idyll, see Bakhtin, "Forms of Time and of the Chronotope in the Novel."

6. This confluence of regionalism and naturalism might be compared with the strong repercussion of naturalist thematics in nineteenth-century Argentina, where the opposition between *pampa* and capital (and between barbarity and civilization) has become central to definitions of national identity. Eugenio Cambaceres's practically contemporary novel *Sin rumbo* (1885) provides numerous parallels with *Los Pazos* (a genealogical crisis, the voyaging between city and country, the countryside as repository of physiological health, atavistic patriarchal violence, etc.). See also the reading by Culasso, *Geopolíticas de ficción*, ch. 2. For a comparative study of the naturalist novel, see Castro, *De la península hacia Latinoamérica*.

7. Castro, *De la península hacia Latinoamérica*, 19–20.

8. According to Moretti, naturalism provides fertile ground for his thesis of literary geography according to which "a plot from the core" is complemented by a "style from the periphery." See "Evolution, World-Systems, *Weltliteratur*," 118. In this regard, he adduces Antonio Candido's pioneering comparative study of naturalism, *O discurso e a cidade*.

9. See Casanova, *La république mondiale des lettres*, 155. The more orthodox followers of Zola (Eduardo López, Alejandro Sawa) are, on the contrary, of minor literary stature; see Schmitz, *Spanischer Naturalismus*, 76. See also Caudet, *Zola, Galdós, Clarín*; López, introduction to Pardo Bazán, *La madre naturaleza*, 22–29.

10. On this paradox, see Parnes, Vedder, and Willer, *Das Konzept der Generation*, 180–81.

11. Soriano, "Una conferencia con Emilio Zola." See also Davis, "Catholicism and Naturalism."

12. See also Clemessy, "De *La cuestión palpitante* a 'La tribuna'"; Davis, "Catholicism and Naturalism."

13. Pardo Bazán, *La cuestión palpitante*, *Obras Completas*, 574.

14. Ibid., 624.

15. Hemingway, "Grace, Nature, Naturalism, and Pardo Bazán."

16. Pardo Bazán, *La cuestión palpitante*, *Obras Completas*, 582.

17. Ibid., 639.

18. Ibid., 643.

19. Ibid., 647.

20. See especially the section of *La cuestión palpitante* entitled "Genealogía," concerned with the European origin of the novel, and especially with Spanish-French relations (chs. 6–7):

> En achaque de novelas hemos madrugado bastante más que los franceses. Hartos estábamos ya de producir historias caballerescas, y florecía en nuestro Parnaso el género picaresco y pastoril, mientras ellos no poseían un mal libro de entretenimiento en prosa, si se exceptúan algunas *nouvelles*" (595).

> [Concerning the vice of novels we got up much earlier than the French. We are already fed up with producing chivalrous histories, and in our Parnassus flowered the picaresque and the pastoral genre, while they did not possess one bad book of entertainment in prose, with the exception of some *nouvelles*.]

On the debate of national priority, see Caudet, "La querella naturalista."

21. "La imitación entre naciones no es caso extraordinario ni tan humillante para la nación imitadora como suele decirse." [The imitation among nations is not an extraordinary occurrence, nor is it so humiliating for the imitating nation, as is often claimed.] Pardo Bazán, *La cuestión palpitante*, *Obras Completas*, 590.

22. Martí-López, *Borrowed Words*, ch. 2. For an extended discussion of the reception of naturalism in Spain, see Schmitz, *Spanischer Naturalismus*, esp. 70–80; on Pardo Bazán, 166–75. On Pardo Bazán's critical adaptation of naturalism, see also Hemingway, "Emilia Pardo Bazán."

23. For a detailed analysis of the text along these lines, see Lee Bretz, *Voices, Silences and Echoes*, 90–99.

24. Pardo Bazán, *La cuestión palpitante, Obras Completas*, 1002, 1093.

25. On this aspect, and generally the problem of ideological hybridity in Pardo Bazán, see Nitsch, "Nervöse Martyrien: Wissenschaftlicher und religiöser Diskurs in Pardo Bazáns *Los Pazos de Ulloa*," in Matzat, *Peripherie und Dialogizität*, 205–21, esp. 211.

26. See also Labanyi, *Gender and Modernization*, 61: "The motif of isolation is arguably more significant in novels of the North than in those of the South. [. . .] The lack of exchange or contact with the outside world causes the internal and isolated social worlds depicted to fester and degenerate."

27. This kind of ethnographic perspective might be indebted to the contemporary genre of travel literature: "Just as we may discern the degree of influence that travel books of other Europeans exerted upon early nineteenth-century Spanish writing through being perceived by outsiders, something which arguably encouraged self-observation, so too in the regional novel the figure of the visitor becomes part of a necessary discovery of the terrain." Sinclair, "The regional novel: evolution and consolation," 57. On the figure of the foreign observer, see also Wolfzettel, *Der spanische Roman*, 280.

28. Pardo Bazán, *Los Pazos de Ulloa*, 590. All quotations refer to this edition with page numbers in the text (*LPU*).

29. This multicausality has been interpreted as overcoming the Spanish novel's earlier more exclusive focus on the faculty of the imagination. See Gullón, *La novela del XIX*, 81–97, esp. 85–87.

30. Pavel, *La pensée du roman*, 349: "Dans la recherche de l'idéalisme moderne les romanciers espagnols ont-ils évité d'emblée la confrontation entre les positions extrêmes représentées par l'enchantement de l'interiorité et par la réduction de l'être humain à son milieu."

31. See Guillén, "Entre la distancia y la ironia."

32. Bakhtin, "Forms of Time and of the Chronotope in the Novel," 246.

33. Although of much shorter length, this scene has obvious structural parallels in the moments of genealogical excursus that occur relatively early on both in Galdós's *Fortunata y Jacinta* and Clarín's *La Regenta* (vol. 1, ch. 4, 239–42.; for Galdós, see previous chapter). See also the first two chapters of Clarín, *Su único hijo*, esp. 162; 176.

34. "Con las antiguallas que allí se pudrían, pudiera escribirse la historia de las costumbres y ocupaciones de la nobleza gallega, desde un par de siglos acá" (*LPU*, 227). [With the old things that were rotting there, one could write the history of the customs and occupations of the Galician nobility, from several centuries ago until now.]

35. Carr, *Spain*, 8–11 (8).

36. Labanyi, *Gender and Modernization*, 343–46.

37. Pardo Bazán, "Apuntes autobiográficos," *Obras Completas*, 3:727.

38. As Maurice Hemingway argues, "This is how she initially conceived the novel and probably continued to think of it, even though by the time it was completed it could no longer be accurately described in this way." See *Emilia Pardo Bazán*, 27–28. See also Mayoral, introduction to Pardo Bazán, *Los Pazos de Ulloa*, 13: "En la Pardo Bazán la longitud de las novelas parece estar sobre todo en función del estudio psicológico de los personajes, más que en el análisis de aspectos sociológicos o históricos, de la visión totalizadora de una época o de una clase social, como sucede en Galdós."

39. Baguley, *Naturalist Fiction*, 107.

40. Wolfzettel, *Der spanische Roman*, 290.

41. This motif of dislocation and the shuttling between different spaces is typical for the novels of Pardo Bazán. See Henn, *Early Pardo Bazán*, ch. 2, esp. 38. See also Dorca, *Volverás a la región*, ch. 6, esp. 125–27.

42. See also Mayoral, introduction to Pardo Bazán, *Los Pazos de Ulloa*, 71–85.

43. Hart, "Gendered Gothic in Pardo Bazán's *Los Pazos de Ulloa*." Hart insists on the sociohistorical origins of the Gothic genre, suggesting that it reflects the "fading ghost of the nobility" in peripheral places (226).

44. Koschorke, *Die Heilige Familie und ihre Folgen*, 57–63.

45. See also Matzat, *Peripherie und Dialogizität*, 212–13.

46. Other novels by the author, however, lay a somewhat greater stress on determinist hereditary traits. See Dendle, "Racial Theories of Emilia Pardo Bazán."

47. It is through the figure of the abbot of Nayal, a confidant of Julián, that the context of politics is first introduced (ch. 12). We learn that Nayal, embodying the conservative view of the clergy, is concerned with the fact that the Queen Isabella II has fled into French exile and a provisional government is established (*LPU*, 244).

48. See Mayoral, introduction to Pardo Bazán, *Los Pazos de Ulloa*, 95.

49. For the most thorough discussion of the political context, see Henn, *Early Pardo Bazán*, 125–33.

50. See also the scene in *La madre naturaleza*, where Gabriel expresses to Juncál the idea that Spain is far from ready for a constitutional democracy:

> Antes que aquí se formen costumbres en armonía con el constitucionalismo, tiene que ir una poca de agua a su molino de usted. Decía cierto hombre político que el sistema parlamentario era una cosa excelente, que nos había de hacer felices dentro de setecientos años" (*LMN*, 190–91).

> [Before customs will be formed here in harmony with constitutionalism, some water will have to go down the river. A certain politician said that the parliamentary system was an excellent thing, that it would make us happy within seven hundred years.]

51. Labanyi, *Gender and Modernization*, 346–47.

52. Carr, *Spain*, 366–79, 367: "The main charge against *caciquismo* at the turn of the century was that it transformed what was legally and formally a democratic monarchy into an oligarchy." My comments on *caciquismo* rely largely on this account.

53. Carr, *Spain*, 369; Henn, *Early Pardo Bazán*, 132.

54. On the author's political standpoint, see the comment by Marina Mayoral in her substantial introduction: "La crítica social de la Pardo Bazán no va nunca en un sentido moderno, democrático, de denuncia de privilegios o injusticias. Ella es aristócrata por nacimiento y por convicción y carece de talento democrático; muy al contrario, tiene espíritu de clase y sus ideales reformistas se dirigen hacia una sociedad jerarquizada, paternalista que suple mediante la caridad las inevitables diferencias y las posibles injusticias." Introduction to Pardo Bazán, *Los Pazos de Ulloa*, 92.

55. Darwin, *Origin of Species*, 460. See also Beer, *Darwin's Plots*. More specifically on the Spanish context, see Litvak, *El tiempo de los trenes*, 108–12; Kirby, "Pardo Bazán, Darwinism and 'La Madre Naturaleza.'"

56. See Zola, *La fortune des Rougon*, 29: "Règnent encore la végétation puissante et le silence frissonante de l'ancien cimetière." For an extended analysis of this key scene in Zola's novelistic project, see Warning, "Zola's Rougon-Macquart."

57. Pardo Bazán, *La madre naturaleza*. All quotations refer to this edition with page numbers in the text (*LMN*).

58. Weigel, *Genea-Logik*, 29–37.

59. For a succinct characterization of Darwin's *Origins* along these lines, as well as its relation to literary Naturalism, see Shideler, *Questioning the Father*, ch. 1, esp. 60.

60. For a detailed discussion, see López, introduction to Pardo Bazán, *La madre naturaleza*, 35–37.

61. See also the interesting discussion by Wolfram Nitsch, who (using the narratological categories of Lotman) understands "the strict serialization of a radically sharpened conflict as the productive problematization of the realist *sujet*" (Nitsch, *Nervöse Martyrien*, in Matzat, *Peripherie und Dialogizität*, 208). In contrast to other contemporary examples of literary realism, Pardo Bazán's two novels are modeled not on a linear but on a cyclical pattern that "combines event-driven progression and event-deprived repetition" (208). It is precisely this infinite serialization of conflict, caused by the historical pessimism of Pardo Bazán, that might be understood as a formal innovation with respect to conventional realism (Balzac, Galdós), as well as the naturalism of Zola (similarly pessimist, yet apocalyptic—and hence not cyclical—in structure). On the cyclical nature, see 206–11.

62. The sudden change toward a plural voice nicely illustrates on a grammatical level the stated fact, namely that the category of generation mediates between the individual and the nation.

63. Labanyi, *Gender and Modernization*, 372.

64. In 1870 Pardo Bazán had traveled for the first time to France and returned with "apostolic zeal" to work toward the regeneration of the country. See Pardo Bazán, *La madre naturaleza*, 172n157. Bearing in mind Pardo Bazán's exceptional condition as an autodidactic woman, one finds certain parallels between the intellectual formation of Gabriel Pardo (!) and the author herself. In "Apuntes autobiograficos" (1886) she reports on her readings of Krause and Kant (*Obras Completas*, 3:710) and speaks generally of regenerative projects of her own generation: "En aquellos años de 1879 a 1880 empezaba a destacarse ya la generación hija de la Revolución de septiembre del 68." See also Clemessy, *Emilia Pardo Bazán, romancière*, 458–59.

65. On the interconnectedness of decadence and regeneration, both in Darwinian and literary discourse, see Davis, "Decadence and the Organic Metaphor," esp. 139.

66. See also Tobin, *Time and the Novel*, 42–43: "Once the novel's historical time becomes contaminated or haunted or enriched by the mythical and primitive, the one impossible distance from beginning to end is a straight line." See Urey, "Incest and Interpretation in *Los Pazos de Ulloa* and *La Madre Naturaleza*." Among twentieth-century novels thematizing the involution of genealogy by incest, one may cite works by William Faulkner, Gabriel García Márquez, and Robert Musil.

67. Lévi-Strauss, *Die elementaren Strukturen der Verwandtschaft*, 73.

68. Freeland, "Evolution and Dissolution." See also Lourenço, "Eça de Queirós e o incesto na literatura naturalista ibérica"; Almeida Moura, "*Os Maias*, ensaio alegórico sobre a decadência da nação."

69. For such an argument, see Lee Six, "Buenos Seamos, que dios nos ve."

Chapter 6 · Dissolution and Disillusion

1. Eça de Queirós to Oliveira Martins, 1884, quoted in Coleman, *Eça de Queirós and European Realism*, 195.

2. Ferreira da Cunha, "A história literária e a 'invenção da tradição,'" 98: "A história literária, enquanto narrativa da trajectória da literatura portuguesa, consiste assim numa sequência de movimentos e gerações que procuraram retratar Portugal e redimi-lo da decadência com que foi diagnosticado, em particular desde Herculano." See also Machado Pires, *A ideia de decadência na Geração de 70*; Serrão, *Temas da cultura portuguesa—II*.

3. For a useful comparison of the respective influence of French naturalism in Spain and Portugal, see Reis, "Eça de Queirós e Clarín ou o romance como discurso ideológico."

4. "Respeitamos a memória dos nossos avós: Memoremos piedosamente os actos deles: mas não os imitemos." Quoted in Ribeiro, *História crítica da literatura portuguesa*, 6:88.

5. Gilman, "Political Theory and Degeneration."

6. Queirós, *Os Maias*. All quotations refer to this edition with page numbers in the text (*OM*). English translations follow *The Maias*, marked with (*TM*).

7. For a detailed analysis of the temporal and narrative structure, see also Prado Coelho, *A contrário de Penélope*, 167–70.

8. Koselleck, *Vergangene Zukunft*, 313; Dilthey, "Über das Studium," 36.

9. For the literary representation of the bachelor in nineteenth-century literature, see Parnes, Vedder, and Willer, *Das Konzept der Generation*, 164–73.

10. See also Reis, *Introdução*, 135. This is also the view of Freeland, *O leitor e a verdade oculta*, 141: "It is in the generation of the son Pedro, the period of the Regeneration, where the authority of the father is definitely usurped, leading to the betrayals and confusions that condemn the last generation of the Maias."

11. The allegorical association of an oedipal rivalry between father figures and sons with a situation of intranational conflict—namely, the civil war of 1828–34—has famously been explored in the founding text of the modern Portuguese novel, Almeida Garrett's *Viagens na minha terra* (*Travels into my Homeland*, 1846).

12. The name Tancredo is undoubtedly an allusion to Benjamin Disraeli's novel *Tancred*. See also Eça's essay on Disraeli, "Lord Beaconsfield," where he mocks his qualities as a novelist as "this disordered monument of idealism" (554), a form of literature hopelessly outmoded in the modern age (544). In "Cartas de Inglaterra," in *Obras*, 2:543–56.

13. This has been argued by Coimbra Martins, *Ensaois Queirosianos*, 268–87. For a historical and comparative perspective, see Nonnenmacher, *Natur und Fatum*.

14. Rothwell, *Canon of Empty Fathers*, 65. What is new is not the disturbance of familial order as such—this is indeed a classical topic of the bourgeois novel—but the emergence of the protagonist-as-dandy in Eça's later, postrealist novels. According to Tony Tanner's observations about Henry James, this marks precisely the "decline of the bourgeois novel as such. . . . One is tempted to say that the emergence of the artist-as-hero is coincident with a sense of the family-as-ruin." *Adultery in the Novel*, 99.

15. On this problem of the character's indeterminacy, see also Vilela, "Histórias de ausência n'*Os Maias*," esp. 61–62.

16. In this sense, Abraham and Torok have modified Freud's understanding of the uncanny as *nescience,* an "unknown knowledge," as usefully formulated by Esther Raskin: "Abraham [. . .] suggests that the psychological effect of something seeming familiar and strange at the same time can be explained through the specific configuration in which something is unknown (*unheimlich*) to the subject in one generation and secretly 'known' or 'within the family house' (literally *heimlich*) in the preceding one." *Family Secrets and the Psychoanalysis of Narrative,* 30. *Os Maias* would thus lend itself to Raskin's thesis that family secrets function as the very generator of narrative (45).

17. See Pires da Lima, *As máscaras do desengano,* 47–49. Not in formal but in thematic terms, the portrayal of generational/regenerational hopes and disillusions, *Os Maias* might also be compared to the Spanish generation of 1898, as represented for example by Azorín's *La voluntad* (1902).

18. See also Brooks, *Reading for the Plot,* ch. 7. For the "plot of resignation" and the "static and repetitive," discontinuous nature of Flaubert's model of naturalism in contrast to Zola's more "clinical" and "dynamic" version, see Baguley, *Naturalist Fiction,* 90. For a comparison with Flaubert's novel of disillusion, see Grossegresse, *Konversation und Roman,* 146–47.

19. Mazzoni, *Teoria del romanzo,* 292.

20. "Realismen, Literaturtheorien des," in Nünning, *Metzler Lexikon Literatur- und Kulturtheorie,* 608–9.

21. On the relation between incest and Romanticism, see Lourenço, "Eça de Queirós e o incesto na literatura naturalista ibérica," esp. 110–12.

22. See also Seabra Pereira, "Decadence and Fin-de-siècle Literature in Portugal," 106: "As an antirational and spiritualist reaction against Positivism and Scientism, [. . .] Decadence embodied an artificial revival of romantic tendencies, in symbiosis with an agonizing pessimism and morbid aestheticism."

23. As David Weir puts it, decadence is "less a period of transition than a dynamics of transition." *Decadence and the Making of Modernism,* 15.

24. See also Grossegresse, *Konversation und Roman,* 149. Grossegresse argues that "conversational speech in the ambivalent zone between conversational speech and narration" sets out "to dissolve the pertinence of narrative and explanatory patterns." With historical hindsight, we might see here an anticipation of later developments in the form of the novel. On the symptomatic substitution of plot with conversation in the modernist novel, see also Sarraute, *L'ère du soupçon.*

25. One of the most authoritative students of Eça's work, Carlos Reis, proposes a schematization according to which Eça passed from a Romantic phase (1866–67) to a naturalist (1876–80) and finally to an "eclectic" one (1880–99). See *Introdução,* 12.

26. Ibid., 33–34.

27. Coleman, *Eça de Queirós and European Realism,* 203. The medical doctor becomes a stock figure and self-reflexive metonym for naturalism in the Iberian novel of the late nineteenth century, most prominently in Clarín's *La Regenta.*

28. In his book *Portugal contemporâneo* (1881, 2:299), the historian Oliveira Martins repeatedly employs metaphors that stress the "sick" state of the nation, a "collective pathology," as in this densely metaphorical passage:

Há, sem dúvida, uma patologia colectiva sem o estudo da qual o historiador jamais poderá iniciar-se no íntimo dos sentimentos de um povo. As doenças místicas do catolicismo do XVII século constituem um corpo de sintomas eminentes; e Portugal, cujo organismo raros momentos gozou de uma saúde perfeita; Portugal, cujo último ataque de febre monárquico-católica estudámos em 26–33; Portugal, que desde a implantação do liberalismo, ou em colapso, não se movia, ou passava da inacção à fúria, Portugal apresenta um sintoma curioso para diagnóstico ao médico político.

Quoted in Almeida Moura, "*Os Maias*, ensaio alegórico sobre a decadência da nação," 51. On organicist thinking in Martins, see also Freeland, "Evolution and Dissolution," esp. 326–27.

29. Pires de Lima, *As máscaras do desengano*, 180.

30. Coleman, *Eça de Queirós and European Realism*yes, 198.

31. Alan Freeland notes how this role of chance and other antiprogressive, antievolutionary aspects go against the program of positivist science and its assumption of a strict relation between cause and effect. *O leitor e a verdade oculta*, 150–53.

32. See also Reis, *Introdução*, 58.

33. See also Coleman, *Eça de Queirós and European Realism*, 209.

34. For a discussion of Portuguese-English relations in this context, see Rothwell, *Canon of Empty Fathers*. Rothwell argues that the two nations stand for two competing paternal lines (Monforte vs. Maia), in turn represented by "two competing educational models" (72) and the clash between two economic models: "what Maria Monforte represents through her father is the brutal excess of exchange where bodies quite literally operate as currency, in a trade that was the unrepentant backbone of capitalist economies" (76).

35. With reference to modern Greece, Gregory Jusdanis writes that peripheral societies "internalize the incongruity between western originals and local realities as a structural deficiency." *Belated Modernity and Aesthetic Culture*, xiii.

36. "The descending scale of copies implies an original from which the copies are derived." Freeland, "Evolution and Dissolution," 334. See also idem., *O leitor e a verdade oculta*, 123–25.

37. For an interesting discussion of the phenomenon of cultural globalization, see a passage from Eça's "Ecos de Paris," where he notes that London and Paris set the universal standard for civilization: "Mas, dentro em pouco, nem ruínas, nem monumentos haverá dignos de viagem; cada cidade, cada nação, se está forçando por aniquilar a sua originalidade tradicional, e nas maneiras e nos edifícios, desde os regulamentos de polícia até à vitrina dos joalheiros, dar-se a linha parisiense. [. . .] O mundo vai-se tornando uma contrafacção universal do Boulevard e da Regent Street." *Obras*, 2:1114–15.

38. Ferreira da Cunha, *A construção do discurso*, 217, 223. According to da Cunha, the significance of the generation of 1870 consists in the fact that it signals the establishment of a national intelligentsia, as well as the construction of Portugal as a cultural nation: "Descontente com o Portugal da Regeneração, esta geração põe em grande plano a questão do lugar de Portugal na Europa e na Humanidade, enfatizando a decadência dos povos peninsulares" (218).

39. Ibid., 232.

40. Santiago, "Eça, autor de *Madame Bovary*," 65. In his Borgesian reading Santiago suggests that another often-remarked "defect" of Eça's novels, his incapacity to represent characters with a convincing psychology, might actually be read as a sign of modernity: as a negation of introspection (60).

41. Machado de Assis, *Obras completas*, 39: "O Sr. Eça de Queirós é um fiel e aspérrimo discípulo do realismo propagado pelo autor do *Assommoir*."

42. For a concise review of this famous critical quarrel, see also Santos, "Machado de Assis, Critic of Eça de Queirós."

43. Queirós, *Obras*, 2:1647–848.

44. Zola, *Thérèse Raquin*, 9.

45. Queirós, *Obras*, 2:813–14.

46. Ibid., 2:819

47. Ibid., 2:822–23.

48. See also Ferreira da Cunha, *A construção do discurso*, 24.

49. "This consciousness of the passing of time, of the 'weight' of the years, is probably the one single distinguishing element that is wholly new to the dense fabric of *Os Maias*." Coleman, *Eça de Queirós and European Realism*, 123.

50. For a detailed development of this argument, see Gledson, *Por um novo Machado de Assis*, 136–42.

51. Certeau, *Writing of History*, 100.

52. The symbolic status of the statue of Camões is similarly invoked at the end of the third edition of *The Crime of Father Amaro* (1880). See *O crime do padre Amaro*, 527.

53. Such a turn toward traditional, rural values may also be detected in other representatives of Eça's generation, such as Antero de Quental and Oliveira Martins. On the conflict between urban and rural values in Eça's work generally, see Candido, "Entre campo e cidade," esp. 49: "In this passage from city toward countryside, *Os Maias* occupies a key position, for it signifies that definitive liquidation of Lisbon civilization, and because in its plot it is the country seat of Santa Olávia that establishes a countermeasure and source of moral energy."

Chapter 7 · Surface Change

1. See Reiss, *Against Autonomy*, 16–18.

2. Anderson, *Imagined Communities*.

3. Casanova, *La république mondiale des lettres*, 36. It will suffice to mention the magisterial work of literary historiography by Antonio Candido, *Formação da literatura brasileira*, a study concerned with the problematic formation of a system of literary communication in the case of the Arcadian and the Romantic movements during the eighteenth and early nineteenth century.

4. The social exclusivity of literacy is, of course, generally characteristic of late nineteenth-century Latin America, but it was particularly pronounced in Brazil. See Rama, *Lettered City*, 64–66.

5. This has been detailed by Seixas Guimarães, *Os leitores de Machado de Assis*. In the following paragraph I rely heavily on this account.

6. Ibid., 73.

7. Machado de Assis, "Notícias da atual literatura brasileira: Instinto de nacionalidade," in *Obras completas*, vol. 3.

8. Casanova, *La république mondiale des lettres*, 157: "Dans le cas des 'petites' littératures, l'émergence d'une nouvelle literature est indissociable de l'apparition d'une nouvelle 'nation.'" On the antinationalist implications of Machado's essay, see the extended reading by Barros Baptista, *Em nome do apelo do nome*, ch. 1.

9. Machado de Assis, *Obras completas*, 802.

10. Ibid., 803.

11. Gledson, *Machado de Assis*.

12. Schwarz, *Um mestre na periferia do capitalismo*; idem., *A Master at the Periphery of Capitalism*; Chalhoub, *Machado de Assis, historiador*.

13. Schwarz, "La capriola di Machado," 288.

14. For a recent discussion that polemicizes against the common critical tendency to label Machado's work as a hyphenated form of realism ("critical realism," "allegorical realism," etc.), see Bernardo, *O problema do realismo de Machado de Assis*, esp. 65, 71. However, it seems clear that the historical formation of the practice of realism is a major reference point for Machado's novels, even as they contest, or deconstruct, this realism.

15. Gledson, *Machado de Assis*, 169.

16. Bosi, "Brás Cubas em três versões," 311.

17. Meira Monteiro, "Absence of Time," 352–54. On the critical debate, see also Fischer, "Geography and Representation in Machado de Assis."

18. Gledson, *Machado de Assis*, 225.

19. All quotations refer to Machado de Assis, *Esaú e Jacó*, with page numbers in the text (*EJ*). English translations follow *Esau and Jacob*, with page numbers in the text (HC). A newer translation is also available from the Oxford Library of Latin America: Machado de Assis, *Esau and Jacob*, trans. Elizabeth Lowe (Oxford: Oxford University Press, 2000)

20. For a reading of late Machado that draws on Benjamin's idea of a "ruined" allegory, see Costa Lima, "Sob a face de um bruxo," in *Dispersa demanda*, 57–123.

21. Schwarz, *Um mestre na periferia do capitalismo*, 87.

22. See in this regard the painting *O último baile da monarquía*, by Aurélio Figueiredo. Painted directly after the coup of 1889, it shows a festive congregation on the Ilha Fiscal embodying the "last dance" of the monarchy while in the sky appears a female symbol of the Republic surrounded by her followers and the Brazilian flag. For a reproduction of the painting, see Bueno, *Brasil*, 234–35.

23. See also Castro Rocha, *Literatura e cordialidade*.

24. For reproductions of such images, see Martins, *O despertar da República*, 13, 15; as well as the detailed discussion of the allegorical iconography in Carvalho, *A formação das almas*, ch. 4.

25. For a discussion of this iconographic tradition, see Banti, *L'onore della nazione*, ch. 1.

26. Moreover, as Gilberto Freyre has speculated, the feminized iconography of the Republic was probably also connected to the liberal classes' opposition to the paternalist character of the imperial order as embodied by D. Pedro II. See *Ordem e progresso*, 204. However, as Murilo de Carvalho has shown, this iconography became soon "desacralized" when the female Republic was increasingly represented in a negative or parodic fashion, for example as a harlot. See *A formação das almas*, 89.

27. Needell, *Belle époque tropical*, 31–32.

28. For Machado, this event signifies the worst aspects of corrupt, exploitive monetary capitalism, as can be gleaned from the *crônicas* of the series *A semana* (1892–93). Machado de Assis, *A semana*. See the numerous entries for *encilhamento* in the index.

29. On Machado's ambiguous relation to the Republic, see the brief remarks by Facioli, "Várias histórias para um homem célebre," 51–52.

30. Carvalho, *A formação das almas*, 30.

31. These practices have already been satirized, in a rather heavy-handed allegorical fashion, in Joaquim Manuel de Macedo's novel *A carteira de meu tio* (A letter from my uncle, 1855). In another related novel by Macedo, *Memórias do sobrinho de meu tio* (1868), liberal and conservative politicians are described as "twin brothers." See Süssekind, "O sobrinho do meu tio," 16.

32. Hirschman, *Rhetoric of Reaction*, 43.

33. Quoted after Martins, *O despertar da République*, 27.

34. Viotti da Costa, *Da monarquia à República*, 268.

35. Ibid., 273.

36. Bueno, *Brasil*, 230.

37. Viotti da Costa, *Da monarquia à República*, 274.

38. Carvalho, *Os bestializados*, 36.

39. Ibid., 36.

40. Ibid., 43, 56.

41. Santiago, *O cosmopolitismo do pobre*, 222.

42. Salles, *Joaquim Nabuco*, 27.

43. As Flora Süssekind has shown in her study of the Brazilian novel, the second half of the nineteenth century witnessed the emergence of the figure of the national historian as a paradigm for the narrator of fiction. See *O Brasil não é longe daqui*, esp. 189–90.

44. Woll, *Machado de Assis*, 183–85.

45. Almeida Magalhães, *Repensar o romance histórico*, 83–87, 118. I am indebted to the author for many fruitful discussions on this topic.

46. Barros Baptista, *Autobibliografias*, 406

47. Gledson, *Machado de Assis*, 162.

48. For Machado's conscious departure from the naturalist tradition via constellations of sterile or dubious genealogies, see the suggestions in Süssekind, *Tal Brasil, qual romance?*, 74–77.

49. Caldwell, introduction to Machado de Assis, *Esau and Jacob*, ix.

50. Chalhoub, *Machado de Assis, historiador*, 97–107.

51. Gledson, *Machado de Assis*, 214.

52. Machado de Assis, *Memórias póstumas de Brás Cubas*, ch. 160, p. 254: "Não tive filhos, não transmitiu a nenhuma criatura o legado da nossa miséria." [He had no sons or daughters and did not transmit to any creature the legacy of our misery.]

53. Bosi, "Brás Cubas em três versões," 312.

Chapter 8 · *The Last of the Line*

1. Tobin, *Time and the Novel*, 24.

2. Kern, *Culture of Time and Space*, 64.

3. Bakhtin, "Forms of Time and of the Chronotope in the Novel," 231.

4. Candido, "Literatura e subdesenvolvimento," 172.

5. Casanova, *World Republic of Letters*, 336–37.

6. See the comparative analyses by Toller Gomes, *O poder rural na ficção*; Standley, "Here and There."

7. The common motivations for this comparative dimension of 1930s literature are well underlined by Fitz, *Brazilian Narrative Traditions in a Comparative Context*, 130.

8. See also Gollnick, "Regional Novel and Beyond."

9. Banfield, "Remembrance and Tense Past," 48.

10. Wainwright, *Darwin and Faulkner's Novels*, 175.

11. Freyre, *Casa-grande & senzala*, 56–57. On the parallel Brazilian Northeast / American South, see also the remarks in the classic study by Ellison, *Brazil's New Novel*, 3.

12. Freyre, *Masters and Slaves*, xix–xx.

13. Freyre, *Manifesto regionalista*, 32–35.

14. Ibid., 58: "The current novelists, narrators, and writers have fear to appear as regionalists, forgetting that the novel of Hardy is regional, the poetry of Mistral, the best of the Spanish essay: by Ganivet, Unamuno, or Azorín."

15. Melo, "Os mundos misturados de Gilberto Freyre," 36.

16. Freyre, *Casa-grande & senzala*, 44.

17. Freyre, *Masters and Slaves*, xxxvii.

18. Ibid., xxxviii.

19. Lund, *Impure Imagination*, ch. 9. For an extended discussion of the relation Freyre and Lins do Rego, see also Trigo, *Engenho e memória*, 51–66.

20. Freyre, *Masters and Slaves*, xxxvii.

21. Ventura, *Estilo tropical*, esp. 126. See also Candido, "Um romancista da decadência," 57–62. For a discussion of the melancholic chronotope of the Big House theme in postnaturalist Brazilian literature of the 1950s and 1960s, see Lopes, *Nós os mortos*. The theme continues in still more recent authors, such as Raduan Nassar, Milton Hatoum, Francisco Dantas.

22. Ventura, *Estilo tropical*, 124–25.

23. The Brazilian regionalism of this period was typified by the successive elaboration of given narratives into cyclical series, similar to the roman-fleuve. See also Süsskind, *Tal Brasil, qual romance?*, 116–18.

24. Bakhtin, "Forms of Time and of the Chronotope in the Novel," 233.

25. Lins do Rego, *Menino de engenho*. All quotations refer to this edition with page numbers in the text (*ME*).

26. For a view of Lins do Rego's style as "spontaneous" and "instinctive," generally typical for the early criticism, see, for instance, Montenegro, *O romance brasileiro*, 173, 177.

Chapter 9 · *Death of a Prince, Birth of a Nation*

1. Robert, "Origins of the Novel," 169.

2. For Lampedusa's questioning of historical representation and change, see the reading in Lucente, *Beautiful Fables*, ch. 7.

3. For a comparative reading of these texts, see Tobin, *Time and the Novel*.

4. On the Oedipal complex and the Freudian family romance as a master plot of the modern novel, see Robert, "Origins of the Novel," 166–69. Francesco Orlando sees the literary originality of the novel precisely in the fact that Don Fabrizio combines the roles of intellectual and father. See *L'intimità e la storia*, 34–36.

5. The implied allusion is most obvious in the names of the respective protagonists: Fabrizio / Fabrizio del Dongo. For Lampedusa's supreme valuation of Stendhal, see Tomasi di Lampedusa, "Lezioni su Stendhal," in *Opere*, 615–47. See also Orlando, *L'intimità e la storia*, 148–49; Ragusa, "Stendhal, Tomasi di Lampedusa, and the Novel."

6. Colletta, *Plotting the Past*, 78: "The ideology of the novel was generally identified with that of its protagonist, Prince Fabrizio of Salina, and that of Prince Fabrizio with the author's."

7. As quoted in Vitello, *Giuseppe Tomasi di Lampedusa*, 230. See also Orlando, *L'intimità e la storia*, 95. I am much indebted to the insights of Orlando's study. For a more biographical perspective, see also idem., *Ricordo di Lampedusa*.

8. Tomasi di Lampedusa, *Il Gattopardo*. All quotations refer to this edition with page numbers in the text (*G*). The English translations (occasionally altered) follow *The Leopard*, marked with (*L*). I refer generally to the novel with its original title, which in fact refers to a sort of ocelot rather than a leopard.

9. Lansing, "Structure of Meaning in Lampedusa's *Il Gattopardo*."

10. Frank, "Spatial Form in Modern Literature."

11. Finley, Mack Smith, and Duggan, *History of Sicily*, 177.

12. Auerbach, *Mimesis*, ch. 18; esp. 444, 458.

13. See also Orlando, *L'intimità e la storia*, 27: "È dunque necessario ammettere che i lettori del romanzo, a milioni, si siano interessati soprattutto a qualcosa di più discontinuo che una trama. E non saprei dire a che cosa, se non a questo: al riflesso intimo d'un tempo quotidiano, storicamente significativo, entro una coscienza—quella appunto di Don Fabrizio."

14. On the different functions of narrative prolepsis, see Ricoeur, *Temps et récit*, 2:157.

15. Kermode, *Sense of an Ending*, 46.

16. "Saranno 24 hore della vita di mio bisnonno il giorno dello sbarco di Garibaldi." Lanza di Tomasi, "Premessa," in Tomasi di Lampedusa, *Opere*, xli. See Gilmour, *Last Leopard*, 129.

17. For a detailed analysis of this aspect, including the interesting suggestion that Lampedusa contrasts an aristocratc with a bourgeois conception of time, see Luperini, "Il 'gran signore' e il senso della temporalità."

18. In "Letteratura inglese" (Lectures on English literature) Lampedusa briefly expresses his interest in representing the specific, initial moment of political crisis: "se avessi la minima competenza e quindi la possibilità di occuparmi di storia politica, quel che più mi atttrarebbe sarebbe lo studio della crisi, anzi, ho detto male, lo studio del *inizio* della crisi, la considerazione di quell'impercettibile abbassamento del barometro" (*Opere*, 1126) [if I had a minimal competence, and hence the possibility to occupy myself with political history, what would be most appealing to me would be the study of the crisis, or better, the study of the *beginning* of the crisis, the consideration of that imperceptible lowering of the barometer].

19. In "Letteratura inglese" Lampedusa writes about Woolf:

Nei romanzi della Woolf sarebbe inutile cercare un 'intreccio' nel senso tradizionale della parola. Vi si può trovare soltanto quello che per lei era l'equivalente di un intreccio, una situazione nella quale la vita si é cristallizata, una situazione comprendente un certo numero di persone e una succesione di 'momenti' nelle loro vite reagenti l'una sull'altra" (*Opere*, 1253).

[In the novels of Woolf it would be useless to look for a "plot" in the traditional sense of the word. One can find there only that which for her was the equivalent of a plot, a situation in which life has become crystallized, a situation comprising a certain number of characters and a succession of "moments" in their lives as they react upon each other.]

20. Tomasi di Lampedusa, *Opere*, 1257: "Sono episodi staccati di quattro momenti della vita di una famiglia, dal 1880 ad oggi [. . .]; la mutevole identità delle generazioni." [These are isolated moments of four moments of the life of a family, from 1880 until today (. . .); the changing identity of the generations.]

21. On the modernist concern with the discontinuity of time, see also Kern, *Modernist Novel*, 109–11.

22. For a succinct contrast with De Roberto, see Dombroski, *Properties of Writing*, 156–57.

23. Ibid., 159.

24. For a sampling of this criticism, see Gilmour, *Last Leopard*, ch. 13.

25. Moe, *View from Vesuvius*. See also Luzzi, "Italy without Italians."

26. Moe, *View from Vesuvius*, 22.

27. Dainotto, *Europe*, 164–66.

28. Ibid., 168.

29. For a critique of these concepts from the perspective of subaltern studies, see Chakrabarty, *Provincializing Europe*, esp. ch. 4.

30. See also the illuminating and wide-ranging overview of the North/South dinstinction in literature by Leersen, "The Rhetoric of National Character." For a brief reference to Lampedusa, see 276.

31. Riall, "Garibaldi and the South," 106.

32. Hirschman, *Rhetoric of Reaction*, 43: "Starting from different premises [Gaetano] Mosca and [Vilfredo] Pareto had come more or less independently to the same conclusion toward the latter part of the nineteenth century. In the case of Mosca, the immediate 'sense data' by which he was surrounded as a young man in Sicily." For brief references to Lampedusa, see also 58, 77. For the possible influence of these thinkers on Lampedusa, see Stagl, "Vergänglichkeit und Wiederkehr im *Gattopardo*," 150–51.

33. On the issue of grafting metaphors and genetic hybridity, see also Meyers, "Symbol and Structure in *The Leopard*."

34. See also Orlando, *L'intimità e la storia*, 103.

35. Lampedusa himself was actually obsessed with the problem of Sicily/Italy as a cultural backwater, as can be see by the series of increasingly polemical comments in the latter part of his *Letteratura inglese*, where he laments the much-belated reception of writers such as Jane Austen or Henry James. See Tomasi di Lampedusa, *Opere*, 1187. See also Gilmour, *Last Leopard*, 57–58, 123–24.

36. For an extended discussion of the contemporary reception, see Reichel, "Geschichtsdenken und Gegenwartsdeutung in *Il Gattopardo*," 31–35.

37. Koschorke, *Wahrheit und Erfindung*, 237.

38. Saccone, "Nobility and Literature."

39. Ibid., 172.

40. In the context of the history of Sicilian colonization, however, they were not really an entirely new phenomenon, since a similar, parasitical division of power had operated for centuries on the island. The "compromise" between the prince and Don Calogero echoes the rivalry, as well as the strategic cooperation, between "poor" landowners and the small elite of cash-ready "new men" during the period of the 1860s. See also Finley, Mack Smith, and Duggan, *History of Sicily*, 183. The figure of the rentier, or *gabelloto* (a kind of "gentleman capitalist" and absentee landlord, often faulted for the uncompetitive state of Sicilian agriculture) actually goes back to the eighteenth century: "By the 1770s these *gabelloti* were already rich and aspiring to become aristocrats themselves. They had the reputation of being more ruthless than the landlords," reducing the peasants to a state of absolute dependence (126).

41. When Napoleon III, siding with the pope, resisted Garibaldi's plans to turn Rome into the new capital, the state's troups under General Pallavicino forced a military defeat upon Garibaldi and his voluntary army on the mountain of Aspromonte (Calabria), where Garibaldi was shot in the foot by Pallavicino, whom he thereafter befriended. See also Duggan, *Force of Destiny*, 245–46.

42. An exception is Meyers, "Greuze and Lampedusa's *Il Gattopardo*." I agree with Meyer's observation that "this particular painting is the symbolic core of the novel" (309).

43. See also Fried, *Absorption and Theatricality*, 65.

44. See Helgerson, *Adulterous Alliances*, 166–69.

45. For a reading of the painting as emblematic and anticipatory of an "un-heroic, bourgeois" death of the prince, see Tappert, "Kunstwerke im *Gattopardo*," 169.

46. This "balanced" view of the problem appears to have been the opinion of Lampedusa himself. See Gilmour, *Last Leopard*, 183: "It could be argued that Lampedusa's criticism of the Risorgimento came from both sides, from the viewpoints of both Gramsci and the Bourbons. In his opinion it should have been a real revolution or nothing at all" (183).

47. For a transhistorical and wide-ranging discussion of how the historiography of feudalism has shaped the self-understanding of modernity in relation to its own past, see Davis, *Periodization & Sovereignty*, ch. 1.

Chapter 10 · *The Perspective from the End*

1. Baltasar Porcel, introduction to Llorenç Villalonga, *Bearn o La sala de las muñecas* (2006) 7–14 (12). The editorial history of Villalonga's novel is complex insofar as he first wrote the text in Catalan (*Bearn o la sala de las nines*), then published it in Spanish—and only gained literary success in 1961 with the publication of the Catalan version. All further references refer to Llorenç Villalonga, *Bearn o La sala de las muñecas* (2011).

2. Wagner, "Mallorca und die Universalität der Lumières."

3. Villalonga, *Bearn*, 132.

4. Ibid., 118.

5. Ibid., 156, 193.

6. Ibid., 193, 262, 387.

7. Kern, *Modernist Novel*, 205; see also 132.

8. Casanova, *World Republic of Letters*, 338–42.

9. Bouju, *La transcription de l'histoire*. See also Caruth, *Unclaimed Experience*.

10. Ribaupierre, *Le roman généalogique*, esp. 140–43.

11. Benson, *Fenomenología del enigma*, 185: "El espacio textual que conforma el discurso benetiano apela precisamente a la mente en continuo estado de creación de imágenes que fluyen rítmicamente y cujo sentido ultimo no podemos descifrar. Representan el horror de una guerra civil que rompió el país y destruyó tanto la familia y la infancia del autor com la de tantos otros españoles."

12. Ibid., 181.

13. Casanova, *World Republic of Letters*, 340–42.

14. Herzberger, "Theme of Warring Brothers in *Saúl ante Samuel*."

15. Benet, *Saúl ante Samuel*, 236: "Las ideas también son afectivas y se hermanan o distancian más por razones generacionales y de simpatía que por su parentesco en un mismo sistema del juicio."

16. Wiltshire de Oliveira, "*Auto dos danados*," 16–32; Rothwell, *Canon of Empty Fathers*, 2007.

17. Lobo Antunes, *Auto dos danados*.

18. Le Bigot, "Le roman aux prises avec l'histoire."

19. Camaert, *L'écriture de la mémoire*, 47–48.

20. Bernhard, *Auslöschung*.

21. Ibid., 201.

22. See also Schönthaler, *Negative Poetik*, 93–95.

23. Bernhard, *Auslöschung*, esp. 113–14.

24. Ibid., 201.

Primary Sources

Assis, Joaquim Maria Machado de. *Esau and Jacob.* Translated by Helen Caldwell. Berkeley: University of California Press, 1965.

———. *Esaú e Jacó.* Rio de Janeiro: Garnier, 2005.

———. *Memórias póstumas de Brás Cubas.* Edited by Antônio Medina Rodrigues. São Paulo: Ateliê, 2001.

———. *Obras completas.* Edited by Afrânhio Coutinho. Rio de Janeiro: Nova Aguilar, 1997.

———. *A semana.* Edited by John Gledson. São Paulo: Hucitec, 1996.

Benet, Juan. *Saúl ante Samuel.* Barcelona: Random House Mondadori, 2009.

Bernhard, Thomas. *Auslöschung: Ein Zerfall.* Frankfurt am Main: Suhrkamp, 1988.

Cambaceres, Eugenio. *Sin rumbo.* Edited by Claude Cymerman. Madrid: Cátedra, 2005.

Clarín [Leopoldo Alás]. *La Regenta.* Edited by Juan Oleza. 2 vols. Madrid: Cátedra, 2004.

———. *Su único hijo.* Madrid: Cátedra, 2005.

Darwin, Charles. *The Origin of Species.* London: Penguin, 1985.

De Roberto, Federico. *Romanzi, novelle e saggi.* Edited by C. A. Madrignani. Milan: Mondadori, 1984.

———. *I Viceré.* Turin: Einaudi, 1990.

Edgeworth, Maria. *Castle Rackrent; an Hibernian Tale, Taken from Facts, and from the Manners of the Irish Squires, before the Year 1782.* Edited by George Watson. Oxford: Oxford University Press, 1999.

———. *Castle Rackrent and Ennui.* New York: Penguin, 1992.

Lins do Rego, José. *Menino de engenho.* Rio de Janeiro: José Olympio, 2008.

Lobo Antunes, António. *Auto dos danados.* Lisbon: Dom Quixote, 1986.

Pardo Bazán, Emilia. *La madre naturaleza.* Edited by Ignacio Javier López. Madrid: Cátedra, 2007.

———. *Obras completas.* Madrid: Aguilar, 1973.

———. *Los Pazos de Ulloa.* Edited by Marina Mayoral. Madrid: Clásicos Castalia, 1986.

Pérez Galdós, Benito. *La desheredada.* Madrid: Alianza, 2000.

———. *Fortunata y Jacinta: Dos historias de casadas.* Edited by Francisco Caudet. 2 vols. Madrid: Cátedra, 2002.

———. *Obras completas.* Edited by Carlos Robles. 6 vols. Madrid: Aguilar, 1951.

————. *Obras inéditas.* Edited by Alberto Ghiraldo. 11 vols. Madrid: Renacimiento, 1923–33.

————. "Observaciones sobre la novela contemporánea en España." In *Ensayos de crítica literaria*, edited by L. Bonnet, 115–24. Barcelona: Península, 1972.

Queirós, Eça de. *O crime do padre Amaro.* Porto, Portugal: Porto Editora, 2009.

————. *Os Maias: Episódios da vida romântica.* Lisbon: Porto Editora, 2002.

————. *The Maias: Episodes from Romantic Life.* Translated by Margaret Jull Costa. New York: New Directions, 2007.

————. *Obras de Eça de Queiróz.* Porto, Portugal: Lello & Irmão, 1979.

Scott, Walter. "Essay on Romance." In *Essays on Chivalry, Romance, and the Drama*, 129–16. Freeport, NY: Books for Libraries Press, 1972.

————. *Ivanhoe.* Edited by Ian Duncan. Oxford: Oxford University Press, 1996.

————. *Waverley; or, ' Tis Sixty Years Since.* Edited by Andrew Hook. London: Penguin, 1985.

Strindberg, August. *I Havsbandet.* Edited by Hans Lindström. Stockholm: Almqvist & Viksell, 1982.

Tomasi di Lampedusa, Giuseppe. *Il Gattopardo.* Milan: Feltrinelli Editore, 2003.

————. *The Leopard.* Translated by Archibald Colquhoun. New York: Pantheon, 1988.

————. *Opere.* Milan: Mondadori, 1995.

Verga, Giovanni. *Lettere a Luigi Capuana.* Edited by Gino Raya. Florence: Le Monnier, 1975.

————. *I Malavoglia.* Edited by Ferruccio Cecco. Turin: Einaudi, 1997.

————. *Tutte le novelle.* Edited by Giuseppe Zaccaria. Turin: Einaudi, 2011.

Villalonga, Llorenç. *Bearn o La sala de las muñecas.* Palma, Spain: Institut d'Estudis Baleàrics, 2006.

————. *Bearn o La sala de las muñecas.* Barcelona: Random House Mondadori, 2010.

Zola, Émile. *La fortune des Rougon.* Paris: Gallimard, 1981.

————. *Thérèse Raquin.* Paris: Gallimard, 2004.

Secondary Sources

Almeida Magalhães, Pedro Armando de. "Repensar o romance histórico: Leituras de 'Esaú e Jacó' de Machado de Assis e 'L'oeuvre au noir' de Marguerite Yourcenar." PhD diss., Universidade do Estado do Rio de Janeiro, 2007.

Almeida Moura, José de. "*Os Maias*, ensaio alegórico sobre a decadência da nação." *Cadernos de Literatura* (Instituto Nacional de Investigação Científica / Centro de Literatura Portuguesa da Universidade de Coimbra), 14 (1983): 46–56.

Anderson, Benedict. *Imagined Communities: Reflections on the Origin and Spread of Nationalism.* London: Verso, 1991.

Armstrong, Nancy. *How Novels Think.* New York: Columbia University Press, 2005.

Asor Rosa, Alberto. *Storia europea della letteratura italiana.* 3 vols. Turin: Einaudi, 2009.

Auerbach, Erich. *Mimesis: Dargestellte Wirklichkeit in der abendländischen Literatur.* Bern: Francke, 1986.

Augieri, C. A. "La struttura della parentela come codice narrativo, in 'Vita dei campi.' " In *Verga, ideologia e strutture narrative, il "caso" critico*, edited by Romano Luperini, 13–59. Lecce, Italy: Milella, 1982.

Baglio, Salvatore. "*I Malavoglia*: La famigliuola e il paese." In *Famiglia e societá nell'opera di G. Verga: Atti del convegno nazionale 1989*, edited by Norberto Cacciaglia, Ada Neiger, and Renzo Pavese, 313–24. Florence: Olschki, 1991.

Baguley, David. *Naturalist Fiction: The Entropic Vision*. Cambridge: Cambridge University Press, 1990.

Bakhtin, Mikhail M. "Forms of Time and of the Chronotope in the Novel." In *The Dialogic Imagination*, edited by Michael Holquist, translated by Caryl Emerson and Michael Holquist, 84–258. Austin: University of Texas Press, 1981.

Baldi, Guido. *L'artificio della regressione: Tecnica narrativa e ideologia nel Verga verista*. Naples: Liguori, 1980.

Banfield, Ann. "Remembrance and Tense Past." In *The Cambridge Companion to the Modernist Novel*, edited by Morag Shiach, 46–52. Cambridge: Cambridge University Press, 2007.

Banti, Alberto Mario. *L'onore della nazione: Identità sessuali e violenza nel nazionalismo europeo dal XVIII secolo alla Grande Guerra*. Turin: Einaudi, 2005.

Barros Baptista, Abel. *Autobibliografias: Solicitação do livro na ficção e na Ficção de Machado de Assis*. Lisbon: Relógio d'Água, 1998.

———. *Em nome do apelo do nome: Duas interrogações sobre Machado de Assis*. Lisbon: Litoral, 1991.

Beer, Gillian. *Darwin's Plots: Evolutionary Narrative in Darwin, George Eliot, and Nineteenth-Century Fiction*. London: Routledge and Kegan Paul, 1983.

Beizer, Janet L. *Family Plots: Balzac's Narrative Generations*. New Haven, CT: Yale University Press: 1986.

Benson, Ken. *Fenomenología del enigma: Juan Benet y el pensamiento literario postestructuralista*. Amsterdam: Rodopi, 2004.

Bernardo, Gustavo. *O problema do realismo de Machado de Assis*. Rio de Janeiro: Rocco, 2011.

Bernecker, Walter R., and Horst Pietschmann, *Geschichte Spaniens*. Stuttgart: Kohlhammer, 1993.

Bhaba, Homi K. *The Location of Culture*. New York: Routledge, 1994.

Bly, Peter A. *Galdós' Novel of the Historical Imagination: A Study of the Contemporary Novels*. Liverpool: Francis Cairns, 1983.

Boheemen-Saaf, Christine van. *The Novel as Family Romance: Language, Gender, and Authority from Fielding to Joyce*. Ithaca, NY: Cornell University Press, 1987.

Borri, Giancarlo. *Come leggere "I Viceré" di Federico De Roberto*. Milan: Mursia, 1995.

Bosi, Alfredo. "Brás Cubas em três versões." *Teresa: Revista de literatura brasileira* 6/7 (2006): 279–317.

Bouju, Emmanuel. *La transcription de l'histoire: Essai sur le roman européen de la fin du XXe siècle*. Rennes: Presses Universitaires de Rennes, 2006.

Brandes, Georg. "World Literature" [1899]. In *World Literature: A Reader*, edited by Theo d'haen, César Domínguez, and Mads Rosendahl Thomsen, 23–27. New York: Routledge, 2012.

Brooks, Peter. *Reading for the Plot*. New York: Vintage, 1985.

Brown, David. *Walter Scott and the Historical Imagination*. London: Routledge, 1979.

Bueno, Eduardo. *Brasil: Uma história*. São Paulo: Ática, 2005.

Burgess, Miranda. "The National Tale and Allied Genres, 1770's-1840's." In *The Cambridge Companion to the Irish Novel*, edited by John Wilson Foster, 40–59. Cambridge: Cambridge University Press, 2006.

Butler, Marilyn. *Maria Edgeworth: A Literary Biography*. Oxford: Clarendon, 1972.

Buzard, James. *Disorienting Fiction: The Autoethnographic Work of Nineteenth-Century British Novels*. Princeton, NJ: Princeton University Press, 2005.

Calabrese, Stefano. "Cicli, genealogie e altre forme di romanzo totale nel XIX secolo." In *Il romanzo*, edited by Franco Moretti, 4:611–40. Turin: Einaudi, 2004.

Camaert, Felipe. *L'écriture de la mémoire dans l'oeuvre d'Antonio Lobo Antunes et de Claude Simon*. Paris: L'Harmattan, 2009.

Candido, Antonio. "Entre campo e cidade." In *Tese e antitese*, 39–60. Rio de Janeiro: Ouro sobre Azul, 2006.

———. *Formação da literature brasileira*. Belo Horizonte, Brazil: Itatiaia, 1959.

———. "Literatura e subdesenvolvimento." In *A educação pela noite*, 140–62. Rio de Janeiro: Ouro sobre Azul, 2006.

———. "O Mundo-Provérbio." In *O discurso e a cidade*, 83–106. Rio de Janeiro: Ouro sobre Azul, 2010.

———. "Um romancista da decadência." In *Brigada ligeira*, 57–62. Rio de Janeiro: Ouro sobre Azul, 2004.

Carr, Raymond. *Spain, 1808–1975*. Oxford: Clarendon, 1982.

Caruth, Cary. *Unclaimed Experience: Trauma, Narrative and History*. Baltimore: Johns Hopkins University Press, 1996.

Carvalho, José Murilo de. *Os bestializados: O Rio de Janeiro e a República que não foi*. São Paulo: Companhia das Letras, 2006 [1987].

———. *A formação das almas: O imaginário da República no Brasil*. São Paulo: Companhia das Letras, 1990.

Casanova, Pascale. *La république mondiale des lettres*. Paris: Éditions du Seuil, 2008.

———. *The World Republic of Letters*. Translated by M. B. DeBevoise. Cambridge, MA: Harvard University Press, 2004.

Castelnuovo, Enrico, and Carlo Ginzburg. "Zentrum und Peripherie." In *Italienische Kunst: Eine neue Sicht auf ihre Geschichte*, 1:21–92. Berlin: Wagenbach, 1987.

Castro, Percio de, Jr. *De la península hacia Latinoamérica: El naturalismo social en Emilia Pardo Bazán, Eugenio Cambaceres y Aluísio Azevedo*. New York: Peter Lang, 1993.

Castro Rocha, João Cezar de, ed. *The Author as Plagiarist—the Case of Machado de Assis*. Vols. 13/14 of *Portuguese Literary & Cultural Studies*. Dartmouth, MA: Center for Portuguese Studies and Culture, University of Massachusetts Dartmouth, 2005.

———. *Literatura e cordialidade: O público e o privado na cultura brasileira*. Rio de Janeiro: Editora Universidade do Estado do Rio de Janeiro, 1998.

———. "Machado de Asis: The Location of an Author." In Castro Rocha, *Author as Plagiarist*, xix–xxxix.

Caudet, Francisco. "La querella naturalista: España contra Francia." In *Realismo y naturalismo en España en la segunda mitad del siglo XIX*, edited by Yvan Lissourges, 58–74. Barcelona: Editorial Anthropos, 1988.

———. *Zola, Galdós, Clarín: El naturalismo en Francia y España*. Madrid: Universidad Autónoma de Madrid, 1995.

Celati, Gianni. *Finzioni Occidentali: Fabulazione, comicità e scrittura*. Turin: Einaudi, 1986.

Certeau, Michel de. *The Writing of History*. Translated by Tom Conley. New York: Columbia University Press, 1988.

Chakrabarty, Dipesh. *Provincializing Europe: Postcolonial Thought and Historical Difference*. Princeton, NJ: Princeton University Press, 2000.

Chalhoub, Sidney. *Machado de Assis, historiador*. São Paulo: Companhia das Letras, 2003.

Clemessy, Nelly. "De 'La cuestión palpitante' a 'La tribuna': Teoria y praxis de la novela en Emilia Pardo Bazán." In *Realismo y naturalismo en España en la segunda mitad del siglo XIX*, edited by Yvann Lissorgues, 485–95. Barcelona: Editorial Anthropos, 1988.

———. *Emilia Pardo Bazán, romancière: La critique, la théorie, la pratique*. Paris: Centre de Recherches Hispaniques, 1980.

Coimbra Martins, António. *Ensaios Queirosianos*. Lisbon: Publicações Europa-America, 1967.

Coleman, Alexander. *Eça de Queirós and European Realism*. New York: New York University Press, 1980.

Colletta, Cristina Della. *Plotting the Past: Metamorphoses of Historical Narrative in Modern Italian Fiction*. West Lafayette, IN: Purdue University Press, 1996.

Colley, Linda. *Britons: Forging the Nation, 1701–1837*. New Haven, CT: Yale University Press, 1992.

Contarino, Rosario. "Il Mezzogiorno e la Sicilia." In *Letteratura italiana: Storia e geografia*, 3:711–90. Turin: Einaudi, 1989.

Costa Lima, Luiz. *Dispersa demanda: Ensaios sobre literatura e teoria*. Rio de Janeiro: Francisco Alves, 1981.

Culasso, Adriana G. *Geopolíticas de ficción: Espacio y sociedad en la novela argentina (1880–1920)*. Buenos Aires: Corregidor, 2006.

Dainotto, Roberto. "'All the Regions Do Smilingly Revolt': The Literature of Place and Region." *Critical Inquiry* 22, no. 3 (1996): 486–505.

———. *Europe (In Theory)*. Durham, NC: Duke University Press, 2007.

———. *Place in Literature: Regions, Cultures, Communities*. Ithaca, NY: Cornell University Press, 2002.

Damrosch, David. "World Literature in a Postcanonical, Hypercanonical Age." In *Comparative Literature in an Age of Globalization*, edited by Haun Saussy, 43–53. Baltimore: Johns Hopkins University Press, 2006.

Davis, Gifford. "Catholicism and Naturalism: Pardo Bazán's Reply to Zola." *Modern Language Notes* 90 (1975): 282–87.

Davis, Kathleen. *Periodization & Sovereignty: How Ideas of Feudalism & Secularization Govern the Politics of Time*. Philadelphia: University of Pennsylvania Press, 2008.

Davis, Whitney. "Decadence and the Organic Metaphor." *Representations* 89 (2005): 131–49.

Deane, Seamus. *The Writer as Witness: Literature as Historical Evidence*. Cork: Cork University Press, 1990.

Dekker, George G. *The Fictions of Romantic Tourism: Radcliffe, Scott, and Mary Shelley*. Stanford, CA: Stanford University Press, 2005.

Del Porto, Heriberto. *La decadencia de la familia aristocratica y su reflejo en la novela española moderna*. Miami, Florida: Ediciones Universal, 1984.

Dendle, Brian J. "The Racial Theories of Emilia Pardo Bazán." *Hispanic Review* 1, no. 38 (1970): 17–31.

Dilthey, Wilhelm. "Über das Studium der Geschichte der Wissenschaften vom Menschen, der Gesellschaft und dem Staat." In *Gesammelte Schriften*, vol. 5, edited by Georg Misch, 31–73. Stuttgart: Vandenhock & Ruprecht, 1990.

Dombroski, Robert S. *Properties of Writing: Ideological Discourse in Modern Italian Fiction*. Baltimore: Johns Hopkins University Press, 1994.

Domínguez, César. "The South European Orient: A Comparative Reflection on Space in Literary History." *Modern Language Quarterly* 67, no. 4 (2006): 419–49.

Dorca, Toni. *Volverás a la región: El cronotopo idílico en la novela española del siglo XIX*. Frankfurt am Main: Vervuert/Iberoamericana, 2004.

Downing, Eric. *Double Exposures: Repetition and Realism in Nineteenth-Century German Fiction*. Stanford: Stanford University Press, 2000.

Duggan, Christopher. *The Force of Destiny: A History of Italy since 1796*. London: Penguin, 2008.

Duncan, Ian. *Scott's Shadow: The Novel in Romantic Edinburgh*. Princeton, NJ: Princeton University Press, 2007.

Eagleton, Terry. *Heathcliff and the Great Hunger: Studies in Irish Culture*. London: Verso, 1995.

Egenolf, Susan B. "Maria Edgeworth in Blackface: *Castle Rackrent* and the Irish Rebellion of 1798." *English Literary History* 72 (2005): 845–69.

Ellison, Fred P. *Brazil's New Novel: Four Northeastern Masters; José Lins do Rego, Jorge Amado, Graciliano Ramos and Rachel de Queiroz*. Berkeley: University of California Press, 1954.

Facioli, Valentim. "Várias histórias para um homem célebre." In *Machado de Assis* [Antología & Estudos], edited by Alfredo Bosi, José Carlos Garbuglio, Mario Curvello, Valentim Facioli, 51–52. São Paulo: Ática, 1982.

Ferreira da Cunha, Carlos M. *A construção do discurso da história literária na literatura portuguesa do século XIX*. Poliedro. Minho, Portugal: Universidade de Minho, 2002.

———. "A história literária e a 'invenção da tradição.'" *Limes* 2 (2008): 97–114.

Ferris, Ina. *The Achievement of Literary Authority: Gender, History and the Waverley Novels* Ithaca, NY: Cornell University Press, 2002.

———. "Melancholy, Memory, and the 'Narrative Situation' of History in Post-Enlightenment Scotland." In *Scotland and the Borders of Romanticism*, edited by Leith Davis, Ian Duncan, and Janet Sorensen, 77–93. Cambridge: Cambridge University Press, 2007.

Finley, M. I., Denis Mack Smith, and Christopher Duggan. *A History of Sicily*. London: Chatto & Windus, 1986.

Fischer, Sybille Maria. "Geography and Representation in Machado de Assis." *Modern Language Quarterly* 55, no. 2 (1994): 191–213.

Fitz, Earl. E. *Brazilian Narrative Traditions in a Comparative Context*. New York: Modern Language Association, 2005.

Flanagan, Thomas. *The Irish Novelists, 1800–1850*. New York: Columbia University Press, 1959.

Foucault, Michel. *The Order of Things: An Archaeology of the Human Sciences.* New York: Vintage, 1994.

Frank, Joseph. "Spatial Form in Modern Literature" [1991]. In McKeon, *Theory of the Novel*, 784–802.

Freeland, Alan. "Evolution and Dissolution: Imagery and Social Darwinism in Eça de Queirós and Leopoldo Alas." *Journal of the Institute of Romance Studies* 2 (1993): 323–36.

———. *O leitor e a verdade oculta: Ensaio sobre "Os Maias."* Lisbon: Impresa Nacional / Casa da Moeda, 1987.

Freyre, Gilberto. *Casa-grande & senzala.* São Paolo: Global, 2004 [1933].

———. *Manifesto regionalista.* Recife, Brazil: Instituto Joaquim Nabuco, 1967.

———. *The Masters and the Slaves: A Study in the Development of Brazilian Civilization.* New York: Knopf, 1946.

———. *Ordem e progresso.* Rio de Janeiro: Record, 2000 [1957].

Fried, Michael. *Absorption and Theatricality: Painting and the Beholder in the Age of Diderot.* Berkeley: University of California Press, 1980.

Fuchs, Barbara. *Romance.* New York: Routledge, 2004.

Furst, Lilian. *All Is True: The Claims and Strategies of Realist Fiction.* Durham, NC: Duke University Press, 1995.

Gallagher, Catherine. *Nobody's Story: The Vanishing Acts of Women Writers in the Marketplace, 1670–1820.* Oxford: Clarendon, 1994.

Ganeri, Margherita. *Il romanzo storico in Italia: Il dibattito critico dalle origini al postmoderno.* Lecce, Italy: Manni, 1999.

Gilman, Stephen. *Galdós and the Art of the European Novel: 1867–1887.* Princeton, NJ: Princeton University Press, 1981.

Gilman, Stuart C. "Political Theory and Degeneration: From Left to Right, from Up to Down." In *Degeneration: The Dark Side of Progress*, edited by Edward Chamberlin and Sander L. Gilman, 165–98. New York: Columbia University Press, 1985.

Gilmartin, Sophie. *Ancestry and Narrative in Nineteenth-Century Literature: Blood Relations from Edgeworth to Hardy.* Cambridge: Cambridge University Press, 1998.

Gilmour, David. *The Last Leopard: A Life of Giuseppe di Lampedusa.* London: Quartet Books, 1988.

Gledson, John. *Machado de Assis: Ficção e historia.* Translated by Sônia Coutinho. Rio de Janeiro: Paz e Terra, 1986.

———. "The Meaning of Os Maias: The Role of Gambetta." *Bulletin of Hispanic Studies* 96, no. 5 (1992): 147–54.

———. *Por um novo Machado de Assis.* São Paolo: Companhia das Letras, 2006.

Gold, Hazel. *The Reframing of Realism: Galdós and the Discourses of the Nineteenth-Century Novel.* Durham, NC: Duke University Press, 1993.

Gollnick, Brian. "The Regional Novel and Beyond." In *The Cambridge Companion to the Latin American Novel*, edited by Efraín Kristal, 44–58. Cambridge: Cambridge University Press, 2005.

Grana, Giovanni. *"I Vicerè" e la patologia del reale.* Milan: Marzorati, 1982.

Grossegresse, Orlando. *Konversation und Roman: Untersuchungen zum Werk von Eça de Queiróz.* Stuttgart: Franz Steiner, 1991.

Guillén, Claudio. "Entre la distancia y la ironia: De Los Pazos de Ulloa a Insolación." In *Estudios sobre "Los Pazos de Ulloa,"* edited by Marina Mayoral, 103–28. Madrid: Cátedra, 1989.

Gullón, Germán. *La novela del XIX: Estudio sobre su evolución formal.* Amsterdam: Rodopi, 1990.

Gumbrecht, Hans Ulrich. Eine *Geschichte der spanischen Literatur.* 2 vols. Frankfurt am Main: Suhrkamp, 1990.

———. *Zola im historischen Kontext: Für eine neue Lektüre des Rougon-Macquart-Zyklus.* Munich: Wilhelm Fink, 1978.

Hack, Daniel. "Inter-Nationalism: *Castle Rackrent* and Anglo-Irish Union." *Novel* 29, no. 2 (1996): 145–64.

Hart, Stephen M. "The Gendered Gothic in Pardo Bazán's *Los Pazos de Ulloa.*" In *Culture and Gender in Nineteenth-Century Spain,* edited by Jo Labanyi and Lou Charnon-Deutsch, 217–29. Oxford: Clarendon, 1995.

Hechter, Michael. *Internal Colonialism: The Celtic Fringe in British National Development.* London: Routledge, 1975.

Helgerson, Richard. *Adulterous Alliances: Home, State, and History in Early European Drama and Painting.* Chicago: Chicago University Press, 2000.

Hemingway, Maurice. *Emilia Pardo Bazán: The Making of a Novelist.* Cambridge: Cambridge University Press, 1985.

———. "Emilia Pardo Bazán: Narrative Strategies and the Critique of Naturalism." In *Naturalism in the European Novel: New Critical Perspectives,* edited by Brian Nelson, 135–50. New York: Berg, 1992.

———. "Grace, Nature, Naturalism, and Pardo Bazán." *Forum for Modern Language Studies* 16, no. 4 (1980): 341–49.

Henn, David. *The Early Pardo Bazán: Theme and Narrative Technique in the Novels of 1879–89.* Liverpool: Francis Cairns, 1988.

Herzberger, David K. "The Theme of Warring Brothers in *Saúl ante Samuel.*" In *Critical Approaches to the Writings of Juan Benet,* edited by Robert C. Manteiga, David K. Herzberger, and Malcolm Alan Compitello, 100–110. Hanover, NH: University Press of New England, 1984.

Hinterhäuser, Hans. "Benito Pérez Galdós: *La desheredada.*" In *Der spanische Roman: Vom Mittelalter bis zur Gegenwart,* edited by Volker Roloff and Harald Wentzlaff-Eggebert, 253–71. Stuttgart: J. B. Metzler, 1995.

———. *Die "Episodios Nacionales" von Benito Pérez Galdós.* Hamburg: De Gruyter, 1961.

Hirschman, Albert O. *The Rhetoric of Reaction: Perversity, Futility, Jeopardy.* Cambridge, MA: Harvard University Press, 1990.

Hobsbawm, Eric. *The Age of Capital: 1848–1875.* New York: Vintage, 1996 [1957].

Hurst, Michael. *Maria Edgeworth and the Public Scene: Intellect, Fine Feeling and Landlordism in the Age of Reform.* London: Macmillan, 1969.

Iser, Wolfgang. "Möglichkeiten der Illusion im historischen Roman." In *Der implizite Leser,* 132–76. Munich: Fink, 1974.

Jameson, Fredric. "Third-World Literature in the Era of Multinational Capitalism." *Social Text* 15 (1986): 65–88.

———. *The Antinomies of Realism.* London: Verso, 2013.

Jonsson, Stefan. *A Brief History of the Masses: Three Revolutions.* New York: Columbia University Press, 2008.

Jusdanis, Gregory. *Belated Modernity and Aesthetic Culture: Inventing National Literature.* Minneapolis: University of Minnesota Press, 1991.

Kermode, Frank. *The Sense of an Ending: Studies in the Theory of Fiction.* Oxford: Oxford University Press, 2000.

Kern, Stephen. *The Culture of Time and Space, 1880–1918.* Cambridge, MA: Harvard University Press, 1983.

———. *The Modernist Novel: A Critical Introduction.* Cambridge: Cambridge University Press, 2011.

Kiberd, Declan. *Irish Classics.* London: Granta, 2000.

Kirby, Harry L., Jr. "Pardo Bazán, Darwinism and *La Madre Naturaleza.*" *Hispania* 47, no. 4 (1964): 733–37.

Klobucka, Anna. "Theorizing the European Periphery." *symploke* 5, no. 1 (1997): 119–35.

Koschorke, Albrecht. *Die Heilige Familie und ihre Folgen.* Frankfurt am Main: Fischer, 2000.

———. *Wahrheit und Erfindung: Grundzüge einer allgemeinen Erzähltheorie.* Frankfurt am Main: Fischer, 2012.

Koschorke, Albrecht, Nacim Ghanbari, Eva Eßlinger, Sebastian Susteck, and Michael Thomas Taylor, *Vor der Familie: Grenzbedingungen einer modernen Institution.* Konstanz, Germany: Konstanz University Press, 2010.

Koselleck, Reinhart. *Vergangene Zukunft: Zur Semantik geschichtlicher Zeiten.* Frankfurt am Main: Suhrkamp, 1989.

Kreilkamp, Vera. *The Anglo-Irish Novel and the Big House.* Syracuse, NY: Syracuse University Press, 1998.

Kropf, David Glenn. *Authorship as Alchemy: Subversive Writing in Pushkin, Scott, and Hoffmann.* Stanford, CA: Stanford University Press, 1994.

Küpper, Joachim. *Balzac und der effet de réel: Eine Untersuchung anhand der Textstufen des "Colonel Chabert" und des "Curé de Village."* Amsterdam: Grüner, 1986.

———. *Zum italienischen Roman des neunzehnten Jahrhunderts: Foscolo, Manzoni, Verga, D'Annunzio.* Stuttgart: Franz Steiner, 2002.

Labanyi, Jo. *Gender and Modernization in the Spanish Realist Novel.* Oxford: Oxford University Press, 2000.

Lambert, José. "L'éternelle questions des frontiers: Littératures nationales et systems littéraires." In *Langue, dialecte, littérature: Etudes romanes à la mémoire de Hugo Plomteux,* edited by C. Angelet, L. Melis, F. Mertens, and F. Musarra, 355–70. Leuven: Leuven University Press, 1983.

Lansing, Richard H. "The Structure of Meaning in Lampedusa's *Il Gattopardo.*" *PMLA* 93, no. 3 (1978): 409–22.

Le Bigot, Claude. "Le roman aux prises avec l'histoire: Une constante dans la production romanesque de l'Europe de l'ouest (1975–2003); Quelques exemples espagnols, français et portugais." In *Écriture et identités dans la nouvelle fiction romanesque,* edited by Rita Olivieri-Godet, 61–74. Rennes: Presses Universitaires de Rennes, 2010.

Lee Bretz, Mary. *Voices, Silences and Echoes: A Theory of the Essay and the Critical Reception of Naturalism in Spain.* London: Tamesis, 1992.

Leersen, Joep. "The Rhetoric of National Character: A Programmatic Survey." *Poetics Today* 21, no. 2 (2000): 267–92.

Lee Six, Abigail. "'Buenos Seamos, que dios nos ve': *La Madre Naturaleza* and Foucault's Panopticon." *Modern Language Review* 3 (1995): 1019–26.

Lévi-Strauss, Claude. *Die elementaren Strukturen der Verwandtschaft*. Translated by Grete Osterwald. Frankfurt am Main: Suhrkamp, 1983.

Lewis, Pericles. *Modernism, Nationalism, and the Novel*. Cambridge: Cambridge University Press, 2000.

Lewis, Thomas E. "*Fortunata y Jacinta*: Galdós and the Production of the Literary Referent." *Modern Language Notes* 96 (1981): 316–39.

Link-Heer, Ursula. "Über den Anteil der Fiktionalität an der Psychopathologie des 19. Jahrhunderts." *Zeitschrift für Literaturwissenschaft und Linguistik* 51/52 (1983), 280–302.

Litvak, Lily. *El tiempo de los trenes: El paisaje español en el arte y la literatura del realismo (1849–1918)*. Barcelona: Ediciones del Serbal, 1985.

Lopes, Denilson. *Nós os mortos: Melancolia e Neo-Barocco*. Rio de Janeiro: Sete Letras, 1999.

Lourenço, António Apolinário. "Eça de Queirós e o incesto na literatura naturalista ibérica: Simões Dias, Lourenço Pinto, López Bago e Pardo Bazán," in "Eça de Queirós." Special issue, *Leituras* 7 (2000): 109–27.

Lucente, Gregory. *Beautiful Fables: Self-Consciousness in Italian Narrative Fiction from Manzoni to Calvino*. Baltimore: Johns Hopkins University Press, 1986.

Lund, Joshua. *The Impure Imagination: Toward a Critical Hybridity in Latin American Literature*. Minneapolis: University of Minnesota Press, 2006.

Luperini, Romano. "Il 'gran signore' e il senso della temporalità: Saggio su Tomasi di Lampdusa." *Allegoria* 26 (1997): 138–40.

———. "*I Malavoglia* e la modernità." In *Il romanzo*, edited by Franco Moretti, 5:327–45. Turin: Einaudi, 2003.

———. *Simbolo e costruzione allegorica in Verga*. Bologna: Il Mulino, 1989.

Luzzi, Joseph. "Italy without Italians: Literary Origins of a Romantic Myth." *Modern Language Notes* 117 (2002): 48–83.

Machado Pires, António M. B. *A ideia de decadência na Geração de 70*. Lisbon: Vega, 1992.

Makdisi, Saree. *Romantic Imperialism: Universal Empire and the Culture of Modernity*. Cambridge: Cambridge University Press, 1998

Marramao, Giacomo. *Pasaje a Occidente: Filosofía y globalización*. Buenos Aires: Katz, 2006.

Martí-López, Elisa. *Borrowed Words: Translation, Imitation, and the Making of the Nineteenth-Century Novel in Spain*. Lewisburg, PA: Bucknell University Press, 2002.

Martínez Cuadrado, Miguel. *La burguesía conservadora (1874–1931): Historia de España alfaguara*. Madrid: Alianza, 1970.

Martins, Anna Luiza. *O despertar da Républica*. São Paulo: Contexto, 2001.

Matzat, Wolfgang. "Natur und Gesellschaft bei Clarín und Galdós: Zum diskursgeschichtlichen Ort des Realismus/Naturalismus." In Matzat, *Peripherie und Dialogizität*, 13–44.

———, ed. *Peripherie und Dialogizität: Untersuchungen zum realistisch-naturalistischen Roman in Spanien*. Tübingen: Gunter Narr, 1995.

Mazzoni, Guido. *Teoria del romanzo*. Bolgna: Il Mulino, 2011.

McCormack, W. J. *Ascendancy and Tradition in Anglo-Irish Literary History from 1789 to 1939*. Cambridge: Cambridge University Press, 1985.

McKeon, Michael, ed. *Theory of the Novel: A Historical Approach.* Baltimore: Johns Hopkins University Press, 2000.

Meira, Monteiro, Pedro. "Absence of Time: The Counselor's Dreams." In Castro Rocha, *Author as Plagiarist*, 353–72.

Melo, Alfredo Cesar. "Os mundos misturados de Gilberto Freyre." *Luso-Brazilian Review* 43, no. 2 (2006): 27–44.

Mercer, Leigh. *Urbanism and Urbanity: The Spanish Bourgeois Novel and Contemporary Customs, 1845–1925.* Lewisburg, PA: Bucknell University Press, 2012.

Meter, Helmut. *Figur und Erzählauffassung im veristischen Roman: Studien zu Verga, De Roberto und Capuana vor dem Hintergrund der französischen Realisten und Naturalisten.* Frankfurt am Main: Vittorio Klostermann, 1986.

Meyers, Jeffrey. "Greuze and Lampedusa's *Il Gattopardo*." *Modern Language Review* 69 (1974): 308–15.

———. "Symbol and Structure in *The Leopard*." *Italian Quarterly* 9 (1965): 50–70.

Moe, Nelson. *The View from Vesuvius: Italian Culture and the Southern Question.* Berkeley: University of California Press, 2002.

Montenegro, Olívio. *O romance brasileiro.* Rio de Janeiro: José Olympio, 1953.

Moretti, Franco. *Atlante del romanzo europeo, 1800–1900.* Turin: Einaudi, 1997.

———. *The Bourgeois: Between History and Literature.* London: Verso, 2013.

———. "Conjectures on World Literature." In *Debating World Lierarture*, edited by Christopher Prendergast, 148–62. London: Verso, 2004.

———. "Evolution, World-Systems, *Weltliteratur*." In *Studying Transcultural Literary History*, edited by Gunilla Lindberg-Wada, 113–21. Berlin: De Gruyter, 2006.

———. *La letteratura vista da lontano.* Turin: Einaudi, 2005.

———. "Modern European Literature: A Geographical Sketch." *New Left Review* 206 (1994): 98–101.

———. *Opere mondo: Saggio sulla forma epica dal "Faust" a "Cent'anni di solitudine."* Turin: Einaudi, 1994.

———, ed. *Il romanzo.* 5 vols. Turin: Einaudi, 2001–03.

Mortimer, Anthony. "*Castle Rackrent* and Its Historical Contexts." *Etudes Irlandaises* 9 (1984): 107–32.

Needell, Jeffrey D. *Belle époque tropical.* São Paulo: Companhia das Letras, 1993.

Nelson, Brian. "Émile Zola (1840–1902): Naturalism." In *The Cambridge Companion to European Novelists*, edited by Michael Bell, 294–309. Cambridge: Cambridge University Press, 2012.

Neuschäfer, Hans-Jörg. *Der Naturalismus in der Romania.* Wiesbaden: Athenaion, 1978.

Newcomer, James. "*Castle Rackrent*: The Disingenuous Thady Quirk." In *Family Chronicles: Maria Edgeworth's "Castle Rackrent,"* edited by Coilin Owens, 79–85. Totowa, NJ: Barnes and Noble, 1987.

Nonnenmacher, Hartmut. *Natur und Fatum: Inzest als Motiv und Thema in der französischen und deutschen Literatur des 18. Jahrhunderts.* Frankfurt am Main: Peter Lang, 2002.

Nünning, Ansgar, ed. *Metzler Lexikon Literatur- und Kulturtheorie.* Stuttgart: Metzler, 2008.

Oberhelman, David. "*Waverley*, Genealogy, History: Scott's Romance of Fathers and Sons." *Nineteenth-Century Contexts* 15, no. 1 (1991): 29–47.

O'Connell, Daragh. "Degenerative Genre: Federico De Roberto and His Sicilian Legacy." In *The Risorgimento of Federico De Roberto*, edited by Julie Dashwood and Margherita Ganeri, 137–63. Oxford: Peter Lang, 2009.

Onrubia, Carmen Menéndez. "Historia y familia en *Fortunata y Jacinta.*" In *Textos y contextos de Galdós: Actas del Simposio Centenario de "Fortunata y Jacinta,"* edited by John W. Kronik and Harriet S. Turner, 105–14. Madrid: Castalia, 1988.

Orlando, Francesco. *L'intimità e la storia: Lettura del "Gattopardo."* Turin: Einaudi, 1998.

———. *Ricordo di Lampedusa (1962): Seguito da "Da distanze diverse" (1996).* Turin: Bollati Boringhieri, 1996.

Osterhammel, Jürgen. *Die Verwandlung der Welt: Eine Geschichte des 19. Jahrhunderts.* Munich: Beck, 2011.

Parnes, Ohad, Ulrike Vedder, and Stefan Willer. *Das Konzept der Generation: Eine Wissenschafts- und Kulturgeschichte.* Frankfurt am Main: Suhrkamp, 2008.

Parsons, Deborah. *A Cultural History of Madrid: Modernism and the Urban Spectacle.* New York: Berg, 2003.

Pavel, Thomas. *La pensée du roman.* Paris: Gallimard, 2003.

Pellini, Pierluigi. *Naturalismo e verismo: Zola, Verga e la poetica del romanzo.* Milan: Le Monnier, 2010.

Perera, Suvendrini. *Reaches of Empire: The English Novel from Edgeworth to Dickens.* New York: Columbia University Press, 1991.

Pires da Lima, Isabel. *As máscaras do desengano: Para uma abordagem sociológica de "Os Maias" de Eça de Queirós.* Lisbon: Caminho, 1987.

Prado Coelho, Jacinto do. *A contrário de Penélope.* Lisbon: Livraria Bertrand, 1976.

Profeta, Maria Grazia. "'Realismo,' punto di vista, linguaggio: Benito Pérez Galdós, *Fortunata e Giacinta*, 1886–1887." In *Il romanzo*, edited by Franco Moretti, 5:359–73. Turin: Einaudi, 2003.

Ragusa, Olga. "Stendhal, Tomasi di Lampedusa, and the Novel." *Comparative Literature Studies* (1973): 200–208.

Rama, Angel. *The Lettered City*, edited and translated by John Charles Chasteen. Durham, NC: Duke University Press, 1996.

Raskin, Esther. *Family Secrets and the Psychoanalysis of Narrative.* Princeton, NJ: Princeton University Press, 1992.

Reichel, Edward. "Geschichtsdenken und Gegenwartsdeutung in *Il Gattopardo*: Tomasi di Lampedusa, die 'nouvelle histoire' und das Ende der Nachkriegsepoche in Italien." *Italienische Studien* 4 (1981): 31–43.

Reis, Carlos. "Eça de Queirós e Clarín ou o romance como discurso ideológico." In *Estudos Queirosianos: Ensaios sobre Eça de Queirós e a sua obra*, 93–102. Lisbon: Presença, 1999.

———. *Introdução à leitura d' "Os Maias."* Coimbra, Portugal: Livraria Almedina, 1978.

Reiss, Timothy. *Against Autonomy: Global Dialectics of Cultural Exchange.* Stanford, CA: Stanford University Press, 2002.

———. "Mapping Identities: Literature, Nationalism, Colonialism." In *Debating World Literature*, edited by Christopher Prendergast, 110–47. London: Verso, 2004.

Riall, Lucy. "Garibaldi and the South." In *Italy in the Nineteenth Century, 1796–1900*, edited by John A. Davis, 132–53. Oxford: Oxford University Press, 2004.

Ribaupierre, Claire de. *Le roman généalogique: Claude Simon et Georges Perec.* Brussels: La Part de l'Oeil, 2002.

Ribbans, Geoffrey. "Contemporary History in the Structure and Characterization of *Fortunata y Jacinta.*" In *Galdós Studies,* vol. 1, edited by J. E. Varey, 90–113. London: Tamesis, 1979.

———. "History and Fiction." In Turner and López de Martinez, *Cambridge Companion to the Spanish Novel,* 102–19.

Ribeiro, Maria Aparecida, ed. *História crítica da literatura portuguesa.* 7 vols. Lisbon: Verbo, 1994.

Ricoeur, Paul. *Temps et récit.* Vol. 2, *La configuration dans le récit de fiction.* Paris: Seuil, 1984.

Robert, Marthe. "Origins of the Novel" [1980]. In McKeon, *Theory of the Novel,* 160–78.

Rosendahl Thomsen, Mads. *Mapping World Literature: International Canonization and Transnational Literatures.* London: Continuum, 2008.

Rothwell, Philip. *A Canon of Empty Fathers: Paternity in Portuguese Narrative.* Lewisburg, PA: Bucknell University Press, 2007.

Saccone, Eduardo. "Nobility and Literature: Questions on Tomasi di Lampedusa." *Modern Language Notes* 106 (1991): 159–78.

Salles, Ricardo. *Joaquim Nabuco: Um pensador do Império.* Rio de Janeiro: Topbooks, 2001.

Santiago, Silviano. *O cosmopolitismo do pobre: Crítica literária e crítica cultural.* Belo Horizonte, Brazil: Universidade Federal de Minas Gerais, 2004.

———. "Eça, autor de *Madame Bovary.*" In *Uma literatura nos trópicos,* 47–65. Rio de Janeiro: Rocco, 2000 [1978].

Santos, João Camilo dos. "Machado de Assis, Critic of Eça de Queirós: A Symptomatic Misunderstanding." In Castro Rocha, *Author as Plagiarist,* 105–28.

Sarasin, Philip. *Darwin und Foucault: Genealogie und Geschichte im Zeitalter der Biologie.* Frankfurt am Main: Suhrkamp, 2009.

Sarraute, Nathalie. *L'ère du soupçon.* Paris: Gallimard, 1987.

Schirmer, Gregory A. "Tales from the Big House and Cabin: The Nineteenth Century." In *The Irish Short Story: A Critical History,* ed. James F. Kilroy, 21–44. Boston: Twayne, 1984.

Schmitz, Sabine. *Spanischer Naturalismus: Entwurf eines Epochenprofils im Kontext des "Krausopositivismo."* Tübingen: Niemeyer, 2000.

Schönthaler, Philipp. *Negative Poetik: Die Figur des Erzählers bei Thomas Bernhard, W. G. Sebald und Imre Kertész.* Bielefeld: transcript, 2011.

Schulze, Hagen. *Staat und Nation in der europäischen Geschichte.* Munich: Beck, 2004.

Schwarz, Roberto. "La capriola di Machado." In *Il romanzo,* edited by Franco Moretti, 5:287–307. Turin: Einaudi, 2003.

———. *A Master at the Periphery of Capitalism,* translated by John Gledson. Durham, NC: Duke University Press, 2001.

———. *Um mestre na periferia do capitalismo.* São Paolo: Duas Cidades, 1990.

Seabra Pereira, J. C. "Decadence and Fin-de-Siècle Literature in Portugal." In *A Revisionary History of Portuguese Literature,* edited by Miguel Tamen and Helena C. Buescu, 105–23. New York: Garland, 1999.

Seixas Guimarães, Hélio de. *Os leitores de Machado de Assis: O romance machadiano e o público de literatura no século 19*. São Paolo: Editora da Universidade de São Paulo, 2004.

Serrão, Joel. *Temas da cultura portuguesa—II*. Lisbon: Livros Horizonte, 1983.

Shideler, Ross. "Borg's Lost Children: Darwin and Strindberg's *I Havsbandet*." In *Studies in German and Scandinavian Literature after 1500: A Festschrift for George C. Schoolfield*, edited by James A. Parente Jr. and Richard Erich Schade, 181–95. Columbia, SC: Camden House, 1993.

———. *Questioning the Father: From Darwin to Zola, Ibsen, Strindberg, and Hardy*. Stanford, CA: Stanford University Press, 1999.

Shields, Juliet. "From Family Roots to the Routes of Empire: National Tales and the Domestication of the Scottish Highlands." *English Literary History* 72 (2005): 919–40.

Sieburth, Stephanie. *Inventing High and Low: Literature, Mass Culture and Uneven Modernity in Spain*. Durham, NC: Duke University Press, 1990.

Sinclair, Alison. "The Regional Novel: Evolution and Consolation." In Turner and López de Martinez, *Cambridge Companion to the Spanish Novel*, 49–64.

Siskind, Mariano. "The Globalization of the Novel and the Novelization of the Global." In *World Literature: A Reader*, edited by Theo d'haen, César Domínguez, and Mads Rosendahl Thomsen, 329–51. New York: Routledge, 2012.

Soriano, Rodrigo. "Una conferencia con Emilio Zola." *Revista de España*, 137 (1891): 226–32.

Spitzer, Leo. "L'originalità della narrazione nei *Maravoglia*." *Belfagor* 11 (1956): 37–53.

Stafford, Fiona J. *The Last of the Race: The Growth of a Myth from Milton to Darwin*. Oxford: Clarendon, 1994.

Stagl, Justin. "Vergänglichkeit und Wiederkehr im *Gattopardo*." In Tappert, *Vom Bestseller zum Klassiker der Moderne*, 139–52.

Standley, Arline R. "Here and There: Now and Then." *Luso-Brazilian Review* 23 (1986): 61–75.

Süssekind, Flora. *O Brasil não é longe daqui: O narrador, a viagem*. São Paulo: Companhia das Letras, 2006 [1990].

———. "O sobrinho do meu tio." *Papéis avulsos* (Rio de Janeiro: Fundação Casa de Rui Barbosa) 20 (1995): 9–32.

———. *Tal Brasil, qual romance? Uma ideología estética e sua história: o naturalismo*. Rio de Janeiro: Achiamé, 1984.

Tanner, Tony. *Adultery in the Novel: Contract and Transgression*. Baltimore: Johns Hopkins University Press, 1979.

Tappert, Birgit. "Kunstwerke im *Gattopardo*." In Tappert, *Vom Bestseller zum Klassiker der Moderne*, 153–71.

———, ed. *Vom Bestseller zum Klassiker der Moderne: Giuseppe Tomasi di Lampedusas Roman "Il Gattopardo."* Tübingen: Stauffenburg, 2001.

Tellini, Gino. *Il romanzo italiano dell'Ottocento e Novecento*. Milan: Bruno Mondadori, 1998.

Tobin, Patricia Drechsel. *Time and the Novel: The Genealogical Imperative*. Princeton, NJ: Princeton University Press, 1978.

Toller Gomes, Heloisa. "Plantation Boy: The Memory of Loss." In *Brazil 2001: A Revisionary History of Brazilian Literature and Culture*, edited by João Cezar de Castro Rocha,

167–76. Portuguese Literary & Cultural Studies 4/5. Dartmouth: University of Massachusetts, 2001.

―――. *O poder rural na ficção.* São Paulo: Ática, 1981.

Toscano Liria, Teresa. *Retórica e ideología de la Generación de 1868 en la obra de Galdós.* Madrid: Editorial Pliegos, 1984.

Trevor-Roper, Hugh. "The Invention of Tradition: The Highland Tradition of Scotland." In *The Invention of Tradition,* edited by Eric Hobsbawm and Terence Ranger, 15–36. Cambridge: Cambridge University Press, 1983.

Trigo, Luciano. *Engenho e memória: O nordeste do açucar na ficção de José Lins do Rego.* Rio de Janeiro: Topbooks, 2002.

Trumpener, Katie. *Bardic Nationalism: The Romantic Novel and the British Empire.* Princeton, NJ: Princeton University Press, 1997.

―――. "Cosmopolitismo periferico: La Scozia, l'Irlanda e il romanzo inglese." In *Il romanzo,* edited by Franco Moretti, 3:205–28. Turin: Einaudi, 2002.

―――. "National Character, National Plots: National Tale and Historical Novel in the Age of *Waverley,* 1806–30." *English Literary History* 60 (1994): 685–732.

Turner, Harriet S. "Family Ties and Tyrannies: A Reassessment of Jacinta." *Hispanic Review* 1 (1983): 1–22.

―――. "The Realist Novel." In Turner and López de Martinez, *Cambridge Companion to the Spanish Novel,* 81–101.

Turner, Harriet, and Adelaida López de Martinez, eds. *The Cambridge Companion to the Spanish Novel from 1600 to the Present.* Cambridge: Cambridge University Press, 2003.

Urey, Diane F. "Incest and Interpretation in *Los Pazos de Ulloa* and *La Madre Naturaleza.*" *Anales Galdosianos* 22 (1987): 117–31.

Uriarte, Fernando. "El comercio en la obra de Galdós." *Atenea* 72 (1942): 136–40.

Valente, Joseph. "Upon the Braes: History and Hermeneutics in *Waverley.*" *Studies in Romanticism* 25, no. 2 (1986): 251–76.

Vecchi, Roberto, Silvia Albertazzi, and Barnaba Maj. *Periferie della storia: Il passato como rappresentazione nelle culture omeoglotte.* Macerata, Italy: Quodlibet, 2004.

Veglia, Federica. "Il 'maestro' e il 'discepolo': Su alcune immagini di Zola nell'epostolario di Verga." In *Il verismo italiano fra naturalismo francese e cultura europea,* edited by Romano Luperini, 23–53. Lecce, Italy: Manni, 2007.

Ventura, Roberto. *Estilo tropical: História cultural e polêmicas literárias no Brasil.* São Paolo: Companhia das Letras, 1991.

Vilela, Ana Luísa. "Histórias de ausência n'*Os Maias.*" *Leituras: Revista da Biblioteca Nacional* 7 (2000): 47–63.

Viotti da Costa, Emília. *Da monarquia à República: Momentos decisivos.* São Paulo: Brasiliense, 1985.

Vitello, Andrea. *Giuseppe Tomasi di Lampedusa.* Palermo: Sellerio Editore, 1987.

Wagner, Birgit. "Mallorca und die Universalität der Lumières: *Bearn o la sala de les nines* von Llorenç Villalonga." *Zeitschrift für Katalanistik* 1 (1988): 52–61.

Wainwright, Michael. *Darwin and Faulkner's Novels: Evolutionism and Southern Fiction.* New York: Palgrave, Macmillan, 2008.

Walter, Klaus-Peter. "Normierte Wunschwelten und realistischer Diskurs: Die Präsenz des Populärromans in Pérez Galdós' *Novelas Contemporáneas.*" In *Peripherie und*

Dialogizität: Untersuchungen zum realistisch-naturalistischen Roman in Spanien, edited by Wolfgang Matzat, 45–68. Tübingen: Gunter Narr, 1995.

Warning, Rainer. "Zola's Rougon-Macquart: Compensatory Images of a 'Wild Ontology.'" *Modern Language Notes* 2 (1991): 705–33.

Weigel, Sigrid. *Genea-Logik: Generation, Tradition und Evolution zwischen Kultur- und Naturwissenschaften*. Munich: Fink, 2006.

———, ed. *Generation: Zur Genealogie des Konzepts; Konzepte von Genealogie*. Munich: Fink, 2005.

Weir, David. *Decadence and the Making of Modernism*. Amherst: University of Massachusetts Press, 1995.

Welsh, Alexander. *The Hero of the Waverley Novels*. New Haven, CT: Yale University Press, 1963.

Wiltshire de Oliveira, Maria Lúcia. "*Auto dos danados*: Cenas de uma família condenada." In *Facts and Fictions of António Lobo Antunes*, edited by Victor K. Mendes. Dartmouth, MA: Tagus Press, 2011.

Wohlgemut, Esther. "Maria Edgeworth and the Question of National Character." *Studies in English Literature, 1500–1900* (1999): 645–58.

Wolff, Erwin. "Sir Walter Scott and Dr. Dryasdust: Zum Problem der Entstehung des historischen Romans im 19. Jahrhundert." In *Dargestellte Geschichte in der europäischen Literatur des 19. Jahrhunderts*, edited by Wolfgang Iser and Fritz Schalk, 17–26. Frankfurt am Main: V. Klostermann, 1970.

Wolfzettel, Friedrich. *Der spanische Roman von der Aufklärung bis zur frühen Moderne*. Tübingen: Francke, 1999.

Woll, Dieter. *Machado de Assis: Die Entwicklung seines erzählerischen Werkes*. Braunschweig, Germany: Georg Westermann, 1972.

Woloch, Alex. *The One vs. the Many: Minor Characters and the Space of the Protagonist in the Novel*. Princeton, NJ: Princeton University Press, 2003.

Wright, Julia M. *Ireland, India, and Nationalism in Nineteenth-Century Literature*. Cambridge: Cambridge University Press, 2007.

imitation, peripheral modernity and,
134–39, 142
immobility, narrative, 176; peripheral
modernity and, 134–40; Sicily, 151,
181, 183–84
incest, 14, 72, 114–16, 127–28, 130, 201;
aristocracy, 195; bourgeoisie, 82; nature, 110;
Romanticism, 222n21; symbolism, 102; in
twentieth-century novels, 220n66

James, Henry, 196, 221n14, 229n35
Jameson, Fredric, 66, 206n22
Joyce, James, *Ulysses*, 176
Jusdanis, Gregory, 222n35

Kermode, Frank, 228n15
Kern, Stephen, 196, 226n2
Koschorke, Albrecht: on discourse of
modernity, 205n9, 206n20; on Holy family,
219n44; on modern concept of history, 16,
205n4, 206n11; on periphery, 9; on time and
modernity, 229n37
Koselleck, Reinhart, 16, 221n8
Kreilkamp, Vera, 26
Küpper, Joachim, 213n23

Labanyi, Jo, 97, 212n18, 216n57, 218n36, 219n51,
220n63
Lansing, Richard H., 228n9
Lawrence, D. H., 43, 160, 171; *The Rainbow*, 171
Le Bigot, Claude, 231n18
Lévi-Strauss, Claude, 9, 116
Lewis, Thomas E., 213n31
Link-Heer, Ursula, 211n45
Lins do Rego, José, 14, 159–70; *Fogo morto*, 164,
169; *Menino de engenho*, 163–64, 171
Lotman, Jurji M., 9, 220n61
Lund, Joshua, 227n19
Luperini, Romano, 45, 228n17

Macedo, Joaquim Manuel de, 226n31
Mann, Thomas, 1, 3, 164, 171; *Buddenbrooks*, 72,
123, 171, 173
Manzoni, Alessandro, *I Promessi sposi*, 186
Márquez, Gabriel García, 1, 3, 171, 220n66; *Cien
años de soledad*, 171
Marramao, Giacomo, 206n27
Martí-López, Eliza, 91, 212n17

Martins, Oliveira, 121, 222n28, 224n53
Mayoral, Marina, 219n48
Mazzoni, Guido, 222n19
McCormack, W. J., 207n6
Melo, Alfredo Cesar, 162
memory, 176; and narration, 171; and time,
164–69
Mercer, Leigh, 213n20
modernism, 90, 159–64, 173–74, 176–77, 194,
196, 198; postwar, 196–98
modernity, 52–53, 72–76, 114; ambivalence
toward, 79; bourgeois, 127; Brazil, 150–51;
community, family, and, 39–40; cultural,
175; domestic sphere of, 34; homogenizing
forces of, 56; naturalism and, 88–90, 129;
of Paris, 141; parody of, 140; and past, 186;
Portuguese, 136; and social world, 170;
Spain's lack of, 84–85; and time, 47–48;
universal, 43
modernization, 27, 60, 70; accelerated,
160; belated, 63–64; and economic
transformation, 164; historical
change and, 180, 195–96; nation, periphery,
and, 5–12; past and, 30; political, 106–7;
social, 195
Moe, Nelson, 180
Montesquieu, Charles Louis de Secondat,
7, 180
Moretti, Franco, 7–9; on center and periphery,
20, 64–65, 207n7, 216n5; on family saga,
205n1; on naturalism, 205n16, 217n8
Murilo de Carvalho, José, 153, 225n26

Nabuco, Joaquim, 153, 163
narration, 18; memory, time, and, 164–66, 169;
voice of, 172
nation, 144, 158; character, 132, 137, 162–63, 180,
182; community, 146; crisis of, 61–63;
decline, 123; genealogy and, 61–63;
generation and, 111–17; identity, 163; novel,
63–66, 142–44; periphery, 5–12; politics, 105,
143, 152; Portugal, 146–47; and region, 41,
87–92; and time, 27–31, 36; union/unity, 35,
157, 182
national tale, 18, 188
naturalism, 4, 13; de Assis's departure from,
226n48; dissolution/crisis of, 129–33;
doctrine, 59; French, 39, 55, 76, 91, 222n18;

Staël, Madame de, 7, 180
Stendhal, 171, 176, 228n5; *La chartreuse de Parme*, 171
Strindberg, August, 4
surface change, 142–46
Süssekind, Flora, 226n43, 226n48

Taine, Hippolyte, 55
Tanner, Tony, 221n14
Tappert, Birgit, 230n45
Thackeray, William Makepeace, 164
Thomsen, Mads R., 6–7
time/temporality, 2–5, 7, 9–10, 22, 27–30, 35–36, 43; anachronistic, 174; and change, 47, 51; chronological/linear, 140, 158–59, 165, 176; circularity, 60; continuity, 44, 66; counterhistorical, 116; cyclical, 107, 173; extension, 47–48, 60, 67, 139, 146, 164–66, 170–72; literary representation of, 154–58; modernity's conception of, 187; progression, 159, 173; self-enclosed, 165; simultaneity, 198; stasis, 199; subjective representation of, 161, 194; suspension of, 196
Tobin, Patricia Drechsel, 3, 226n1
Tolstoy, Leo, *Anna Karenina*, 66
Tomasi di Lampedusa, Giuseppe, 10–13, 15, 25, 151, 162, 170–72, 194; *Il Gattopardo*, 59, 107, 136, 151, 162, 170–71, 194–95, 202
Torok, Maria, 221n16
trauma, 97, 199, 202
Trumpener, Katie, 17, 207n4

union: amorous, 188; national, 188; sexual, 35, 89, 102; social, 186
Uriarte, Fernando, 214n34

Valera, Juan, 88
Ventura, Roberto, 163, 227n22
Verga, Giovanni, 13, 38–39, 60, 159, 172; *Duchessa de Leyra*, 48; *I Malavoglia*, 39–40, 55; *Mastro-don Gesualdo*, 48, 172; *Vita dei campi*, 43–44
verismo, 38–39, 52
Villalonga, Llorenç, 194–96, *Bearn o La sala de las muñecas*, 194–96, 202, 230n1
Viotti da Costa, Emília, 226n34, 226n37

Wagner, Birgit, 230n2
Wainwright, Michael, 227n19
Weigel, Sigrid, 220n58
Weir, David, 222n23
Wiltshire de Oliveira, María Lucia, 231n16
Wolfzettel, Friedrich, 219n40
Woll, Dieter, 226n44
Woloch, Alex, 81
Woolf, Virginia, 176, 228n19; *The Years*, 176
world literature, 6, 160, 203, 206n40

Zola, Émile, 4–5, 13, 39–41, 53, 55, 76, 79, 89–91, 109, 121, 131, 217n9; *L'assommoir*, 40, 121, 133, 137, 220n61, 222n18, 224n44; *Le docteur Pascal*, 40; *La faute de l'abbé Mouret*, 40, 102, 137; *La fortune des Rougon*, 40, 109; *Le roman expérimental*, 40; *La terre*, 41, 131